OUDTESTAMENTISCHE STUDIËN

DEEL XV

OUDTESTAMENTISCHE STUDIËN

NAMENS HET OUDTESTAMENTISCH
WERKGEZELSCHAP IN NEDERLAND

UITGEGEVEN DOOR

P. A. H. DE BOER

LEIDEN

DEEL XV

LEIDEN
E. J. BRILL
1969

THE PRIESTLY CODE
AND
SEVEN OTHER STUDIES

BY

J. G. VINK, J. C. H. LEBRAM, CHR. H. W. BREKELMANS,
H. A. BRONGERS, J. SCHONEVELD, N. A. VAN UCHELEN,
NIC. H. RIDDERBOS, M. J. MULDER

LEIDEN
E. J. BRILL
1969

INHOUD

THE DATE AND ORIGIN OF THE PRIESTLY CODE IN THE OLD TESTAMENT

BY

J. G. VINK

CONTENTS

PREFACE

The starting-point of the present inquiry was an investigation of the relationship between Shiloh and the Priestly Code, in order to verify the hypothesis provisionally worked out in our commentary "Leviticus uit de grondtekst vertaald en uitgelegd", Roermond 1962, pp. 8-10. As a result, we no longer are convinced of the thesis defended there; the study of the most relevant text, Josh. xviii 1, put us on a quite different track. It convinced us that a far more general question should be tackled, viz. the date and origin of the Priestly Code. On this point the Wellhausenian system was never put to the test, an omission resulting in a deadlock in the traditio-historical exegesis of the Priestly Code.

If we are going to advocate a "late" date for the Code, we mean "late" compared with the dating of the priestly texts in the Wellhausenian system. Our procedure has been a comprehensive one. A wide range of data was investigated. Both the biblical and extra-biblical texts were examined for any references to post-exilic history. In a cursory commentary all the texts of the Priestly Code itself have been commented upon. Finally, our conclusions have been compared with the data of the early pre-exilic cultic history of Israel.

The reader should be well aware of the difference between the fifth Chapter and the previous ones. The elaboration of the thesis proper is finished at the end of the fourth Chapter. What follows is a sort of corollary of a far more provisional and hypothetical nature, added because we were interested in certain analogies between our findings and recent research. The Chapter should be judged quite apart from the rest of the work.

The purpose of the work as a whole is best formulated as: the criticism of a hypothesis. The Wellhausenian view of the Pentateuch is accepted, but it is criticized on a special point, viz in what it has to say about the Priestly Code, which is the final contribution to and the framework of the Pentateuch. A new hypothesis on the Priestly Code is offered, evidence for which has been gathered from within and from without the Priestly Code; from biblical and extra-biblical material.

It might be asked whether source-criticism is not a superseded stage of Old Testament scholarship. Should not our attention rather go out towards form-criticism and traditio-historical analysis, that is, to the history of the text prior to its final written form? Has not everything been said that could be said about the various sources? Our answer is that the Priestly Code takes up a special place. Far more than the older strata of the Pentateuch (Yahwist, Elohist and Deuteronomy) it was from the outset conceived as a literary work. Its origin was at a time when Israel was cut off from its traditional country-bound features: their cult, kingship, and identity as a nation. Whatever progress in exegesis form-criticism and traditio-historical analysis may have brought us, a student of the Priestly Code should never forget that he has to do with a literary work in written form, recasting older written traditions.

To the second question our answer is that it would be a mistake to think that form-critical research cannot be applied to a literary work of a relatively late date. On the contrary, the present work tries to integrate the progress made in this respect into the study of the Priestly Code. Any reader of the Chapters III-IV will see there the application of the so-called aetiological method, to which a special paragraph will be devoted.

The starting-point of the present study is the conviction that the deadlock in the study of the Priestly Code can only be overcome by the integration of form-critical research with the traditional source-critical approach.

The final result of the inquiry is that it provides us with a picture of the Priestly Code which is quite different from the traditional one, still found in a good many Introductions to the Old Testament. If we should find adhesion, some of our views may also have consequences for the exegesis of the Books of Ezra and Nehemiah; some might be further developed with regard to the Deuteronomist and Ezechiel.

Those who are not convinced by our argument could help us by suggesting alternative answers to these questions, raised by the "traditional" exegesis.

I would like to thank Mr. Louis GROOTEN for his suggestions as regards the linguistic and stylistic form of this work.

LIST OF ABBREVIATIONS

AJSLL	American Journal of Semitic Languages and Literature
ANET	J. B. PRITCHARD, *Ancient Near Eastern Texts relating to the Old Testament*, Princeton 1950.
ASTI	Annual of the Swedish Theological Institute
ATD	Das Alte Testament Deutsch
BA	Biblical Archeologist
BHT	Beiträge zur Historischen Theologie
BJ	Bible de Jérusalem
BJRL	Bulletin of the John Rylands Library
BL	Bibel und Leben
BOT	Boeken van het Oude Testament
BWANT	Beischrifte zur Wissenschaft des Alten und Neuen Testaments
BZAW	Beihefte zur Zeitschrift der alttestamentlichen Wissenschaft
CV	Communio Viatorum
DBS	Dictionnaire Biblique Supplément
EP	Elephantine Papyri (ed. COWLEY)
ET	Evangelische Theologie
GTT	Gereformeerd Theologisch Tijdschrift
HAT	Handkommentar zum Alten Testament
HTR	Harvard Theological Review
ICC	International Critical Commentary
i.l.	*in loco (respectivo huius commentarii)*
IZBG	Internationale Zeitschriftenschau für Bibelwissenschaft und Grenzgebiete
JAOS	Journal of the American Oriental Society
JBL	Journal of Biblical Literature
JNES	Journal of Near Eastern Studies
JSS	Journal of Semitic Studies
JTS	Journal of Theological Studies
KHAT	Kurzer Handkommentar zum Alten Testament
l.c.	*loco citato*
LXX	Septuagint
MT	Massoretical Text
NRT	Nouvelle Revue Theologique
NTT	Nederlands Theologisch Tijdschrift
OA	Oriens Antiquus
PC	Priestly Code
RB	Revue Biblique
RGG	Religion in Geschichte und Gegenwart, 3rd ed.
RSV	Revised Standard Version
TLZ	Theologische Literaturzeitung
TvT	Tijdschrift voor Theologie
ThZ	Theologische Zeitschrift
VT	Vetus Testamentum
VTS	Vetus Testamentum Supplements
WMANT	Wissenschaftliche Monographien zum Alten und Neuen Testament
ZAW	Zeitschrift für die alttestamentliche Wissenschaft
ZThK	Zeitschrift für Theologie und Kirche

BIBLIOGRAPHY

Albrecht ALT, "Die Rolle Samarias bei der Entstehung des Judentums", *Kleine Schriften zur Geschichte des Volkes Israels* II (2nd ed.), München 1959, pp. 316-337.

W. R. ARNOLD, "The Passover Papyrus from Elephantine", *JBL* XXXI 1912, pp. 1-33.

E. AUERBACH, "Der Aufstieg der Priesterschaft zur Macht im Alten Israel", *VTS* IX 1963, pp. 236-249.

——, "Die babylonische Datierung im Pentateuch und das Alter des Priester-kodex", *VT* II 1952, pp. 334-342.

B. BAENTSCH, *Exodus* (HAT), Göttingen 1900.

——, *Numeri* (HAT), Göttingen 1903.

I. BENZINGER, *Die Bücher der Chronik* (KHAT), Tübingen 1901.

Walter BEYERLIN, *Herkunft und Geschichte der ältesten Sinai-Traditionen*, Tübingen 1961.

R. BORCHERT, Stil und Aufbau der priesterschriftlichen Erzählung (Diss. Maschinenschrift), Heidelberg 1957.

BOWMAN, "Samaritan Studies", *BJRL* XL 1956-1958, pp. 298-327.

John BRIGHT, *A History of Israel*, Philadelphia s.d.

R. J. BULL and G. E. WRIGHT, "Newly discovered temples on Mt. Gerizim in Jordan", *HTR* LVIII 1965, pp. 234-237.

Alex. VON BULMERINCQ, *Der Prophet Maleachi* (Acta et Commentationes Universitatis Tartuensis-Dorpatensis XXIII ff.), Tartu 1931-1932.

H. CAZELLES, "La mission d'Esdras", *VT* IV 1954, pp. 113-140.

——, "Pentateuque" IV: Textes sacerdotaux, DBS fasc. 39, Paris 1964.

R. J. COGGINS, "The Interpretation of Ezra iv 4", *JTS* XVI 1965, pp. 124-127.

A. COWLEY, *Aramaic Papyri of the fifth century B.C.*, Oxford 1923.

Fr. M. CROSS, "The Development of the Jewish Scripts", in: *The Bible and the Ancient Near East*, Essays in honor of W. E. Albright (ed. G. E. WRIGHT), Garden City 1961.

Mathias DELCOR, "Hinweise auf das samaritanische Schisma im Alten Testament", *ZAW* LXXIV 1962, pp. 281-291.

J. DUCHESNE-GUILLEMIN, *La Religion de l'Iran ancien*, Paris 1962.

Jan DUS, "Der Brauch der Ladewanderung im alten Israel", *ThZ* XVII 1961, pp. 1-16.

——, "Noch zum Brauch der Ladewanderung", *VT* XIII 1963, pp. 126-132.

——, "Der Beitrag des benjaminitischen Heidentums zur Religion Israels" CV VI 1963, pp. 61-80.

——, "Josua 22", *ThZ* XVII 1961, pp. 15-16.

Otto EISSFELDT, *Einleitung in das Alte Testament* (3d ed.), Tübingen 1964.

——, *Hexateuch-Synopse*, Leipzig 1922.

Karl ELLIGER, *Leviticus* (HAT I, 4) Tübingen 1966.

——, "Sinn und Ursprung der priesterlichen Geschichtserzählung", *ZThK* XLIX 1952, pp. 121-143.

J. A. EMERTON, "Did Ezra go to Jerusalem in 428 B.C.?", *JTS* XVII 1966, pp. 1-19.

G. FOHRER, "Priesterschrift", RGG, *Tübingen* 1961 (V, pp. 568 f.).

J. DE FRAINE, *Genesis* (BOT I, 1), Roermond 1963.

——, *Esdras en Nehemias* (BOT V, 2), Roermond 1961.

R. N. FRYE, *The heritage of Persia*, London 1962.

Kurt GALLING, *Studien zur Geschichte Israels im persischen Zeitalter*, Tübingen 1964.

M. GASTER, *The Samaritans* (Schweich Lectures 1923), London 1925.

Roman GHIRSMAN, *Perse*; *Proto-iraniens, Mèdes, Achéménides*, Paris 1963.

G. B. Gray, *Numbers* (ICC), Edinburgh 1903.

P. Grelot, "Le Papyrus Pascal d'Eléphantine", *VT* IV 1954, pp. 349-384.

——, "Le Papyrus Pascal d'Eléphantine et le problème du Pentateuque", *VT* V 1955, pp. 250-265.

——, "La dernière étape de la rédaction sacerdotale", *VT* VI 1956, pp. 174-189.

H. H. Grosheide, "Juda als onderdeel van het Perzische Rijk", *GTT* LIV 1954, pp. 65-76.

A. H. J. Gunneweg, *Leviten und Priester*, Göttingen 1965.

M. Haran, "The nature of the " 'Ohel Mo'edh" in Pentateuchal Sources", *JSS* V 1960, pp. 50-65.

——, "Shiloh and Jerusalem. The origin of the Priestly Tradition in the Pentateuch", *JBL* LXXXI 1962, pp. 14-24.

J. Hempel, *Geschichten und Geschichte im Alten Testament*, Gütersloh 1964.

——, "Priesterkodex", in: Pauly-Wissowa XXII 1954, col. 1945 ff.

M. L. Henry, "Phänomene religiöser Lebensbewegungen in der jahwistischen und priesterlichen Ueberlieferung", *ThLZ* LXXXV 1960, pp. 145-148.

Siegfried Herrmann, "Das Werden Israels", *ThLZ* LXXXVII 1962, pp. 561-574.

J. Hoftijzer, "Enige opmerkingen rond het israelitische 12-stammen-systeem", *NTT* XIV 1959, pp. 241-263.

H. Holzinger, *Exodus*, Tübingen 1900.

——, *Genesis* (KHAT), Freiburg i. Br. 1898.

——, *Numeri* (KHAT), Tübingen 1903.

S. H. Hooke, "Introduction to the Pentateuch", in: Peake's *Commentary on the Bible* (ed. M. Black and H. H. Rowley), London 1963, pp. 168-174.

Flemming Hvidberg, "The Canaanite Background of Gen. I-III", *VT* X 1960, pp. 285-294.

W. H. Irwin, "Le sanctuaire central israélite avant l'établissement de la monarchie", *RB* LXXII 1965, pp. 161-184.

Alfred Jepsen, "Zur Chronologie des Priesterkodex", *ZAW* XLVI 1929, pp. 251-255.

A. S. Kapelrud, "The Date of the Priestly Code (P)", *ASTI* III 1964, pp. 58-64.

J. Kaufmann, "Probleme der israelitisch-jüdischen Religionsgeschichte", *ZAW* XLVIII 1930, pp. 23-43.

M. Kegel, *Die Kultusreform Esras*, 1921. This work was inaccessible to us.

R. H. Kenneth, "The origin of the Aaronite Priesthood", *JTS* VI 1904-1905, pp. 161-186.

R. Kilian, "Die Hoffnung auf Heimkehr in der Priesterschrift", *BL* VII 1966, pp. 39-51. Now also in: *Wort und Botschaft* (ed. J. Schreiner), Würzburg 1967, pp. 226-243.

R. Kittel, *Geschichte des Volkes Israel* III, 2 (1st and 2nd ed.) Stuttgart 1929.

Klaus Koch, *Die Priesterschrift von Exodus 25 bis Leviticus 16*, Göttingen 1959.

——, "Sühne und Sündenvergebung um die Wende von der exilischen zur nachexilischen Zeit", *ET* XXVI 1966, pp. 217-238.

E. G. Kraeling, *The Brooklyn Aramaic Papyri*, Yale 1953.

H. J. Kraus, *Gottesdienst in Israel* (2nd ed.), München 1962.

S. R. Kuelling, *Zur Datierung der "Genesis-P-Stücke"*, Kampen 1964.

A. Kuschke, "Die Lagevorstellung der priesterschriftlichen Erzählung", *ZAW* LXIII 1951, pp. 74-105.

S. Lehming, "Erwägungen zur Zelttradition", in: *Gottes Wort und Gottes Land* Festschrift H. W. Herzberg ed. H. Graf Reventlow), Göttingen 1965, pp. 110-132.

B. A. Levine, "The Descriptive Tabernacle Texts of the Pentateuch", *JAOS* LXXXV 1965, pp. 307-318.

Jean L'Hour, "L'alliance de Sichem", *RB* LXIX 1962, pp. 5-36, 161-184.
J. Lindblom, "The Political Background of the Shiloh Oracle", *VTS* I 1953, pp. 78-87.
Johann Maier, *Das altisraelitische Ladeheiligtum* (BZAW 93), Berlin 1965.
A. Menès, "Tempel und Synagoge", *ZAW* L 1932, pp. 268-276.
J. Morgenstern, "The Dates of Ezrah and Nehemiah", *JSS* VII 1962, pp. 1-11.
S. Mowinckel, *Tetrateuch-Pentateuch-Hexateuch*, Berlin 1964.
——, *Erwägungen zur Pentateuch Quellenfrage*, Oslo 1964.
——, *Zur Frage nach dokumentarische Quellen in Joshua 13-19*, Oslo 1964.
——, *Studien zu dem Buche Ezra-Nehemia I: Die Listen*, Oslo 1964.
    II:Die Nehemia-Denkschrift, Oslo 1964.
    III: Die Ezra-Geschichte und das Gesetz Moses, Oslo 1965.
J. M. Myers, *Ezra-Nehemiah* (The Anchor Bible), Garden City 1965.
E. W. Nicholson, "The meaning of the expression ʿam haʾareṣ in the Old Testament", *JSS* X 1965, pp. 59-66.
E. Nielsen, *Shechem: a traditio-historical Investigation*, Copenhagen 1955.
F. S. North, "Aaron's Rise in Prestige", ZAW LXVI 1954, pp. 191-198.
M. Noth, "Zur Anfertigung des 'Goldenes Kalbes' ", *VT* IX, 1959, pp. 419-422.
——, *Das Buch Josua* (2nd ed.), Tübingen 1953.
——, *Das zweite Buch Mose. Exodus* (ATD), Göttingen 1959.
——, *Geschichte Israels* (5th ed.), Göttingen 1963.
——, *Ueberlieferungsgeschichte des Pentateuchs*, Stuttgart 1948.
——, "Ueberlieferungsgeschichtliches zur zweiten Hälfte des Josuabuches", in: *Alttestamentliche Studien* (Festschrift Noetscher), Bonn 1950.
——, *Ueberlieferungsgeschichtliche Studien* I, Halle 1943.
W. Nowack, *Die Kleine Propheten*, Göttingen 1903.
H. M. Orlinsky, "The tribal system of Israel and related groups in the period of the Judges", OA I 1962, pp. 11-20.
G. von Rad, *Das erste Buch Mose. Genesis. Kap. 1-25, 18* (ATD II, 3), Göttingen 1952.
——, "Die Nehemia-Denkschrift", ZAW LXXVI 1964, pp. 176-187.
——, *Die Priesterschrift im Hexateuch* (BZAW 13), Stuttgart 1934.
——, "Zelt und Lade", in: *Gesammelte Studien zum Alten Testament*, München 1961, pp. 109-129.
Bo Reicke, *Neutestamentliche Zeitgeschichte. Die biblische Welt 500v-100 n. Chr.*, Berlin 1965.
Rolf Rendtorff, *Die Gesetze in der Priesterschrift*, Göttingen 1954.
L. Rost, "Zu den Festopfervorschriften von Num. 28 und 29", *TLZ* LXXXIII 1958, pp. 329-334.
——, "Zum geschichtlichen Ort der Pentateuchquellen", *ZThK* LIII 1956, pp. 1-10.
——, "Der Leberlappen", *ZAW* LXXIX 1967, pp. 35-41.
——, *Vorstufen zur Kirche und Synagoge im Alten Testament* (BWANT) Stuttgart 1938.
J. Roth, "La tradition sacerdotale dans le Pentateuque", *NRT* XC 1958, pp. 696-721.
H. H. Rowley, "Sanballat and the Samaritan Temple", *BJRL* XXXVIII 1955, pp. 166-198.
——, "The samaritan Schism in legend and history", in: *Israel's prophetic heritage* (Essays in honour of J. Muilenburg, ed. B. W. Anderson and J. Harrelson), London 1962, pp. 208-222.
W. Rudolph, *Ezra und Nehemia* (HAT), Tübingen 1949.
Lothar Ruppert, *Die Josephserzählung der Genesis. Ein Beitrag zur Theologie der Pentateuchquellen*, München 1965.

H. H. Schaeder, *Esra der Schreiber* (BHT 5), Tübingen 1930.

Werner H. Schmidt, *Die Schöpfungsgeschichte der Priesterschrift* (WMANT 17), Neukirchen 1964.

W. Schneemelcher, "Esra", in: *Reallexikon für Antike und Christentum* IV 1965, pp. 595-612.

A. Schulz, *Das Buch Josua*, Bonn 1924.

H. Seebass, *Mose und Aaron. Sinai und Gottesberg*, Bonn 1962.

E. Sellin, *Gilgal. Ein Beitrag zur Geschichte der Einwanderung Israels in Palästina*, Leipzig 1917.

Rudolf Smend, *Jahwekrieg und Stämmebund*, Göttingen 1963.

N. H. Snaith, "The Date of Ezra's arrival in Jerusalem", *ZAW* LXIII 1951, pp. 53-66.

E. A. Speiser, *Genesis* (The Anchor Bible), Garden City 1964.

G. te Stroete, *Exodus* (BOT I, 2), Roermond 1966.

A. Thomson, "An inquiry concerning the Books of Ezra and Nehemiah", *AJSLL* XLVIII 1931-1932, pp. 99-132.

R. de Vaux, *Les institutions de l'Ancien Testament* II, Paris 1960.

J. G. Vink, *Leviticus* (BOT II, 1), Roermond 1962.

H. C. M. Vogt, *Studie zur nachexilischen Gemeinde in Esra-Nehemia*, Werl 1966.

Julius Wellhausen, *Die Composition des Hexateuchs und der historischen Bücher des Alten Testaments* (3rd ed.), Berlin 1899.

——, *Prolegomena zur Geschichte Israels* (6th ed.), Berlin 1927.

F. V. Winnett, "Re-Examining the Foundations", *JBL* LXXXIV 1965, pp. 1-19.

E. Wuerthwein, *Der ʿamm haʾarez im Alten Testament* (BWANT IV 17), Stuttgart 1936.

W. Zimmerli, "Sinaibund und Abrahambund", *ThZ* XVI 1960, pp. 268-280.

I. THE PRIESTLY CODE IN CRITICAL SCHOLARSHIP

For those who accept the critical analysis of the Pentateuch as a valid method of scholarly research, Eissfeldt's [1]) second criterion viz unity in language and literary style, proves to be very fruitful indeed when applied to the Priestly Code (PC), so markedly different from the other strata in vocabulary. The relative development of cultic and political ideas, Eissfeldt's 3rd criterion, was subjected to a revolutionary change in the approach to the PC in the first period of critical biblical scholarship. It was long thought, indeed up to 1866-1869 [2]), that the PC, on account of its chronology and its seemingly accurate way of describing the course of Israel's history and that of the surrounding world, was the very *Grundschrift* or basic literary stratum of the Pentateuch. Pentateuchal criticism did

---

[1]) Otto Eissfeldt, *Einleitung in das Alte Testament*, Tübingen 1964³, pp. 241-246. The first criterion is the use of the divine name; the fourth, the literary relationships of groups of texts.

[2]) *Ibidem*, p. 218-219. Cf. S. R. Kuelling, *Zur Datierung der "Genesis-P-Stücke"*, Kampen 1964. Cf. our remarks in *TvT* V 1965, pp. 452-453.

not reach its full development until REUSS, GRAF, KUENEN and WELLHAUSEN had completely turned upside down the relative order of the Pentateuchal strata. It was now recognized that P was not the first but the last in historical order. From that time onwards the early post-exilic date of the PC is a rarely challenged datum of Pentateuchal analysis, in fact its cornerstone.

Some have tried to evade the difficult problem of precise chronology of the PC by saying that its early and late materials prove that it is the product of a schoool more or less co-existant with Israel's history. Such is E. A. SPEISER's [1]) opinion. P is a school with an unbroken history reaching back to early Israelite times. The final result would thus represent the carefully nurtured product of some permanent scholastic committee, as it were, in regular session since the beginnings of ethnic consciousness in Israel. However, for this hypothesis to be tenable, there should be positive indications from other biblical writings showing P's influence or at least not proving the contrary. The supposition might also be ruled out if it could be shown that the PC has an inner cohesion and is closely linked up with certain well-defined historical circumstances.

After the propagation of the Wellhausenian system in its above-mentioned final form, the defenders of a pre-exilic origin of the PC have become very scarce indeed. J. KAUFMANN [2]) defends the thesis

---

[1]) E. A. SPEISER, *Genesis*, Garden City 1964 (The Anchor Bible), p. XXVI.

[2]) J. KAUFMANN, "Probleme der israelitisch-jüdischen Religionsgeschichte", *ZAW* XLVIII 1930, pp. 23-43. Cf. MOWINCKEL's criticism in: *Erwägungen zur Pentateuchfrage*, Oslo 1964, p. 44. When KAUFMANN says (p. 24) that Israel did not know a theocratic or rather a hierocratic ideal even in post-exilic times, he quotes Ezr. ix 8-9; Neh. ix 36 f. and Neh. ix as a whole. As we shall see in Ch. II, p. 27-33, both texts are Maccabean and cannot be quoted for the relevant Persian period. KAUFMANN omits to quote Ezr. vi 22, the royal rescript in Ezr. vii, and Zech. xi 10. He duly stresses (p. 28-31) the prophetocratic ideal of the PC, but, as we shall see in our note on Num. xx 1-13, 22-29 (Ch. iv 31, p. 121 f.) it is one of P's specific aims to emphasize the end of the great revelatory period, characterized by the great prophet Moses. It is now time for the officials to take over the rule of the community.

The military character of the camp (p. 28) is no evidence of P's prophetocratic structure; neither is the *Landnahme* in the PC a military undertaking (see our note on Num. xxvii 12-23, Ch. iv, 34, p. 124 f.). When KAUFMANN concludes from this prophetocratic structure and from non-centralization of the cult (see our note on Ex. xii 16; Ch. iv, 16, p. 97 ff.) that P is pre-Deuteronomic, he seems to know only two alternatives. P is either early post-exilic or pre-Deuteronomic. Our answer is: "*tertium datur.*" In a late post-exilic chronology it can easily be understood why the PC should not condemn (p. 32) the cult of the *bamôt*, whereas it does condemn idolatry, service of Moloch and adultery. The local cult at

that P is a pre-Deuteronomic record of the cult of the *bamôt*, the high-places. The *tent of meeting* is not a retrojection of the temple of Jerusalem, but a place of oracles (cf. Ex. xxxiii 7-11) and revelation, the *Urbild* of the numerous cultic sites in Palestine. This is a revival of DE WETTE's thesis of 1805, as quoted by WELLHAUSEN [1]). DE WETTE and KAUFMANN hold that there is no stress on cultic centralisation in the PC; WELLHAUSEN calls that opinion "superficial, to say the least". In spite of WELLHAUSEN's rejection, we think KAUFMANN's views on cultic centralisation and decentralisation in P highly valuable, although his argument will not leas us into accepting his view on the pre-Deuteronomic origin of the PC.

On the basis of a rather hypothetical reconstruction of the priestly chronology JEPSEN [2]) argues that this chronology points to the first temple; a confirmation, to him, of the thesis of the pre-exilic origin of P.

The central position of Abraham in the PC makes HEMPEL [3]) think that P might represent the cult-legend, i.e. the sacred story about the beginnings and the fixed order of the cult, of the sanctuary of Hebron. According to him, the expression Abraham, the "father of kings" (Gen. xvii 6) is understandable only in pre-exilic times. In our view the focus of interest is not in Jerusalem, in spite of the reference to kings; at the contrary, there is a polemical note against political messianism in Jerusalem. Such a polemical attitude would also explain the fact that the dimensions of the temple in P, and other cultic regulations, are different from those in Jerusalem. But a full evaluation of HEMPEL's thesis will have to wait until the fourth Chapter.

Another theory of P as a pre-exilic cult-legend of a non-Jerusalemite sanctuary was worked out by Jan DUS in a number of articles [4]).

---

the *bamôt* was no longer a reality. As to the connection of the *Urim-Tummim* oracle and the tent of meeting in P, this points to a hierocratic ideal which Israel *did* know in the late Persian period.

[1]) J. WELLHAUSEN, *Prolegomena zur Geschichte Israels*, Berlin 1927 (3rd ed.) pp. 34-35.

[2]) Alfred JEPSEN, "Zur Chronologie des Priesterkodex", *ZAW* XLVI 1929, pp. 251-255. According to him, the exact chronological numbers from before the Flood are to be found in the Samaritan text, those from after the Flood in MT.

[3]) J. HEMPEL, *Geschichten und Geschichte im Alten Testament*, Gütersloh 1964. *Idem*, "Priesterkodex", in: Pauly-Wissowa XXII, 1954, pp. (col.) 1945.

[4]) Jan DUS, "Der Brauch der Ladewanderung im alten Israel", *ThZ* XVII 1961, pp. 1-16. *Idem*, "Noch zum Brauch der Ladewanderung", *VT* XIII 1963, pp. 126-132. *Idem*, "Der Beitrag des benjaminitischen Heidentums zur Religion Israels", *CV* VI 1963, pp. 61-80.

In his view, 1 Sam. vi 7-9 is of central importance; the text describes a basic cultic custom in Israel before the monarchy. After a period of seven years the Ark was carried on a cart to another sanctuary chosen by the godhead himself. In this series of central sanctuaries Shiloh was the last site of the Ark. It may be assumed that prescriptions existed for this sanctuary of the Ark, making sure of it being transportable and full of splendour. Now it is a striking fact, according to this author, that the sanctuary of the PC, presenting both these characteristics, according to Josh. xviii 1 was located at Shiloh, where the custom of carrying the Ark on a cart is assumed to have ended, and where the transportable sanctuary of the Ark must have been incorporated into the existing temple. Is it not reasonable then to conclude, Dus says, that P is the cultic legend of the changeable cultic centre (Dt. xii 5) of the Israelite tribes? In explaining the PC this way, Jan Dus distinguishes between two strata: *shilonic P* and *Nob-P*, the latter dating from after the overthrow of the Shiloh sanctuary. It has stronger Zadokite elements and is a *Programmschrift* for a new sanctuary, the place of which is still left open. The role of the Ark, and why Dus's description of it is unacceptable to us, will be dealt with in the last Chapter; what is relevant at this moment is the important place Dus attributes to Josh. xviii 1; in his opinion, as well as in the present writer's view, in this text the PC reaches a climax, rewarding special study.

Among the small number of scholars who have paid attention to Josh. xviii 1 is M. HARAN [1]). For him the description of the tent of meeting is not a retrojection of the temple of Jerusalem, nor is it entirely unhistorical, as is most often alleged. Actually, it is based on a stratum of authentic tradition representing the cult legend of the sanctuary of Shiloh, older than that of Jerusalem. The literary form of that legend is, however, of a later date. Unlike Dus, HARAN does not change the classic datation of the PC.

Unfortunately, he does not provide us either with a formal literary analysis summing up the evidence of such an older stratum within P. But HARAN's revaluation of Josh. xviii 1 does remain interesting.

Summarizing, we do not think the authors mentioned so far have made a convincing defence of a pre-exilic origin of the PC or part of it. Their views do not invalidate the Wellhausenian argument about

---

[1]) M. HARAN, "Shiloh and Jerusalem. The origin of the Priestly Tradition in the Pentateuch", *JBL* LXXXI 1962, pp. 14-24.

the exilic-postexilic origin of P, in so far as this argument provides us with a *terminus a quo*.

In this survey of the *status quaestionis*, attention should therefore now be paid to the evidence advanced for the exilic date of the PC.

One of the pillars of the Wellhausenian argument is the relative chronology of P; that is its relation to the other Pentateuchal strata [1]). He points out that in P the unity of cult is no longer explicitly prescribed as in D, but silently presupposed. This would be easily understandable, if the PC dated from the time of the Exile. But even if the argument is valid, we must not forget that this provides no more than a *terminus a quo*. In our view, the argument is valid only in a limited way; as we shall see later on, the unity of cult is presupposed not in a legalistic way, but as a primeval basic datum (*Urbild*).

A further important ground of exilic datation is the *programmatic* character of the Code; in this respect it may be compared with the programmatic parts of the Book of Hezekiel [2]). As EISSFELDT (l.c.) says, the Code's programmatic character pertains to the restoration of the people as well as of the cult.

Important as it is, to the best of our knowledge, no special study has yet appeared on the subject of this programmatic character of the PC. Hence a brief discussion will not seem out of place here. First of all, the concept of the programmatic character of P is very much dependent on one's view about *the extension* of P. Those who hold that P is not represented in the Book of Joshua will say that the PC is only programmatic in regard to the cult. To those however who, like CAZELLES [3]), hold that P *is* present there, the Code is a programmatic approach to the new *Landnahme* after the Exile (CAZELLES); it is written "dans le calme de l'Exil". KILIAN [4]) says that P is absent from Joshua and therefore knows of no *Landnahme*; its open ending, however, is like Moses's situation on Mount Nebo.

---

[1]) EISSFELDT, l.c. *Einl.*, p. 275.

[2]) *Ibidem*.

[3]) H. CAZELLES, "Pentateuque", IV: Textes sacerdotaux. DBS, fasc. 39, Paris 1964, col. 822.

[4]) R. KILIAN, "Die Hoffnung auf Heimkehr in der Priesterschrift", *BL* VII 1966, pp. 39-51. The author depends on NOTH and ELLIGER in rejecting any *Landnahme-Bericht* in P; no further argument is given (p. 39). We agree that the figure of Moses is stressed in P, but he is not represented as leading his people out of *slavery* (p. 45-48). The cause of their discontent was not that they were kept in a foreign land against their will (p. 50). On the contrary, they are unwilling to exchange their happy state for an uncertain future. The chronological conclusion (P as a reflection upon the events of 587 B.C.) is therefore unconvincing.

The Code testifies to an intense longing to return to the Holy Land. In the same way as Moses was prevented from entering it by divine judgment, so the exiles were mourning about the catastrophe of 587 B.C., preventing *them* to return.

FOHRER [1]) defends the presence of P in Joshua, but avoids a specific conclusion. P is a *Programmschrift* for the post-exilic cultic community; the cult is to be realized in their own country. With him we find no explanation whatsoever about the interrelationship of land and cult in the programme as laid down in the PC.

It is important to know whether the attention of the authors of the Code was directed towards the sacred past or towards the future. If they intended to shed light on the traditions on which the present cult was based, their work was one of *legitimation*. If they intended to outline a future cultic project, their work is called *programmatic*. Both such a programme and legitimation are mentioned side by side in many expositions. But in how far are they related? Is, for instance, the long description of the Ark meant for the future or only as a commemoration of an object from the past? And is the unity of cult a programme for the future, or only a landmark of the *Urbild* of cult in the *Urzeit* of the people, in the same way as the unity of the camp was replaced by numerous cities and the one and single prophet by a number of prophets? [2])

An important passage on the programmatic character of P is found in G. TE STROETE [3]). The specific contributions of P, for example its reworking of pre-existing texts, prescribe magnificent decorations of the sanctuary. The sober post-exilic sanctuary in Jerusalem does not in any way correspond to this description. Furthermore, the question is whether such a realisation would have been technically possible at all. For TE STROETE, a supporter of the theory of the exilic origin of P, there is only one way out: the programme of P is *une utopie visionnaire* (STEINMANN); a theological construction rather than an architectural blue-print. However, it may be asked whether for P divine commandments are materials with which to build utopian visions. To us, TE STROETE's thesis is a good indication of what the real dilemma is. We have either to accept the exilic origin of the PC and to explain away the programmatic action as an *"utopie visionnaire"*, or to accept the PC as a programmatic

---

[1]) G. FOHRER, "Priesterschrift", RGG, Tübingen 1961 (3rd ed.), V, 568 f.
[2]) Cf. J. KAUFMANN, l.c. "Probleme" p. 40.
[3]) G. TE STROETE, *Exodus*, Roermond 1966 (BOT I, 2), p. 191 f.

action originating from a situation of great prosperity; in the latter case the early post-exilic origin of the PC is to be rejected. Apart from the wealth and splendour of the cultic project, mentioned by TE STROETE, one could also point to the Ark as something equally problematic with regard to programmatic action in early post-exilic times.

TE STROETE realizes that P's early-post-exilic origin is irreconcilable with its programmatic nature; most authors are less clear on this point. Talking as they are about legitimation as well as programmatic action, about commemoration of the glorious past as well as about a building programme they try to eat this cake and have it. They should be asked: what is your criterion in distinguishing between these features?

In view of such questions, the position of MOWINCKEL [1]) is even more unclear. The PC is written, this author says, in Jerusalem after the Exile for the community already re-established, in order to legitimate its cult. MOWINCKEL finds evidence for this thesis in the lists of geographical names in Joshua; they are not drawn from documents but betray the knowledge of an author writing within the country itself. But if P was written not at a far and safe distance, but in the shadow of the temple, how can MOWINCKEL defend the legitimation of the cult as its purpose? Under these circumstances, how ever is the absence of the Ark and all the other differences between the post-exilic temple and the temple of P to be explained?

But we may go even further. With the modern scholars mentioned above we have missed a balanced view of what is past and what is future in the priestly description of the cult. Some of them have also cast doubts upon the Jerusalemite character of that description. As VON RAD [2]) points out, Ark and Aaronite theology take up a much too prominent place in the PC for its Jerusalemite character to go unchallenged ELLIGER [3]) even goes so far as to question (rather hesitantly) the possibility that P was perhaps programmatic in regard to some cultic institution (tent of meeting) *in the Exile*, to be erected as a cultic *Provisorium* in order to know the will of God and to provoke Him once more into saving action [4]) According to

---

[1]) S. MOWINCKEL, *Erwägungen zur Pentateuch Quellenfrage*, Oslo 1964, pp. 183-185.

[2]) G. VON RAD, *Die Priesterschrift im Hexateuch*, Stuttgart 1934, pp. 183-185.

[3]) K. ELLIGER, "Sinn und Ursprung der priesterlichen Geschichtserzählung", *ZThK* XLIX 1952, pp. 121-143, esp. p. 142 f.

[4]) Cf. Ch. II, p. 55, n. 1 about Kasifja.

Klaus Koch [1]) the actual priestly text lends itself to formal literary analysis, revealing a *Vorlage* that is representative of the cultic traditions of a Palestinian, non-Jerusalemite sanctuary during the period of the monarchy. (Rendtorff [2]) however, his predecessor in this kind of literary analysis, says that the two different strata may represent two successive stages within the development of the cult in Jerusalem.) There seems to be a growing consensus that in the Wellhausenian system the PC is too easily assumed to have its origin in Jerusalemite priestly circles, such attribution being essential to the classical datation. But, surely, as soon as the Jerusalemite origin of the PC is doubted, the whole chronological construction should be questioned.

In conclusion: the second pillar of the early post-exilic dating of the PC, viz its relation to the Jerusalemite cult and its programmatic character, has turned out to be inadequate in many respects. Authors disagree about which sanctuary P is bound up with; there is difference of opinion as to the extent of its programmatic structure (country, cult, Ark, priesthood). The interdependence of legitimation and programmation, i.e. the description of the past and the description of what is meant to be future, is never made clear, and its impact on history is never examined.

Exilic or early post-exilic chronology is also supported by secondary arguments. Auerbach [3]) draws attention to the calendar system in the priestly Code, pointing to the battle of Karkemish (603 B.C.) as the starting-point of the Babylonian calendar system in Palestine (cf. Jer. xxxvi 9), which had the year begin in spring time. It is clear, however, that this evidence, though reliable, is only a *terminus a quo* and has to be supplemented. The same may be said about the absence of monarchical elements in P, to which Cazelles [4]) has drawn attention, and also about the direct and indirect polemical reaction to the Babylonian civilisation (Rost) [5]). That the Code was meant to

---

[1]) Klaus Koch, *Die Priesterschrift von Exodus 25 bis Leviticus 16*, Göttingen 1959.

[2]) R. Rendtorff, *ThLZ* XC 1965, pp. 591-593 (book-review of Koch).

[3]) E. Auerbach, "Die babylonische Datierung im Pentateuch und das Alter des Priesterkodex", *VT* II 1952, pp. 334-342. In so far as this article is a refutation of Kaufmann's pre-Deuteronomic dating, we agree with Auerbach; cf. the previous note 2 on p. 9.

[4]) H. Cazelles, l.c. "Pentateuque", col. 822.

[5]) L. Rost, "Zum geschichtlichen Ort der Pentateuchquellen", *ZThK* LIII 1956, pp. 1-10.

comfort those in misery and distress, as ROTH [1]) says, is not obvious
to us, even after spending a good many years on the theology of P.
According to HENRY [2]), the priestly theology is stressing the divine
order in creation over against the sceptical tendencies in exilic times;
but the exilic chronology of P is here supposed rather than demonstrated. An important external argument is put forward by KAPEL-
RUD [3]). He argues that Second Isaiah knew of P's creation story and
Exodus narrative, and that therefore P should be dated not later than
550 B.C. There is only room left for some minor adjustments and a
few later additions after this date. The argument requires serious
examination in our second Chapter (E, 1).

We have not found any defender of a late Persian date of the PC.
HOOKE [4]) mentions a prestly school of writers and editors who
produced a document P in the Persian period. But he seems to refer
to the well-known classical thesis, because later on he mentions "the
post-exilic editors emerging from the purifying experience of the
captivity". WINNETT [5]) dates P at about 400 B.C., but he does not
seem to attribute the same meaning to the symbol P as do the other
authors. He calls it "an official revision". J and E are also different,
J being post-exilic. No further argument is given.

A later Persian origin, however, *is* defended for a group of texts
within the Code. The first scholar attempting this new line of approach
is H. CAZELLES [6]). For the first time the most recently published
Elephantine papyri (the "Brooklyn papyri") have been evaluated as
regards the PC. He sheds light on the connection between the
mission of Ezra, dated at the beginning of the fourth century B.C.,
and the contents of the PC. The post-exilic datation, however, still
seems to be axiomatic to him: "if there is anything new in the legalistic contribution by Ezra, it should be looked for *within* the PC",

---

[1]) J. ROTH, "La tradition sacerdotale dans le Pentateuque", NRT XC 1958,
pp. 696-721, esp. p. 698.

[2]) M. L. HENRY, "Phänomene religiöser Lebensbewegungen in der jahwistischen und priesterlichen Ueberlieferung", *ThLZ* LXXXV 1960, pp. 145-148.

[3]) A. S. KAPELRUD, "The Date of the Priestly Code (P)", *ASTI* III 1964,
pp. 58-64.

[4]) S. H. HOOKE, "Introduction to the Pentateuch", in: PEAKE's Commentary
on the Bible (ed. M. BLACK and H. H. ROWLEY), London 1963, pp. 168-175,
esp. p. 169 and 174.

[5]) F. V. WINNETT, "Re-Examining the Foundations", *JBL* LXXXIV 1965,
pp. 1-19.

[6]) H. CAZELLES, "La mission d'Esdras", *VT* IV 1954, pp. 113-140.

and so he draws our attention to the *ger* and *'ezraḥ* additions [1]). GRELOT [2]) developed this point in a valuable series of articles. Not only should this *ger-'ezraḥ* formula be dated after 419 B.C. (the date of the Pascal-papyrus of Elephantine) but we should do the same with quite a number of texts, all of them permeated with the Dispersion piety of the Jews. They consist of excommunication formulas, Dispersion terminology (allusions to "all the places where they live"), allusions to the "community" and references to purity. But, GRELOT says, "this list is not exhaustive. Special study of this point might reveal more criteria. The number of additional chapters, belonging to the latest *mise au point* of the PC may be fairly high" [3]). The present study is meant to be an answer to this invitation. It not only confirms the findings of GRELOT, but it challenges the assumption, taken for granted, as in CAZELLES's study, of an early post-exilic origin of the PC. This axiom has impressed GRELOT so much that he is disturbed by the fact that the excommunication formula in Gen. xvii 14 does not look like a *pièce rapportée* and tries to demonstrate that it *is*. In spite of this difference of opinion, it will be clear to the reader of the following pages how much the present author owes to CAZELLES and GRELOT, whose ideas have put him on the road outlined in this work.

We want to show that the entire PC is to be tied up with the Ezra mission as dated in the late Persian period (398 B.C.).

After this survey of the literature on the PC since WELLHAUSEN, the following questions suggest themselves.

1. What is the extent of the PC? Is it present in the Book of Joshua? If so, does the *Landnahme* play any part in its programmatic intentions? What is the role of Shiloh?

2. What is the role of the cult in P? Is its background centralistic and Jerusalemite? Or have Deuteronomic concepts been read into it since WELLHAUSEN?

3. In what respect does it express a divinely commanded programme of action for the nearby future? Does this help in pinpointing more exactly the date and origin of P and its theological outlook?

---

[1]) *Ibidem*, p. 126. Italics are ours.
[2]) P. GRELOT, "La dernière étape de la rédaction sacerdotale", *VT* VI 1956, pp. 174-189.
[3]) *Ibidem*, p. 182.

Our detailed research on the PC along these lines has convinced us that in this field of biblical scholarship a fairly large number of unadequately founded assumptions have too long remained unchallenged.

II. THE PRIESTLY CODE IN POST-EXILIC HISTORY

A. *Exile and Return in Israel and Judah*

A preliminary condition to any understanding of the political situation during the Persian empire is an exact knowledge of the specific differences between Exile and Captivity in Israel and in Judah. We owe to A. ALT [1]) an excellent survey of the issue. He emphasizes the fact that the Assyrian structure of the province of Samaria had transferred itself into the social and political structure of that part of the Persian empire. It was characteristic of Assyrian policy to substitute the political superstructure of the countries they had conquered for one founded on elements of population taken from remote areas of their empire. Relying upon the loyalty of those groups of the population, they could easily incorporate the conquered territories into the provincial system of their empire. Such an exchange of population seems to have taken place more than once (cf. Ezr. iv 2, 10). The result at any rate was a very strong link with the court. ALT stresses the fact that this socio-political superstructure (*soziale Oberschicht*) naturally benefited by keeping aloof from the original population (whose major part was left behind in the country), since this aloofness was the best guarantee for its good relations with the Assyrian, and later the Persian court.

This approach seems more realistic than the view advanced by H. H. ROWLEY [2]). He takes the biblical record of the exchange of population in Samaria (2 Kgs. xvii; Ezr. iv 2. 10) to be wholly legendary. That 2 Kgs. xvii from a historical point of view is biased can hardly be denied, but that there would have been no exchange at all would run contrary to all we know of Assyrian policy.

---

[1]) A. ALT, "Die Rolle Samarias bei der Entstehung des Judentums", *Kleine Schriften* II, pp. 316-337. Cf. also: E. WUERTHWEIN, *Der ʿamm haʾarez im Alten Testament*, Stuttgart 1936, p. 60: "Wir haben also durch eine historische Analyse feststellen können, dass die aus dem Osten nach Samarien verpflanzte Bevölkerung eine besondere Mission hat, nämlich einen Ersatz zu bilden für die deportierten Oberschicht ... Sie nimmt in ihrem Gebiet mutatis mutandis dieselbe Stellung ein, die einst der judäische ʿamm haʾarez in Juda innegehabt hatte".

[2]) H. H. ROWLEY, "The Samaritan Schism in legend and history", in: *Israel's prophetic heritage*, London 1962, pp. 208-222, esp. p. 212.

As for Judah, here the situation was quite different. The neo-Babylonians had left the political structure of that province hanging in the air. On the one hand they had removed the élite of the population, but on the other they had not transformed Judah into a neo-Babylonian province. The discontentment of the exiled Judeans about the situation is not surprising. They were left in what ALT calls a *Provisorium*, looking forward to their return. Jer. xxix 24-28 sums up their spiritual attitude; it is a protest against any suggestion of resignation to the actual state of affairs.

The different after-effects of the exile in Samaria and in Judah are important for a good understanding of the course of events under the Achemenides. In Samaria the leading noblemen continued to maintain strong ties with the Persian court, like they did with the Assyrian and neo-Babylonian, "they were eating the salt of the palace" (Ezr. iv 14) and maintained their supervision over Judah as well as over the northern region. On several occasions a strong influx of well-prepared returning Judeans, who from the beginning of the exile had been very keen on returning, tried to improve the uncertain situation of their country, by putting an end to the Samaritan tutelage and gaining independence [1]).

It is here that the source of the conflicts described in Ezra and Nehemiah is to be found. The hypothesis we will develop in the present work will utilize ALT's thesis: in our view, Ezra's mission and the PC have an impact on both Samaria and Judah. The whole of the Palestinian community is involved, and therefore a knowledge of the differences between its various parts is essential.

From ALT's thesis it is clear that we must not underestimate the extent to which pre-exilic traditions were retained among the Judean exiles, nor the formation of priestly and lay genealogies. MOWINCKEL would seem to make this mistake [2]). If the exiles consisted of the leading and most able strata of the population of Judah, if their

---

[1]) H. H. GROSHEIDE, "Juda als onderdeel van het Perzische Rijk", *GTT* LIV 1954, pp. 65-76: Nehemiah would never have called the governors of Samaria "his predecessors" in the office of *peḥa* in Neh. v 15, because he did not do so either in Neh. ii 10. Therefore Judah had been an independent province long before Nehemiah.

But, in our view, Neh. ii 7, 9 suggests that Sanballat and Tobiah received the information because they were governors; that Nehemiah does not call them so has the same reason why he stresses their bad behaviour as governors in Neh. v 15, viz his hostility to them.

[2]) S. MOWINCKEL, *Studien zu dem Buche Ezra-Nehemia* I, *Die Listen*, Oslo 1964, pp. 75-77.

exile was only a half-way measure not followed by the establishment of a provincial rule by the conquering empire in their homeland, then all their hopes and expectations must have been set on their return and the restoration.

Summing up, two factors provide the key to an understanding of the history of Palestine during the Persian empire: the consciously segregational and non-Israelite attitude of the Samaritan authorities (the ʿam haʾareṣ of Ezr.-Neh.), and the loyalty to the Persian court of both the Judean and Samaritan authorities, even though their reasons for it were different. In the North it was the *status quo*, in the South the final attainment of political independence.

The discussion about the meaning of ʿam haʾareṣ goes on. Adhering to ALT's view as expounded above, we cannot agree with COGGIN [1]). The opposition of the ʿam haʾareṣ against the construction of the temple would have been caused by their Yahwistic-nationalistic feelings, which would turn down any settlement imposed by a foreign dictator. Oversimplifying things, COGGIN extends WUERTHWEIN's approach to the post-exilic situation.

Equally unacceptable is NICHOLSON's view [2]) that the term ʿam haʾareṣ has no specific meaning at all and means nothing more than "indigenous population". ALT rightly points to Ezr. iv 14 to shed light on their relations with the Persian court. That court was the source of their authority in Samaria.

A well-balanced synthesis of Israelite history in Persian times has been given by K. GALLING [3]). The new Achemenid policy of tolerance in religious affairs is too well-known to need elaboration here. Nor have we to dwell on GALLING's criticism of the Chronicler's recording of a collective return of exiles in 538 B.C., as mentioned in Ezr. i. Important, however, is GALLING's correction of his former view of a return under Cambyses [4]). He now considers even such a date as too early. To him Ezr. ii- Neh. vii is a list presented to the visitator Tatnaï (Ezr. v 3 ff.). The return, then, is only of recent date; there is no reference to a reigning sovereign. Therefore the first large-scale (Neh. vii 5) return is to be put during the reign of Darius I in 521 B.C. The direct occasion of that return is supposed to be the loyalty of

---

[1]) R. J. COGGINS, "The Interpretation of Ezra IV, 4", *JTS* XVI 1965, pp. 124-127.

[2]) E. W. NICHOLSON, "The meaning of the expression ʿam haʾareṣ in the Old Testament", JSS X 1965, pp. 59-66.

[3]) Kurt GALLING, *Studien zur Geschichte Israels im persischen Zeitalter*, Tübingen 1964.

[4]) L.c. *Studien* . . . p. 56-60.

the Jews to Darius in the revolt of Gaumata and Nidintu-Bel; the indirect occasion, according to GALLING, the governmental structure of the western part of the Persian empire, well-established by now. GALLING holds the absence of this structure in 538 B.C. a decisive argument against a return under Cyrus.

A difficulty that can be brought against GALLING's view is the different impression one gets from Haggai's prophecies, which date from exactly the same time. How are we to explain the messianic excitement in Palestine in 520 B.C., commonly associated with the rebellious movements in 522-520 B.C. [1]), if there had just been an influx of Persian-loyal Babylonian Jews? Does the prophet lend his voice to those sections of the population that had never been in exile? On the other hand, is it the influence of just-returned exiles which caused the messianic movement to end so soon? More about this in the present Chapter under E, 2.

Another difficulty is the community's poverty stressed by Haggai, in contrast to the supposed great wealth of the returning exiles (cf. GALLING's explanation [2]) of slaves being mentioned in Neh. vii 67).

In spite of these difficulties arising from Haggai, GALLING's thesis seems better founded than the one advanced by W. RUDOLPH [3]) who defends a first return close in time to the Cyrus decree of 538 B.C. The two grounds of his argument,

(*a*) an influx of Persian-loyal Jews must have been attractive to Cyrus no less than to Darius; and

(*b*) the absence of financial support is understandable because of the lack of organisation of the empire, are mutually exclusive. One might object that this problem is outside the scope of the present study. Yet it may be of indirect interest to us, since the *de facto* rule of the Samaritan non-Israelite leading classes over Judah might be strengthened so long as the Judean return was delayed.

If ALT is right, a further conclusion is that the usual picture of the religious state of affairs in Samaria as syncretistic is probably incorrect. From a historical point of view the presentation in 2 Kgs. xvii 24-41, viz that the whole population was given to syncretism, is not unbiased. ROWLEY (l.c.) sees in Hezek. viii an indication that Jerusalem itself was a stronghold of syncretism. There is reason to suppose that

---

[1]) Because of this messianism of Haggai, the statement of J. M. MYERS, *Ezra-Nehemiah*, Garden City 1965, p. XXV: "There is no overt adverse judgment against the Persians in the exilic or postexilic prophets or in the words of the Chronicler", would ask for some qualification.

[2]) L.c. *Studien* . . . p. 101.

[3]) W. RUDOLPH, *Ezra und Nehemia*, Tübingen 1949, p. 63.

genuin Yahwism was predominant in the northern part of the country. It was not the northern Yahwists who were responsible for the conflicts about cultic participation. Neither were the Persian authorities, as ROWLEY suggests, unless "Persian authorities" stands for the leading classes loyal to the Persian court, which obviously is not what ROWLEY means. It was of paramount importance for those leading classes to take share in the Jerusalemite cult in order to confirm their political rule not only over northern Israel but over Judah as well. Unfortunately they were utterly unacceptable to the Yahwists because they kept aloof from genuine Israelite traditions. Now there is, as we are going to show in the following pages, a fundamental difference in the way Nehemiah and Ezra dealt with this situation.

In discussing Ezra and Nehemiah we take our startingpoint from the now wide-spread view that the order of Ezra and Nehemiah in the actual biblical text should be inverted. For a summary of the issue and the relevant authors we refer to EISSFELDT [1]). To the authors defending the Chronicler's order should be added Bo REICKE [2]) and J. MORGENSTERN [3]); to the authors defending a date in the later years of Artaxerxes I M. NOTH [4]); to the authors defending the 7th yeart of Artaxerxes II W. SCHNEEMELCHER [5]) and P. GRELOT whose studies will be viewed in detail. J. M. MYERS [6]) refuses to choose between the middle and late chronology.

B. *Nehemiah*

An interesting point is made by MOWINCKEL [7]), when he uses Is. lvi 3-5 to shed light on Nehemiah's personality. In view of his office at the Persian court, it is only reasonable to suppose that Nehemiah

---

[1]) EISSFELDT, l.c. *Einl.* p. 751 ff.

[2]) Bo REICKE, *Neutestamentliche Zeitgeschichte*. Die biblische Welt 500 v.-100 n. Chr. Berlin 1965.

[3]) J. MORGENSTERN, "The Dates of Ezrah and Nehemiah", *JSS* VII 1962, pp. 1-11.

[4]) M. NOTH, *Geschichte Israels*, Göttingen 1963, p. 289.

[5]) W. SCHNEEMELCHER, "Esra", in: Reallexikon für Antike und Christentum VI 1965, pp. 595-612, col. 597.

[6]) J. M. MYERS, l.c. *Ezra* . . . p. XXXVII.

[7]) S. MOWINCKEL, *Studien zu dem Buche Ezra-Nehemia* II Die Nehemia-Denk-schrift, Oslo 1964, p. 81. G. VON RAD, "Die Nehemia-Denkschrift", *ZAW* LXXVI, 1964, pp. 176-187 refers to the biographical inscriptions of Egyptian magistrates. In earlier publications MOWINCKEL had pointed to Asiatic royal inscriptions, but according to VON RAD, far closer parallels are to be found in the inscriptions of magistrates in the late periods of the Egyptian reign. Note VON

was a eunuch. Instead of longing for survival by progenity his longing must have been for survival by means of a memorial in the temple in the way the Isaiah text promises. More is indeed to be said for considering Nehemiah's text as meant for a perpetual memorial in the temple (*Denkschrift*) rather than as a report of his acts as governor, intended for the Persian court (*Rechenschaftsbericht*). If it was to be cut in stone, the stone, MOWINCKEL tells us, would not need to have been much bigger than the Mesha-stone. It is even possible to fancy that, in case his view is right, in some future time such a memorial stone might be excavated on the actual temple site. Anyhow, the question is not without some relationship to our subject; if the performance of great feats, to be commemorated within the temple enclosure, was foremost in Nehemiah's mind, the exclusiveness and purity of the cult in Jerusalem may have been more important to him than a political compromise with the Samaritan leading classes, as is shown in the expulsion of the high priest's son. The circumstances that led to his mission are, however, nationalistic; as regards Nehemiah's sorrow on the miserable state of Jerusalem many exegetes refer to Ezr. iv 7-23.

MORGENSTERN [1]) also ties up Nehemiah's mission with Ezr. iv 7-23; he incorporates both data into his theory of the year of catastrophe 485 B.C. The temple which, according to the inscription discovered in 1937, was destroyed by Xerxes in that year is supposed by him to have been the temple of Jerusalem. Ezr. iv 16, however, seems to be incompatible with this theory. Is it likely that a written complaint would be sent to the Persian administration at the beginning of Xerxes's reign, one in a series of many complaints of the same kind, when just then a calamity of the size MORGEN-STERN has in mind, occurred? Not only biblical scholars but orientalists as well consider the temple referred to in the inscription to be Babylonian [2]).

From the viewpoint of the Persian court it is no doubt strange that Artaxerxes I should agree to Nehemiah's request thereby granting independence to Judah so soon after his favourable answer to the Samaritan demand to stop the building of Jerusalem's walls.

RAD's remark on p. 187: "Es ist die Einstellung eines Tat-menschen, dem priesterlich-kultische Probleme im Grunde fremd sind. Dass Nehemia die öffentlichen Dinge in Jerusalem in Ordnung bringen wollte, spricht noch nicht für einen theologische Eifer. Darum ist es doch recht merkwürdig, dass Nehemia, den man so gern für einen der Väter des "Nomismus" gehalten hat, sich so wenig oder gar nicht von der Frage der Erfüllung des Gesetzes bewegt zeigt"

[1]) L.c. "The Dates . . ." p. 1-11.

[2]) J. DUCHESNE-GUILLEMIN, *La Religion de l'Iran ancien*, Paris 1962, p. 156. R. KITTEL, *Geschichte des Volkes Israel* II, 2, Stuttgart 1929 (1st and 2nd ed.), p. 485.

GALLING's answer [1]) to this difficulty is that Aitaxerxes had got the worst of his dispute with Megabyzos, whom he had to maintain as satrap of Syria [2]). He had therefore to counterbalance this uncertain factor by introducing a more stable element of loyalty in the person of the governor of the province of Judah, now independent. At the same time he could use him and his province as a spearpoint against Egypt. The position of Judah as bulwark against ever-turbulent Egypt remains throughout the whole period the constant element in the Persian policy towards the Judean province. More difficult is the question as seen from the viewpoint of the Babylonian Jewry. Was for them the movement that led to Nehemiah's mission at the same time the starting-point for the mission of Ezra, which aimed at a reformation of far wider range, as NOTH [3]) suggests? We do not think so. In our view, the differences in outlook and background of these two missions are so great as to make a certain distance in time between them plausible. Hence we do not favour the Ezra date of NOTH (shortly after Nehemiah, during the reign of Artaxerxes I). Is it not more probable that Nehemiah shared the nationalistic feeling of the Palestinian community [4]), whereas the Babylonian Jews were more Persian-loyal in outlook?

Far more important and in a way basic to our study is the *Deutero-nomic* character of Nehemiah's activity, as indicated by CAZELLES [5]). The religious and social measures undertaken by Nehemiah, viz the protection of the poor landowners, his concern about the sabbath and about mixed marriages go entirely back to the prophets and Deuteronomy. A striking example is Neh. xiii 15 and 28, as compared with Dt. vii 3.

In one instance CAZELLES seems to trim the evidence to his thesis [6]), attributing the quotation of Dt. xxiii 4-6 to Nehemiah himself, but the first person here is not a singular but a plural form; the quotation therefore is Chronistic.

CAZELLES has been the first to draw attention not only to this fact, but also to its importance for the study of the PC. It is even possible, we think (as we shall see later on), to conclude from this more than CAZELLES does.

---

[1]) L.c. *Studien* . . . p. 156.
[2]) R. KITTEL, l.c. *Geschichte* . . . p. 487 f.
[3]) L.c. *Geschichte Israels* . . . p. 299.
[4]) Cf. p. 22, n. 7 of the present Chapter.
[5]) H. CAZELLES, l.c. "La mission . . ." p. 120.
[6]) *Ibidem*. The two forms *niqra'* and *nimṣa'* might also be *niphal*.

There is one more feature in the Nehemiah memorial-text which in our view could be used to reconstruct the sequel of historical events, viz the end of the canonical Book of Nehemiah (xiii 29).

According to RUDOLPH [1]), the whole text, up to v. 31, belongs to the Memoirs of Nehemiah, except v. 30a, which is a gloss. But with CAZELLES [2]) we hold that v. 29b might be an addition by the Chronicler's hand, explaining in his favourite way the defilement of the priesthood.

Now if RUDOLPH were right, v. 29b would be by the hand of Nehemiah himself; in this case the text reflects a clear insight on his part into the possible consequences of his measures against Sanballat's son-in-law. He could not, of course, have ended the text of his temple memorial on a gloomy note, but his official oral or written report to the Persian court may have expressed far more misgivings about the course of events in the province of Palestine. Therefore the matter of authenticity of v. 29b is not of final importance; the expulsion of the high priest's son could not fail to have consequences important for the Persian court. This expulsion was bound to threaten the delicate Deuteronomic alliance of priests from northern Israel and from Jerusalem, and stir up the demand for a sanctuary in the North, which found strong support in the text of Deuteronomy itself. ROWLEY [3]) is certainly right in stressing the fact that Jerusalem's claims to be the Deuteronomic cultic centre (Dt. xii) were considerably less strong than those of the North. Only the discovery of the Book of Deuteronomy in Jerusalem under Josiah's reign gave a decisive turn to history in favour of that city. Not until then could the central sanctuary of Dt. xii be identified with the temple of Jerusalem. This is often overlooked in discussions about the Samaritan Schism.

Anyway, the tension between Jerusalem and Samaria may have influenced the choice of Nehemiah's successor as governor of Judah. GALLING [4]) says the date of succession of Bagoas is unknown to us. Bagoas, according to the Elephantine papyri, was certainly in office in 411 B.C.. Did Nehemiah's mission end at the death of Artaxerxes? More important is the fact that a Persian, not a Jewish successor was appointed. GALLING thinks that a man neutral in religious matters was chosen in order to lessen the tension with Samaria.

[1]) L.c. *Ezra.*, p. 210 f.
[2]) L.c. "La mission . . ." p. 135.
[3]) L.c. "The Samaritan Schism." p. 210 f.
[4]) L.c. *Studien* p. 157 f.

In fact, the Elephantine papyri indicate that Bagoas did respect Samaritan opinion. In any case, the balance between the Samaritan and Judean interests within the structure of the Persian common-wealth must have been a matter of lasting concern to the Persian court. It may well have been that the nomination of the Persian Bagoas was counterbalanced by an invitation from the court to the Babylonian Jews to prepare a new legislation aiming at a greater unity of the Palestinian community. It must have become clear, especially at the end of Nehemiah's career, that the prevailing Deuteronomic legislation in Palestine was inadequate to effect that unity between the two parts of Palestine. Our concept of the ties between Nehemiah's and Ezra's work is therefore different from NOTH's above-mentioned view. In our opinion, Nehemiah's term as a governor was a decisive test-case of relationships in Palestine. Up to Nehemiah's coming the political centre of the country was Samaria, its cultic centre Jerusalem. Judah had been made a separate province. It was not to be expected that the cultic predominance of Jerusalem could be maintained, at least so long as the prevailing Deuteronomic legislation was left as it was. The dominating position of the Jerusalemite temple was a legacy from the monarchical period of Israelite history; the Zadokite priesthood had taken care to provide for a legal backing of that position. Yet it was not self-evident that this domination was to continue during the Persian empire. Nehe-miah's rigoristic and provocative attitude, although based on other grounds than an attachment to Zadokite traditions, laid bare the weak spot in that Jerusalemite domination, throwing back the northerners on Deuteronomy, that is, on the old cultic traditions from the North. It was now up to the Persian court to decide what to do about the unity of that region which was of such great strategical value against Egypt. That loyal Jewish subjects should be ordered to prepare a new codification of religious and cultic traditions would be quite in harmony with all we know about the Persian practice of government. Whether any such campaign was likely to succeed, we will see later on.

C. *Ezra*

I. *Preliminary literary criticism of the relevant texts*

a. Neh. viii-x

It is not our intention to repeat here all the efforts of the com-mentators to disentangle the literary problems of the book. A few remarks about the texts closely connected with our subject are, however, necessary.

First of all there is the problem whether Neh. viii is in its proper place or whether the Chapter was transferred from between Ezr. viii and ix to its actual place. If the latter alternative is right, as is commonly believed, then the purpose of the transfer must have been the same as that of the two glosses Neh. viii 9 and xii 33, viz to create an artificial connection between the work of the two great Jewish reformers. There is almost general agreement that this connection was made by the Chronicler. The first to challenge this consensus was MOWINCKEL [1]). In his view the entire structure of Neh. vii-x ("the whole chaos" he says) derives from the hand of a redactor, posterior to the Chronicler, probably living in the Maccabean period.

The most important evidence for MOWINCKEL's view is the fact that Flavius Josephus was not aware of any connection between the two reformers. According to Josephus, Ezra was dead before Nehemiah started on his mission. In other words, Josephus *did* know the actual order of the books, but did *not* know about any simultaneous appearance of the two men, as in the actual text. (It is good to keep in mind that these two problems are indeed not connected). The conclusion is therefore justified that the first Greek translations did not know of such a connection. MOWINCKEL also adduces 3 Esdras (LXX: Esdras A) as evidence against the connection of Ezra and Nehemiah. But this evidence is questionable, since 3 Esdras ix 37 can hardly be anything else than a summary of the synoecism of Nehemiah (Neh. vii 4-5; 72). Although in 3 Esdras we get a better representation of the historical order of events, the writer did not avail of any information independent of MT in its actual form. J. M. MYERS [2]) thinks that probably the first serious attempt to rearrange the various episodes was made by the compiler of First Esdras (= 3 Esdras or Esdras A of the LXX). As for Josephus, the same author says (ibid.) that Josephus is often seen to follow the same order as the First Esdras.

Further evidence for MOWINCKEL's thesis is the identification of Nehemiah and Tirshata in Neh. viii 9 which is not in the spirit of the Chronicler, for whom Tirshata is probably Sorobabel (Ezr. ii 63). The identification must have been the result of moving the Chapter

---

[1]) L.c. *Studien* I p. 45 ff.
[2]) L.c. J. M. MYERS, *Ezra* ... p. XLII.

to its actual place behind Neh. vii and the redactor responsible for that move must therefore be different from the Chronicler.

According to MOWINCKEL, not only the insertion of Neh. viii but also the whole composition of Neh. ix is by a redactional hand. We agree with him against RUDOLPH (i 1.) that Neh. ix cannot have been taken from after Ezr. ix-x. There is no connection at all, MOWINCKEL says, between the "separation from the b^enej nekar" in Neh. ix 1 and the measures concerning mixed marriages in Ezr. ix-x. Neither can the transition from Neh. viii to Neh. ix have been in the original: psychologically as well as cultically the alleged transition from joy to penance is impossible. Moreover, the secondary character of the list in Neh. vii 6 ff. (taken from Ezr. ii) and of the originally independent document of Neh. x also strongly suggests that Neh. vii 6-x 40 as a whole is a late redactional arrangement. If the Chronicler, as MOWINCKEL holds, is to be dated at the beginning of the second century B.C. (cf. the Seleucid anachronism Ezr. vi 22),—and indeed that date is not irreconcilable with EISSFELDT's *terminus ad quem* [1])— then the whole construction should be assigned to Maccabean times.

We are inclined to accept MOWINCKEL's analysis of the text and there may even be internal evidence of the Maccabean redactor's theological motives. It seems to have been overlooked so far that the long section on the walls (Neh. vii 1-vii 43) constitutes a unity structured by an *inclusio* consisting of vii 1-5a, the completion of the walls, and xii 27-43, their dedication. Is the whole passage perhaps meant to give a theological explanation of the city walls of Jerusalem? Is it intended to express the fact that those city walls are, literally, "a wall around the Law" [2])? We see the whole community of Israel (vii 4-72 and xi 1-xii 26) before us, in three 'congregations', confessing their loyalty to the Law of God. Such a theological construction would be typical of the Maccabean period. From quite a different starting-point, therefore, we have arrived at a confirmation of MOWINCKEL's thesis. Moreover, the end of Neh. ix (v. 36 f.) with its undertones of slavery and submission, cannot very well be an expression of piety during the Persian period and is certainly not by the Chronicler's hand (cf. Ezr. vi 22). RUDOLPH (i.l.) is silent about this. The mood of this passage would be entirely in accord with the Maccabean period [3]) (cf. also Neh. ix 30 in contrast with Ezr. iv 4).

---

[1]) L.c. *Einl.* p. 733.
[2]) Cf. 1 Macc. i, 36-40.
[3]) Cf. 1 Macc. ii 11.

Likewise, the composition of the entire Chapter of Neh. ix must have been due to the fact that Neh. viii was too joyful to the Maccabean redactor. It did not reflect the state of affairs during his time. During the Persian time, on the other hand, any stress on the Day of Atonement (*Yom Kippur*) would not have corresponded to the triumphal feelings of this period.

All this may help us to solve another well-known problem. For a long time exegetes have noticed that in Neh. viii the liturgical calendar of Lev. xxiii, to all appearances, has not been followed. Ezra reads to the people from the Law on the first day of the seventh month. On the second day the people hear the prescriptions about the Feast of Tabernacles in the Law. Is *Yom Kippur* left out and is the author unaware of the priestly calendar of Lev. xxiii? Such a deviation from the priestly calendar would be strange in view of the fact that v. 18 of the same Chapter is so close to the priestly calendar. According to MORGENSTERN [1]) and others, this is convincing proof that Ezra was ignorant of both the regulations about *Yom Kippur*, the most forcibly imposed observance of Judaism, and of the exact date of the Feast of Tabernacles. If indeed the argument were conclusive, there would be no connection between Ezra and the PC.

But *is* the argument conclusive? RUDOLPH (i.l.) calls it "*ein vorschnelles argumentum e silentio*". According to him the reasons Ezra may have had to omit the Day of Atonement are to be looked for in v. 9-12: at that moment the people would hardly bear to be reminded of *Yom Kippur*. More acceptable seems MOWINCKEL's [2]) theory when he says that a day of repentance was not called for after the national law had been renewed. Now *Yom Kippur* was indeed the day in which the ritual of atonement for the sins against the Law was performed. NOTH [3]) says that the author wanted to have done with the joyful feast before going to speak about the day of penance. Apart from the problem of the literary criticism of Ch. ix, this theory seems unacceptable because of its artificiality.

But did the author mean to say that Ezra ignored or neglected the Day of Atonement? In any case, this does not seem to have been the opinion of the redactor of Ch. ix. For in v. 1 he dated his (fictitious) congregation on the 24th, after the Feast of Tabernacles, according to the priestly calendar. In our view the redactor inter-

---

[1]) L.c. "The Dates . . ." p. 10.
[2]) L.c. *Studien* I, p. 51.
[3]) M. NOTH, *Ueberlieferungsgeschichtliche Studien* I, Halle 1943, p. 148 f.

preted Ch. vii in the right way. In viii 9-12 it is told how Ezra
tried to allay the overwhelming sorrow of the people, and in the
same context (v. 13) there follows how, on the second day, Ezra
and his helpers looked for even stronger remedies against the sorrow
of the people, and then they announced the celebration of the most
joyful feast of the Jewish religion. Any mention of *Yom Kippur* would
be out of place, either because it would only make sense after a year
of observance of the newly established Law, or even more so because
there would be no point in the Chronicler mentioning it now that he
has reached the climax of his edifying work. Now for the Maccebean
redactor the situation was just the other way round. The state of
Israel was miserable; not content, therefore, with the bright colours
of Ch. viii, he inserts a penitential liturgy, known to him, and
suggests it to have taken place not on the 10th, which would have
been the right thing to do if he had assumed Ezra had omitted *Yom
Kippur*, but on the 24th. Thus the literary reason for leaving out
Yom Kippur in the Chronicler's work is parallel to the Maccabean
insertion of the penitential liturgy of Neh. ix.

b. Ezr. vii 1-x 44

Obviously, the second part of this section (Ch. ix and x) on
Ezra's measures against mixed marriages, is of great importance to
anyone who tries to outline the reformer's mental attitude. Is, as is
often said, exclusiveness and rigorism an outstanding feature of his
character? To us the authenticity of these Chapters seemed even
more questionable than that of the arrangement of Neh. viii-x. In
our view Maccabean characteristics abound here.

(1) In Ezr. ix 1.2.11; occurs the expression *'ammej ha'araṣôt*, an
odd double plural, which has not been given due attention. One
cannot agree with RUDOLPH [1]) (quoting WUERTHWEIN) that this is a
simple equivalent of the singular *'am ha'areṣ*. The singular expression
is so firmly rooted in the language that it does not give way even
when the verb is in the plural, as in Ezr. iv 4. Moreover, where the
plural occurs, the texts are interdependent. In Ezr. iii 3 it occurs in
a gloss (cf. RUDOLPH i.l.), concerned with the site of the altar among
the enemies; this is the spirit of Neh. ix and Ezr. ix. The interdependence is shown by the following survey:

Ezr. ix 1: *nibdal . . . me'ammej ha'araṣôt*

---

[1]) L.c. "Esra." p. 28. Cf. WUERTHWEIN, l.c. p. 51-71, esp. 55.

Ezr. x 11: *nibdal . . . me'ammej ha'areṣ* (the second part of the expression is in the singular form, like in Ezr. x 2)

Neh. ix 2: *nibdal . . . ẓera' jisra'el . . . benej nekar*

Neh. x 29: *nibdal . . . me'ammej ha'araṣôt*

Looking for the sense of this double plural and its possible date, we are helped by the *Maccabean* text Dan. ix 6. From this text it is evident that in the Maccabean period the expression *'am ha'areṣ* (in the singular form) meant: "the people of Israel" [1]). It was therefore no longer suitable to indicate the enemies of Israel in the Holy Land. That the newly coined expression *'ammej ha'araṣôt* mostly implied two plurals (cf. the survey) may reflect the hellenistic cultural situation. That culture comprised a variety of peoples and countries (cf. also 2 Chr. xiii 9).

(2) The terminology in Ezr. ix and x is close to that of Qumran, more than in any other chapter of the Book of Ezra. J. M. MYERS (i.l.) points *inter alia* to the above-mentioned double plural *'ammej ha'araṣôt* in 1 QM 19,9 and 1 QH 4,26 (where the meaning of the words is very general). To the words listed by MYERS should be added the biblical *hapax ta'anît* (self-abasement) in Ezr. ix 5; cf. Hf. 22,3; 4QpPs 37: 1,9.10; CD 6,19.

(3) Important internal evidence is to be found in Ezr. ix 12. The Hebrew text *we̱lo' . . . tidre̱šu še̱lomam we̱tobatam* is often translated as if *šalom* and *tobah* are the results of the efforts (*tidre̱šu*) of the Israelites (BJ: ne vous souciez jamais de leur paix), but it is clear that this translation is not the obvious sense of *daraš*. Better is RSV: and never seek their peace or prosperity. The Hebrew should be read as a warning not to be attracted and allured by the real brilliance and material prosperity of the surrounding peoples. It might be objected that the text is a quotation from Dt. xxiii 7, the only difference being the singular of the verb, but the new context gives a different meaning to the quotation. In Dt its context was cultic; in Ezr. ix 12 the text is preceded by a rejection of mixed marriages and followed

---

[1]) E. WUERTHWEIN, l.c. *Der 'amm . . .* p. 54, erroneously states that this text being a summary is wholly dependent upon Jer. xliv 21. It must be obvious to anyone comparing the two texts that there is a remarkable shift in Dan. ix 6 by means of the new copula, the repetition of *'el* and the addition of *kol*. It is therefore surprising to say the least, when he writes: "Deshalb kann natürlich *'amm ha'areẓ* in Dan. ix 6 auch nicht verwendet werden als Zeuge für den Gebrauch von *'amm ha'areẓ* in der Zeit der Entstehung des grösseren Zusammenhanges, in dem sich Dan. ix 6 befindet".

by the admonition to preserve the good (*tub*) of their own land and to hand down the heritage to their progeny. Between these two parts of the sentence the expression *lo' tidre šu* etc. is most naturally explained as an exhortation to avoid the attraction and allurement of the peoples around.

If this exegesis is right, its conclusion is obvious. A danger for the Jewish faith from the side of the brillant Hellenistic civilisation was specific for the Maccabean period.

(4) Besides this indication of the historical situation in the regions around Israel, there are also indications of the condition of Israel itself. The expression *zera' haqqodeš*, the holy race (Ezr. ix 2), only occurs in a very late text (Is. vi 13b), a gloss not even to be found in LXX and therefore possibly originating from the renaissance of the Hebrew language during the Maccabean period, to which also the Qumran vocabulary has some relationship. In the gloss on Isaiah the expression *zera' haqqodeš* expresses the notion of Holy Remnant, a concept also influencing the canticle of Ezr. ix (cf. ix 8). Once more there is a relationship with Neh. ix, where the expression *zera' jisra'el* occurs in v. 2. We know of no texts from the Persian period where the idea of the Holy Remnant was expressed in such racial terms; cf. also the "abominable peoples" in Ezr. ix 14.

(5) What we said about Neh. ix 36-37 is also true of Ezr. ix 8: these expressions of slavery [1]) do not match at all with the proud and triumphal feelings of the Persian period (Ezr. vi 22; Ezr. vii). The description and mood agree with other canticles from the Maccabean period (Dan. ix 4-19; Dan. iii 25-45 and Bar. i and iii).

The same may be said about Ezr. ix 9 and x 7; the region mentioned is too small for it to have been described in the Persian period (Ezra's rescript uses so wide a geographical term as 'Transeuphratene'). Cf. also the three-days journey in x 8, suggesting a small region (NOWACK i.l.). The word *gader* in Ezr. ix 9 is often understood as pointing to Nehemiah's city walls and the text interpreted as evidence of Ezra's coming to Jerusalem after Nehemiah. But, as MYERS (i.l.) says, PRITCHARD's discoveries in Gibeon suggest that the term should be read in the sense of the vineyard of Is. v 5 f. This would be more in accordance with the term *bîhudah ûbřušalajim* following upon it.

---

[1]) This is why Is. lxiii 7-lxiv 11 and Dt. xxxii are no parallel texts to Ezr. ix, in spite of what is said by H. H. SCHAEDER, *Esra der Schreiber*, Tübingen 1930, p. 65.

SNAITH [1]) had already noticed that neither interpretation of *gader* would bring us very far.

(6) The picturesque detail about the rainfall in Ezr. x 9 reminds us of apocryphal literature [2]).

(7) The distinction between Levites on the one hand and singers and doorwaiters on the other (Ezr. x 23-24) is post-Chronistic [3]).

(8) A further link with the Maccabean section of Neh. is the meaning "lay-people" given to the word 'Israel' in Ezr. x 25 and ix 1; cf. Neh. xi 3.

(9) There may be some importance In the expression evening-*minḥah* in Ezr. ix 4-5, cf. the Maccabean text Dan. vi 11; ix 21.

(10) Notice the late word *maʿîdîm*, trembling, in Ezr. x 9; it occurs only here and in Dan. x 11. Also the expression (ix 9) *malkej Paras* the kings of Persia; the plural occurs only in Est. x 2; Dan. viii 20; x 13. (The singular form *melek Paras* is Chronistic).

(11) The summary of peoples in Ezr. ix 1 is dependent both on Dt. vii 1-4 and on Dt. xxiii 4-6 and xxiii 8-9. The texts are, however, applied and re-interpreted in a rigoristic and incorrect way. In Dt. xxiii 4-6 it is only cultic participation which is excluded; in xxiii 8-9 an indulgent attitude towards Edomites and Egyptians is recommended. We know of no text about Ezra or from the PC so openly clashing with Deuteronomy.

The conclusion seems justified that the two chapters concerning Ezra's measures in the matter of mixed marriages are unauthentic and legendary; they cannot be relied upon to outline the mission and character of Ezra but only to testify to the exclusiveness and rigorism [4]) of the Jewish minority so hard-pressed in the Maccabean period [5]).

---

[1]) N. H. SNAITH, "The Date of Ezra's Arrival in Jerusalem", *ZAW* LXIII 1951, pp. 53-66, esp. p. 59.

[2]) A. THOMSON, "An inquiry concerning the Books of Ezra and Nehemiah", *AJSLL* XLVIII 1931-1932, pp. 99-123, p. 123 and 127.

[3]) Cf. Ezr. ii 41; iii 10; vii 7; cf. J. DE FRAINE, *Esdras en Nehemias*, Roermond 1961, p. 71.

[4]) There is no reference to mixed marriages in 1 and 2 Macc., but there seem to be references in the Book of Wisdom (iii 16 and iv 6) and in Ecclesiasticus (xlvii 19-20 LXX).

[5]) To what dilemma a Chronistic attribution of Ezr. ix-x will lead, is demonstrated by H. C. M. VOGT, *Studie zur nachexilischen Gemeinde in Esra-Nehemia*, Werl 1966. Because he has to reconcile Ezr. vi 21 and Ezr. ix-x, he arrives at statements like these: ". . . die Bundestreue dadurch beweisen, dass sie sich von

c. The priestly genealogies

In our quest for the historical foundations of Ezra and the PC [1] the reliability of the priestly genealogies constitute an important issue.

(aa) The case of Neh. x 1-8 is extremely weak.

RUDOLPH's [2] defence that the list is a gloss and yet at the same time part of the original document quoted in the Chapter, is hardly convincing. He admits the literary evidence that the list as we have got it now, is an insertion. But, according to him, the Chronicler must have come across the list somewhere else in the documents he used. If the Chronicler had it all made up himself, he would have put Ezra at its head, not Nehemiah. MOWINCKEL's opinion about the Maccabean redaction seems to us far more convincing. Additional evidence for the thesis we think to have found in v. 29. There occurs the expression "to separate oneself from the peoples of the lands", *ʿammej haʾaraṣôt*. It is irrelevant whether this expression belongs to the framework of the list or to the list itself because, as the note in BJ points out, the list seems to interrupt an older context, which now constitutes the setting of the list. The Maccabean period seems to be the earliest possible date of the Chapter. We therefore disagree with KITTEL [3] who relies on Neh. x in arguing that there is a gradual post-exilic expansion of the ideas of the PC. According to him, the priestly concept of the genealogies of Phinehas and Ithamar reaches its final point (the 24 classes of 1 Chr. xxiv) through the intermediate stage of Neh. x, where we see the appearance of 21 or 22 priestly families instead of 4. The starting-point of the development was the division of the priests in 3 or 4 groups: Ezr. ii 36-39 = Neh. vii 39-42 (cf. Ezr. x 18-22) and Neh. xi 10-14 [4]).

---

ihren feindlichen *Brüdern* trennt" (p. 160). "Zwar sind die abgefallenen Israeliten im Augenblick noch Feinde der Gemeinde . . ." (*ibidem*). The fact that Ezr. ix-x "als Formular einer Bundesurkunde angelegt zu sein scheint" (p. 7) is in itself no sign of antiquity, cf. Qumran.

[1]) A useful survey of the relevant texts in: A. VAN DEN BORN, *Kronieken*, Roermond 1960, tabel 36, p. 265.

[2]) L.c. Esra p. 173 ff.

[3]) R. KITTEL l.c. *Geschichte* p. 685 and 406.

[4]) E. AUERBACH, "Der Aufstieg der Priesterschaft zur Macht im Alten Israel", VTS IX 1963, pp. 236-249. In this article an interesting hypothesis is defended for the decrease in numbers of the priests, and the absence of Harim in the list of Neh. xi.

(bb) As KITTEL (l.c.) admits, the case for Neh. xii 1-26 is no stronger; it clearly interrupts the context of xi 34-xii 27. RUDOLPH (i.l.) contends that the redactor who inserted the list wished to make a synchronistic link between the high priest Joiakim and both Ezra and Nehemiah [1]). But this is exactly in the spirit of the Maccabean redactor who composed the structure of Neh. viii-x [2]). As for Ezra's date that redactor might have relied on a superficial reading of Ezr. vii 7, where Artaxerxes could be taken to be Artaxerxes I, in whose reign Joiakim is supposed to have lived [3]). As for Nehemiah's date the redactor's synchronism disagrees with Neh. iii 1 and xiii 28, but the Maccabean redactor either overlooked this disagreement or let it stand. Evidence that not only v. 26 but the whole list is of Maccabean origin, is further revealed by the expression in v. 22 of 'Darius the Persian'. In spite of RUDOLPH's argument (i.l.) we think that this expression implies that the Persian period is finished. A comparison with Herodotus is not valid, because Judeans mentioning Darius were referring to their own king, as appears from the authentic parts of Ezra and Nehemiah.

If Darius the Persian is Darius II (424-404 B.C.), as is defended by J. DE FRAINE (i.l.) the redactor of the list seems to have been at pains to place the extended classification of priests (in 22 or 24 classes) in the period between the Return and the historical occurrence of Ezra.

For those who want to date Ezra's mission after Nehemiah (it should be stressed that KITTEL did not do so), the conclusion, though negative, is important; before Ezra's coming to Palestine the authentic genealogies do not show any characteristics of the genealogical structure of the PC.

Furthermore, there turns out to be a far greater unity in the Maccabean reworking of Ezra-Nehemiah than has been advanced by MOWINCKEL.

(cc) The systematical listing of priests in 1 Chr. xxiv offers a connection between the Phinehas-Ithamar system of the PC and pre-exilic history. Phinehas is linked up with Zadok and is given a dominant position, whereas Ithamar is connected with Ahimelek

---

[1]) It seems better not to isolate v. 26, as done by J. DE FRAINE, l.c. *Esdras.*, p. 129, but to consider it as the "seal" of the interruption xii 1-26.

[2]) We disagree therefore with BJ i.l., where this synchronism is said to be the Chronicler's work.

[3]) J. DE FRAINE, l.c. *Esdras* ... p. 127.

and therefore with Ebjathar. The rivalry of the two priests, who had parted company in the early years of king Solomon, seems to have been forgotten in this perfectly balanced genealogy. MOWINCKEL [1]), however, has no belief in the authenticity of this list in 1 Chr. xxiv. It does not fit into the context; after 1 Chr. xxiii one does not expect a list of priests, nor is the introductory formula in xxiii 3 adapted to Ch. xxiv. The promotion of Joiarib's family from the 17th (Neh. xii 6) to the 1st rank, is clear proof of the Maccabean provenance of the list. DE VAUX [2]) thinks that this promotion is only an adaptation of the list to Maccabean circumstances and no infringement upon its basic reliability. Against DE VAUX it can be brought that the mutual order of the priestly groups in 1 Chr. xxiv is not just peripheral but belongs to the very heart of the text. Its aim seems to be the legitimation of the internal order of families and especially of the predominance of the Joiarib family. This is why we side with BENZINGER's [3]) opinion rather than with MOWINCKEL's. According to the former, the list is Hasmonean rather than Maccabean. If the above defence of the Maccabean povenance of Neh. xii, where Joiarib is 17th, is reliable, our conclusion is bound to be that 1 Chr. xxiv is Hasmonean. This is in harmony with its double glossar character: xxiii 3-37 is added to xxiii 1-2 cf. xxviii 1; xxiv 1 comments upon xxiii 3. We also agree, however, with BENZINGER when he says that the connection of the Phinehas-Ithamar system with Zadokites and Ebjatharides may well be of ancient date, at least in so far as it reflects the claims of those who returned with Ezra. The extent to which these claims are historically reliable must remain an open question here.

(dd) As final and in a way most important text remains therefore Ezr. viii 2. Here Ezra's mission is linked up with a characteristic feature of the Priestly Code, viz the Phinehas-Ithamar system. According to MOWINCKEL [4]) the text is unauthentic, but here we cannot follow him. First of all, MOWINCKEL seems to have worked from an uncritical translation; how else could he speak about 'Artaxerxes, the king of Babel' as part of Ezr. viii 1, when the Hebrew text clearly connects *mibbabel* with *'olim*? Secondly, why does MOWINCKEL repeat his argument in 1964 without any reference to the

---

[1]) L.c. *Studien* I p. 120. Cf. A. VAN DEN BORN, l.c. *Kronieken*, p. 104.
[2]) R. DE VAUX, *Les institutions de l'Ancien Testament*, II Paris 1960, p. 266.
[3]) I. BENZINGER, *Die Bücher der Chronik*, Tübingen 1901, pp. 71 f.; 127.
[4]) L.c. *Studien* I, p. 116-123.

refutation by Rudolph (i.l.) in 1949? Mowinckel holds the beginning
of the list to be pleonastic, but neither Rudolph nor we can find any
trace of pleonasm. Mowinckel's contention that the list is an interruption of the context, is dismissed by Rudolph as "grotesque",
and we cannot but side with the latter here. His remark that the
suffixes of 'abôtekem and hitjaḥsam are without a reference is incom-
prehensible in view of vii 28 and the following 'olim (cf. Ezr. ii 62).
How can it be an objection (rather than a confirmation) that not one
of the names in the list occurs in viii 16? Mowinckel's remark that
all genealogies give evidence that the distribution of families over
Phinehas and Ithamar is pure theory, is no more than a *petitio principii*.

The historically valuable thing about Ezr. viii 2 *is* indeed the link
between Ezra's mission and the priestly genealogical system. That
traces of this system are fairly rare in other genealogical lists in the
Bible is not to be wondered at if the late chronology of Ezra's mission
is correct. With Eissfeldt[1]), we would prefer to defend the reliability of the text. Even Mowinckel himself, for that matter, has to
admit that the material of the list seems trustworthy and has nothing
in it which might put in doubt the authenticity of the document
underlying it [2]). De Vaux [3]) rightly sees in this text an indication
of a concordat arrived at in Babylonia between two groups of
priests in view of the return under Ezra. A parallel movement may
have taken place in Palestine, he says, but this statement is gratuitous,
because there is no text proof for it at all. It may well be that De
Vaux supports the wide-spread assumption that the PC was present
in Palestine shortly after 538 B.C. Whether or not those groups
were historically identical with the families of Zadok and Ebjathar
is, we repeat, irrelevant to our point. What *is* important, is that in
the Dispersion, not in Palestine, a group of priestly people vindicated
the old rights of the Ebjathar family against the Zadokites, still
so jealous of their rights in Hez. xliii 19; xlv 15. In view of Ezra's
undertaking, a sort of peace treaty seems to have been of the highest
urgency to all parties concerned.

II. *The historical data*

If our view of the end of Nehemiah's career is right, it must have
become clear to the Persian authorities of the time that the prevailing

---

[1]) L.c. *Einl.*, p. 74 .
[2]) L.c. *Studien* I, p. 122 f.
[3]) R. de Vaux, l.c. p. 264 f.

Deuteronomic legislation threatened to split up the Palestinian community because of the opposite claims being based upon it. A wholly new legislation was called for. It is therefore important to investigate whether the available historical data about Ezra suggest that promulgating such a new legislation was his task.

Mowinckel [1]) strongly opposes this idea. His argument is three-fold. He is against the interpretation of Ezra's title *saphar di 'elohah šᵉmajjah* as reflecting a high ministerial office in matters of Jewish religion at the Persian court. Secondly, according to him, the rescript in Ezr. vii clearly indicates that the Law was known already in Palestine. Thirdly, Neh. viii does not record the proclamation of a new Law but records a sort of "revival"-celebration, in which the observance of the Law is once more inculcated.

As for the first point [2]), Schaeder's [3]) opinion in his study of 1930, admittedly, is no more than a hypothesis; his main argument is the situation under the Parthes and Sassanides. This theory, however, is not decisive for our question. The Persians may very well have used the pious Ezra whether or not they bestowed upon him the high title, going with some court-office. A second question, quite apart from the previous one, is whether the author of the History of Ezra used that title in full knowledge of its Persian implication or whether he regarded it only as an expression of Ezra's piety towards the Law. Mowinckel says that the author would certainly have mentioned such a high office. Either he did not know of it or he deemed it more tactful not to stress the fact. Although we personally are inclined to adhere to Schaeder's hypothesis, the question may remain open; it is not of vital importance.

As for the second point [4]), Mowinckel says that Ezra could not possibly present himself as the promulgator of a new law, *even if he was so*, because this would have made his mission impossible. Now this is forcing an open door because the principle applies to anyone in Israel having anything to do with the Law. There was no pattern of thought about the Law outside the Mosaic one. Moreover, it invalidates what Mowinckel says about the text of the rescript. What is said in Ezr. vii 14, 25 f. is exactly what Mowinckel demands of

---

[1]) S. Mowinckel, *Studien zu dem Buche Ezra-Nehemia* III Die Ezra-Geschichte und das Gesetz Moses, Oslo 1965, pp. 121-123, 126-127; 131-136.

[2]) *Ibidem*, p. 121-124.

[3]) H. H. Schaeder, l.c. *Esra* . . . p. 39-59.

[4]) S. Mowinckel, l.c. *Studien* III p. 121-126.

anyone whose task it was to proclaim the Mosaic Law, even if that proclamation concerned a new literary form of that Mosaic Law. Within that Mosaic pattern the rescript is bound to say that a number of things in Judea are not in harmony with that Law (v. 14); that judges and magistrates may take the matter in hand (v. 25); and that some people are singled out as having expert knowledge of that Law (v. 25). Moreover, nobody claims that the legislation introduced by Ezra was so 'new' as to sound unfamiliar to all ears. We should not forget that the situation in Palestine during Bagoas's office was loaded with dispute and strife. It was Ezra's mission to introduce decisive judicial measures with the backing of both the Mosaic Law, applied to these circumstances, and of the Persian governmental power. This is the obvious sense of v. 25 and 26. The weakness of MOWINCKEL's argument is that he considers the data of Ezr. vii and Neh. viii purely by themselves. It is our conviction that all biblical and extra-biblical data should be compared so as to provide an overall picture. When this is done, the rescript too will appear in a new light.

There is an important detail in the text (overlooked up to now, we believe), suggesting that we have to do with a new legislative corpus. "Whatever seems good to you and your brethren to do with the rest of the silver and gold, you may do, *according to the will of your God*" (Ezr. vii 18). The final clause certainly does not mean that Ezra will have to use the rest of the money according to some personal reve- lation. The text obviously implies the existence of some *written* cultic prescriptions apart from those about sacrifices (= v. 17) for which heavy expenses will be needed. Is it justified to think of the tent of meeting in the PC? Nothing would clarify this passage better.

Furthermore, is not the implication of the heavy sanctions mention- ed in v. 26 that some new kind of legislation (although within the framework of the Mosaic revelation) is to be introduced? This verse has a striking parallel in the PC, viz the renewal of the "apodictic" death and excommunication sentences. We disagree with GALLING [1]) that the verse only bears on Ezra's dealings with the royal treasurers (v. 21-22). It is not at all convincing that v. 23 would have been the final clause and that v. 26 belonged to v. 21-22.

Nor is there any ground for RUDOLPH's statement (i.l.) that the Persians had nothing to do with the codification but only with the promulgation of this new legal corpus. This question can only be

---

[1]) L.c. *Studien* p. 167.

dealt with after questioning all the available evidence, especially the PC itself.

As for the third point [1]), the deep impression made upon the people when they heard the Law read out to them is certainly not the only ground for assuming that a new legislation was introduced, as MOWINCKEL contends. Nor is the assembly a regular liturgical reunion [2]) on the occasion of New Year's Day, as he holds. First of all, the assembly is held on profane territory, on the square near the Water-Gate (v. 1). Furthermore, the initiative for bringing the Book of the Law is ascribed to the people (ibid.). Nothing is told about the liturgical rites prescribed in the Law for festive celebrations, and the reading took a long time (v. 3). Ezra is standing on a wooden structure "especially made for that occasion". Furthermore, a delegation of noble laymen stands beside him (v. 4), so as to stress the governmental and even juridical implications of the assembly. The only religious gestures mentioned (v. 6) express acceptation and consent; no mention is made of sacrifices, incense or blessing of the people. The meaning of $m^ephora\check{s}$ in v. 8 is disputed; the translation "to read in sections" has been defended [3]). If, however, the meaning should be "providing it with explanations", then this may be an indication that the impression made upon the people was not due to the "revival"-character of the assembly, but to the implications of the Mosaic Law for everyday life. The examples advanced by MOWINCKEL to prove that a new legislation would have met with opposition and bitter resentment rather than with penitential tears, are inadequate. Since all legislation moved within the sacred framework of Mosaic revelation, there is little point in comparing, as MOWINCKEL does, this promulgation with the first preaching of the Gospel, meeting with fierce opposition in pagan northern Europe, nor with the strife in the Reformation period. That people can be deeply stirred by the words of an able preacher is true enough, but this is a truism, which hardly qualifies for argument.

It is doubtful whether 2 Kgs. xxiii is sufficient proof that for the introduction of a new legislation an assembly of a very different kind would be needed. Things were different when Israel was a kingdom.

---

[1]) L.c. *Studien* III, pp. 129-132.
[2]) L. M. MYERS, l.c. *Ezra* p. 153. The non-liturgical character is also apparent from the role of those taking part.
[3]) BOWMAN, "Samaritan Studies", *BJRL* XL 1957-1958, pp. 298-327.

Moreover, it has been argued [1] that the assembly in Neh. viii *is* indeed an imitation of that of 2 Kgs. xxiii, and, as we have seen, there are numerous details in Neh. viii, that point to the special character of the assembly. MOWINCKEL has to admit that in Neh. viii 15, 17 we have a concrete case of new legislation. But there was only a difference in reading (*lectio varians*), he says, between the text with which Ezra was familiar and the text known in Palestine. Does that justice to the text of v. 17?

Once more, MOWINCKEL's position is weakened because the PC itself is not taken into account. But the Book of Ezra itself provides some information here.

That Ezra's mission began a considerable renewal in the cultic life in Palestine is suggested by some indications of his journey as a *new Exodus*. In Ezr. viii 31 it is said that he left on the 12th day of the first month. According to MORGENSTERN [2], this is proof, "and quite decisive proof", that Ezra did not know of the PC because he would never have left just before the Feast of Passover [3]. But this argument could be reversed. We might read in this verse an indication of the *pascal* character Ezra wanted to impart to his enterprise. That impression is strengthened by v. 31b, "he *saved* us from the hand of the enemy". RUDOLPH (i.l.) did not give the literal translation of this word, but he preferred the vaguer "he *protected* us" because to him in view of the peaceful circumstances of the journey "to save" was an exaggeration. This is not so, because in Ezra's mind it stood for the New Exodus he was undertaking. There is also a kind of adaptation of the Exodus *haggada* in viii 21-22, reporting how Ezra refused the accompaniment of royal troops.

Not only the biblical data are important but also the synthesis of these data with the extra-biblical history. Several recent authors have attempted to achieve this. Historians will underline the revolutionary character of Persian history in the Ancient Near East. The religious tolerance of the Achemenides was a strikingly new phenomenon. Whether it is to be explained by a kind of philosophico-religious liberalism or just by political cleverness is still an open question. The admiration for that new religious policy, however,

---

[1] *Ibidem.*

[2] L.c. "The Dates . . ." p. 10.

[3] Cf. the answer by J. A. EMERTON, "Did Ezra go to Jerusalem in 428 B.C.?", *JTS* XVII 1966, pp. 1-19; esp. p. 10: was a journey necessarily incompatible with a festival?

tends to hide a less favourable aspect of the political strategy of the Persian court in this period. ALT [1]) points out that in their rule over the provinces the Persian authorities were not wont to reflect upon their measures and their consequences. It all came about piece-meal; changes in the existing situation were only worked out on the initiative of those who were interested; the impact of those measures was awaited before any supplementary measures were taken, to be followed later on by equally incomplete acts.

A source of information of immense value for this period are the Elephantine papyri. Their edition, completed in 1952 and 1953 with the "Brooklyn papyri" [2]) has launched a series of studies on the PC. In 1954 CAZELLES [3]) wrote a lucid article on Ezra's career. His starting-point was the fact, shown by the recently published papyri, that the Jewish military colony in southern Egypt did not, as generally thought, come to an end with the death of Darius II in 404 B.C., but only after the early years of Artaxerxes II. The Elephantine papyri clarify the policy of the Persians in the period that their rule in Egypt was threatened. Its aim was to strengthen their loyal Jewish subjects by giving royal authority and sanction to the newly codified religious traditions of the Jews themselves. These Jewish traditions were codified by Jewish scribes, in close touch with the Persian court and then, by royal decree, imposed upon the Jewish community or, what was even more important, upon the Persian governor of Egypt. CAZELLES invites us now to look for measures of the same kind meant for the province of Judah in the first years of the reign of Artaxerxes II, because when Egypt had been lost, i.e. in the first years of Artaxerxes II, as we now know, this province had become the cornerstone of the Persian empire. That empire was already in dire stress as a result of the rebellion of Cyrus, Artaxerxes' brother, and his allies, the Greek Ten Thousand. Moreover, many Greeks lived in the coastal regions of Palestine. If the Persians would give greater inner strength and unity to that part of their empire, this would be of great advantage to them. Achemenid policy would ensure that inner unity by ordering a new comprehensive codification of old religious traditions. If CAZELLES's conclusion [4]) is

---

[1]) A. ALT, "Zur Geschichte der Grenze zwischen Judäa und Samaria", *Kleine Schriften* II, München 1959, pp. 346-362, esp. p. 355.

[2]) E. G. KRAELING, *The Brooklyn Museum Aramaic Papyri*, Yale 1953. Cf. *idem*: *BA* XV 1952, pp. 50-67.

[3]) H. Cazelles, l.c. "La mission . . .".

[4]) Cf. in the present work: Ch. II, B, p. 24.

correct that under Nehemiah the only prevailing legislation was
Deuteronomy, it is worth looking into the PC for traces of those
Persian measures more than anywhere else. It confirms VAN HOON-
ACKER's well-known theory that Nehemiah's mission preceded that
of Ezra. It could be expected that some Persian delegate—and no
one else than the towering figure of Ezra can be envisaged—would
collect the ancient traditions of temple and priesthood and adapt
them to recent needs. In fact, we find in the PC a number of duplicates
of ancient laws, all of which are remarkable because of the addition
that there is one and single legislation for *ger* and *'ezraḥ*, for strangers
and indigenous (Lev. xxiv 20 ff: *lex talionis* cf. Ex. xxi 24; Lev. xxiv
16: blasphemy, cf. Ex. xxii 27; Num. xxxv 15: cities of refuge,
cf. Ex. xxi 13; Ex. xii 48: Passover, cf. Ex. xii 14; Ex. xii 19; Azymi,
cf. Ex. xiii 7). The same formula is to be found in Num. ix 14, Lev.
xvi 29, xvii 10-14, Num. xv 16 and 29, Lev. xix 34, xviii 26. The wide-
spread translation of this term *ger* (already found with the LXX and
the Chronicler) is *proselyte*. According to CAZELLES, however, this
is contrary to the Hebrew root and to a number of texts where *gerim*
evidently refers to the Israelites themselves. Nor are they the northern
Israelites, the Samaritans, because the record of Ezra's work does
not betray the same hostility between Judeans and Samaritans as
was felt under Nehemiah. Hence CAZELLES's suggestion that the
gerim should be identified with the Exiles wishing to resettle in
Palestine and the *'ezraḥim* with the Samaritans, who claimed continuous possession of the country. Ezra's life-work might be summed
up by the formula "one law for either category" i.e. the unification
of the country.

Except for his view on the *gerim* and *'ezraḥim*, CAZELLES's brilliant
exposition explains the whole situation; it explains how the Samaritans
came to accept the Pentateuch whereas they did not accept the pre-
exilic *northern*-Israelite prophets Amos and Hosea. It provides us
with a new confirmation of the late chronology of Ezra. It draws
valuable conclusions from the Elephantine papyri for a period in
Israel's history about which our information was scanty.

In the same year 1954 GRELOT [1]) published the first of his three
studies about the Persian period. The first, on the pascal papyrus

---

[1]) P. GRELOT, "Le Papyrus pascal d'Elephantine", *VT* IV 1954, pp. 349-384.
The text of the Passover Papyrus is given in ANET p. 491 (= COWLEY EP 21):
"[To] my [brethren Yedo]niah and his colleagues the [J]ewish gar[rison], your
brother Hanan[iah]. The welfare of my brothers may God (litt. "the gods")

of Elephantine, is in some way basic. He compares his method with the work of a biologist who reconstructs a prehistoric animal, starting from only one excavated bone. The "Pascal papyrus" consists of two parts, the first (v. 1-3) being a decree of the king (Darius II) in his fifth year (419 B.C.) for Yadeniah the leader of the Jewish military colony, by the hand of Hananiah. Hananiah must have been a Jewish priest or scribe connected with the administration of Arsham, the governor of Egypt. The fact that he possibly uses a polytheistic formula of salutation, "May the gods grant you prosperity" need not cast doubt on the orthodoxy of the sender of the document. It may derive from a subordinate scribe. The text itself of the royal decree is lost; there have been numerous attempts of reconstruction on which we need not dwell. The second part (v. 4-9) is the famous regulation about the Passover feast. It contains rules about date, about purity, abstinence from work, food and drink. There are gaps in the text and the name of the feast in question is lacking, but GRELOT is certainly right in stressing the identity between the calendar formula in the papyrus and those in the biblical texts. Any reasonable doubt is excluded; nothing else but Passover is meant (cf. Hez. xlv 21; Lev. xxiii 6; Num. xxviii 16; Ex. xii 6). The rule for purity in connection with Passover in v. 6b and 7a reminds us of Num. ix 1-14 where in case of impurity a celebration of Passover in the second month is allowed. We find a similar celebration in 2 Chr. xxx 1-22. An explicit reference to the Law of Moses is made in 2 Chr. xxx 18, probably to Lev. vii 20-21. If this is correct, then the Passover meal is compared to the consumption of the *šelamim* sacrifices, but in xxx 17 purity seems to be tied up with the *immolation* of the animals. This, likewise, appears to be the idea expressed by the Chronicler in Ezr. vi 20. The reason may be that to the Chronicler the Passover sacrifice was mainly a temple-sacrifice, not a family-celebration. It is, however, still, or again, a family-celebration in the texts of the PC, esp. Num. ix 1-14. The pascal papyrus is related especially to the latter text.

[seek at all times]. Now, this year, the fifth year of King Darius, word was sent from the king to Arsa[mes saying, "*Authorize a festival of unleavened bread for the* Jew[ish [garrison]". So do you count fou[rteen days of the month of Nisan and] obs[erve the *passover*], and from the 15th to the 21st day of [Nisan observe the festival of unleavened bread]. Be (ritually) clean and take heed. [Do n]o work —[on the 15th or the 21st day, no]r drink [beer, nor eat] anything [in] which the[re is] leaven [from the 14th at] sundown until the 21st of Nis[an. For seven days it shall not be seen among you. Do not bring it into your dwellings but seal (it) up between these date[s. By *order of King Darius*. To] my brethren Yedoniah and the Jewish garrison, your brother Hanani[ah].

The term "beware" (*'ezdaharu*) is a more general one, but in this context of priestly jurisdiction it may be compared with the closing section of the Code of Purity (Lev. xv 31) and with 2 Chr. xix 10. The latter text puts us in mind Hez. iii 17-21; xxxiii 1-9. All these texts testify to a characteristic feature of post-exilic priestly piety, viz of integrating into the priestly task the prophetic task of warning Israel.

The conclusions from this study are applied by GRELOT to the problem of the Pentateuch [1]) in a second article. The papyrus demanding purity for the Passover feast, without however permitting a celebration of the feast in the second month, clearly reflects a less developed stage of legislation than does Num. ix 1-14. There is no proof that Hananiah refers to Lev. vii 19b-21, because Lev. vii 19b-21 and Num. ix 1-4 must be studied together; the formulas in both texts are similar in outlook. Both texts probably play the same role in the cultic system, connecting the pascal law with the law of purity on the one hand and the sacrificial law with the law of purity on the other.

Secondly, all kind of work is forbidden on the 15th and on the 21st day of Nisan in the papyrus (v. 6-7). But in Lev. xxiii and Num. xxviii and xxix there is a restriction on the law of abstaining from work; only the work of *'abodah*, the work reserved for servants, is forbidden on these festive days. Complete abstention is required only on sabbath and *Yom Kippur*. Ex. xii forms a sort of intermediate stage; only cooking of food is permitted. It is obvious that the rules in Lev. and Num. are the most elaborate ones. They are the ones most adapted to practical life. The same conclusion is therefore justified: certain texts in the PC represent a later stage of development than the Pascal papyrus of 419 B.C. With regard to the indication of the days of the Azymi feast, quite different from the Deuteronomic approach (Dt. xvi 1-8), the papyrus comes closest to Ex. xii 18-20, but in the actual text Ex. xii is similar in terminology to Num. ix 13-14. The papyrus may therefore be dependent upon a formulation of the rule in Ex. xii at an earlier stage of development. Hence we may conclude that the PC is not a monolithic block but represents a *tradition juridique*; a collection of legal statutes, of which at least the final part is from after 419 B.C.

In his third article [2]), to us the most important, GRELOT takes a

---

[1]) P. GRELOT, "Le Papyrus pascal d'Elephantine et le problème du Pentateuque", *VT* V 1955, pp. 250-265.
[2]) P. GRELOT, "La dernière étape de la rédaction sacerdotale", *VT* VI 1956, pp. 174-189.

closer look at the texts shown by the Elephantine papyri to be later than 419 B.C. First of all he investigates the *ger-'ezrah*-formula, to which CAZELLES had already drawn attention. GRELOT agrees with CAZELLES that the term reflects the policy of the Persian court, viz to unify the different parts of the Jewish people in the Persian empire. The formula is found in many places, even in Josh. viii 30-35 and Hez. xlvii 22. According to GRELOT, Josh. viii 30-35 may confirm CAZELLES's opinion that the formula may have something to do with the Samaritans, if it would be possible to see a discreet allusion to the Samaritans in that text. It is not to be wondered at that the texts presenting this formula reflect the viewpoint of the Persian administration in their concern for the community: *qahal* or *'edah*. At the same time they tend to circumscribe the community by enumerating the cases of exclusion and demanding purity. Cf. Ex. xii 9; Num. ix 6-13, Lev. vii 19-21; xvi 29b-31 (the end of the Code of Purity); Lev. xvii 15-16; Lev. xviii (esp. v. 24-30); Lev. xx 22-35 (compared with Ch. xviii); Num. v 1-4; perhaps also Num. vi (cf. v. 7, 11, 12b). In all these texts the *ger-'ezrah*-formula is linked up with excommunication and with an extreme preoccupation with purity. GRELOT stresses the interrelation of all these data within the pattern of Dispersion-piety. A strict observance of purity rules, as well as regulations concerning the Azymi, circumcision, sabbath and food are its characteristic features.

According to GRELOT, all this also confirms [1]) the opinion of those exegetes who have refused to see in Nehemiah's measures of expulsion a completion of the Samaritan schism. The Samaritan schism was after Nehemiah's time, for the Samaritans accepted the Pentateuch which now turns out to have found its final form not before 419 B.C. GRELOT agrees with CAZELLES that it is reasonable to identify this effort of unifying the Jewish community at the end of the fifth or the beginning of the fourth century with Ezra's mission according to the late chronology (398 B.C.). GRELOT would seem to have overlooked, however, his remark about the absence of *Yom Kippur* in Neh. viii in his first article [2]), a problem with which anyone is faced who connects Ezra with the PC (see pp. 29-30 of the present Chapter).

It is of essential importance here to investigate the meaning of *ger* and *'ezrah*. According to CAZELLES, as we have seen, the *'ezrahim*

---

[1]) L.c. "La dernière . . ." p. 186.
[2]) L.c. *VT* V 1955, p. 252.

are the Samaritans, the *gerim* the returning Judeans. According to GRELOT, the *'ezraḥim* comprise both the Judean and the Samaritan Jews, the *gerim* are Jews from the Dispersion, coming to Jerusalem for the celebration of the feasts [1]). To us, neither opinion is convincing. The evidence of CAZELLES that *gerim* can point to Jews and could therefore be used of Jews returning to Judah, is not conclusive. The text 1 Chr. xvi 19 refers to the Patriarchs; 2 Chr. xv 9 to refugees from other tribes, Ezr. i 4 to those living in the Persian empire, 1 Kgs. v 11 and similar texts to the Canaanites. GRELOT rightly asks [2]) whether the name *gerim* would be appropriate so long after the return, i.e. at the end of the fifth century. Certainly we would not expect the word to be used by the resettled Jews themselves. This would be the case according to CAZELLES, since it is in their literature that we find the formula. They could not afford to call themselves *gerim* in their disputes about property; neither could they do so in their exclusive claims to the local cult.

To GRELOT on the other hand Ex. xii 32-39 is a key passage for understanding the formula. The *gerim* are allowed to share the Passover meal only after they have given proof that they are circumcised. But they form a single community with the *'ezraḥim*; in Lev. xviii 24-26 the two categories together are being opposed to the former inhabitants of Canaan. Therefore he concludes that the *gerim* are the Jews from the Dispersion who wish to take part in the Jewish feasts. But GRELOT's explanation of Ex. xii is unacceptable. Dispersion Jews cannot be meant by the term *gerim* in this Chapter, since in xii 43 it is said as a basic principle of law that the *gerim* are excluded from the pascal meal. In v. 48 no more than a concession is made: if they are prepared to let themselves be circumcised they are allowed to take part. How can GRELOT read in this passage that the *gerim* are only asked to show that they are circumcised? (How does he imagine this to have happened?) Ex. xii 43-49 can indeed be used as a key passage but the methodical approach should be different. Obviously, the *gerim* were people asking for participation in the Jewish cult. That request seemed acceptable to the priestly authors as far as, for instance, the sacrificial laws were concerned. As a special condition, circumcision was required for the most specific Jewish rite, the Passover meal. For all the rest, P states emphatically that the *gerim* belonged to the community of Israel and were worthy of love and

---

[1]) L.c. *VT* VI 1956, p. 178.
[2]) *Ibidem*.

respect (Lev. xix 33-34; Num. xv 14-16). The only group of people we know of to have asked for participation in the Jewish cult are the Samaritan leading classes (Ezr. iv 2 and vi 21). It is they who from Ezra's viewpoint are rightly called *gerim* and to whom all the relevant priestly texts are most suitably applicable. In spite of their claims for cultic participation, they deliberately cautioned to keep aloof from the Israelite population, because they "eat the salt of the royal palace" (Ezr. iv 14). Those claims were a source of continuous conflict; their emancipation among the Palestinian community was of the utmost importance to the royal court. It is to them also that the exegesis of Num. xv 14-16 (cf. Ch. iv, 27) refers.

GRELOT at the end of his third article remarks that his list is not exhaustive. "A thorough-going examination of the PC might lead to the conclusion that the number of additional pericopes, later than 419 B.C., is in fact even higher". It is precisely such an examination that we have in mind. The classical thesis about the early post-exilic origin of the PC was held to be unassailable by CAZELLES [1]) as well as by GRELOT. They only went so far as to label as insertions those texts which they found to have some relationship with Ezra's mission of 398 B.C. We want to challenge this limitation and discuss the question whether we have to do with insertions here, or with indications of the origin of the PC as a whole. The answer will be decisive of our verdict on the Wellhausenian view of the PC.

Kurt GALLING's [2]) study is more historical and less involved in exegetical problems than those by CAZELLES and GRELOT. His work is a brilliant confirmation of their hypothesis about the ties between the PC and the Persian time. Whereas Bo REICKE [3]) holds that Ezra's mission cannot possibly be dated under Bagoas because of the disputes about cult and temple that took place during his term as governor (cf. Josephus [4]), GALLING, using all the data from the Elephantine papyri [5]), Flavius Josephus and Ezra's career, arrives at

---

[1]) L.c. "La mission . . ." p. 126.
[2]) Cf. p. 000 note 00 of the present Chapter.
[3]) L.c. *Neutestamentliche* . . . p. 12 f.
[4]) Ant. xi 7.
[5]) ANET p. 491-492 (= COWLEY EP 30): "To our lord Bagoas, governor of Judah, your servants Yedoniah and his colleagues, the priests who are in the fortress of Elephantine. May the God of Heaven seek after the welfare of our lord exceedingly at all times and give you favor before King Darius and the nobles a thousand times more than now. May you be happy and healthy at all times. Now, your servant Yedoniah and his colleagues depose as follows: In the month of Tammuz in the 14th year of King Darius, when Arsames (5) departed and went

the opposite conclusion. He maintains that Bagoas, a Persian, was appointed as governor by Darius II in order to lessen the tensions with Samaria that had grown during the office of Nehemiah. This hypothesis seems to be confirmed by the Elephantine papyri. It appears from EP 32 that the negotiators from the military colony of Yeb

---

to the king, the priests of the god Khnub, who is in the fortress of Elephantine, conspired with Vidaranag, who was commander-in-chief here, to wipe out the temple of the god Yaho from the fortress of Elephantine. So that wretch Vidaranag sent to his son Nefayan, who was in command of the garrison of the fortress of Syene, this order, "The temple of the god Yaho in the fortress of Yeb is to be destroyed". Nefayan thereupon led the Egyptians with the other troops. Coming with their weapons to the fortress of Elephantine, they entered that temple and razed it to the ground. The stone pillars that were there they smashed. Five (10) "great" gateways built with hewn blocks of stone which were in that temple they demolished, but their doors *are standing*, and the hinges of those doors are of bronze; and *their* roof of cedar-wood, all of it, with the ... and whatever else was there, everything they burnt with fire. As for the basins of gold and silver and other articles that were in that temple, they carried all of them, and made them their own.—Now, our forefathers built this temple in the fortress of Elephantine back in the days of the kingdom of Egypt, and when Cambyses came to Egypt he found it built. They knocked down all the temples of the gods of Egypt, but no one did any damage to this temple. (15) But when this happened, we and our wives and our children wore sackcloth, and prayed to Yaho the Lord of Heaven, who has let us see our desire upon that Vidaranag. The dogs took the fetter out of his feet, and any property he had gained was lost; and any men who have sought to do evil to this temple have all been killed and we have seen our desire upon them.—We have also sent a letter before now, when this evil was done to us, (to) our lord and to the high priest Johanan and his colleagues the priests in Jerusalem and to Ostanes the brother of Anani and the nobles of the Jews. Never a letter have they sent to us. Also, from the month of Tammuz, year 14 of King Darius, (20) to this day, we have been wearing sackcloth and fasting, making our wives as widows, not anointing ourselves with oil or drinking wine. Also, from then to now, in the year 17 of King Darius, no meal-offering, in[cen]se, nor burnt-offering have been offered in this temple. Now your servants Yedoniah, and his colleagues, and the Jews, the citizens of Elephantine, all say thus: If it please our lord, take thought of this temple to rebuild it, since they do not let us rebuild it. Look to your well-wishers and friends here in Egypt. Let a letter be sent from you to them concerning the temple of the god Yaho (25) to build it in the fortress of Elephantine as it was built before; and the meal-offering, incense, and burnt-offering will be offered in your name, and we shall pray for you at all times, we, and our wives, and our children, and the Jews who are here, all of them, if you do thus, so that that temple is rebuilt. And you shall have a merit before Yaho the God of Heaven more than a man who offers to him burnt offering and sacrifices with a thousand talents of silver and (because of) gold. Because of this we have written to inform you. We have also sent the whole matter forth in a letter in our name to Delaiah and Shelemiah, the sons of Sanballat the governor of Samaria. (30) Also, Arsames knew nothing of all that was done to us. On the 20th of Marheshwan, year 17 of King Darius.

For the text of EP 21 see p. 43, n. 1; EP 22: p. 104, n. 2; EP 33 see p. 60, n. 3 of the present Chapter; EP 32: see p. 76, n. 1 of Chapter III.

returned home with the permission to rebuild their temple of Yahu; a permission that was granted to them by the governor Bagoas and by Deliah and Shelemiah, the sons of Sanballat, the Samaritan governor. Bagoas had had to consult the Jewish authorities in Jerusalem, Johanan and Ostanes, who could not, understandably, give their assent. Another and fiercer conflict was to follow between Judah and Samaria. It is reasonable to suppose some relationship between this strife about the Yahu temple and what Josephus [1] tells us about the murder in the temple. Bagoas was a friend of Jeshua, the brother of Johanan the high priest. If he was the brother expelled by Nehemiah (Neh. xiii 28), then that friendship would be mutually advantageous, but we have no confirmation of this guess. Bagoas had promised the office of highpriest to Jeshua. When the latter recklessly started a dispute in the temple, his irritated brother, the high priest, killed him then and there. The incident led to the profanation of the temple by Bagoas and to the suppression of the people and taxation of the cult. There was only one way out for the Palestinian Jews, namely, intervention through the Dispersion Jews in Babylonia. It was, GALLING says, "die Stunde Esra's".

Reading Josephus' text only, one is led to believe that the Bagoas of the temple conflict was the famous military commander of Artaxerxes III (350-338 B.C.). But this possibility, already tenuous in itself, is ruled out by the Elephantine papyri in which Johanan and Bagoas are mentioned together, as was already pointed out by COWLEY (l.c.). This author, on the other hand, reverses the order of the conflicts about the temple murder and the Yahu temple. According to him, the tension stirred up by the Jerusalem conflict may explain the absence of Johanan's name from the document giving permission to rebuild the temple in Yeb. This absence, however, is easily accounted for by the prevailing Deuteronomic legislation. If, on the other hand, the high priest's murdered brother was the person expelled by Nehemiah, the fact that he was in Jerusalem is not easily accounted for. His presence and, even more so, the promise of promotion made to him might be explained by a policy of *rapprochement* to Samaria on the part of Bagoas, if the dispute on the Yahutemple had preceded. Although neither thesis can claim convincing evidence, GALLING's reconstruction is to us the most plausible. In

---

[1] On the difficulties of chronology implied in this text, see A. COWLEY, *Aramaic Papyri of the fifth century B.C.*, Oxford 1923, pp. 108-109.

this view the suppression of the cult in Jerusalem at the end of Darius II's reign constitutes an excellent basis for the theory of its restoration by Ezra in 398 B.C.

BRIGHT's [1]) objection against dating Ezra in 398 B.C. is that according to the pascal papyrus the priestly calendar was already well-known in Jerusalem in 419 B.C., since it was probably sent by way of Jerusalem, especially if the sender Hananiah was Nehemiah's brother (Neh. vii 12). If this is what happened, it is not clear by what authority Hananiah should write from Jerusalem, bypassing the high priest Johanan. The Aramaic parallel Ezr. iv 6-vi 18 indicates that letters to this effect were sent from the Persian court by means of Jewish officials closely related to the Court. Moreover, as GRELOT has shown, the papyrus is prior to the actual text of the priestly calendar. Besides, if P would have existed and been in legal force, how could a clash have been avoided with the Deuteronomic legislation, also well-known in Jerusalem, according to which the celebration of Passover outside Jerusalem was forbidden?

Another objection against the reconstruction given above is drawn from Ezr. x 6 and advanced by BRIGHT (l.c.). If the Johanan mentioned there is the high priest and murderer of Josephus' story, would the stern reformer have so consorted with a murderer who had disgraced his sacred office? Leaving aside the problems of literary criticism of Ezr. x, we can quote EMERTON's answer to this objection[2]), that the text of Josephus suggests that the murdered man was himself the agressor and had conspired with Bagoas. GALLING's [3]) remark may be helpful that Ezra, although being himself of priestly family, does not wish to get involved in priestly functions (Ezr. viii 24-30; viii 35 and viii 36) and appears to have maintained Johanan in his office, assuming the murder to have been the effect of provocation. One should keep in mind that his mission was less a moral reformation than an effort of reconciliation in a situation where the tension ran high indeed.

D. *The Samaritan Schism*

If Ezra's mission is shown to be so closely tied up with the tensions between Judeans and Samaritans, one cannot evade the question of its success or failure. Biblical records are silent about this aspect

---

[1]) John BRIGHT, *A history of Israel*, Philadelphia s.d. p. 384.
[2]) J. A. EMERTON, l.c. "Did . . ." p. 11 f.
[3]) L.c. *Studien*, p. 179.

of his work, which silence is due to the literary *genre* of the History of Ezra and the Memorial text of Nehemiah.

The three volumes on these writings published by Mowinckel, to which we gave so much attention above, are excellent in this respect. The aim of Ezra's History was pious edification; Nehemiah's text was probably intended to be cut into a memorial stone in the temple. In such writings we can hardly expect any interest in political matters, and certainly not an emphasis on political failures. We have to rely therefore upon indirect information, e.g. such as we have from the *ger-'ezraḥ*-formula. The Samaritan schism is in a way the negative expression of what was meant by this formula, namely, the unification of the Palestinian community. Of the various opinions about the schism we shall mention only those which bear on Ezra and the PC. Mowinckel [1]) defends a very early date for the temple on Mt. Gerizim. He thinks that its erection must have been part of Darius II's organisation of the empire. A military colony like Samaria (Neh. iii 34: *ḥel šomron*) should be provided with a temple. Of the story related by Josephus [2]) we should discard the Hellenistic chronology, polemical and biased as it is, but its historical nucleus can be retained. According to Mowinckel, this nucleus must have been Sanballat's request to Darius II. The fact that the Samaritans accepted the Pentateuch as canonical literature, is to Mowinckel no objection against this early date of the Samaritan schism, because the formation of the Pentateuch is to be detached from Ezra (who should be dated under Artaxerxes II) and likewise to be given an early date (under Darius II). Mowinckel's view that the Pentateuch must already have had legal force during the reign of Darius II cannot be followed for many reasons. Such an early date of the Pentateuch is unacceptable in view of Nehemiah's Memoirs and the post-exilic prophets. But above all, the thesis is irreconcilable with the Elephantine papyri. The petition for the rebuilding of the Yahu temple would certainly have contained a reference to the temple on Mt. Gerizim, and would have been addressed to the priesthood of Samaria as well. It may be ruled out that the Samaritans would have accepted the Pentateuch without any Persian Act of government at a time when we know there was a good deal of Jewish-Samaritan hostility already. As for Mowinckel's deduction from Flavius Josephus' text of a royal permission to build a Samaritan temple under Darius II, it is highly

[1]) L.c. *Studien* II, p. 118.
[2]) Ant. xi 7-8.

improbable that the legendary elaboration of Neh. xiii 28 in Josephus should stem from a historical nucleus.

According to ALT [1]), the building of the temple on Mt. Gerizim is merely the logical consequence of Judah becoming a separate province and gaining its independence from the Samaritan administration. Before, there had only been a single administrative region, with Jerusalem for its cultic centre and Samaria for the administrative one. When Jerusalem had become both a cultic and administrative centre, Samaria was bound to aspire to achieve the same. All the evidence suggests that this occurred at the end of the Persian empire. This theory, however, fails to account for the influence of the old Yahwistic traditions, especially in Deuteronomy, which were so much in favour of a sanctuary in the North.

It is ROWLEY [2]) who stressed the importance of this point. The biblical suggestion (esp. in 2 Kgs. xvii) that syncretism was stronger in Samaria than in Judah is a polemical note without sufficient historical justification. Opposition against the cult in Jerusalem only came from the side of the Persian authorities. When Nehemiah expelled the high priest's son, the political opposition assumed religious colour as well and the old longing for a cultic centre in the North, which had been silenced because Deuteronomy had become the spiritual property of the Josianic movement in Jerusalem, could not fail to grow in strength. But cultic independence did not necessarily stand for a schism, as Elephantine testifies. ROWLEY is inclined to give credit to the traditions of the Samaritans themselves and to lay the schism at Ezra's door. Samaritan literary traditions are, in fact, very hostile to Ezra and, according to ROWLEY, inexplicable if the theory of CAZELLES and GRELOT were right that Ezra's mission was meant to bring Judeans and Samaritans together.

ROWLEY gives too much credit here to the traditions of the Samaritans themselves. He mainly relies on GASTER [3]). In various ways these traditions appear to take their starting-point not from reliable historical tradition, but from written *Jewish* sources. They found their origin in later periods and had polemical intentions. They follow for example the Chronistic order of Ezra and Nehemiah [4]) and present a legend about the disappearance of the Ark that seems to be the exact counterpart of 2 Macc. ii 4. Their

---

[1]) L.c. "Die Rolle . . ." p. 337.

[2]) L.c. "The Samaritan . . ." *passim*. Cf. also H. H. ROWLEY, "Sanballat and the Samaritan Temple", *BJRL* XXXVIII 1955, pp. 166-198.

[3]) M. GASTER, *The Samaritans*, London 1925.

[4]) *Ibidem*, p. 31.

main objection against Ezra is that he caused the separation between the two communities to come about by introducing the new script for the Jewish Bible. This looks more like a learned speculation from behind the writing-desk than a sound argument from history, leaving alone the fact that the Samaritans themselves may have introduced the new alphabet in the first century [1]). It has been defended by Fr. M. Cross [2]) that the final split between Jews and Samaritans occurred not until the end of the second century, because it was then that the independent history of the Samaritan script began.

The Samaritans might well have been equally ignorant of the exact historical circumstances of the split as the Jews. Did neither tradition survive the disturbances connected with the beginnings of the new Hellenistic period?

ROWLEY, like MOWINCKEL, is compelled to dissociate Ezra from the imposition of the Pentateuch. He quotes a study of 1912 [3]) when defending, like BRIGHT does, that the pascal papyrus proves the existence of the priestly calendar. This point has already been discussed by us above. ROWLEY, too, fails to explain how the Samaritans came to accept the Pentateuch as canonical literature, whereas they did not accept the pre-exilic prophets from northern Israel, and how this acceptance came about in the hostile atmosphere before the coming of Ezra.

ALT's view that it was the Samaritan leading classes which were at the back of the opposition to the building of the temple of Jerusalem is to be preferred to ROWLEY's view that it was the Persian authorities. But ROWLEY is certainly right over against ALT when he stresses the fact that the genesis of the Samaritan cultic autonomy is not just a matter of imitating Jerusalem events but one of developing the authentic old traditions found in Deuteronomy. GALLING [4]) gives a far more accurate picture, not so much of the schism itself but rather of the circumstances leading up to it. The Elephantine papyri betray the divergence of opinion in the two provinces on the very important subject of the Yahu temple in Yeb. The opposition of the priests in Jerusalem, on the one hand, and the more liberal attitude of

---

[1]) According to ALBRIGHT and EERDMANS, quoted by ROWLEY, l.c. "Sanballat and . . ." p. 194.

[2]) Fr. M. CROSS, "The Development of the Jewish Scripts", in: *The Bible and the Ancient Near East*, Essays in Honor of W. F. ALBRIGHT (ed. G. E. WRIGHT), Garden City 1961. Quoted in G. E. WRIGHT, "The Samaritans at Shechem", *HTR* LV 1962, pp. 257-366, esp. p. 360, note 8.

[3]) W. R. ARNOLD, "The Passover Papyrus from Elephantine", *JBL* XXXI 1912, pp. 1-33, esp. 13 f.

[4]) L.c. Studien p. 161-165.

the high administrative circles in Samaria, on the other, were bound
to clash. It is all but certain that the Persian authorities agreed with
the Samaritan view; for those who follow CAZELLES and GRELOT,
Ezra too must have been in favour of the temple in Yeb [1]).

In our view the Samaritan schism is the logical and inevitable
consequence of the Persian policy in religious matters. GRELOT [2])
remarks that the priestly Passover ritual, which is supposed in the
pascal papyrus and described in Ezr. xii 21-43, belongs to the old
rites of Ex. xii 1-14 and omits the Deuteronomic innovations of
Dt. xvi 2 and 5-7. The PC and the pascal papyrus, therefore, return
to Passover in its old character of family rite and seem to bypass the
Deuteronomic reformation, which had turned it into a temple feast.
In fact, the PC assumes that the rite can be observed in the Dispersion,
as can the sabbath, food regulations and circumcision. By sending
the pascal papyrus to Elephantine the Jewish officials in the Persian
administration took a decisive step regarding the Deuteronomic
traditions. This decision implied a deviation from the Deuteronomic
law that was in force in Palestine. It is easy to see how full of consequences this decision was. By introducing this anti-Deuteronomic
measure the Jews that were loyal to Persia tied their own hands in
the subsequent discussion about the temple at Elephantine. Once
they had allowed the pascal cult to be officiated outside the temple
and Palestine, they could be expected to give a similar permission
where the rebuilding of the temple of Yeb was concerned. The
conclusion is obvious: the Persian policy, intended to unify the loyal
Jews everywhere in the empire by granting them religious independence, had precisely the opposite effect in Palestine itself. There was
the danger of a rift between the two parts of the Palestinian community. For both sides the solution seemed to be to make an appeal to
the Babylonian Jews; the Judeans expected from them a favourable
influence at the Persian court to counteract Bagoas's repressive
measures; the Samaritans and the Persian court expected a mitigating
influence on the rigorous Judeans so as to persuade them to accept
the broader views of the administrative circles. Influencing them by
way of legislation or written documents was not enough; the personal
presence as well as the wealth of these Jews imbibed with the Persian
spirit would be needed. This is indeed the picture given by the

---

[1]) Cf. the interpretation of Kasifja (Ezr. viii 17-22) as a cultic centre in the
Dispersion: S. MOWINCKEL, l.c. *Studien* III, p. 28.

[2]) L.c. *VT* V 1955, pp. 259-262.

Bible of Ezra's mission: a solemn act of proclamation of the Law is supported by a return of Jews in the spirit of a new Exodus. In the same way as the Israelites had marched out of Egypt, bowed down under the treasures of the Egyptians, thus the Jews now returned from Babylon, carrying with them the treasures collected not only from among their compatriotes living there, but also from among the Babylonians. Rudolph [1]) suggests that the Babylonians, getting rid of dangerous rivals, may have paid not unwillingly. As we shall try to show in Ch. iv, the description of the Exodus from Egypt in the PC is the aetiology of this New Exodus. In other words, the original Exodus provides the inspiration and legitimation (down to the smallest details) of this new beginning of sacred history. To us, one of these aetiological ties is the link between the wealth of the returning Jews in Ezra's time and the exuberance and splendour of the cult in the PC. By means of the royal rescript financial provisions were safeguarded even for the future. When we look at it from the Persian point of view, however, Ezra's undertaking stood no chance of succeeding. Since it envisaged the imposition of a common Law on the two parts of the Palestinian community, the new legislative additions, formulated in the spirit of the Dispersion, had to be knit together with the Deuteronomic traditions at the time in force in Palestine. Moreover, as Eissfeldt [2]) rightly points out, the body of texts had to be limited to what is now called the Pentateuch, since the Persians did not care for the sacred story to get military overtones, for instance in the Book of Joshua. The prophets, too, were excluded, probably likewise because of their nationalistic tendencies. Hence the Samaritans acknowledged the Pentateuch as canonical literature, but did not accept their own pre-exilic northern Israelite prophets. As a result, Deuteronomy became detached from the Deuteronomistic historical writings. The cultic centralisation, in Deuteronomy itself if anything pointing to the North, was separated from the Davidic covenant which had Jerusalem for its centre. Under these circumstances obedience to the newly imposed Law seemed to compel the northerners to start a cult around ancient Shechem. So there was no need of a special initiative or dispute to set off a schism; it was implied in the legislative situation itself. This, in our view, is the reason why neither community kept a reliable record of the origins of the

---

[1]) W. Rudolph, *Esra und Nehemia*, Tübingen 1949, pp. 73-77.
[2]) Eissfeldt, l.c. *Einl.*, p. 342.

schism, although the legends in Josephus and the Samaritan chronicles soon satisfied the demands for an explanation. If the complicated situation itself had not got out of hand of the Persian authorities, the political and military calamities in the Syrian satrapy, foreboding the end of the empire, would anyhow have frustrated the hopefully planned compromise.

When the conquests of Alexander started a new epoch, the schism had reached its most dramatic form; both parties had it on divine authority that the other violated the holiest laws of God about the legitimate cult.

Archaeology may soon bring a good deal of light here if the remains excavated by BULL and WRIGHT [1]) should indeed turn out to be those of the Samaritan temple discussed here.

E. *The post-exilic Prophets*

1. It is a well-known fact that there are many points of similarity between *Deutero-Isaiah* and the PC. Recently KAPELRUD [2]) has concluded from them that the PC was prior to Second Isaiah. "The indications of Second Isaiah's knowledge of P's creation-story and Exodus-narrative seem to date P not later than 550 B.C. There may be a few later additions and some minor adjustments, but mainly and in practically every detail the P-work was finished before 550 B.C. in the form it now has in the Tetrateuch".

To us, the author's conclusions are not convincing. That in Second Isaiah's speaking about God (xl 21 ff.; xli 25 ff.; xliv 24 ff.; xlvi 5 ff.;xli 8 ff.) and its use of *bara'* (to create) there is a bridge to the terminology of P is true enough. But KAPELRUD seems to take the priority of P for granted and to consider his material as merely providing confirmation of the early date of P. Otherwise he surely would have considered whether the opposite explanation, dependence of P from Second Isaiah, was not one of the alternatives. His main evidence does not stand up to examination. A combination of covenant, Noah and the flood in the same context is indeed peculiar to P and to Second Isaiah (liv 9-10), but this same text indicates that a dependence or posteriority of P is more probable. In Isaiah, the Noah-story is only an example of that which is primarily meant, the covenant with

---

[1]) R. J. BULL and G. E. WRIGHT, "Newly discovered temples on Mt. Gerizim in Jordan", *HTR* LVIII 1965, 234-237.
[2]) A. S. KAPELRUD, "The Date of the Priestly Code (P), *ASTI* III 1964, pp. 58-64.

Israel. In P the outlook is far more universalistic; as we will see later on, the covenant with Noah is the priestly expression of God's work among all mankind. The second important text to which KAPELRUD refers is the one about the Exodus. Ex. xiv 28-29 offers some parallels with Is. xliii 16-17 mainly as regards the terminology "chariots and horsemen, chariot and horse, army and warrior". The parallel is not evident; other details stand for a dependence or posteriority on the part of the PC. In Isaiah the Exodus-story is applied to the destruction of Babylon; in P the outlook is once again more universalistic; the celebration of Passover is open, on certain conditions, to the non-Israelites as well (Ex. xii 48-49, Num. ix 14).

As for the creation-story, HEMPEL[1]) has pointed to the fact that the description in P is more dualistic than in Second Isaiah (cf. Is. xlv 7), which again suggests posteriority of the PC.

2. It seems reasonable to assume that *Haggai*'s messianism (ii 7, 20) was connected with the insurrections in many parts of the Persian empire at the moment of Darius' accession (522 B.C.). As we have seen above, at first sight this might seem contrary to GALLING's view that the first great influx in Palestine of returning Jews had something to do with the Jewish loyalty to the king. But here an observation by NOWACK[2]) may be helpful. He says that the opposition to the building of the temple in Jerusalem may have been due to the fact that the exiled Jews had got used to their worship without a temple. Extending this view, we wonder whether Haggai may not testify to more points of tension between the long-established Palestinian community and the newly-returned exiles. Is there a connection between four characteristic points in Haggai, his predilection for temple worship, his ideas on kingship, on messianism and his attitude of exclusiveness (ii 10-14)? Are they the counterparts of the ideas of those Persian-loyal Jews who had lived in Babylonia not as exiles, but as Persian subjects, even adopting Persian names (Ezr. ii 14; Neh. vii 19)? The PC adopts a quite different viewpoint in all respects. Haggai would provide one more indication that in the early post-exilic period the Palestinian community was not influenced by the PC.

3. In *Zechariah* the most important text for our purpose is iii 1-9. This judicial scene is usually interpreted as Joshua, the priest in filthy garments, symbolizing the repentant people. In our view this

---

[1]) L.c. PAULY-WISSOWA XXII, col. 1946.
[2]) W. NOWACK, *Die Kleine Propheten*, Göttingen 1903, p. 327 f.

explanation leads us nowhere. To begin with, why would—if this were true—any literary relationship with the two passages explicitly speaking about the repentant people (viii 18-19 cf. vii 11-14) be lacking? Moreover, if the whole nation had been meant, the only suitable term to use would not have been "election", but "re-election" of Jerusalem. Above all, would the Accuser not have been called upon to speak if the purpose of the pericope was parenetic (cf. vii 7-13)? There can hardly be any doubt that the text refers to a dispute about the priests of Jerusalem and their resumption of office. Since the issue of the debate is linked up with the Sion-covenant (v. 2), the priests involved can only be the Zadokites. The text clearly says that the filthy garment stands for a real guilt on the part of the priesthood (v. 4). This fully agrees with the impression given in Hez. viii about the idolatrous goings-on in the temple of Jerusalem. That is why we disagree with KENNETH [1]) and NORTH [2]). They both maintain that Zech. iii describes a dispute about the legitimacy of priestly functions, but they think the priesthood involved to be that of Bethel, allegedly Aaronitic and keeping to the functions in Jerusalem which they had taken over during the Exile. In this case, what would the meaning be of the filthy garment of the high priest? One would rather expect the priesthood of Bethel, safeguarded from the calamities of Jerusalem, to be clothed in garments of triumph. In fact, the situation appears to have been one of strife because of the dispute about the Zadokite priesthood. This state of affairs seems to have occurred before the existence of the PC which settles the discussion by going back to the newly-emphasized priestly figure of Aaron who united in his person the rival parties. Furthermore, as in Haggai, there is some connection between the attachment to the temple of Jerusalem and royal messianism (iii 8; vi 11-13). A detailed study of Zechariah does not, therefore, tend to support the theory of an early post-exilic presence of the PC in Palestine.

4. Of essential importance to our subject is the prophet *Malachi*. It is an exegetical commonplace that Malachi, in spite of his cultic interest, is not at all familiar with the PC. The abuses he condemns are the opposite of what the PC stands for. This enables KITTEL [3])

---

[1]) R. H. KENNETH, "The origin of the Aaronite Priesthood," *JTS* VI 1904-1905, pp. 161-186.
[2]) F. S. NORTH, "Aaron's Rise in Prestige", *ZAW* LXVI 1954, pp. 191-198.
[3]) L.c. *Geschichte* p. 658.

to say that the book sounds like a preparatory document, paving the way for the programmatic intentions of the PC. Malachi's concern on mixed marriages makes most people date the prophet shortly before Nehemiah's mission. However, both the Targum and Hieronymus and, more recently, VON BULMERINCQ [1]) identify the messenger of iii 1 with Ezra. Since the three of them keep to the traditional dating of Ezra, this identification does not lead them to a late chronology of the Book of Malachi. EISSFELDT [2]) opposes that identification of Ezra and the messenger of Mal. iii 1, since he dates Ezra after Nehemiah; he thinks that such a late date for Malachi is impossible. But is it? He gives no evidence at all and it may well be that he merely shrinks back from the inevitable consequence, a late date for the PC. Fairly strong evidence of a late date for Malachi is provided by his place in the Canon. The book bears no name and comes after two other anonymous appendices of the Dodekapropheton, viz Second and Third Zechariah. Of these appendices Second Zechariah (see the commentaries) almost certainly dates from the Hellenistic period. Furthermore, Mal. i 11, whether applied to the Dispersion (cf. EP 32, 1-9; Ch. III of the present work, p. 76, n. 1) or to a monotheistic interpretation of the Persian cult, suggests a rather late date [3]). The hostility to Edom in Ch. i is no objection to this. Since the hostility between Arabs and Edomites mentioned in Jer. xlix 7 ff.; xxvii 2-7;

---

[1]) Alex VON BULMERINCQ, *Der Prophet Maleachi*, Tartu 1932, previously published in: Acta et Commentationes Universitatis Tartuensis (Dorpatensis), B. Humaniora, XXIII ff. Tartu 1931 f.; cf. XXIII p. 336:
"Sind wir mit der Ansetzung der vorliegenden Rede in die Zeit unmittelbar vor der Ankunft Esras im Recht (s. Bd. I, IV, 5, S. 118-121), dann dürfte es nicht unwahrscheinlich sein, dass Maleachi die himmlische Gestalt des Volksglaubens menschlich-geschichtlich umgedeutet hat: für ihn ist der erwartete Vorläufer Gottes niemand anders als der eben im Aufbruch von Babel nach Jerusalem befindliche Priester und Schriftgelehrte Esra (vgl. II 7)".

[2]) L.c. *Einl*. p. 598.

[3]) For the text of EP 32, 1-9 see p. 76, n. 1 of Chapter III. Cf. Also ANET p. 492 (EP 33): "Your servants Yedoniah the son of Ge[mariah] by name 1, . . ., 5 men in all, Syenians who [hol]d proper[ty] in the fortress of Elephantine, say as follows: If your lordship is [favo] rable, and the temple of our God Yaho [is rebuilt] in the fortress of Elephantine as it was [formerly built], (10) and n[o] sheep, ox, or goat are offered there as burnt offering, but (only) incense, meal-offering, [and drink-offering], and (if) your lordship giv(es) orders [to that effect, then] we pay into your lordship's home the s[um of . . . and] a thousand *ardabs* of barley".

For the literary and exegetical problems of Mal. i 11, see E. COTHENET, "Parfums", DBS VI col. 1291-1331, esp. col. 1322. COTHENET's eschatological interpretation of Mal. i 11 enervates the parenetical strength of v. 11 with regard to v. 10 and 12.

xxv 9 occurs too early for our argument, the text can only point to the hostility between Edomites and Nabateans, since we have no other post-exilic historical data. This fact, too, would point to the end of the Persian time rather than before Nehemiah.

Let the reader assume for a moment that the messenger of iii 1 is indeed Ezra, then he will have to admit that the section ii 17-iii 5 provides no difficulties. It sets out to describe how the ungodly prosper in their ways. The forthcoming messenger is going to purify the cult; his coming must be an answer to the present situation.

The only alternative to this assumption is to consider the messenger as a supra-mundane transcendent being. But is not such an exegesis difficult to accept in view of ii 17? This verse is the expression of a factual situation of some sort of suppression by mighty people. The suppression of cultic freedom by governor Bagoas would fit in very well with this verse. The cultic purification will imply a coming of the Lord to his temple; that is understood by v. 1b: the Lord whom *you seek*, i.e. whose cult is now taken away from you by others. It stands to reason that a purification of the cult will also result in an internal improvement of the circumstances of sacrifice (i 7 f.), but ii 17 in combination with $m^e baqq^e \check{s} \bar{i}m$ of iii 1b suggests that there was external interference as well.

We think that exegesis should put greater emphasis on KITTEL's word above; Malachi seems to be the cult-*nabi'* of Ezra, the forerunner of him that as messenger will prepare the way of Yahweh [1]).

5. In the Dodekapropheton we may have found a precious witness from the time *after* the Ezra-mission presenting us with the glimpse of an understanding of its political failure. That text is to be found in the prophecy of *Second Zechariah* xi 1-14. In our view the text becomes clear if v. 10 is understood as referring to the end of the Persian empire. The period of the Persian empire is thought of as a time of covenant with all peoples, a concept which has a parallel in the PC (Gen. ix).

Zech. xi 4 indicates how a shepherd's task is imposed on the prophet. V. 5 explains why the flock is called a flock doomed to slaughter. It sums

---

[1]) Cf. Andrew THOMSON, "An inquiry concerning the Books of Ezra and Nehemiah", *AJSLL* XLVIII 1931-1932, pp. 99-132, esp. p. 121: "Just as in the work of Zerubbabel and Joshua Haggai and Zechariah prepared the way for and cooperated with them, and in the time of Nehemiah Trito-Isaiah, so Ezra was preceded by Malachi . . . Therefore God is about to send his messenger who will purify the sons of Levi".

up the groups for whom the prophecy is meant; the verse as a whole is resumed in the expression *likᵉnaʿanijjeʾ* (the accepted emendation of MT cf. v. 11) in v. 7, which verse is a repetition of v. 5 from the viewpoint of the prophet. It is therefore methodically incorrect to introduce the expression *kᵉnaʿanijje* when explaining the symbolic staffs, as is done in two recent studies on this text by CAZELLES [1]) and DELCOR [2]). Only v. 6 can be used for such an explanation, because v. 5 sums up those for whom the prophecy is intended (cf. 7a), whereas it is only in v. 6 that the contents of the prophecy are told. V. 6 has two parts. The first part speaks about the inhabitants of "this land"; the other considers a wider geographical context, because it speaks about "each man falling into the hand of his shepherd and king". There must be a correspondence, it seems to us, between these two parts of this verse and the two staffs. In view of the date of Second Zechariah it is reasonable to think of the end of the Persian period as the background of this pericope. Not until then did the end of a period of peace for the Palestinian Jews coincide with the disturbances and calamities among many other peoples, Syria being an important battlefield in these upheavals. In v. 7 the prophet mentions the names of his staffs. The name of the first, *noʿam*, Grace, does not provide any grammatical difficulties; the second one, however, does. MT has *ḥobᵉlim*, "pawnees". The LXX, Aquila and Symmachus read *ḥabalim*, "cords", interpreting these cords as symbolizing territorial rights. Most modern translators follow the interpunction of LXX, understanding it as "Union" and we agree with them because it corresponds with v. 14. The two above-mentioned studies, however, keep to MT and identify the "pawnees" with the mighty Samaritans and also with the priests of Jerusalem. They think these pawnees are to be identified with the "Canaanites" of v. 7a. From this point onwards their explanation gets confused. DELCOR sees in v. 10 the end of the troubles caused by the neighbouring peoples, and in the staff *noʿam* a favourable signification, "the faithful flock". This obviously disagrees with v. 6. In CAZELLES's view the staff "Grace" represents the universalistic aspirations of the Israelites, dispersed among all nations. He thinks that the breaking of the staff symbolizes the end of these universalistic tendencies. This would be approved by the high authorities in Jerusalem and the prophet himself, both of them symbolized by the "Canaanites of the flock, who knew that it was the word of the Lord" (v. 11). In CAZELLES's view, the prophet opposed Ezra's universalistic spirit. That all this can be deduced from v. 11 is most surprising. Finally, how can CAZELLES at the same time say that the staff "Grace" represents the faithful flock?

In our view, the text is clear enough once the unjustified connection between the Canaanites of v. 7a and one of the staffs is dropped. What is meant by v. 8 can of course only be clarified if we knew more about the historical facts of the period. The allusions to money in v. 5 and 12 f.

[1]) L.c., La mission . . .", p. 138 f.
[2]) Mathias DELCOR, "Hinweise auf das samaritanische Schisma im Alten Testament", *ZAW* LXXIV 1962, pp. 281-291, esp. p. 286 f.

may refer to the current practice in the Persian period to buy political and strategical favours by means of tremendous bribes. From this role of money in the text derives our suggestion that the "Canaanites of the flock" should be identified with the Greeks, but its discussion is out of place in the present context.

Summary

The findings of this Chapter can be summarized in a double proposition. The biblical and extra-biblical historical data outside the PC proper contain no trace at all of an early post-exilic presence of the PC in Palestine. Secondly, the same data suggest that the PC should be linked up with the mission of Ezra and both should be dated in the first decade of the reign of Artaxerxes II, early fourth century B.C. We studied the roots of the Palestinian situation in the Persian time by comparing the Exile in Israel and Judah. The restoration itself was the next subject of inquiry. Nehemiah's mission proved to be Deuteronomic in inspiration. The Elephantine papyri were studied both for what they tell us about the Palestinian Jews and about the central Persian governmental policy in religious affairs.

The investigation into Ezra's work was preceded by a literary analysis of the relevant texts, revealing a substantial Maccabean contribution to the Book of Ezra and Nehemiah. The ger-'ezrah-formula is shown to have a central place in Ezra's mission as instigated by the central Persian administration in view of the reconciliation of the Samaritan leading classes and the Judeans. We defend the thesis, that the gerim are the leading classes in Samaria, strongly under Persian influence, and that the PC urges the necessity for them to form one community with the Israelite population, the 'ezrahim.

The origin of the Samaritan schism was studied; it was found to result from the Persian administrative measures. In a final paragraph the data of the Dodekapropheton and Second Isaiah were considered; they provided some new details.

III. THE PRIESTLY CODE IN THE BOOK OF JOSHUA

A. Josh. xviii 1-10

There have been numerous complaints that the traditio-historical study of the PC has been neglected and that its exegesis has not kept up with the progress made in other fields of Old Testament research [1].

---

[1] Cf. R. Rendtorff, ThLZ XC 1965, p. 591 (cf. Ch. I, p. 15, n. 1).

In our view, progress was blocked by a kind of *circulus vitiosus*; on the one hand the extension of the PC was not agreed upon because its inner meaning was not well understood; on the other hand the investigation of its theological meaning could not avail itself of a number of important texts of which the P-attribution was widely rejected. For this reason we have begun our study of the PC proper with the problems concerning its extension, i.e., its final sections. It is often useful to start the study of biblical books with their final pericopes, because these will often shed light on their structure and purpose.

As for Josh. xviii 1-10, two basic facts should be kept in mind:

1. From WELLHAUSEN to Martin NOTH there was no reasonable doubt about the presence of P in Josh. xiii-xxii;

2. From WELLHAUSEN up to the present day there has been unanimity about the displacement of Josh. xviii 1 from either before xiii 1 or before xiv 1.

Ad 1. EISSFELDT, dealing with the literary criticism of Josh. xiii-xxii in his *Hexateuch-Synopse* [1]) is very confident in his statement, "P takes up such a large share that up to Ch. xx it is in a dominating position. There can be *no doubt* about the attribution to P of the parts mentioned in the synopse". With no less assurance NOTH [2]) defends the opposite opinion. "It can be demonstrated with a *certainty unusual* in matters of literary criticism that the attribution of Josh. xiii-xix to P is an erroneous statement". NOTH's opinion and confidence do not stand a critical examination of the evidence, however. NOTH agrees that it is characteristic of P to compile lists and catalogues like those we find in these texts and that the introductory and concluding formulas of those lists are written in the terminology of P. According to him, however, these formulas are too short to be attributed to P. But NOTH's argument is by no means convincing. Fragments of smaller size are admitted by NOTH and other exegetes as evidence to find out about J, E and D. Why should we not be satisfied with them here? According to NOTH, the word *matteh*, tribe, admittedly P-style, could have been of more widespread post-exilic usage. Of course it *could*, but methodically it is better to keep

---

[1]) Otto EISSFELDT, *Hexateuch-Synopse*, Leipzig 1922, p. 75. (Author's translation).

[2]) M. NOTH, *Ueberlieferungsgeschichtliche Studien* I, Halle 1943, p. 226 (= 184). Author's translation and italics.

to what statistical lexicography tells us. Of unmistakable P-style, according to NOTH, is Josh. xiv 1b; xix 51a, mentioning 'the committee' and Eleazar, cf. Num. xx 28 = P; and xviii 1, mentioning the *ʿedah* and the *ʾohel moʿed*. "But these very sentences are easily shown to be additions and by that very fact it is certain that for the rest of Josh. xiii-xix the priestly hand is absent." (l.c., author's translation). For the argument we are referred to NOTH's commentary [1]).

The original text (to NOTH that is the non-priestly text) is alleged by him to have been: v. 1a, 4, 5, with *benej jisraʾel* as subject and *nahal (qal)* as verb. V. 1b is considered an addition because it is a second relative clause depending on the word *ʾelleh*; which was added as a correction to the first relative clause and is a literal quotation from Num. xxxii 28. Still later v. 2 a + b, alpha was added, mentioning the execution of the commandments of Num. xxxiii 54; xxxiv 13. But the argument is not conclusive. NOTH has to admit that *ʾereṣ kenaʿan* is a priestly phrase (1a), but has "therefore" to be reckoned among the secondary data. NOTH omits to tell us that *ʾelleh ʾaśer* and *benej jisraʾel* in the same part of v. 1 are likewise expressions in the manner of P, so that only one word, *nahal*, is left to the *nucleus* of the alleged non-priestly text. But even *nahal* is not incompatible with P, it is merely of wider use. Can all this still be called literary criticism? Secondly, the construction with double *ʾaśer*, dependent upon *ʾelleh*, can hardly be called a construction of two relative clauses dependent upon a single *nomen regens*. *ʾAśer* is rather close to a *wau* copulative in this case. Furthermore, v. 1b is not a correction to v. 1a, but is entirely in the style of P, favouring a sequence of clauses that will describe things in a gradually more detailed manner. The same can be said of v. 2a + b, alpha, which need not be labelled an addition at all.

There is no reason to see a gap in v. 5, which does not mention the divine commandment to Joshua referred to in Josh. xiii 7. This text xiii 7 being itself an addition, as NOTH admits, it can hardly be adduced as evidence against our text. It is quite in the spirit of P to connect the whole occupation of the land, also of Western Palestine, with a divine commandment given to Moses.

The double formula with *benej jisraʾel* as subject and *nahal (qal)* as verb on the one hand, and the committee as subject and *nahal (piʾel)* as verb on the other, occurs again in xix 49a and 51. There is, however, no reason to eliminate, as NOTH does, the second and retain only the first; on the contrary, the fine harmony of the double formula both at the beginning and at the end of the section on the repartition of the land does not fit in well with the glossal character of one of its parts. The literary style of xix 49-51 is in harmony with what we shall find in the next Chapter to be a permanent structure in P, viz the evolution of subject-matter being

---

[1]) M. NOTH, *Das Buch Josua*, Tübingen 1953, p. 83 (Josh. xiv 1); p. 80 (Josh. xviii 1); p. 123 (Josh. xix 51).

interrupted for the sake of the elaboration of some detail. The story of the repartition of the whole land has to be completed before the granting of a small part to Joshua himself can be told; this makes another concluding formula necessary (v. 51). As for xviii 1, NOTH refers to the displacement since WELLHAUSEN, of this text (cf. our next paragraph).

At the end of this analysis we can only endorse CAZELLES's remark [1] that in spite of NOTH's authority the PC is to be found in Josh., a view for that matter defended since WELLHAUSEN.

NOTH's thesis about the absence of P in Josh. xiii-xxii and its attribution to a late Deuteronomistic compiler was rejected also by S. MOWINCKEL, first in a study in 1946 [2]), to which NOTH answered in 1950 [3]). MOWINCKEL has resumed the argument in a recent work (1964) [4]).

NOTH gives no other argument, MOWINCKEL says [5]), than that P is not interested in the *Landnahme* but only in the cultic Sinai legislation. MOWINCKEL's answer is that even before the Book of Joshua the P narrative has a trend towards the occupation of the land in quite a number of texts: Num. xxvii 12-33; Num. xiii 2; xx 12b; xxii 1 (we may add xxvi 53 f., 55 f.). Important are here the commandments given to Moses (Num. xxxii and xxxiii 50-xxxiv 29), the carrying-out of which is told in Josh. xii-xix. Even in the first part of the Book of Joshua there are traces of P. Ch. xxii with its stress on legitimate cult forms a worthy conclusion of the whole corpus of P. For all these reasons MOWINCKEL returns to the pre-NOTH P-attribution.

To what sort of painful dilemma NOTH's thesis may lead is clearly demonstrated by ELLIGER's study on the PC [6]). He almost dogmatically follows the opinion that in P no *Landnahme* is narrated. By studying the theology of P, he finds himself compelled, however, to stress the importance of Canaan in all parts of the PC. The *'ohel mo'ed* is the place of revelation of the divine guidance to Canaan; the Exodus is the manifestation before the Egyptians of God's

---

[1]) Cf. Ch. I, p. 000. note 00.

[2]) S. MOWINCKEL, *Zur Frage nach dokumentarische Quellen in Josua 13-19*, Oslo 1946 (Avhandlinger utgitt av Dat Norske Videnskaps-Akademi).

[3]) M. NOTH, "Ueberlieferungsgeschichtliches zur zweiten Hälfte des Josuabuches", in: *Alttestamentliche Studien* (Festschrift Noetscher), Bonn 1950 (Bonner Biblische Beiträge 1), pp. 152-167.

[4]) S. MOWINCKEL, *Tetrateuch—Pentateuch—Hexateuch*, Berlin 1964 (BZAW 90), pp. 51-76.

[5]) L.c. *Tetrateuch*, p. 55.

[6]) K. ELLIGER, "Sinn und Ursprung der priesterlichen Geschichtserzählung", *ZThK* XLIX 1952, pp. 121-143, esp. p. 140.

might in fulfilling his promise. The only answer he gives to his own question ("Why is there no record of the occupation of Canaan?") is that basically the PC is not a historical narrative, *keine Geschichts-erzählung*. In our view such a statement is an obvious *reductio ad absurdum* of NOTH's thesis.

Ad 2. Throughout all these authors, however, one thing remains unchanged, viz the critical approach to Josh. xviii 1. Would not the discussion have been more successfull if that critical analysis had been re-examined? "There seems to have been a minor transposition in the text", WELLHAUSEN says, "involving an important modification in the whole scene" [1]. Josh. xviii 1 must have preceded xiv 1-5, because this is the only place in P where the phrase "the land lay subdued before them" makes sense. Why should the casting of lots have been imposed upon *all* the tribes in Western Palestine, and have taken place for only seven of them, if xviii 1 is read in its actual place?

That question is indeed a fundamental one, not only for the exegesis of the Book of Joshua but for the whole of the PC. After this question WELLHAUSEN suggests that xviii 1 was transferred in order to streng-then the alleged JE-tradition in xviii 2-10, according to which Judah and Joseph had settled in Palestine before the other tribes. Apart from the difficulty of finding traces of J and E outside the Pentateuch, it is quite unlikely that the procedure of the committee and the description of the land in xviii 2-10 should belong to JE instead of to P. V. 7 with its strong Levitical interest also points to P. Another well-known argument is that "Shiloh" and the "camp" in this context are incompatible; that "the camp" is the original text and "Shiloh" an addition. EISSFELDT (l.c.) remarks that the viewpoint of v. 5, "in between Judah and Joseph" can only refer to Gilgal.

The camp in xviii 1 is not necessarily that of Gilgal. Gilgal has been latest referred to in xiv 6, but this is a secondary text, parallel to xv 13. Further back, both camp and Gilgal occur in x 43. But this sentence is the end of the war-story of the capture of Jericho and Ai (Josh. vi 1-viii 29) and of the legend-like summary of the conquest of southern Palestine (ix 1-x 43) (cf. the note in BJ on Ch. x and xi). The fact deserves notice that in both sections on warfare the tent of meeting is not mentioned in contrast with xviii 1. Not only is this section alien to P as regards termino-

---

[1]) Julius WELLHAUSEN, *Die Composition des Hexateuches und der historischen Bücher des Alten Testaments*, Berlin 1899, p. 128.

logy, but most of all so because it is not in agreement with the pacifism of the PC.

As for the priestly author's geographical standpoint midway between Judah and Joseph, we should not forget that Shiloh is just half way the distance between the two post-exilic governmental centres of Jerusalem and Shechem. From a literary point of view, there is no reason to eliminate, as NOTH (l.c.) does, "Shiloh" in v. 9 and 10, his only evidence being that it would be in disharmony with "here" in v. 8 or "the camp" in v. 9. As in Num. xxxii and Josh. xxii, the repetition of the main word is deliberate. It is stressed that Shiloh at that moment is the cultic centre (v. 8); the centre of the gathering of the Israelites (v. 9), where the cultic and ritual act of the partition of the land has to be performed (v. 10).

Only VON RAD [1]) finds some justification for thus locating the 'ohel mo'ed in Shiloh, after the preparatory demarcation of the Ephraim area. He refuses however to admit that it was the priestly author who numbered the tribes, that were to receive their portion of land, from one to seven in Ch. xix [this is an obvious error of VON RAD's for xviii 11-xix 51], "because there is no trace of any objective motive for this new partition of the land". He comes near NOTH's position, who attributed to the priestly glossator the idea that first the area of Ephraim ought to have been in the complete possession of the tribe before there could be any question of the tent of meeting being placed there.

Even MOWINCKEL [2]) agrees with NOTH and all the others that xviii 1 is out of place and that the camp of Ch. xviii is Gilgal. The reason for this unanimity among exegetes is no doubt that they could not think why the partition of the land should have occurred in two stages, before and after the placing of the tent of meeting in Shiloh. The so-called literary analysis of xviii 1 and its displacement are in fact a cover for this exegetical dilemma. The critical argument in itself is quite unconvincing.

So the first thing we have to do is to detach this question from literary criticism and see it as a primarily exegetic problem.

Can this remarkable construction in the PC have been deliberate? We think the answer will be in the affirmative after the introduction of a new methodical approach, viz the aetiological one.

---

[1]) Gerhard VON RAD, *Die Priesterschrift im Hexateuch*, Stuttgart 1934, p. 158.
[2]) L.c. *Tetrateuch*, p. 45.

Excursus: *The aetiological method*

An excellent *ex professo* treatment of the question of aetiology is given by S. MOWINCKEL [1]). He maintains that aetiology is a story or element of a story providing an answer to the question in the readers' or hearers' minds why a certain intriguing or bewildering phenomenon is as it is. He then refers to the recent debate [2]) between NOTH and ALBRIGHT about the degree of historical reliability involved in this kind of aetiological stories.

ALBRIGHT, referring to his personal experiences with Arab people, states that aetiology is no more than a "mnemotechnic, didactic aid" to keep alive a mainly reliable historical tradition. But MOWINCKEL rejects this view, saying that ALBRIGHT's examples are taken from recent history, whereas aetiology as such is concerned with phenomena dating back to an immemorable past (cf. Gen. xxxii 23-32). He contends that ALBRIGHT errs when he says that a story is historically reliable as soon as some of its details are confirmed by archeology. It can be proved from many literatures (MOWINCKEL actually quotes from Norwegian literature) that aetiological stories indeed contain some elements of historical value or interest. But this does not mean to say that the allusions to historical data constitute the primary element of aetiology. The primary reference to historical reality is rather the phenomenon asking for explanation: an archaic saying (Ex. iv 26), a heap of stones (cf. Josh. iv 6! vii 26), the imposing ruins of an ancient city-wall (Josh. viii 1-29; Josh. vi) etc.

According to MOWINCKEL, it is essential to aetiology that with regard to historical reality the story as such is the secondary element. ALBRIGHT would therefore not be correct in stating that the legendary character of an aetiological story ought to be supported by external evidence. On the contrary: without any counterproof it should be held that aetiological stories as such are unhistorical.

Of course aetiological stories have many points of contact with historical reality. Sometimes there is an object, e.g. the tower of Babel, the *zikkurat*, the historical reality of which is indisputable. But its very existence raised many problems in the Israelite mind, to which the aetiological story tried to give an answer. Very often aetiological stories were attached to well-known personalities, e.g.

---

[1]) L.c. *Tetrateuch*, p. 78-86.
[2]) M. NOTH, "Der Beitrag der Archäologie zur Geschichte Israels", VTS VII 1960, pp. 262-282.

the Hebrew Patriarchs, or to certain historical situations, for instance the nomadic wandering in the desert.

MOWINCKEL then refers to 2 Sam. vii, to point out that there also occur *gelehrte Aitia*, i.e. sophisticated aetiological stories. In 2 Sam. vii an aetiological explanation is given of the fact that Solomon, and not David, had built the temple.

The occurrence of sophisticated aetiological stories is important to us, because it is exactly under this heading that we would like to classify the stories of the Priestly Code. Aetiology was not limited to certain popular sayings or phenomena intriguing the popular mind. Aetiological stories provided an answer to theological problems as well. To us it seems possible that such a theological aetiology also provided a vista on the future and suggested a programme of action. This view of the priestly literature would be correct if it could be proved that its authors re-wrote the old traditions in a consistent manner. The programmatic nature of aetiology is in agreement with the fact that Israelite historiography served *practical* aims, as is now widely recognized. If, for example, someone would wonder about our conclusions from Josh. xviii 1-3 and would object that the text might equally well be a vivid way of describing a historical tradition, he should be well aware of his own western, non-semitic idea of historiography. Of course the mere assumption that a certain text *might* be aetiological and programmatic, is not sufficient. We have therefore strengthened our argument by demonstrating that the traditional non-aetiological explanations will lead to a deadlock. Furthermore, our method is often confirmed by findings from archeology, lexicography, and onomatography. Together with the fact that our aetiological reconstruction shows such a consistency, these two confirmations constitute the backbone of what we think to be a valid demonstration.

We are not the first defenders of aetiological explanation of Josh. xviii 1.

Some authors have defended the idea that Josh. xviii 1 is an aetiological reflection of the premonarchical history of Shiloh. They have, however, not presented a critical analysis of the text. KRAUS [1]), followed by BEYERLIN [2]), considers that the tradition about the tent of meeting standing in Shiloh is historically trustworthy for the very reason that the juxtaposition

---

[1]) H. J. KRAUS, *Gottesdienst in Israel*, München 1962 (2nd ed.), p. 206 f.
[2]) Walter BEYERLIN, *Herkunft und Geschichte der ältesten Sinai-Traditionen*, Tübingen 1961, p. 137.
Cf. in the present work, Ch. V, 4, p. 136-139.

of such divergent notions as that of Shiloh with its stone temple and the wandering sanctuary of the tent could not have been invented by a redactor. M. HARAN [1]), too, claims historical value for the traditions of the tent of meeting, which should not be seen as a mere retrojection of Solomon's temple. According to him, the story of the tent of meeting contains a nucleus of an ancient, authentic tradition, namely, the one of a shrine of pre-Jerusalemite Shiloh, the main witness of which is P in Josh. xviii 1. HARAN even favours these priestly texts about a tabernacle above the texts mentioning a "house" i.e. a temple building in Shiloh. We cannot agree with such a preference because 2 Sam. vii 6-7 can be explained more easily. Furthermore, it is difficult to see the pre-exilic Zadokite priesthood of Jerusalem being so unselfish as to give a description in P of the Shiloh shrine-legend. It is unlikely that they unconsciously should have transferred the splendour of their own temple upon the image of a rival one.

Another aetiological interpretation of Josh. xviii 1, as reflecting pre-monarchical Shiloh, comes from Jan DUS [2]). As we have seen in Ch. 1, his starting-point is the ritual "trek" of the Ark, *der Brauch der Ladewanderung*. For DUS Dt. xii 5 refers to the periodically changing place of the Ark. The description of how the Ark came there he finds in 2 Sam. vi 1-6: a waggon drawn by a pair of oxen was said to have brought the Ark to its new site, not guided by human hand but by the will of God. In Shiloh this ritual custom found its end and a stone temple was built there. The sanctuary around the wandering Ark must have been mobile, but at the same time full of splendour. For this reason it can only correspond to the sanctuary of P in Ex. xxv ff. which therefore is not the retrojection of the temple in Jerusalem but the shrine-legend of Shiloh, where in fact the ʾohel moʿed is placed according to Josh. xviii 1.

DUS's hypothesis is, however, not convincing. If his cultic interpretation of 2 Sam. vi is already stretching the evidence, his application of Dt. xii 5 to the time of the Judges is equally hazardous. Furthermore, DUS says that the wandering sanctuary was henceforward contained *within* the temple at Shiloh. In Ex. xxv ff., on the other hand, a tent is described containing within itself a kind of rectangular structure. Moreover, the thesis supposes the pre-monarchical origin of the Ark, which is a questionable basis. Also, to assume the existence of a double PC, one from Shiloh and the other from Nob, is an unnecessary complication. DUS has recourse to it in order to explain the vanishing of the idea of the Ark as Yahwe's throne and to explain the Zadokite elements in the actual text of the PC.

But above all, it may be advanced against HARAN and DUS that an aetiological reading of Josh. xviii 1 need not refer *a priori* to the pre-monarchical period. Aetiological landmarks in the text ought to be spotted by means of a study of the context.

---

[1]) Menahem HARAN, "Shiloh and Jerusalem; the origin of the Priestly Tradition in the Pentateuch", *JBL* LXXXI 1962, pp. 14-24.

[2]) Jan DUS, "Noch zum Brauch der Ladewanderung", *VT* XIII 1963, pp. 126-132. *Idem*, "Der Brauch der Ladewanderung im alten Israel", *ThZ* XVII 1961, pp. 1-16.

In order to arrive at an adequate aetiological exegesis of Josh. xviii 1 the following points should be noted:

1. It is *a long time* (xviii 3) *after* "Judah" and "Joseph" have settled in the Holy Land, that a number of Israelites are urged by Joshua to do likewise.

2. "The land lay subdued before them"; this, to the author, was decisive for the new start in xviii 1.

3. The settlement is tied up with an important and decisive *cultic installation*, symbolized in a sanctuary that is a rallying-point to the Israelites;

4. This wandering sanctuary and rallying-point is placed at a site traditionally known as the site of the destroyed temple-building.

If aetiology necessarily is the retrojection of the circumstances of the author's time into the foundation-period of Israel's history, we have only to look for that period which fits all these conditions best. This is the period of Ezra's mission at the end of the Persian period. In this period there were two well-defined groups in the Holy Land, the Judeans and the Samaritans, both of them looking back on a *long* period of settlement. That period of settlement is characterized by the absence of wars and external dangers within the structure of the Persian empire ("the land lay subdued before them"). That people should be called upon to settle in Palestine in such an intensely parenetic way, or rather reproachfully (*mitrappim*), does not fit in with the period of the first *Landnahme*, nor with the time immediately after the Exile, but only with the later Persian period, when Jews lived in prosperity in the Dispersion. In the Persian administration socio-political measures were tied up with a *cultic* reorganisation. Both the sociological and the cultic reorganisation were impossible without the resettlement of a large number of Jews from the Dispersion. With their wealth they would have to support the sumptuous cult; with their loyalty to the Persian empire they were to be the backbone of the community in that important part of the empire; with their detachment from the age-old sanctuaries in the country they were expected to put an end to the disputes flaring up in the Palestinian community about Jewish cultic centres in the Persian empire.

If our hypothesis on Josh. xviii is correct, it would shed light on all that has been said in the preceding Chapter on the relations between Ezra's mission and the PC. In this case the PC would describe the ancient history in such a way that it is relevant for its own days, that it is a mirror of what has happened in the time of its authors or, rather more, a programme and a norm.

B. *Josh. xxii*

Remarkably little attention has been paid to this as yet mysterious Chapter of the Book of Joshua. WELLHAUSEN [1]) and NOTH [2]) point to the terminology and ideas of P in v. 9-34, viz. Phinehas and the tribal leaders (*nᵉsiᵖim*); the community (*ᶜedah*), and Shiloh. According to EISSFELDT [3]) there must have been a pre-existant story in J or E about the building of an altar by the tribes of Gad and Ruben; this author assumes this to P scandalous story to have been re-interpreted and legitimated in the actual P-text. Such a purely conjectural reconstruction does not explain anything at all, however. This is simply conjuring away by means of words the problem how to reconcile the priestly text with the generally accepted ideas about the Code. NOTH (l.c.) thinks that the first version was a local aetiological text, but that nothing more can be said about it because it has been so very much transformed by P into a warning against illegitimate cultic centres. But *is* it this? Is it not rather, as EISSFELDT says, a legitimation of such a centre? MOWINCKEL [4]), too, considers the section to be a parenetic warning against illegitimate cults. He, for one, refuses to look for any pre-existing stages recasted by P.

Such a stand in the question is important: if the reference to the altar is not an archaic element in the text, the vital question is what form of worship the authors had in mind. There are three possibilities:

(*a*) Israelite worship actually occurred near the Jordan at some time on Israel's history;

(*b*) the description of worship near the Jordan is of a legendary character, but actually bears on separate forms of Jewish worship elsewhere in the world;

(*c*) the description of an age-old form of worship in the Jordan Valley was aetiologically used in defence of forms of separate Jewish worship in the Dispersion.

Surprisingly, the first and third assumptions stand now a good chance of being substantiated. The Dutch excavating party at Deir

---

[1]) L.c. *Die Composition* . . . p. 133.
[2]) L.c. *Das Buch Josua* i.l.
[3]) L.c. *Hexateuch-Synopse*, p. 79.
[4]) L.c. *Tetrateuch*, p. 60.

'Allā (in the Jordan Valley) [1]) has unearthed an Israelite temple-building, in continuous use all through the Israelite period, including an uncertain period of the Persian times. The finds have not yet been fully published; we rely on a personal communication by Dr. H. J. FRANKEN (4-10-1967). Dr FRANKEN was the first to point to Josh. xxii 9 ff. to illustrate the existence, amazing enough, of an Israelite sanctuary even after the Josianic reform. His full discussion of this text in relation to his find is still to come.

In the meantime the following provisional remarks may be useful for our purpose.

We think that the altar near the Jordan as discovered by FRANKEN cannot have been the sole and direct theme of Josh. xxii 9 ff., because in this case it would be difficult to see why the priestly author says that a Holy War was planned against those who took the initiative to build the altar. The sanctuary of Deir 'Allā appears to have escaped the cultic purge of Josiah. Apparently, it remained undisturbed by official circles in central Palestine. (The archeologist says its cultural leanings were towards Syria, not towards central Palestine). It would, therefore, not have been in the priestly author's line to present the history of this sanctuary as clashing with the orthodox views. If for this reason the first assumption would be ruled out, in the light of the recent discoveries at Deir 'Allā the third becomes more probable. In our view, the priestly author in that case would have used the reference to the sanctuary, which must have been well-known in Palestine (even if Josh. xxii 9 ff. were the only biblical reference) to discuss aetiologically a problem very much alive in his own days.

The Deir 'Allā discoveries might well prove to be a turning point in the exegesis of Josh. xxii. Yet it seems useful to give attention to those older efforts of explanation which may be said to use the aetiological method. Such an attempt was made by A. MENÈS [2]).

In this Chapter he finds evidence that the Jewish community

---

[1]) H. J. FRANKEN, "Texts from the Persian period from Tell Deir 'Allāh", *VT* XVII, 1967, pp. 480-481. In this article is referred to the forthcoming edition of the results of the expeditions: *Tell Deir 'Allā*, Vol. I, Leiden (1969).

The excavation-party found: . . . "a sacred mound, which was known to have been in existence from the 16th century till about the 5th century B.C. The new excavation started east of the excavated squares and in levels of a later (Persian) period . . . It became at once clear that we were dealing with one large building, of which eight rooms were excavated . . ., the disaster was caused by earthquake" (l.c. *VT* XVII 1967, p. 480).

[2]) A. MENÈS, "Tempel und Synagoge", *ZAW* L 1932, pp. 268-276.

in the Babylonian Exile began those forms of worship later known as synagogues. The texts of Hez. xi 14 ff and Hez. xx 32 and 39-40 testify to the Babylonian Jews yearning for a cultic centre of their own as a counter-balance to the arrogance of those who had remained in Palestine (cf. Ps. li 17 ff. and Ps. lxix 31 f.). A development set in, of which the final stage is to be found in the Talmud, where it says that the recitation of the regulations of the Law concerning sacrifices is tantamount to these sacrifices themselves. This is why the concepts of temple and sacrifice could assume such a predominant place in the Exile; through the concept of the tent of meeting they were detached from any particular chosen site.

A serious objection against MENÈS's theory is that Hez. xi 14 ff. cannot be used as evidence for it. The situation in this text is entirely opposed to that of Josh. xxii. In Hez. Yahwe himself is safeguarding the claims which the Babylonian *Golah* still has on the land. The Palestinians are not to think of divine protection as necessarily tied up with the temple in Jerusalem. Yahwe is no less present among his people in Babylon. In Josh. xxii 19, however, the situation is completely different. The people addressed have no plans at all to leave their homes in the non-Israelite area, and it is rather the Palestinian community's advice to come over to the ancient Holy Land instead of striving after cultic centres of their own. MENÈS is right in looking for an aetiological solution of this puzzle. Most authors agree that the pericope is of very late origin; there is nothing in the tribal history of Israel—so it was said up to FRANKEN's discoveries—to warrant the present story [1]. Only Jan DUS [2] has tried to find an explanation in the context of his above-mentioned theory of the wandering Ark. He tells us that the oxen would never have crossed the Jordan with their sacred burden. This was a disadvantage to the tribes east of the Jordan and the reason why they threatened to

---

[1] KAUFMANN's thesis (Cf. Ch. I, p. 9, n. 2 and the commentary on Ex. xii 16, p. 98 f.) that P represents the cult of the *bamot* leads to a dilemma in his exegesis of Josh. xxii (p. 38). According to him, there is in P a *de facto* Deuteronomism in the primeval period (*Urzeit*), in so far as the cultic place, the tent of meeting, was at the same time the place of revelation and the single cultic site of that basic period. This principle is quite correct, but KAUFMANN is wrong when he sees it at work in Josh. xxii, since that scene occurs *after* the primeval period. If he, rightly, attributes the Chapter to P, he is bound to recognize the post-Deuteronomic character of P, because this is a scene in which the priestly views clash with the older Deuteronomic concepts. Moreover, the altar is *not* said to be incompatible with the cult in the tent of meeting.

[2] Jan DUS, "Josua 22", *ThZ* XVII 1961, pp. 15-16.

effect a schism. Under the influence of this threat the cultic use of
the wandering Ark came to an end because the Shiloh sanctuary was
substituted for it. This fanciful reconstruction cannot be expected to
get much assent. Far more grounds for aetiological explanation are
to be found in the post-exilic period. In critical scholarship this road
has always been blocked by the early post-exilic dating of the PC.
The only realistic approach is to see the PC as addressing in this
Chapter the Jews in the Dispersion. This is clear from v. 24-25; it
is unthinkable that tribes living so near to Palestine should not have
been recognized as brethren when they came up to Jerusalem to
worship (v. 27). On the other hand, the Jews living far away in the
Dispersion were proud to be Israelites, in a way even more so than
their brethren this side of the Jordan, because they could claim a
territorial allotment immediately deriving from Moses (v. 9). In
v. 1-8 we find a summary of Num. xxxii 6-32, which is a complete
theology of the Dispersion. Only if it speaks about life in the Dispersion, v. 19 gets its full sense. The dispute that arose between the
two parts of the people of Israel was fierce enough to be described
in the terms of the Holy War (v. 12). (Note that in the story of the
Holy War in Judg. xx a gloss in v. 27 f. mentions the Ark and Phinehas. It seems that in the mind of the priestly author the symbol of the
Ark was tied up with a peaceful solution of strife between the Israelite
tribes.) The threat of war, however, is turned off into a judicial
session in Shiloh, the cultic rallying-point of the tribes (as in Josh.
xviii 1). In defence of the Transjordanian tribes it is emphasized that
the idea of the altar is not one of sacrifice but of symbol and witness.
Four times this point is repeated (v. 23, 26, 28, 29). Compare Num.
xxxii = P, where the injunction to take part in the battle for Canaan
is repeated six times (v. 17, 20, 27, 29, 30, 32). The conclusion
therefore is that the pericope is by no means urging a unity of cult;
its whole purpose is to approve solemnly (v. 30, 31, 33) the existence
of altars with a limited cultic use also outside Palestine. Recourse
to a pre-existing stage of the story is just fancy.

It is certainly surprising that, to the best of our knowledge, the
parallel with the altar at Yeb and its use for non-bloody sacrifices[1]

---

[1] Cf. ANET p. 492: "Memorandum of what Bagoas and Delaiah said to me:
Let this be an instruction to you in Egypt to say before Arsames about the house
of offering of the God of Heaven which had been in existence in the fortress of
Elephantine since ancient times, before Cambyses, and was destroyed by that

(EP 32) should have gone unobserved. As GALLING [1]) remarks, this very dispute threatened to cause a deep rift between the Judean and Samaritan Jews. It is reasonable to suppose that the occasion of Ezra's mission was exactly this dispute. If our hypothesis in the previous paragraphs is correct, Shiloh must be seen as a sort of symbol of that mission. In all probability, Ezra must have shared the broad viewpoint of the Persian administration in the matter of the temple request of Elephantine. In view of all this there seems ground for the hypothesis that in Josh. xxii we have a further point of contact between the mission of Ezra and the PC.

C. *Josh. viii 30-35*

It stands to reason that this text is not discussed as part of the PC. But it has strong ties with P and seems to be close to the final stages of the Pentateuch.

As EISSFELDT [2]) says, this text is among the most disputed sections of the Old Testament. A glance at the problems discussed in the commentaries shows that we are faced with:

1. The place of the pericope in its actual context;
2. Its Deuteronomistic language and its non-Deuteronomistic contents;
3. Its dependence upon Dt. xi and Dt. xxvii;
4. Its dependence upon P in the *ger-'ezrah*-formula;
5. Its dependence upon the Covenant Law as regards the altar-stones;
6. Its connection with Josh. v 13-15.

Most commentators attribute the passage to a pre-Deuteronomistic source, mostly to E. They know quite well that although language and style are Deuteronomistic in character, the story of the building of an altar outside Jerusalem can never be attributed to the Deuteronomist. While adopting this view, NOTH [3]) and HOLZINGER [4]) are not sufficiently aware, however, that the attribution of this text to

---

wretch Vidaranag in the year 14 of king Darius: to rebuild it in its site as it was before, and the meal-offering and incense to be made on (10) that altar as it used to be". (EP 32)

[1]) K. GALLING, l.c. *Studien.*, p. 163 f.
[2]) L.c. *Hexateuch-Synopse*, p. 281.
[3]) L.c. *Das Buch Josua*, p. 51 f.
[4]) *Ibidem*, p. 28 f.

E will merely evade the problem. The only result of such labelling is to obscure the real dilemma. EISSFELDT (l.c.) attributes the text to a *Bundesbuch-Interpolator*, an interpolator working in the spirit of the Covenant Law. He considers the attribution to E impossible, because E is not familiar with the Covenant Law at all. In our view the intrusion of the Covenant Law is a problem that only concerns Deuteronomy and not Josh. viii 30-35. We believe the exegesis of Josh. viii 30-35 to have been bedevilled by two facts:

1. The favourable attitude of the text to an altar outside Jerusalem has automatically been interpreted as pointing to an early origin [1]);

2. Too little attention has been paid to the differences of the passage in regard to Dt. xxvii.

It is along these lines that we shall attempt to arrive at a satisfactory solution.

The very first word "*ʾaz*" is important. It is an introductory formula in aetiological texts to state that a well-known cultic use or phrase had its origin in the *Urzeit* (cf. Ex. iv, 26b). It suggests that our text as well might belong to the genre of aetiology. The quotation from Deuteronomy may have served a very special purpose, viz the legitimation of an existing situation.

Another point of interest is the title of Moses, *ʿebed Jahweh* (v. 32). This title is also given to Moses in Dt. xxxiv 5 (a redactional formula, see the commentaries) and likewise occurs both at the beginning and at the end of the Book of Josh. (i 1; in xxiv 29 it is applied to Joshua). Has Josh. viii 30-35 something to do with the final redactors of the Pentateuch and of the Book of Joshua? The alleged Deuteronomistic style is no objection, since this seems primarily due to the fact that the Book of Deuteronomy is quoted. Where the text does not follow Dt. it is rather awkward and clumsy. HOLZINGER [2]) has pointed to the fact that the style of very late portions of the Book of Joshua tends to have a Deuteronomistic colour. Its late origin might as well explain the fact that it does not fit into the context. The sudden change of scene after the conquest of Jericho and Ai from Gilgal to Mt. Hebal, and the return to Gilgal again in ix 6 are well-known

---

[1]) The hypothesis that Josh. viii 30-35 is a "concoction" of a late redactor, was defended by Ed. NIELSEN, *Shechem*, a Traditio-historical Investigation, Copenhagen 1955, pp. 74-80. His view that the redactor was from Jerusalem is, in view of the altar at Shechem, not convincing.

[2]) L.c. *Das Buch Josua*, p. 49.

facts. This change of scene cannot be explained by saying that the story of the conquest of Jericho and Ai has been inserted between the connected texts v 13-15 and viii 30-35, as SELLIN [1]) does. The text is intimately connected with the conquest-story through the Ark. Thirdly, there is far stronger emphasis on the altar and its site on Mt. Hebal than in Deuteronomy. The order of things has changed. In Dt. we first have the writing of the Law on the stones painted with chalk; and next the building of the altar; in Josh. the altar comes first. The crossing of the River Jordan is no longer mentioned, which shifts the emphasis on to Mt. Hebal. There is no reason to look for a Mt. Hebal near the Jordan, as SCHULZ [2]) does. Furthermore, there is a change in the concept of the Law; in Dt. it is the living and pro-phetic Word that is recorded; in Joshua we have a written text that has been *copied* and read aloud. In v. 32 the word *mišneh*, copy, is used. The Law was written down by Moses before all the Israelites (*liphne*, v. 32). It is almost a juridical contract. Is that compatible with E? Contrary to what Dt. tells us, the reading takes place in the presence of the Ark and of the whole community (*qahal*, v. 35) with its full hierarchical range. This, too, strengthens the impression that the author wants to give a description of a highly solemn act, with grave juridical consequences.

A fifth point of difference is hidden in the admittedly enigmatic term *berišonah* at the end of v. 33. What does it refer to? To Moses (RSV: "as Moses had commanded at the first")? To the people of Israel in precedence of other peoples (BJ: "*pour donner la bénédiction au peuple d'Israel en premier lieu*")? More probably it refers to *'aharej ken*, immediately following. The benediction of the people (By whom? Is the word *lebarek* dependent upon *'omedin*, as seems most probable?) would then become a preparatory ritual ceremony previous to the reading of the Law (cf. the sign of the Cross!). This would be a considerable shift of meaning indeed, proving the pericope to be very late.

The *ger-'ezrah*-formula, however awkwardly inserted, fully justifies GRELOT's conclusion: "*si l'on voyait là une discrète allusion aux Samari-tains, la thèse de H. Cazelles se trouverait renforcée*" [3]).

---

[1]) E. SELLIN, *Gilgal*. Ein Beitrag zur Geschichte der Einwanderung Israels in Palästina, Leipzig 1917, p. 38.

[2]) A. SCHULZ, *Das Buch Josua*, Bonn 1924, p. 30 f.

[3]) P. GRELOT, l.c. La dernière . . ., p. 178.

Summary

Let us sum up the cumulative evidence we have found for the hypothesis that Josh. viii 30-35 alludes to the mission of Ezra:

1. The text is of very late origin [1]),

2. It has to do with the composition of the Pentateuch,

3. It is concerned about the imposition of the Law upon the community of northern Israel (v. 35 reminds us of Neh. viii 3);

4. At the same time it proclaims the legitimacy of a form of cult of their own.

There seems to be a mutual confirmation between our explanation of Josh. viii 30-35 and of Josh. xxii.

IV. THE PRIESTLY CODE IN THE PENTATEUCH

The priestly text-material that has something to do with the mission of Ezra was shown to be more extensive than GRELOT supposed; an inquiry into the rest of the PC is now asked for. Although not all the evidence is of the same value, we have chosen to follow the order of the PC itself; at the end we try to give a more systematic summary of the results.

It is not our intention to give a full commentary to the relevant passages; we only want to shed light on the elements that are important for the dating. For the aetiological method, see the Excursus in Chapter III.

The Book of Genesis

1. *Gen. i 1-ii 4*

For the study of the story of creation in the PC we can now rely on a recent work by Werner H. SCHMIDT [2]). According to him, the creation-story of P is a thorough-going priestly reworking of an older *Tat-Bericht*. This priestly reworking has a good many features of priestly theology, such as creation through the Word; reduction of mythical elements; *Ordnungsdenken*, i.e. a predilection for a divinely

---

[1]) That the text is later than the Deuteronomist was also recognized by Jean L'HOUR, "L'alliance de Sichem", *RB* LXIX 1962, pp. 5-36, 161-184, esp. 178-181. (L'HOUR also refers to GRELOT and CAZELLES). But his thesis that the pericope points to the old covenant tradition of Shechem, does no right to the late postexilic situation of the text.

[2]) Werner H. SCHMIDT, *Die Schöpfungsgeschichte der Priesterschrift*, Neukirchen 1964.

established order; precise information from the viewpoint of contemporary natural science, and the participation of cosmic nature in salvation history. Of more direct interest here are SCHMIDT's remarks about the preparatory stages of the priestly text. He compares its cosmological viewpoint with the cosmological material of the Ancient Orient, and his conclusion is that it is nearest to the Babylonian creation myth both in order and in details [1]. No conclusive evidence can be derived from the chaos of water and the element of "separation" (between the sea and earth etc.); both of these are familiar features in the cosmogonies of the Ancient Near East. But the story does agree with *Enuma eliš* as regards the order of creation: heaven and earth, the stars and mankind, and also in God's resting in the end. They agree even in details, both of them enumerating the heavenly bodies, although no astronomical descriptions are given in Genesis like there are in *Enuma eliš*. In both cosmogonies the creation of mankind is preceded by a solemn divine proclamation. There is also some kinship between the *Tiamat* of *Enuma eliš* and the *tᵉhom* of the Bible. In which form did the priestly writers handle the Babylonian epic of creation? SCHMIDT defends the thesis that the epic went through Canaanite hands before the priestly writers knew of it. He gives three reasons.

(*a*) Far closer relationship would have to be expected if the Israelites had become familiar with it in the Babylonian Exile;

(*b*) in that case we might have expected a direct polemical approach, which is now absent in Gen. i;

(*c*) the traditio-historical evolution of Gen. i must have taken too long for it to have taken place during the Exile [2].

The third of these points is of course far less stringent once the late post-exilic date of P is accepted. In our view P has gone through a very long time of spiritual evolution because its origin is in the Dispersion, not in the Exile. The second point is not convincing either. Cannot a controversy be direct and yet tacit? It has even been argued that direct controversy is the whole *raison d'être* of Gen. i [3]. Notice the elements left out from *Enuma eliš* by the priestly author,

---

[1]) *Ibidem*, p. 30; p. 177.

[2]) *Ibidem*, p. 32; 36 f.

[3]) Flemming HVIDBERG, „The Canaanite Background of Gen. I-III", *VT* X 1960, pp. 285-294. We disagree, however, with the application of the thesis to the cultic drama of the Palestinian Canaanite New Year and Autumn feasts, since the Chapter is not of hymnical nature.

as summed up by SCHMIDT[1]): the "theogony", i.e. the genesis of the gods themselves; the "theomachy", i.e. the battle amongst the gods and the battle against the sea and the dragons. All of them had to be excluded by the author because of his Yahwism; this very exclusion is a polemical one. The same may be said about the omission of an important element, the building of the temple at the end of creative activity. In our view the priestly authors had a direct contact with the Babylonian epic, either since the beginning of the Exile, or afterwards.

SCHMIDT's objection sub (a) would seem to us to have been answered at the same time as that sub (b). The author is straining our credulity when he says that many more points of agreements could be expected in case of a direct contact. What more could have been taken over from the Babylonian story if the author had to remain within the limits of Yahwistic orthodoxy? (About the omission of the building of the temple, see below). The priestly author's utmost care for theological accuracy is noticed by many authors. It explains his selection from the different elements of the Babylonian cosmogony.

SCHMIDT is right in stressing that the Chapter is not of a hymnical nature[2]); it is far more doctrinal in purpose, and this agrees with what HEMPEL[3]) says about P as a whole. Such doctrinal interest may likewise point to the Dispersion.

Is it not remarkable that the priestly author is silent about the erection of the temple, which he found mentioned in the Babylonian epic at the climax of creation? This reference to the temple was not taken over even in the form of a prospect of the future. It may be said that he left it out in order to remain within the limits of Yahwism, knowing about the temple only in the course of salvation-history; but did not the author open up a perspective on the Sabbath? Is it compatible with the traditional view on P's interest in the temple of Jerusalem and the retrojection of that temple into the desert period? As we have seen (p. 8), the latter view has already been opposed by VON RAD, ELLIGER and KUSCHKE[4]). The point is worth

---

[1]) l.c. *Die Schöpfungsgeschichte* . . ., p. 30.
[2]) *Ibidem*, p. 180 f.
[3]) J. HEMPEL, l.c. „Priesterkodex"; col. 1947 f.
[4]) G. VON RAD, l.c. *Der Priesterschrift* . . . p. 188 f.
K. ELLIGER, l.c. „Sinn. ." p. 142 f.
A. KUSCHKE, „Die Lagervorstellung der priesterlichen Erzählung", *ZAW* LXIII 1951, pp. 74-105, esp. p. 88.

discussing whether the omission of the temple from the creation epic is not a negative parallel to the specifically priestly concept of *'ohel mo'ed*. The omission may be a first hint how to interpret P's cultic legislation.

Anyhow (this matter will be discussed in the commentary on Ex. xii 16), at its very beginning the PC describes the whole universe as having a religious significance and also stresses the religious qualification of all mankind (man as the image of God) without any particular cult being mentioned. The domination of the world (i 28) is not something to be realized merely around the temple of Jerusalem and the Davidic kingship, as many prophecies, also post-exilic ones, had it; the theological concepts of the PC have outgrown these narrow nationalistic views [1]).

A further indication of its late origin and perhaps a reminder of Persian influence is the slightly *dualistic* remark that Elohim has created only the light, not the darkness, notoriously in contrast to Is. xlv 6-7.

HEMPEL [2]) has drawn attention to this fact, but he does not draw from it any conclusions as regards a date. SCHMIDT [3]) fails to notice any dualism; but he does point out the privileged place the creation of light gets in the text. He defends the opinion that v. 4b originally belonged to v. 2 and that v. 3 is a critical reaction to that original text. His idea is that in the original text mention was made of twilight, a mixture of light and darkness as part of the chaos and that God created by separating the two elements. V. 3 was to be a correction: God is not dependent upon a pre-existing chaos. SCHMIDT himself, however, sums up the difficulties against this view and we fully agree with him: the hypothesis would require the further supposition that the text of v. 2 had been changed, because there is no mention at all of a state of twilight, only of the darkness over the abyss. The word *wajjabdil* is a word of the final priestly redaction, not of the *Vorlage*. There is, furthermore, no reason why in the *Vorlage* the creation of light should not have been mentioned. That there *is* something peculiar about the creation of the light appears in fact from v. 4a. The formula of approbation has indeed a special form in this verse. Only here the object of creation is expressly mentioned in the formula of approbation and in a very conspicuous place. The formula, moreover, is put before the reference to divine activity (*Tat-Bericht*) (4b) in contrast with its other occurrences in Gen. i. The preference given to the light is still noticeable in v. 5a from the order of the sentence. These remarks made by SCHMIDT are a useful

---

[1]) J. HEMPEL, l.c. *Geschichten* . . ., p. 200.
[2]) J. HEMPEL, l.c. Priesterkodex, col. 1946.
[3]) W. H. SCHMIDT, l.c. *Die Schöpfungsgeschichte* . . ., p. 99, n. 2; literary analysis, p. 95-100.

confirmation of HEMPEL's observation about the dualistic flavour of the creation story.

It is worth noticing that the creation story is narrowly bound up with the other parts of P. SCHMIDT [1]) stresses the fact that the double literary structure in Gen. i, *Wort-Bericht* und *Tat-Bericht* (creation by making and creation through the Word) is found everywhere in P. Prescriptive and descriptive accounts (*Ausführungsberichte*) are in perfect balance (e.g. Gen. vi 13-21 related to vi 22 + vii 13-16; vii 16-17 related to viii 18-19; Ex. vii 8-9 related to vii 10; Ex. xxv ff. related to Ex. xxxv ff.). A close literary parallel is found in Num. xx, where an old story (from J) has been reworked in the spirit of P just like in Gen. i. In the old form of the narration Moses was reported to have struck the rock; in the P-version he is said to have spoken to it (v. 8a, alpha; 9 and 11a constitute the old *Tat-Bericht*).

Another parallel pointed out by SCHMIDT [2]) is the one that runs between the representation of God resting on the seventh day, with its reference to the Mosaic institution of the Sabbath rest, and the acquisition of Machpela's cave for the tomb of Sarah (Gen. xxiii), as pointing to the possession of the land of Canaan.

2. Gen. ix

HEMPEL [3]) has remarked that the Persian government could be satisfied with the Jewish community being kept together by means of cult and circumcision, characterized by a spirit of pacifism, as is apparent from the covenant scene in Gen. ix. It has often been noticed that the covenant with all mankind represented by Noah is specific for the PC; but, less noticed, this fact has implications for the dating of P. Could the spiritual climate of exilic and early post-exilic times really have favoured such a concept of mankind as living in a covenant of peace with God in which the only form of human domination was to be over the beasts of the earth (Gen. i 26, 27; ix 2)? When we compare this with Zechariah and Haggai and likewise with Second Isaiah (xlix 23; xliii 3-4, 14; xlvii 3; xlviii 20), we can really speak of the abolition of messianism in its old nationalistic setting. Once more this asks for an aetiological explanation, to be found in Israel's experience in the Persian empire, especially in the Dispersion. We should not forget the novelty of religious tolerance in the Near East;

---

[1]) *Ibidem* p. 171.
[2]) *Ibidem* p. 185, n. 1.
[3]) Cf. p. 83, n. 1 of the present Chapter.

many Israelites recognized the hand of Yahwe in all this, cf. the "covenant with all peoples" of Zech. xi 10. This priestly evaluation would hardly have been possible at the beginning of the Persian empire; it points forward far into the Persian period [1]).

There is perhaps an even more specific indication of chronology in ix 6-7.

HOLZINGER [2]) contends that ix 4-6 is an insertion made in a spirit of legalism. According to him it disagrees with 8 ff., where the old order is unconditionally restored without anything being offered by man in return. The insertion, on the other hand, introduces some legalistic rules about the prohibition of blood. HOLZINGER thinks it to have its origin in the practice of admitting proselytes. The section would give itself away by the use of 'ak, favoured in legalistic supplementary additions to P, and by the awkward use of "image of God" and the thought of sacrifice (via the reference to blood) before Sinai. Leaving aside for a moment the literary origin of v. 4-6, against HOLZINGER we agree with DILLMANN's suggestion that the conceptual link between v. 6 and 7 is the rejection of war in favour of the propagation of the human race.

We wish to propose the tentative suggestion that v. 6 had a link with v. 7; Israel had come to the experience in the Dispersion that the idea of Holy War, still prevalent in post-exilic messianism, had become an empty one; procreation, not war, had brought Israel to her important position all over the world.

It is doubtful whether a note of pacifism was still actually felt in the symbol of the bow cast into the clouds (Gen. ix 12-17), as originally there certainly had been (qešet, the warrior-bow cast into the clouds after a thunderstorm [3]), manifestation of the divine wrath).

3. Gen. x

The data of the list provide us with non-theological and therefore methodically unbiased, chronological indications of great value. Its very making is an interesting cultural accomplishment. VON RAD [4]) draws attention to its wide scope and calls the making of it an astonishing achievement for a Binnenvolk as Israel was. It can only be explained, he says, if cartography had made its appearance and was available

---

[1]) Cf. Ch. II, p. 21, n. 1.
[2]) H. HOLZINGER, Genesis, Freib. i. Br. 1898, p. 74.
[3]) Ibidem p. 78.
[4]) G. VON RAD, Das 1. Buch Mose. Genesis, Kap. 1-25, 18, Göttingen 1952, p. 119.

to the author [1]). But would this have been the case in Palestine? It is remarkable that Babylon and the Persians should be absent from the scene, but it is possible that they are absent because they form its centre. They might have been the cartographers and the Israelites, in close touch with the centres of imperial government might have relied on them.

All this, of course, remains hypothetical. Stronger indications are to be found in the contents. First of all the predominance of the *b*e*nej Jawan* strikes the attention. HOLZINGER [2]) says that the Jonians bear the same name in the cuneiform texts. Since they appear in v. 4 as a strong people, their being mentioned in the list does not go back to the drive of the Hellenes towards the East from the 13th century onwards, but would refer to the mighty development of the Jonian colonies in Asia Minor in the 8th and 7th century. This is a first and important *terminus a quo.* To designate the Greeks in general, the word *"Jawan"* is only used in the Persian period. In other words, if the analysis of the Chapter itself and of the PC as a whole should point to the Persian period, the translation "Greeks" would be justified.

According to HOLZINGER (l.c.) *me*e*lleh* of v. 5 does not refer to the *b*e*nej Jawan* but to Elisha, Tarshish, Kittim and Rodanim. But why? Is not the most natural explanation that it should refer to the *b*e*nej Jawan*? [3]) If so, the *b*e*nej Jawan* are said to have a mighty position, not only in Asia Minor, but also in the whole area of the Mediterranean. This alone would be reason enough to translate *b*e*nej Jawan* by "Greeks" and to date the list in the Persian period.

This conclusion is confirmed by other data. The identification of the "sons of Jawan" is difficult enough. They are called in the list: ʾElišah, Taršiš, Kittim and Rodanim. But it is significant that the most likely identification of all, viz Kittim = Cyprus, is also the most fruitful assumption in the matter of chronology. Phoenicians had settled all over the island, and of the towns Kition had been longest in the power of the Phoenicians, as HOLZINGER says (l.c.). The connection with Greece was only episodical; not until 410 B.C.

---

[1]) Cf. E. A. SPEISER, l.c. *Genesis*, p. 71: "The whole is thus noteworthy for its wide scope and analytical approach. As such, the table stands out as a pioneering effort among the ethnographic attempts of the ancient world".

[2]) H. HOLZINGER, l.c. *Genesis*, p. 96.

[3]) Cf. J. DE FRAINE, *Genesis*, Roermond 1963, p. 102. Even if the clause "these are the descendants of Japhet" should have dropped out of MT, its natural place is behind *b*ʾarṣotam.*

do we find Euagoras as king of Salamis [1]). As late as 387 B.C. the domination of Greeks is not established [2]). The connection in Gen. x between the *Kittim* and the *b^enej Jawan* points therefore late into the Persian period.

The attribution of Taršiš to the Greeks is equally surprising. In the 7th and 8th centuries the Phoenician power in the west of the Mediterranean was broken, but in this period the Greeks failed to maintain themselves there [3]). Gen. x supposes a powerful return; one more indication of the growth of the Greek might during the Persian period.

The overall picture of Greeks in full power from one end of the Mediterranean to the other brings the list far into the Persian time.

As for *'elišah*, whatever the significance of this name, it is memorable that in Hez. xxvii 7 it is mentioned as supplying Tyrus with purple; so in Hezekiel's time it must still have been in the hands of the Phoenicians.

If the name should really mean Carthago, as many authors think [4]), we are further drawn into accepting a late date. HOLZINGER thinks that its attribution to the sons of Jawan need mean no more than that Carthago had already been detached from Phoenicia. But although the real power had passed to Carthago, Carthago in fact never broke altogether with Tyrus [5]). Hence our text is an obvious indication of the hegemony of the Greeks over the Phoenicians.

As for "Rhodes" (for the generally accepted emendation of the Hebrew text, see the commentaries), information is rather scarce except that its importance for Greece began after the foundation of the city of Rhodes by the merging of three older cities. This occurred in 408 B.C.

The impressive result of the analysis of the list is the astonishingly strong position of the Greeks. The description of the *Asian* world likewise admits of some conclusions. Gomer, first-mentioned among Japhet's sons, apparently is to be identified with the Cimmerians [6]), an Iranian people. Mention is made of a battle between them and

---

[1]) W. J. WOODHOUSE, ,,Cyprus", in: *Encyclopedia Biblica* (ed. CHEYNE and BLACK), London 1914, col. 976.

[2]) E. MEYER, ,,Phoenicians", in: *Enc. Bibl.* l.c. col. 3760.

[3]) *Ibidem*, col. 3757.

[4]) SCHULTHESS, STADE, E. MEYER, in: HOLZINGER, l.c.

[5]) E. MEYER, l.c. The Phoenicians, col. 3757.

[6]) HOLZINGER, l.c. *Genesis*, p. 94. E. A. SPEISER, l.c. *Genesis*, p. 66.

the Assyrians in the 7th century. The fact that in Gen. x they are listed next to the Medes and Greeks, may mean that the battl efor power was a thing of the past and that the Iranians and Medes were then the constituent elements of the Persian empire.

Another striking feature is the classification of the Lydians with the Semites (v. 22). Cheyne [1]) says, "Lydia was never conquered by the Assyrians ... Did P really transfer the circumstances of the Persian age (for Cyrus did conquer and annex Lydia) to the Assyrian period?" Our answer is: P did not transfer them to the Assyrian period, but reflected the circumstances of the Persian age because he was writing in that time.

4. Gen. xi 31

As von Rad [2]) observes, it is remarkable that no motive at all should be given for the strange journey of Terah with Abraham and Lot from Ur of the Chaldeans into the land of Canaan. The departure from Haran seems to be equally decisive in Abraham's life to P as to JE. A departure from Ur has therefore no function in the account; moreover, it clashes with xxiv 4 ff.; xxix 4 f., where Haran is called the homeland of the family (xi 28 is considered a harmonizing gloss). Why such a long journey to the north-west of Mesopotamia if Canaan was Terah's aim? The answer may be that it is an aetiological reflection on the situation of the Mesopotamian Jews. To us P has tightened the ties between the Israelites' forefathers and Mesopotamia.

5. Gen. xii 5; xiii 6

It is characteristic of the pacifism of P that the separation between Abraham and Lot takes place without any rift or dispute [3]). Even more remarkable is the fact that the separation is caused by their wealth (cf. xxxvi 7), a representation quite different from that by the Yahwist. Abraham's wealth on his journey from Mesopotamia has a parallel in the wealth of the Israelites during the Exodus, which is specific for P; both of them may reflect aetiologically a return to Palestine of exceedingly rich Jews in Israel's later history.

The omissions from the Abraham story of J and E are no less significant. As Hempel [4]) remarks, no mention at all is made of

---

[1]) T. K. Cheyne, „Lydia", in: *Enc. Bibl.* l.c. col. 28 f.
[2]) L.c. *Das erste...* p. 131.
[3]) Holzinger, l.c. *Genesis*, p. 124.
[4]) L.c. „Priesterkodex", col. 1948.

disputes with nations outside Israel, such as the relationships between Sarah, Pharao and Abimelek (Gen. xii 10 and xx 2); the expulsion of Hagar (cf. xxv 9); the dishonourable representation of the east-Jordanian peoples (xix 30 ff.) and the strife between Jacob and Esau and that between Jacob and Laban. In the same way Esau's marriage with a Canaanite woman is tuned down to a marriage with a daughter of Ismael (xxviii 9).

6. *Gen. xvii*

In 1960 ZIMMERLI [1]) tackled the interesting problem why the Sinai covenant is missing in P. The covenant with Abraham gets such a strong emphasis there that one wonders why the covenant of Sinai should virtually be eclipsed by it. This is the more problematic because P is emphatic about the Sinai legislation being the basis of the only legitimate cult. According to ZIMMERLI, Lev. xxvi 45, the reference to a covenant with the Sinai generation, was deliberately corrected by means of xxvi 42. Looking for a solution, Zimmerli started from the classical view of P as exilic literature. In his view the shift of interest was caused by the fact that the Abraham covenant was more a covenant of grace than the Sinai covenant was. Even after the disaster of the Exile, caused by the unfaithfulness of Israel to the Sinai laws, Yahwe's grace was not exhausted. For this reason the priestly authors would have felt more at ease in *der reinen Gnadenbund* with Abraham. But HEMPEL [2]) raised objections to this.

(*a*) Is the Sinai covenant as conditional as represented by ZIMMERLI? Ex. xxxiv has no final clause of benediction and malediction, such as is only found in Dt. xxviii 1 ff. and in H (Lev. xxvi).

(*b*) Nor is in P the Abraham covenant without sanctions (Gen. xvii 14).

HEMPEL's own opinion is that P is rooted in early pre-exilic Hebron.

According to him the emphasis on the Abraham covenant is polemical and directed against an overestimation of the Sinai covenant in Jerusalem. This approach, however, seems unacceptable because the indications of a post-exilic origin of P cannot be explained away. For that matter, has there been so much emphasis on the Sinai covenant in Jerusalem?

One may add to HEMPEL's remarks that the priestly authors were so independent in handling the JE-traditions that they would certainly

---

[1]) W. ZIMMERLI, „Sinaibund und Abrahamsbund. Ein Beitrag zum Verständnis der Priesterschrift", *ThZ* XVI 1960, pp. 268-280.

[2]) L.c. *Geschichten* . . . p. 200.

have amplified the graceful character of the covenant of Sinai if they had found it lacking. This is what they did with the Noah and Abraham covenants. The legislative nature of Sinai covenant would have been no objection, because that legislative character is largely due to the priestly authors themselves.

The solution is once more to be found along the lines of aetiological exegesis. In our view the emphasis on the covenant with Abraham is due to the *ethnic* character of the Patriarch. He became the symbol of the Jewish race as it spread all over the near-eastern world. Ethnically, the covenant of Sinai was far too limited. J. ROTH [1]) has said some good things about this aspect of it. The racial progeny of Abraham, including several peoples, is in this covenant far too important for a single people to issue from him. "Nations and kings shall come forth from him" (Gen. xvii 6). Through the covenant with Abraham salvation is not narrowed down to one nation. It shares the spirit of the covenant with Noah, unlimited in space and time and in its turn linked with the universal scope of the creation story. Once more, the Abraham covenant has to be read aetiologically: Abraham is the mirror held up to the wide-spread Jews who recognized themselves in the patriarch travelling across Mesopotamia and from Mesopotamia to Canaan (v. 8: *m^egureka*).

But ROTH is less fortunate when he connects the PC with the miserable state of the exiled Jews. The stress on the wealth of the Patriarch is due to the fact that they were not miserable at all themselves. Far more accurate is HOLZINGER's description [2]); the Patriarchs are described to have lived like the Jews in Exile and in the Dispersion.

We fail to see the strength of HEMPEL's argument that the mentioning of kings in v. 6 pleads against a post-exilic origin of P. There is no reason to limit this word to Israelite kings. Non-Israelite kings, too, were reached by divine salvation as symbolized by the Patriarch. It is only within the spiritual climate of the Persian period that this could have been said.

In our methodical argument we are now at a crucial point of this study. We have before us the first occurrence (v. 14) of an excommunication formula. This belongs to the group of texts that, as GRELOT pointed out, must be dated after 419 B.C. and for which we would suggest the name "Grelot-group". Now this first occurrence is not favourable to his thesis that we have to do with insertions here. The

---

[1]) J. ROTH, „La tradition sacerdotale dans le Pentateuque", *NRT* XC 1958, pp. 696-721, esp. p. 711.
[2]) L.c. *Genesis* . . . p. 126.

formula, on the contrary, seems to be firmly embedded in the context.

GRELOT [1]) himself seems to shrink back from this conclusion. On the one hand he admits that it is not a *"pièce rapportée"*. On the other hand he suggests that the text is an insertion; his evidence, however, is rather weak. The only anomaly he points at is the change from masculine to feminine in the subject and verb of v. 14. But is this really something special in the case of *hannepheš hahi'*? We should not overlook the fact that the masculine form in v. 14a received some emphasis because of the male child that has to be circumcised. For the interchanging of masculine and feminine forms in P, see Lev. ii 1; iv 2, 27; v 1, 2, 4, 15, 17, 21; vii 21.

The formula, moreover, is wholly adapted to the context. If *zara' 'ahareka* in v. 9 and 10 belongs to the heart of the passage, v. 14 is its negative counterpart. If Abraham's progeny is no longer to be identified with a single national entity but is spread out among the nations, a special criterion is needed to indicate who belongs to this community.

V. 14 could not be missed from the literary viewpoint either, forming an *inclusio* with v. 1 and 2. Verse 14b corresponds (negatively) with "walking before Yahweh" of v. 1, verse 14c with the making of the covenant in v. 2.

We have made an important step forward beyond GRELOT's conclusions: an important feature of late chronology is embedded in a context interwoven with essential priestly themes. The universal spreading of Abraham's progeny and its claim to the land of Canaan, the non-nationalistic universalistic outlook and the emphasis upon circumcision and covenant belong to the heart of P's sacred history and legislation.

7. *Gen. xxiii*

For the stylistic difficulties, see the commentaries. The text is important for P because it tells about the *"primitiae"* of the possession of the land and the beginning of the fulfilment of the divine promise. Would Jews in the Exile have recognized themselves in this image of the Patriarch? This is not very probable. Far more likely to do so were the wealthy Jews from the Dispersion.

(Note the recent parallel to this text in the beginnings of Zionism in Palestine).

---

[1]) GRELOT, l.c. „La dernière . . ." p. 176.

8. *Gen. xxv 13 and 20*

All commentators agree that the Nebajot mentioned here, are
the Nabateans. Now the Nabateans are referred to, together with
Qedar, in Assurbanipal's time, in the 7th century B.C. But the fact
that in our text they are called the first-born son of Ismael is important,
as HOLZINGER [1]) observes. It means that they are already a powerful
nation; "it points towards a late time" he says, without drawing
any further conclusions.

According to the information available the Nabateans were a
mighty people in the Hellenistic times. This takes us, therefore,
far closer to the end of the Persian period than to its beginning.

In v. 20 both Bethuel and Laban are called *ha'arami*, Arameans.
This is contrary to what J says about them. In J they belong to the
family of Nachor (xxii 21-23). Exegetes cannot explain this shift [2]).
Is it a retrojection of the marriages of Jews in Mesopotamia with
people of *Semitic* race?

9. *Gen. xxvi 34*

Besides the problem of the different names of Esau's wives in
xxvi 34; xxviii 29; xxxvi 1-5, there is the question of the name of
one of them, Jehudit. If it should be read as "the Jewess", it would
be strange that the name is attributed to a daughter of the Hittites,
the marriage to whom causes distress to Isaac and Rebecca. DE
FRAINE [3]), to our knowledge the only commentator who pays any
attention to the name, thinks it derives from the city of Jehud in
Josh. xix 45, which assumption does not solve the problem of the
parents' sorrow. If the first supposition were true, the name would
indicate the late origin of the text, but we cannot be certain. Without
bringing any more light or other evidence, T. K. CHEYNE [4]) suggests
that the name is a corruption of Horit.

10. *Gen. xxviii 3*

VON RAD [5]) believes that this *q*e*hal* *'ammim* should be interpreted
as a short and summary prophecy of a universal eschatological cultic
community of peoples, since the word *qahal* is generally used for a

---

[1]) L.c. *Genesis* p. 135.
[2]) HOLZINGER, l.c. *Genesis*, p. 173 f.
[3]) J. de FRAINE, l.c. *Genesis*, p. 202.
[4]) T. K. CHEYNE, „Judith", Enc. Bibl. col. 2624.
[5]) L.c. *Das erste...* p. 245

cultic gathering. VON RAD stresses the difference between this promise and its wording in Gen. xvii 6. There the promise of fertility wound up with the forecast that Abraham would be the father of a multitude of peoples; that peoples and kings would issue forth from him. Here the climax of the promise of fertility is the prospect of the *qahal* of peoples. If we compare the latter expression with the other place where it occurs in P (Gen. xlviii 4-6), VON RAD appears to be right, except for the eschatological character of the cultic community. The expression means that the settlement of Jacob's descendants throughout the world, e.g. in Egypt (Gen. xlviii 4-6), is tantamount to establishing a cultic community of peoples. Once more we are far away from the generally accepted view of P as narrowly Jerusalemite in outlook.

Note in xxviii 2 another important shift of approach, compared with JE. The marriage of Jacob is no longer the incidental issue of the journey but its very aim. Commentators have seen in this a post-exilic aversion to mixed marriages.

11. *Gen. xxxi and xxxv*

P differs from J and E in so far as it supposes that all the children of Jacob are born in Paddan-Aram (xxxv 26 in P originally comes probably before xxxi 18; see the commentaries). This would seem to indicate an extended stay in Paddan-Aram, also suggested by xxxi 18. Both features are again well adapted to what the wealthy Dispersion Jews might like to find back in their Patriarchs.

12. *Gen. xxxv 11-12*

It is interesting to see that the divine promise to Jacob in Bethel has the same phrase q^ehal *'ammim* as we found in xxviii 3; but this time it is preceded by the word *goj*. Those periods of national existence which Israel had gone through should indeed be related aetiologically to the Patriarch Jacob-Israel, without however giving up the more basic promise to Abraham of cultic presence among other peoples. HOLZINGER [1] remarks that the last part of v. 12, *'etten 'et ha'areṣ*, is out of place here, "even when allowing for P's loquacity". Is it? If the PC is the expression of and the preparation for a new *Landnahme*, such a separate mention of the divine gift of the land to the later generations would not be superfluous.

---

[1] L.c. *Genesis* p. 185.

13. *Gen. xxxvii-l*

For the Joseph story in P, too, we can rely upon a recent study, from the hand of Lothar RUPPERT [1]). According to him, in P the Joseph story has turned into a Jacob story. The departure of Jacob is described in the same way as that of Abraham and Jacob from Paddan-Aram, viz in great wealth (xii 5 and xxxi 18). It is a real Exodus [2]). The reason of his departure is not a famine in Palestine. The land of Canaan is far too opulent for this (Num. xiv 7) [3]). In P the reason of his journey must be sought in the re-establishment of the family as a unity (xlvi 6 f.; xlix 1a; 28, 29-31; l 12 f.), and the adoption of Ephraim and Manasse (xlviii 3-6a). Jacob is given possession, *'aḥuzah*, of the best of the land (xlvii 6, 11). The testament, death and burial of Jacob is the climax of this Jacob story. The burial in Canaan is the first possession of the land, "earnest-money" as it were. RUPPERT is less fortunate in thinking that this predilection for the land is an argument that the PC was written for the exiles in Babylon; to us there is room for a later return. The aetiology far more points to a prosperous people. Only a very opulent land of Canaan could appeal to them for settlement.

In xxxvii 2 the word *dibbah* is used for the discreditable stories that Joseph communicates to his father. This word is important for P; it is used for the bad rumours that the spies have been spreading about the land of Canaan (Num. xiv 37, cf. xiii 32; xiv 36). RUPPERT [4]) thinks it a difficulty that such an unfavourable word is used in regard to Joseph. But the figure of Joseph is not important to P; it is far more important to him to point out that it is lack of fraternal unity which has caused them to be moved out from the country. A common pattern of thought underlies both passages in which the word *dibbah* occurs.

For this reason there is no need to assume that there is an opposition to the Galilean tribes at the back of the passage and that it supports the theory of the Hebron origin of P [5]). There is no evidence of any anti-Galilean tendency in P, while the use of the word *dibbah* is perfectly explained by the parallel in Num. xiv.

---

[1]) Lothar RUPPERT, *Die Josephserzählung der Genesis*. Ein Beitrag zur Theologie der Pentateuchquellen, München 1965.
[2]) L.c. *Die Josephserzählung*, p. 136.
[3]) *Ibidem* p. 232.
[4]) *Ibidem* p. 32.
[5]) L.c. „Priesterkodex"; col. 1964.

RUPPERT's analysis may be supplemented by the following considerations: HOLZINGER [1]) is right in his explanation of xlviii 5 and 6a that Ephraim and Manasse are going to fill Joseph's place, who has become an Egyptian and has now dropped out in the tribal system that functioned in the partition of the land. Any future children of Joseph will be Egyptians, like their father. But HOLZINGER is wrong in considering 6b as a mistaken gloss. We agree with him when he states that any children to be born afterwards shall be counted as belonging to Ephraim and Manasse, but this need not mean that it is a mistaken gloss. What P means is that such children as will be born in Egypt will not lose the birth-right claims to their share of the land; but when claiming their rights they shall have to stress the fact that they belong to Ephraim and Manasse. Precisely because the PC recognizes that a number of Israelites are living in Egypt the term $q^e hal$ '*ammim* is used in v. 4. The conjunction of these two elements, the *qahal* and the offspring of Joseph in Egypt is a valuable indication of the Dispersion in Egypt. The reference is not even an aetiological, but a direct one.

The Book of Exodus

14. *Ex. vi 2-vii 2*

For the reasons why P left out several parts of the story of Moses we refer without any discussion to HEMPEL's opinion [2]) that the miraculous salvation Ex. ii 1 ff. is left out in order not to infringe upon Moses' equality with Aaron; the killing of the Egyptian and the flight to the Midianites (ii 11 ff.) are suppressed not to dishonour Moses and not to detract from the effect of the anti-Midianite pericopes (Num. xxv 6 ff. and xxxi 1 ff.).

Of greater importance is that the story of Moses, compared with JE, has been converted into a story how the invitation to go to the Promised Land was rejected. This parenetical feature is quite in keeping with the aetiological elements we have already found. This rejection (vi 9) strongly contrasts with the older story iv 31 (v 21 is not a parallel to this priestly text). It may be interesting to see what motives P records for the rejection of their prospects on the Holy Land. They are *qoṣer ruaḥ* and '*abodah qaṣah* (vi 9; RSV: "but they

---

[1]) L.c. *Genesis*, p. 222.
[2]) L.c. Priesterkodex col. 1949.

did not listen to Moses, because of their *broken spirit* and their *cruel bondage*"). The latter is specific for the situation of the Israelites in Egypt; the reader's attention is not directed primarily to the Dispersion. The former, however, can be applied both to people in slavery and to the Jews living in prosperity in the Dispersion. The word occurs only here; the dictionaries give "pusillanimity". The root means "to be short"; in combination with *ruaḥ* the verb accurs in Prov. xiv 29 as "to be impatient". If the word in our context should mean "they were too impatient, they asked for immediate manifestations of divine power", then it would correspond to the plagues in P. Against this interpretation it may be objected that the plagues in P are directed against Pharaoh and his magicians. If we, therefore, prefer the meaning "they were too short-sighted to look beyond their present state", then the word might have its origin in the parenesis of the Dispersion, calling upon the Jews to look beyond their present situation.

Another change in P is that Aaron's function is no longer that of a prophet to the people, as in iv 10-16, but only to Pharao (vii 1); Moses is no longer said to be "slow of speech and tongue" to the people but only to Pharao (vi 30). This undoubtedly has to do with the predominance in P of the divine words Moses is going to mediate to the people; the parenetic strength of these revelations was not to be diminished.

15. *Ex. x 22-26*

This is not an official P-text, but commentators have drawn attention to a few P-words. First the word *mošᵉbotam* at the end of v. 23. As BAENTSCH [1]) remarks, the Hebrews have dwelling-places of their own in this text, while elsewhere in E they are always supposed to share the dwelling-places of the Egyptians. It cannot be J either, because J reserves the land of Goshen for the Hebrews. Furthermore, the Hebrew word is not very common in J or E, but it is common in P. The word is generally considered to be a late addition.

But there is more. As HOLZINGER [2]) points out, there is a lack of smoothness in the passage. In viii 22 (J) (RSV: viii 26) Moses had refused to bring the sacrificial animals into contact with Egyptian beasts. There seems to be a combination of two approaches here.

---

[1]) B. BAENTSCH, *Exodus*, Göttingen 1900, p. 108.
[2] ˙H. HOLZINGER, *Exodus*, Tübingen 1900, i.l.

According to the first (J), Moses demands that the Israelites should take their own cattle with them; according to the other, Moses demands of the Pharao to grant them Egyptian cattle. We seem to have a double conclusion formula, because the *lo* of v. 28 refers back beyond v. 27 (cf. the BJ translation: "Pharaon dit à Moïse"). In v. 25 there is a second P-word, *'asah*, "to sacrifice". HOLZINGER attributes this second approach to E, but is this the only possibility? In E it is stretching the Hebrew demands very far indeed to ask for Egyptian cattle. But are not things different to P if his account is to be seen in the light of the royal edict in Ezr. vii, where the cult is supported by royal finance? If so, this would be another aetiological text about the late Persian situation. But the question must remain an open one, because the evidence pointing to P is limited to the two words mentioned, although v. 27 might to P, too. Anyhow, *mošebotam* remains an interesting word; in the priestly legislation it is often applied to the Dispersion.

16. *Ex. xii*

We have already dealt with the place of this Chapter before Sinai [1]), its pascal prescriptions fitting to the Dispersion, its emancipation therefore of the old pre-Deuteronomic family ritual and the admittance of *gerim*, and who they were. BAENTSCH (i.l.) remarks that the *ger*, on condition of circumcision, is granted permission to celebrate the Passover meal even in his own family; thus he is put on equal terms with the *'ezrah ha'ares*. We believe that these legal arrangements cannot be explained by any other historical situation in Israel than the mission of Ezra in the beginning of the fourth century B.C. There exists no other legislation, BAENTSCH observes, where the "foreigner" is to such a degree incorporated in the very pattern of theocracy. But this author is wrong when he seeks the explanation of this phenomenon in the tendency not to suffer any foreign element near the holy community. The very opposite is true. The tolerance towards the *gerim*, in spite of the priestly system of purity and holiness, fits in with the late Persian empire. Strengthening the ties between the Samaritan and Judean blocks was then a sheer administrative necessity. In view of P's acceptance of a wide-spread Dispersion its

---

[1]) M. NOTH, *Das zweite Buch Mose, Exodus*, Göttingen 1959, p. 75. He thinks the place of the Pascal regulations to have been the result of the weight of tradition and to run counter to the spirit of the PC itself. We cannot agree; it is not in P's line to permit such an infringement upon its fundamental principles.

concepts of legal purity and racial self-consciousness were not the same as those in Judah; this fact, too long neglected, may help us to arrive at a correct interpretation of the PC.

Another interesting detail in v. 16, to which HOLZINGER (i.l.) has drawn attention, brings us to the crucial question of the unity of cult in the PC. An assembly at the sanctuary on the first day after the Passover family ritual would be possible in the fictitious situation of the camp. But in view of Lev. xxiii 2 and the reference to all the later generations (v. 17), it rather looks like as if the PC knew of synagogues. This is also suggested by the fact that the assembly does not prevent people from doing their household work (v. 16).

One finds an excellent treatment of the unity of cult in the PC in an article by J. KAUFMANN [1]). He points to further evidence: the plural "sanctuaries" in Lev. xxvi 31 and its talmudic explanation as synagogues (cf. Lev. xxi 23; Num. v 3; perhaps Lev. xix 30; xxvi 2). According to him [2]), the description of the 'ohel mo'ed should not be interpreted as a *law* about the unity of cult, no more than it is a prohibition of a temple without an Ark or of a cultic stone building. It would be wrong to judge the significance of the tent of meeting by Deuteronomic concepts. Nor are these to be applied in the interpretation of Lev. xvii, a chapter dealing with the question in how far the tent was to be exclusive. In Lev. xvii there is no opposition between the tent of meeting and other sanctuaries, neither between the tent and any other profane sites, but only between the sphere of the holy and the sphere of what is unclean. Cultic holiness is not bound to an *elected site* (D) but to a *sanctified room*. Outside that room looms the danger of demonic forces, to be evaded by means of apotropaeic rites of purification: pascal and Azazel rites, sacrifices of birds for lepers and the ashes of the red cow, etc. These rites have to do with the "open field" (Lev. xiv 7, 53; xvii 5) or with the desert, the region of the demons.

Although we are in agreement with KAUFMANN's view of the cult in the PC, his argument [3]) that the pascal rite in Ex. xii is pre-Deuteronomic and part of the cult of the *bamôt*, is not convincing at all. The correspondence with Ex. xii, 21-27, allegedly J, is no sufficient proof. Neither can the regulations of Lev. xxiii (booths, the counting of weeks in the period of harvest) be called indications of the cult of

---

[1]) Cf. J. KAUFMANN, l.c. „Probleme...", p. 39 f. Cf. Ch. I, p. 9, n. 2.
[2]) *Ibidem* p. 37.
[3]) *Ibidem* p. 35 f.

the high-places. The only alternative is the late post-exilic or rather Dispersion origin of the PC. KAUFMANN, for that matter, also admits that the cultic laws of P did not exist as a "book" before the Exile (ib.), but according to him fragments presenting the tradition that existed amongst *bamôt*-priests were collected in exilic or post-exilic times. However, even this construction, enigmatic in itself, cannot stand a close scrutiny of the text.

17. *Ex. xvi*

As HOLZINGER and NOTH (i.l.) remark, there are indications that the proper place of this pericope is after the Sinai events. In v. 9 the community is called upon to approach before the Lord and in v. 10, stating how they obey this command, they are said to look towards the wilderness. This is unique in P; it may reasonably be supposed that here the "wilderness" is a later substitute for *miqdaš* or *'ohel mo'ed*. As HOLZINGER says, this is one of the very rare cases where the redactor is adopting himself to J and E. Another characteristic is that in v. 2-3 the good life in Egypt is seen by the people in too rosy a light (cf. NOTH i.l.) Perhaps the two phenomena go together. For the first time we come across a special literary genre in P, viz the reversed order of hardship and euphoria in the description of the Exodus. Wealth and prosperity are found at the point of departure; uncertainty lies ahead. In our view this is an aetiology of Dispersion life and of the canvassing for the New Exodus. It is the deliberate purpose of the PC to point to the miraculous provisions Yahwe has granted his people from the very outset of the journey through the desert.

Hence the section on the miraculous feeding had to be put at the beginning of the narrative. Its importance appears from the fact that it is the only event related between the Exodus and Sinai.

18. *Ex. xxv* 1-*Lev. ix* 21

We now come to the culminating point of the PC. Any theory on its origin must be measured by the yardstick of its applicability to this important and extensive cultic legislation.

Up to recently there was all but general consensus about the literary composition of the Chapters: Ch. xxv-xxix = P-*Grundschrift* or Pg; Ch. xxx-xxxi = a secondary shift, or Ps; and Ch. xxxv-xl, a secondary shift, being dependent upon xxx-xxxi. The reasons for ascribing Ch. xxx-xxxi to Ps are not far to seek. The incense-altar is wholly out of place in the pattern of legislation (the Samaritan text puts it after xxvi 35); in the preceding section the altar of the burnt offerings is called *the* altar (xxvii 1-8; cf. xxv 29); other parts of Ch. xxx are introduced by stereotyped formulas (v. 11, 17, 23, 34); the laver of xxx 17-21 is likewise out of place; the anointing-oil of xxx 22-33 is in contrast with xxix 7 (and to Yahwe's glory as ground of consecration in Pg, cf. our note on Leviticus sub (b)).

Ex. xxxi is secondary, as appears from the list in xxxi 7-11, which is dependent upon Ch. xxx. The section xxxi 12-17 is less clear, but because of the introductory formula and the halting construction v. 15-17, and for some other reasons, it has likewise been attributed to Ps.

Chs. xxxv-xl are everywhere dependent upon xxx-xxxi; especially xxxviii 21-31, anticipating Num. i, is clearly secondary. The author of the story how the divine regulations were carried out was not wholly uncritical about Chs. xxv-xxix, which in general he nevertheless wished to maintain; xxvi 9b, 12, 13 he left out because of its inherent difficulties [1]).

Some remains of the original P might be found in xxxix 32-43 and in xl 17.

There is little doubt in classical literary analysis about the nature of the cultic legislation of P-*Grundschrift*. It is clearly expressed by HOLZINGER [2]). This legislation is the fictitious conversion of the temple of Sion into a transportable sanctuary both for cult and revelation.

A new approach was first made by R. RENDTORFF [3]) and, working on a larger scale, by Klaus KOCH [4]).

Literary analysis led them to assume the existence of a cultic text previous to P (*Vorlage*), which was commented on and elaborated by the priestly authors. In this way they disclosed—and we agree with them—two shifts in P's cultic legislation. The older, consisting of what they called *Rituale*, was characterized by short, rythmic sentences, mainly with *waw*-perfecta, constituting short expositions (of 5-10 sentences) of some cultic object or use; they start with its name and end with its meaning. The priestly casting had a different style of writing: longer, less rythmical sentences, with abundant use

---

[1]) NOTH, l.c. *Das zweite*... p. 222.
[2]) L.c. *Exodus*, p. 140.
[3]) Rolf RENDTORFF, *Die Gesetze in der Priesterschrift*, Göttingen 1954.
[4]) Klaus KOCH, *Die Priesterschrift von Exodus 25 bis Leviticus 16*, Göttingen 1959.

of imperfect forms and a predilection for subdivisions, lists of materials, casuistic specifications and careful distinctions of privileges of the priestly groups. A clear example of the two shifts can be found in Ex. xxv 23-30 over against Ex. xxvi 1-5. If all the texts found by means of these literary criteria are set side by side, they turn out to present a coherent pattern of ritual elements. Such coherence is also present in the priestly reworking. In Koch's view it reflects the cult in the Jerusalem temple. The *Vorlage*, however, must have been the expression of the ritual tradition of a sanctuary outside Jerusalem, with a well-developed cult, not prior to the monarchical period [1]).

Two things may be advanced against Koch's thesis. First, his viewpoint has been too exclusively literary. Having performed the task of distinguishing in detail between the Jerusalemite contributions and the elements preceding P, he might have found it useful to draw up a list of all the supposed contents of the *Vorlage*. He would have been surprised at its contents. It would have contained not only the sanctuary of the Ark and all its annexes but also the pre-Deuteronomic pascal-ritual (Ex. xii 43-49), the ordeal in case of adultery (Num. v 11-31), the purification-water from the ashes of the red cow (Num. xix), the prescriptions about the Nazireans (Num. vi) and purification rites in which birds, cedarwood, scarlet stuff and hyssop were used (Lev. xiv 34-53). One can hardly accept all these elements to be pre-exilic and Palestinian. They are so exclusively dominated by obsession with purity, not shrinking back from taking over from other religions the most primitive purification rituals, that it is hard to believe that they are pre-exilic parallels to the Jerusalem cult. Unwittingly, the author may have been influenced by the classical dating of P. If P's origin is exilic, any *Vorlage* framed within the PC is bound to be pre-exilic and Palestinian.

Our second objection to Koch's thesis as a whole is not entirely independent of the first. The author ought to have given more attention to the P-*Vorlage* as occurring in Hez. xliii 19-21; xlv 18-20; xlvi 2-3; xlvi 12. He only deals with these texts in an appendix. Here, too, he may have thought that Hezekiel and the PC are so close in time that the same literary phenomenon occurring in both of them asks for a *tertium comparationis*, a preceding stage to both of them. Once this chronological assumption is rejected, the fact that Hezekiel and the PC have this phenomenon in common becomes an intriguing challenge. Is it not highly interesting that in both these passages the person addressed is a visionary person, the "Son of man" in Hez. xl-xlviii and Moses in Ex. xxv ff.? The ritual texts of

---

[1]) As regards the identification of the *Vorlage* with Shiloh traditions, we have now come to agree with the criticisms raised against our hypothesis in G. TE STROETE, *Exodus*, Roermond 1966, pp. 189-190. We do not share, however, his opinion on P's exilic origin.

Hezekiel are actually in a Zadokite context (xliv 15), whereas the genealogy of the priests goes further back. In Hezekiel the ritual texts acknowledge the *nasi*ʾ, the substitute for the king (xlvi 2), whereas the *nesi*ʾ*im* in P express a deliberate return to a tribal function, the high priest having taken the place of the king. The texts in Hezekiel form a programme with the temple of Jerusalem for its centre, while the P-texts constitute an aetiology with the wilderness as a background for cultic possibilities both in the Dispersion and in Palestine. Taking into account all these elements one is led to the conclusion that there is an evolution from the group of texts in Hezekiel to that in the PC. It is probable that the texts should find their origin within a group of disciples of the prophet Hezekiel, a group familiar with the spirit of prophecy and eager to prepare the old traditions of Israel for the return of the glory of God to his temple (Hez. xliii 1-9). As to the identification, we no longer assent to KOCH's thesis, as we did in our work, *Leviticus uit de grondtekst vertaald en uitgelegd*, Roermond 1962, p. 60.

KOCH's literary analysis as given above leads of course to results different from the classical ones. We should distinguish between:

1. a stage previous to P, which runs across almost the whole of the cultic legislation (to be found in Ex. xxv 10-31, 37 f.; xxvi 7-15, 25 f., 29-37; xxvii 1-8(9); xxviii-xxix 35; xxx 16-21; xl 1-15 and likewise in Lev.);

2. P-*Grundschrift*. The main difference with the classical literary analysis is that according to KOCH the end of P-*Grundschrift* is not at the end of Ch. xxix. Parts of Ch. xxx and xxxi also belong to it, as well as xxxiv 29-35; xxxv 20-29. The dividing line now lies before Ch. xxxvi instead of before Ch. xxx.

3. supplements to P. First of all, a group of texts is concerned with the carrying-out of the divine regulations, which stratum can be shown to be secondary (at this point KOCH's analysis coincides with the classical one); it is to be found in Ex. xxxv-xl; Lev. viii-x. Secondly, a group of texts is concerned with "humanitarian" additions to the sacrificial laws, so as to make them suitable to the means of the poor (e.g. Lev. iv 32-35).

As for our own view, we agree with the classical position over against KOCH that the real mark of division in the complex of texts is xxx 1. KOCH admits that xxx 1-10 is only imitating the style of the ritual texts which he has found in the previous Chapters [1]). We are convinced the same is true for xxx 16 and 18-21, where KOCH is hard put to reveal the presence of the *Vorlage*. V. 16 is only one sentence and in the prescription about

---

[1]) KOCH, l.c. *Die Priesterschrift*... p. 33.

the laver the grammatical forms of the *Vorlage* are only found in v. 18 and 19a. Also, xl 3-8 shows an impressive list of *waw*-perfecta sentences, but the classical analysis rightly stresses its dependence upon admittedly secondary texts. It seems an arbitrary choice to eliminate only the incense-alter (v. 5), as KOCH [1]) does.

We disagree, however, with the classical analysis in the approach to the texts after xxx 1. Both the classical analysis and KOCH have failed to see the inner coherence of xxx 1-xl 35. That inner coherence will become clear when the preoccupations of Jewish Dispersion piety are kept in mind. As for the incense-altar, KOCH [2]) is unable to prove its Jerusalemite origin. We agree with the commentators [3]) that 1 Kgs. vii 48 is a gloss; that incense-offering in pre-exilic Jerusalem was regarded as an exotic luxury. Far too little attention has been paid in this context to Mal. i 11, where reference is made to a world-wide cult, characterized by incense-offering. It makes understandable how Jewish circles, in close touch with the Persian court, could permit to the Jewish colony in Elephantine a cult devoid of burnt-offerings. As we have seen, Josh. xxii should likewise be read in this light. Incense-offerings opened up the prospect of a new universal cult, made possible by the spiritual climate of the Persian Empire.

The second pericope about the obligatory census likewise fits into this picture (xxx 11-16). Great wealth, as we have seen, was part of the aetiological background of the stories about the Patriarchs and Exodus. In the Sinai-legislation, however, the function of wealth is both aetiological and programmatic. The description of generous collections in Israel's holy past is intended to stimulate the generosity of the wealthy Dispersion Jews. Excavated documents have made clear that the exiled Jews gained considerable influence in the financial world of Mesopotamia. But their prosperity can only have begun after the Exile proper had ended and the Jews had become Dispersion Jews. GALLING [4]) has pointed to the fact that the Jews are first mentioned in contracts from the fifth century B.C. It was Sargon II's policy to assign the exiles to agriculture and to put them in ruined cities in order to make them rebuild these cities. In fact, three places where the Israelites are said to have lived are called "Tell" (Hez. iii 15; Ezr. ii 59). The list in Ezr. ii and Neh. vii sums up slaves and

---

[1]) *Ibidem* p. 43.
[2]) *Ibidem* p. 33.
[3]) BAENTSCH, l.c. *Exodus*, p. 259.
[4]) K. GALLING, l.c. *Studien*, p. 52 f.

singers in the service of the returning Jews, but the Babylonian
and even Persian names suggest that these Jews returned a fairly
long time after 538 B.C. It is no real argument to explain the
luxurious decorations of the priestly sanctuary as mere fancy and
dreams about a glorious past. True, the required precious fabrics
alone, as HOLZINGER remarks [1]), would require a market comparable to Tyrus, as described in Hez. xxvii. On the other hand, the
difference between the priestly programme and the programmatic
description of the cult in Hez. xl-xlviii is remarkable. The precious
materials needed for the priestly sanctuary must somehow have
come within the reach of the community in the interval between
the two texts [2]).

The next section Ex. xxx 17-21, about the laver, is in harmony with
the predominant place taken up by purity in Dispersion piety.

As for the anointing-oil (v. 22-33), the anointing of both persons
and objects as it is described here seems to point to *exorcism* [3]). KOCH [4])
did not recognize this and saw himself faced by an inextricable
dilemma. The anointing of all piests (no longer of the high priest
alone) is not a sign of democratic emancipation, because anointing
is no longer seen as a means to confer dignity; it is rather to be
considered in the light of apotropaeic exorcism. If in such a context
the author speaks about "sanctity", this notion is close to ritual
purity. This apotropaeic character of the cult is essential to the PC
and, as we shall discuss in our final Chapter, its main distinction
from the Deuteronomic cult.

It is noteworthy that this section is also marked off by the excommunication formula (v. 33) and therefore belongs to the "Grelot-
group".

The next section about the composition of the incense (v. 34-38)
confirms our impression. NOTH [5]) points to the exorcistic character
of the incense in the Ancient Near East and interprets the passage

---

[1]) HOLZINGER, l.c. *Exodus*, p. 140.

[2]) It is worth noticing that the nearest literary parallel is from the Elephantine
papyri: cf. ANET p. 491 (= EP22): "On the 3rd of Phamenoth, year 5. This is
(sic!) the names of the Jewish garrison which (sic!) gave money to the God Yaho,
[2 shekels] each. (Lines 2-119, 126-135 name 123 contributors of both sexes).

[3]) Cf. E. COTHENET, „Parfums", in: DBS, col. 1229-1331; esp. col. 1293.
Idem „Onction", DBS VI, col. 703. Cf. J. KAUFMANN, l.c. „Probleme..." p. 37.

[4]) L.c. *Die Priesterschrift...*, p. 35. Cf. our discussion in: J. G. VINK, *Leviticus*,
Roermond 1962, p. 45.

[5]) L.c. *Das zweite...*, p. 192.

in this way. HOLZINGER [1]) points to the fact that some ingredients of the composition stank when they were burnt by themselves; he supposes that they were added because of their fame as exorcistic substances. For this reason we cannot accept HOLZINGER's thesis (l.c.) that the literary origin of the incense-altar was due to an exegetical misunderstanding on the part of the priestly authors about the title "altar", sometimes given to the table of the bread of proposition (1 Kgs. vi 20). The origin is non-Israelite rather and due to the influence of exorcistic tendencies on the Dispersion Jews. HOLZINGER still points to Tobias vi 17 f.; viii 2 ff. In v. 38 we have once more the excommunication formula.

The section about the craftsmen required for the building of the sanctuary (Ex. xxxi 1-11) is clearly dependent upon the preceding ones and again characterized by the theme of wealth and splendour. Even the closing section of this first part, about the sabbath to be observed (xxxi 12-18) is characterized by the same idea of sanctification being identified with the separation from other peoples (v. 13). The transitional text between the regulations and their fulfilment (xxxiv 29-35) runs parallel to that of xxiv 15-18. In the same way as Moses was unable to approach the Glory of Yahwe before Yahwe had called upon him, the Israelites dared not approach Moses before he had summoned them. Notice the apotropaeic detail that Moses had to put a veil over his face: there ought to be protection against and separation between what belongs to the Glory of God and the profane world.

As to the long section on the carrying-out of the divine regulations (Ex. xxxv 1-Lev. ix 21), it appears to be dependent upon the objects summed up in Ch. xxx-xxxi and is also linked up with the preceding section by a reiterated reference to the Law on the sabbath. The sabbath seems to be a sort of framework within which everything finds its place (xxxi 12-18 refers to the regulations; xxxv 1-3 refers to their carrying-out).

It deserves attention that the descriptive account (*Ausführungsberichte*) has in fact a double object: the carrying-out of both the divine commandment to Moses, viz to proclaim the Word of God, and of the task assigned to the people and contained in this Word of God. For this reason the sections might also be called "On obedience".

---

[1]) HOLZINGER, l.c. *Exodus*, p. 146. Cf. E. COTHENET, l.c. „Parfums..." col. 1304, on „galbanum". The author disagrees, but without strong evidence.

This fact may be important for an aetiological understanding; it could reflect a special programme to realize once more the splendour of the tent of meeting and also to inspire willingness to participate.

There are some differences between the texts about the regulations and those on their carrying-out. The tent is now given pride of place both in the summary (xxxv 11-19) and in their actual carrying-out (xxxvi 8-34). Is it merely a question of logical order, as NOTH [1]) says? Has it something to do with "architectural conceptualization", as LEVINE [2]) suggests? Or might it be evidence that the tent became important to the priestly authors as soon as they were less dependent upon a *Vorlage*? Probably there is also a relation between its qualification as *'ohel mo'ed* and the *'edah* [3]).

This brings us to our second and even more important point. There is not only an inner coherence between the elements of xxx 1-xl 35, but the whole section has a closer affinity to the pattern of the PC as a whole than xxv 1-xxix 42 has. We hold therefore that which is usually called Ps to belong to P-*Grundschrift*. This also means that to us xxv 1-xxix 42 is closer to the *Vorlage*; that it is integrated into P but not reflecting P's proper intentions.

Our grounds for this assumption are:

1. The prominence of the Spirit of God (*ruaḥ 'elohim*) in xxxi 1 points to the creation story by P. The priestly history is describing here a turning point in the sacred history, to be compared to God's act of creation. That the reference to the Spirit of God is not fortuitous, is clear from the fact that it replaces the *tabnit* of the *Vorlage*. (xxv 9). This substitution is evidence of a new way of theological thinking. The *Vorlage* may have found its origin in prophetic circles since *tabnit* refers to a visionary context (cf. what we said in the excursion about KOCH's theory on the origin of the *Rituale*), the word playing no role at all in the main stream of the PC. This same process of substituting Spirit for *tabnit* is also found in xxxv 31. Note

---

[1]) L.c. *Das zweite...* p. 222.

[2]) B. A. LEVINE, „The Descriptive Tabernacle Texts of the Pentateuch", *JAOS* LXXXV 1965, pp. 307-318. He compares Ex. xxxv-xxxix with 1Kgs. vi-vii and says that the account in Ex. "is a document patterned after archival records. It follows the logic of architectural conceptualization in the arrangement of its materials and employs traditional methods of accounting". It does not become clear how LEVINE sees its relation to the prescriptive texts in Ex. xxv ff.

[3]) L. ROST, *Vorstufen zur Kirche und Synagoge im Alten Testament*, Stuttgart 1938, p. 84.

also that the two other places where the word occurs in its meaning of the "divine model" or "pattern" (RSV) (xxv 40 and xxvii 8) are left out in the descriptive account (xxxvii 17-24 and xxxviii 1-7). This can hardly be a coincidence. The emphasis on the contemplation of the divine world, so prominent in the *Vorlage* (cf. Von Rad's remarks [1]) about xxv 9 and its traces of reworking) did not fit in with the ideas and concepts of the PC proper.

2. The connection between the Spirit of God and the sabbath (xxxi 1-18) is another suggestion of a link with the priestly creation story. Against the objection that the solemn and hieratic style of the creation story deviates too much from the style we find here, it may be argued, first, that the style of P in the creation story is none too smooth either, as Schmidt's study has shown to us. Such difference as there is, is mainly due to the various traditions which the authors had to take into account. This should prevent us from distinguishing sharply between the sacred history of P and its cultic legislation.

3. The excommunication formula found in this second text (xxx 33 and 38) connects it with the priestly story of Abraham. It is only natural that the formula should now receive stereotype treatment, because of the legislative materials, but Gen. xvii shows that it is incorporated in both sections of the priestly tradition.

4. The above-mentioned elements of wealth and generosity on the part of the people connect the section with the priestly story of Abraham and especially with that of Jacob.

5. The descriptive account has an important function; it transforms the preceding sections from legislation into sacred history [2]). Elliger [3]) has underlined the importance of the divine Word as the power at the back of history in P. As R. Borchert [4]) has shown, there is an anti-parallel between the story of the plagues in P and the descriptive accounts of the carrying-out of the cultic laws. The formula "God said, Speak to Aaron" is followed by the narrative of Pharaoh's

---

[1]) G. von Rad, l.c. *Die Priesterschrift* ... p. 181.
[2]) Cf. Levine, l.c. "The Descriptive ...", p. 313. The integration of the materials into the narrative of ancient Israelite history is the exact reason of the difference in form between the Ugaritic, Assyrian and Hittite rituals on the one hand, and the Israelite texts on the other.
[3]) K. Elliger, l.c. „Sinn ...", p. 139.
[4]) R. Borchert, Stil und Aufbau der priesterlichen Erzählung (Diss. Heidelberg; Maschinenschrift), 1957; quoted by Koch l.c. *Die Priesterschrift* ... p. 100, n. 1.

disobedience; on the other hand, the same formula is followed by the story of the obedience of the Israelites.

6. The formal literary parallel between the story of Creation and the descriptive account is even closer than we saw above. The creation story knows of a *Vorlage*, too, viz the so-called *Tat-Bericht* about God's shaping the things. The corresponding *Wort-Bericht* is a double one, as in the cultic texts we are dealing with here. It consists of the proclamation of the Word of God and of the obedience on the part of the things created.

7. The section is narrowly connected with the concepts of the people and its priestly classes as dealt with in Num.; we see this from xxx 11-16 and xxxviii 21-33. The parts of the Book of Numbers are in their turn intrinsically linked up with the *Leitmotiv* of Canaan and its possession.

We think the evidence is sufficient to conclude that the traditional order, *P-Grundschrift* followed by supplements, should be reversed in this way: a *Vorlage* of traditions preceding the PC, in Ch. xxv-xxix; a recasting and integration of these traditions into the body of the PC in Ex. xxx-Lev. ix.

We admit that in the section Ch. xxv-xxix there once more is a division into two shifts. Although we have expressed some hesitation as to minor points, we have no reason to doubt the fundamental correctness of the new analytic approach made by RENDTORFF and KOCH. But it would be beyond the scope of our present inquiry to go into all the details of what could be called the priestly school. Our emphasis is rather on the basic unity of the work, and its relationship with a particular moment of Israel's history.

If Ex. xxx-Lev. ix does indeed belong to the main stream of the PC, the late dating of these Chapters is a further indication of the late date of the Code. There is confirmation of this from linguistic quarters. HOLZINGER [1] has shown that in the Chapters on the carrying-out of the regulations there are some minor changes of language. Thus the expression *'iš 'el 'aḥiw* of Ch. xxv ff. is replaced by the expression *'aḥat 'el 'aḥat*, a phrase also occurring in both groups of Chapters of the Samaritan text. He therefore rightly concludes (and we extend his conclusion to the main body of the PC) that Ch. xxxv ff. show a linguistic pattern which was close in time to the moment when the Samaritans took over the Pentateuch.

---

[1] HOLZINGER, l.c. *Exodus*, p. 148.

19. *Leviticus*

(*a*) This is the right place to point to the new meaning of "atonement" in the Priestly Code. Klaus KOCH, who recently wrote about the subject [1]), filled a gap in biblical scholarship by doing so. His first thesis is that atonement in the sense of removal of sins (*Beseitigung von Sünde*) plays no role in pre-exilic Israel [2]).

His second thesis is that in the Persian period forgiveness of sins was expected from cultic expiatory rites in which God is the only agent and man is freed from the forces of evil unchained by sin, sin having been transferred to an animal [3]). He emphasizes that sin is a rather material entity (*stoff-ähnlich*), but most exegetes were wrong in seeing human achievements (*Selbsthilfe*) or mere acts of blind obedience (*Observanz*) in these expiatory rites. On the other hand, the priestly authors, through a process of generalization, have extended the note of expiation to all kinds of sacrifices [4]).

We agree with KOCH except where he speaks about the date of this shift of emphasis. He says that this date is the exilic period because the priests, without employment (!), turn to sophisticated and fundamental reflection [5]). Now this view on the Exile originates from the study; there is no indication that the priests were left unemployed. The exiled people were employed in rebuilding ruined cities and developing agricultural regions.

Secondly, KOCH underestimates the degree of generalization in these texts. Besides the fact that all parts of cultic life are brought under a common denominator of removing sin, sin itself is only one of those evil forces (illness, sexuality, death, decay, impurity etc.) which threaten human life. As we have seen, the only suitable name

---

[1]) Klaus KOCH, „Sühne und Sündenvergebung um die Wende von der exilischen zur nachexilischen Zeit", *ET* XXVI 1966, pp. 217-238.

[2]) L.c. p. 219.

[3]) *Ibidem* p. 225.

[4]) *Ibidem* p. 231: „In einer grossartigen Vereinfachung werden die vielfältigen vorexilischen Riten auf diesen einen Generalnenner gebracht, mehr oder minder gewaltsam: Brandopfer, Mehlopfer, Räucheropfer, selbst der Levitendienst und das Musterungsgeld. (Nur das Schlachtopfer wird ausgenommen — Lev. 3 —. Das Gewicht der Tradition war anscheinend so gross, dass eine Uminterpretation zur Sühne nicht möglich erschien. Das geschieht erst später beim Chronisten).

[5]) *Ibidem* p. 232: „Ihren Ausgang haben diese Gedanken bei den Priestern im babylonischen Exil. „Arbeitslos" geworden, wenden sie sich gedanklichen Aufgaben und grundsätzlicher Besinnung zu". Besides the fulfilment of the prophecies of disaster, KOCH points to the Babylonian example: „Vielleicht das Beispiel Babyloniens, wo die Sühneriten seit alters eine grosse Rolle spielen".

for the cultic contents of the PC is: apotropaeic rites. All this asks
for a far later date than is given by KOCH.

(*b*) As an example of this we point to the anointment of the
miškan in Lev. viii, which anointment, when compared with the text
of the regulations in Ex. xxix, gets considerable attention. As KOCH [1])
remarks, such emphasis has the inconvenient consequence of inter-
rupting the passage on the ritual bath of the minor priests and their
investment (v. 6 and 13). The anointment of things as well as persons
(v. 10-11) once more seems to be inspired by prophylactic and apotropaeic intentions [2]). The same may be said about the use of sacrificial blood to free the altar from the influence of sin (v. 15). In v. 35
the clause "all this happened that they might not die" is added to
the text of the regulation, in which addition we should see a prophylactic interpretation of the rite. Such a prophylactic viewpoint is
explicitly stated in Lev. ix 6, with theological implications. The
importance of this verse stands out when it is compared with Ex.
xxix 43-46. Ex. xxix 43-46 (RSV): "There I will meet with the people
of Israel, and it shall be sanctified by my glory; I will consecrate the
tent of meeting and the altar; Aaron also and his sons I will consecrate,
to serve me as priests. And I will dwell among the people of Israel,
and will be their God. And they shall know that I am the Lord their
God . . ." Lev. ix 6: "This is the thing which the Lord commanded
you to do; and the glory of the Lord will appear to you". In the first
text sanctification and consecration are the effects of Yahwe's coming
and of his dwelling amongst his people. In the latter text, on the
contrary, sanctification and consecration are preparatory rites, taking
away the impediments to Yahwe's coming and the dangers implied
by that coming. Here we have another piece of evidence that the
Chapters Ex. xxv-xxix, although themselves bearing the imprint
of priestly reworking, have the function of a *Vorlage* included in the
main stream of P.

The implication as far as Leviticus is concerned is that, if the
sacrificial rites in the main body of P are so emphatically prophylactic,
there is no more need to consider the so-called Code of Purity
(Lev. xi-xvi) as a later insertion into P [3]).

---

[1]) L.c. *Die Priesterschrift* . . ., p. 68.
[2]) Cf. B. A. LEVINE, l.c. "The Descriptive . . .", p. 311: "The High Priest is a
sacred vessel and is consecrated as such".
[3]) K. ELLIGER, *Leviticus*, Tübingen 1966, p. 12 f.

(c) The "technical" details in the description of parts of the sacrificial animals suggest that the priestly authors were far removed from the reality of sacrifice. Attention was drawn to this point by L. Rost[1]). He concludes from this fact that the redaction came about in late post-exilic times and did not originate in Jerusalem.

(d) Important for the question of chronology is the relative spiritualization of the cult, which can be observed in Leviticus. Ch. ii, dealing with non-bloody cereal offerings (cf. EP 32, 1-9; Mal. I 11-but cf. i 13), belongs to the last redactional shift, not to the *Vorlage*; RENDTORFF in this point is certainly right over against KOCH[2]). The *minḥah* is drawn near to the incense-offering as well in this Chapter (v. 1, 15).

(e) HEMPEL[3]) has asked why P should have united entities so different among them as the Code of Purity (Lev. xi-xvi) and the Code of Holiness (Lev. xvii-xxvi). The answer, to our view, is to be found in Lev. xi 44-45, where Yahwe's holiness, the holiness of the people, and purity in a ritualistic-material sense are brought together. It is, then, a matter of late chronology, an old pre-exilic[4]) collection being reinterpreted in the spirit of the Dispersion.

(f) The Code of Purity presents numerous analogies to the Persian ritual, for instance, the use of bundles of plants and running water[5]) (cf. *inter alia* Lev. xiv 4-6). Bloody sacrifices were widely practiced during the Achemenides[6]). Seclusion for nine days (cf. Lev. xiii 14) was a well-known rule[7]). There was a general resemblance in purification ceremonies[8]). KITTEL admits the resemblances and has a rather artificial explanation for them. According to him, the Persian

---

[1]) Leonhard ROST, „Der Leberlappen", *ZAW* LXXIX 1967, pp. 35-41, esp. p. 40: „Für die Endredaktion der Opfergesetze in Ex. und Lev. aber ergibt sich, dass sie frühestens im Exil, wenn nicht erst zur Zeit Esras erfolgt sein kann. Dabei ist es wahrscheinlich, dass sie nicht in Jerusalem, sondern in Mesopotamien erfolgt ist. Denn amtierende Priester, die täglich Gelegenheit hatten, die Anatomie der Opfertiere zu beobachten, da sie ja das Opfertier *lineṭaḥim* zu zerlegen hatten, hatten kaum Rinderleber und Kleinviehleber gleich behandelt. Das ist am Schreibtisch fern der Wirklichkeit geschehen".

[2]) L.c. *Die Priesterschrift . . .* p. 49.

[3]) J. HEMPEL, *ZAW* LXXI 1959, p. 252 (in a book-review).

[4]) J. G. VINK, l.c. *Leviticus*, p. 67.

[5]) Cf. J. DUCHESNE-GUILLEMIN, l.c. *La religion . . .*, p. 71 f.

[6]) *Ibidem* p. 100.

[7]) *Ibidem* p. 110.

[8]) *Ibidem* p. 107 f.

analogies would have roused the ancient silent tradition of the Jews into voice [1]). Such an assumption is without any textual support.

A. von Gall [2]) in "demonstrating" the Persian influence in the PC is decidedly overstating his case. The whole Code, according to him, is a matter of retrojected eschatology. To our view the Code is particularly non-eschatological, and there is no point in denying this. Those who tie up the Persian influence on the Old Testament with Zoroastrian forms, are building their case on the uncertain chronology of the Zoroastrian documents. Moreover, von Gall does not take into account the special forms in which the Persian influence on the Jews must have expressed itself *in Babylonia*. With Bo Reicke [3]) we hold that the Jews in Babylonia did not find any existing old-Iranian ritual forms, nor any Zoroastrianism, but that they must have become acquainted with a Chaldaic-Iranian syncretism in an Aramaic translation, about which unfortunately we have very little information. Any influence of this kind is likely to have manifested itself in the form of outward parallels, as outlined above.

(*g*) Lev. xvi, finally, wholly fits in with Ch. viii-xv. Note the conditions of protection (v. 2, cf. viii 35) and the prophylactic preparation ordered for the divine apparition (v. 2, cf. ix 6). There are three preparations: the apotropaeic application of the blood of the sin-offerings, the Azazel rite (v. 7-10), and the use of incense (v. 12-13). As for the late non-Palestinian origin of the Azazel rite, see our commentary on Leviticus [4]). Noteworthy is also the identification of purity and holiness in v. 19.

As for the literary analysis of this Chapter, there is no need to look for many shifts. The Chapter shows the characteristic "sanwich-

---

[1]) R. Kittel, l.c. *Geschichte...*, p. 670, 743; 656.

[2]) Aug. (Freiherr von) Gall, *Basileia tou Theou*. Eine religionsgeschichtliche Studie zur vorkirchlichen Eschatologie (Rel.-wiss. Bibliothek VII), Heidelberg 1926, p. 205.

[3]) Bo Reicke, l.c. *Die neutestamentliche...*, p. 24.

[4]) J. G. Vink, l.c. *Leviticus*, p. 62 f.

On the etymology of "Azazel", cf. D. Eshbal, „Der für Azazel in die Wüste gejagte Bock (Lev. 16, 8.10.22)", *Bet Miqra*ʾ (in Hebrew) XI 1965-1966, pp. 89-102; summary in *ZAW* LXXIX 1967, p. 241. If his thesis that the name derives from "Azaz", a deity of thunderstorm in South-Western Asia is right, this would once more point towards Mesopotamian redaction of the Code.

The text of the Temple Programme for the New Year's Festival at Babylon (so closely parallel to Lev. xvi) is to be found in ANET p. 331-334. Note that the text is from tablets dating from the Seleucid period: the rites may well have been in use from the Akkadian times until after the Persian period.

procedure" of the priestly literature in that the elements required for a further development of ritual get full treatment before the rest of the ritual is described. The following small groups are formed in this way: v. 2-4; v. 5-10; v. 11-14; v. 15-19; v. 20-22; v. 23-25; v. 26-28; v. 29-34.

Thus Lev. xvi is also evidence of the unity and late date of the PC.

The Book of Numbers

The Book of Numbers with its fairly chaotic order of materials is certainly the most vexing part of the PC. It has led scholars into almost unscholarly irritation. We do not pretend to have removed all of its obscurities but we do believe that their number is now reduced.

Basically new proposals are being made here for the exegesis of the following pericopes: Ch. xiii-xiv; xvi 1-35; xxv 1-18; xxxi 1-54; xxxii 1-42.

Minor suggestions are made about i 1-iv 49; vii 1-80; ix 1-14; ix 15-23; xv 1-16; xv 22-31; xv 37-39; xix 1-22; xx 1-13, 22-29; xxvii 12-23; xxviii 1-xxix 39.

20. Num. i 1-iv 49

A contrast is pointed out in the commentaries between iii 14-39 and Ch. iv on the one hand and i 48-54 on the other. The two reports on a census of the Levites are supposed to be in conflict with the prohibition of such a census. The census itself is told in two parallel versions.

But is the former contradiction a real one? Even without having recourse to concordism, it is possible to find a good explanation. Should *paqad* always be translated in the same way? In iii 32b, iii 36 and especially iv 32 and 49 it seems to mean "to appoint", "to assign to a definite service" (cf. HOLZINGER in iv 49). This translation gives us a good explanation of iv 1-33. The corresponding expression *nasa' 'et roš* in iv 2 ff. could mean "to give some dignity". If in iv 1-33 the word *paqad* should differ in meaning from *paqad* in Ch. i and iii, this might be a way out of the difficult exegesis of i 48-53. Strong emphasis must then be put upon v. 49b as compared with 50c; *lo' betok benej jisra'el* is then fully opposed to *sabib lammiškan*. We have seen above P's apotropaeic preoccupations; they continue to assert themselves in the field of personal relations [1]. The sons of Levi

----

[1] H. HOLZINGER, *Numeri*, Tübingen 1903, p. 6.

have the function of a "shield of protection" within the community of Israel. A solution along this way could dispense with any concordism, we think.

For traces of Dispersion origin i 18b may be important. We find there the *hithpa'el* (*hapax*) *wajjitjall^edu* "to get one's descent acknowledged" (KOEHLER-BAUMGARTNER). Is this an aetiological reflection of the typical Dispersoin tendency towards the drawing-up of individual genealogies [1])? Such an impression is confirmed by GRAY's opinion that the list [2]) of names in i 5-15 must have been compiled at a relatively late date by making a scholarly selection from ancient and modern names. Even the contents of the list point to this conclusion, e.g. the composition of names with "Shaddaï", a unique phenomenon among Hebrew personal names. The name of Shaddaï furthermore belongs to the specific terminology of P when it is describing the divine revelation in regions beyond the confines of Israel. It is interesting to note that in one instance this name of Shaddaï is connected with *'ur*, light (compare with what we have said about the creation of light in Gen. i). The conjunction of *padah* and *ṣur*, "the Rock has redeemed" may also be important; this expression could hardly occur during the Exile. But, just like the name of *'ammi-ṣadday* it fits in perfectly with the piety of the Jews in the Dispersion.

21. *Num. v and vi*

The use of the word *satah* in v 12, 14 f., 29 (cf. HOLZINGER i.l.) points to a late time of origin.

The material of the Chapters, especially the ordeal [3]) and the vow of abstention [4]), point to the Dispersion.

22. *Num. vii*

When reading this text we are bound to think of Ezra's difficulty in finding Levites (Ezr. viii 15). It tries to lighten the burden of transport services imposed upon the Levites. The text may, however, be a later insertion; commentators point to its contradiction with iv 25, 31 f., where no wagon transport is foreseen. The question must be left open whether the incompatibility between the two texts is

---

[1]) S. A. COCK, „Genealogies", in: *Enc. Bibl.* col. 1657-1666, esp. col. 1657-1659.
[2]) G. B. GRAY, *Numbers*, Edinburgh 1903, p. 6 f.
[3]) R. N. FRYE, *The Heritage of Persia*, London 1962, p. 105. J. DUSCHESNE-GUILLEMIN, l.c. *La Religion...*, p. 90 f.
[4]) HOLZINGER, l.c. *Numeri*, p. 146.

from before or after the completion and introduction of the PC in Palestine. Anyhow, behind its actual context is, according to B. A. LEVINE [1]), an archival record, which in its simplest terms, is an account of the sanctuary income, resembling numerous similar accounts from Mesopotamia.

A question which must be left open because of the lack of material, is whether the $n^e si^{\prime}im$ of Num. vii are aetiologically the Judean counterpart of the *gerim*, whom with ALT we have considered to be the Samaritan *Oberschicht*.

23. *Num. viii*

The function of v. 1-4 and 23-26 has not yet been discovered [2]). The intermediate pericope is in line with the main body of P; the legal status of the Levites has to find expression in a cultic ceremony. A literary analysis of the Chapter as given by HOLZINGER (i.l.) would seem unnecessary. The composition is perfectly understandable in the light of the "sandwich-procedure" already mentioned.

The Chapter seems to presuppose the existence of all the main parts of the PC; hence, EISSFELDT [3]) is inconsistent when he attributes Num. viii to Pg and several of the Chapters on which it depends to Ps, viz Num. xix (Num. viii 7); Lev. xiv 8-9 (Num. viii 7).

24. *Num. ix 1-14*

As we have seen, the text is a cornerstone in GRELOT's theory. We disagree, however, about its being additional (GRELOT; HOLZINGER i.l.). It is not, we think, an incorrect repetition of Ex. xii 47-49. The resumption of the theme of Ex. xii is highly significant in this part of the PC. The cultic legislation from Ex. xxx onwards is, as we have seen, reinterpreted in an apotropaeic light. Accordingly, it may be that the two pascal regulations form a kind of framework of the cultic legislation, both before and after the cultic laws, conceived in a spirit of ritual cleanness. The second time the rite is extended by purification regulations.

Note the date connecting this passage with Ex. xl 17 and Num. i 1. (There is no conflict between the dates of Num. ix 1 and i 1; on

---

[1]) Cf. B. A. LEVINE, l.c. "The Descriptive...", p. 314 f.
[2]) The word *mar'eh* (v. 4) (corresponding to *tabnit*) seems to assign the fragments to Ex. xxv ff.
[3]) EISSFELDT, l.c. *Einl.*, p. 272.

account of the regulations presented in this Chapter, the pascal
regulations are assigned to the first month).

25. *Num. ix 15-23*

BAENTSCH (i.l.) calls the paragraph a trivial and even childish
development of v. 18. But might it not have more relevance when it
is read aetiologically? We suggest that the Chapter is a theological
reflection on the interruptions and resumptions of cult in Israel's
history. We realize that such a suggestion must be unacceptable to
whom the Jerusalemite cultic centralization is an axiomatic background to P. But we are faced with the following dilemma: either
we accept BAENTSCH's evaluation of this pericope as childish and
trivial, or we try to find some aetiological background. Earlier we
have argued that the priestly creation story deliberately declined to
take over the vista on the temple from the parallel Babylonian
cosmogony. Nor did P wish to integrate the temple into its cultic
programme as was done in the second part of the Book of Hezekiel.
The tent of meeting is placed in Shiloh, which site is the *Urtypus* of
the devastated temple. The pascal rite is restored as a family rite, and
we have found cultic practices in the Dispersion as a probable background for a number of regulations, cf. our note on Ex. xii 16. In
the light of all this the above hypothesis might appear less improbable.
The meaning of v. 23 seems to be that the divine ordinations have
as their object the organization of the cult rather than to indicate
a specific place where the cult should be performed.

26. *Num. xiii-xiv*

Interesting is first of all that P has added Joshua to the spies
(cf. Dt. I 38). BAENTSCH (i.l.) rightly sees a parallel between this
glorification of Joshua and the less favourable attitude towards
Moses and Aaron in xx 1-13. As we shall see there, from an aetiological point of view it was important to the PC to draw a sharp line
between the period of the great founders and the period of the
organizing officials of the Palestinian community. As regards the
names of the spies (v. 4-16), GRAY [1]) remarks that, although there
is no such convergence of evidence as in the case of Num. i 5-15,
there is little ground to assume that the list itself, or all of the names
of which it is composed, is of ancient origin.

---

[1]) GRAY, l.c. *Numbers*, p. 135.

Another interesting fact is that in P the reconnoitering of the country is not a consequence of historical circumstances, nor is it due to a human plan, as in JED, but that it has its origin in a divine order (HOLZINGER i.l.). Indeed, despite NOTH, the country and *Landnahme* are of the highest importance to P. The journey extends across the whole country and not only as far as Hebron, as in JE. As HOLZINGER, quoting WELLHAUSEN, remarks, one feels the atmosphere of the period of Haggai, Zechariah, Nehemiah and Ezra in the way the country is described after the expedition. The people had to be encouraged and the advantages of the Holy Land had to be discovered with the eyes of faith. We can agree with these authors, our only reservations being that it is not apparent from the texts that it is the people *in Palestine* who are addressed. Whether it is they or the Dispersion Jews that are addressed, should be decided by a study of the Code as a whole. The parallel to the reversal of the Exodus termini (the country of prosperity is behind and not before the people, cf. our note to Ex. xvi) might point to the Dispersion Jews.

27. *Num. xv*

The words in v. 2, "When you come into the land", following upon xiv 26-35, on the generation which is not permitted to go into the Holy Land, are generally taken to be out of place and are therefore assumed to belong to Ps. If, however, the preceding section is indeed a parenetical address to the Dispersion Jews, it would be far easier to understand the text continuing with "When you come into the land". Henceforth the PC will be more and more considering the specific Palestinian situation. V. 14-16 give precious information about the *gerim*. The Hebrew text, *weki jagur ʾitkem ger ʾoj ʾašer betokam ledorotekem* may be rendered in several ways. BJ: *Si quelque étranger réside avec vous, ou avec vos descendants* ... seems to us less probable because *ledorotekem* determines *betokekem*. We therefore prefer RSV: "If a stranger is sojourning with you, or any one is among you throughout your generations..." Since the preceding verse speaks of the *ʾezrah*, it seems to us that the verse as a whole is a definition of the *gerim*. The description starting with *ʾoj* is not to be applied to a third group but to the *gerim*. The whole section v. 14-16, cf. v. 29 is about these two groups. This excludes any exegesis explaining the *gerim* as returning Jews or Jews coming up for the pilgrimage to Jerusalem.

The emphasis of the section is so strong that it seems not far-fetched to suppose that the object of this legislation is the emancipation of the *gerim*. The unity of the community is explicitly stated in v. 15 and 16. The beginning of v. 15 is also open to different renderings. Is *haqqahal* a *nomen pendens*, commanding the rest of v. 15, or does it belong to the last verb of v. 14? The first alternative has been chosen by RSV: "For the assembly, there shall be one statute for you and the stranger . . ." The second is chosen by BJ: "*Ainsi que vous faites, ainsi fera l'assemblée* . . ." The final result is the same in both translations; we have here an explicit statement about the *gerim* belonging to the community. That statement is even repeated in v. 16 and 29 (cf. v. 26 and 30).

This unusual stress on the *gerim* has never yet been taken as a starting-point for an exegesis of this Chapter, although it would seem the only promising approach. It explains why the exposition on sin-offerings (v. 22-31) is repeated after Lev. iv. Of all the cases summed up in Lev. iv only that of the community and of the individual person are resumed, and explicitly applied to the *gerim*. The general Israelite legislation is here resumed with special application to the specific Palestinian situation, marked off by the presence of the *gerim* in Samaria; cf. the beginning of the Chapter: "When you come into the land".

With regard to the contents of the Chapter, L. Rost[1]) remarks that we have in Num. xxviii and xxix a Babylonian concept of sacrifice because the sacrifice is expanded into a meal for the divinity with wine and cereal food. His observation may be extended to Num. xv 1-13.

The hypothesis may be defended that the link between these sacrificial meals in Babylonian style and the legislation for the Palestinian community is to be sought in the *gerim* keeping deliberately, as Alt says, to their Mesopotamian customs.

An important indication of Dispersion origin is found in the tassels of v. 37 ff. Baentsch[2]) remarks: "this use seems to have been widespread as is testified by the excavations of Persepolis". This points to Persian times. When we checked this statement, we found an even more specific indication of late origin in the archeological pictures collected by Roman Ghirshman[3]). It is undubitably

[1]) L. Rost, „Zu den Festopfervorschriften von Num. 28 und 29", *TLZ* LXXXIII 1958, pp. 329-334.

[2]) B. Baentsch, *Numeri*, Göttingen 1903, p. 539.

[3]) Roman Ghirsman, *Perse; Proto-iraniens, Mèdes, Achéménides*, Paris 1963, p. 177, picture nr. 223.

It has been objected (oral communication) that the same object is found in

clear that the tassels in the picture from Persepolis belong to noble *Babylonians* in the Persian period. The picture agrees with Num. xv 37 rather than with the four tassels of Dt. xxii 12. Such unbiased, untheological evidence is of the highest value.

28. *Num. xvi*

We cannot agree with the generally accepted attribution of the Datan-Abiram story (v. 1b-2; 12-15; 25-34) to JE.

First of all, its language and terminology do not favour any attribution to JE:

1. *ham^{e}at* in v. 13: in v. 19 it occurs in an acknowledged P-text;

2. The expression "milk and honey" (v. 13) is not exclusively restricted to JE, cf. Lev. xx 24; Hez. xx 6, 15; Jer. xi 5; xxxii 22; Num. xiv 8.

3. Words occurring in JE, but also known to P are *he^{e}elitam* (v. 13), cf. Lev. xi 45; *naḥalah* (v. 14): Gen. xlviii 6; Num. xviii 20-26; xxvi 53. The *hiphil* of the verb *bo'* occurs very often in P (v. 14); *wajjuḥar l^{e}moseh m^{e}od* (v. 15): Num. xxxii 10,13; Num. xxv 3.

4. The following words do not occur in JE at all: *panah 'el* (v. 15), although it does occur in P, Dt. and elsewhere. Of rather late origin is in v. 14 *naqar* (in *pi'el*). In 1 Sam. xi 2 it has the literal sense, to gouge out the eyes, as in Judg. xvi 21; in a metaphorical sense it occurs in Prov. xxx 17; Job. xxx 17; Is. li 1. The word *p^{e}qudah* (v. 29) occurs only in prophetical contexts (cf. Lev. xxvi = P). Equally incongruent with JE is *bara' b^{e}ri'ah* (v. 30), cf. Jer. xxxi 22.

5. Not only is the lexicographical argument unconvincing, but the specific attribution to J or E respectively has not led to any result either.

The contents of the story of Datan and Abiram likewise point away from JE:

1. The double mention of *'alah* in v. 12-14 is generally understood as a refusal to appear before Moses as a judge. This explanation, however, does not stand up to inquiry. In v. 2a the clause *liphne Moseh* suggests that their revolt took place in the very presence of Moses. The word does not express another offence *after* the revolt had taken place but is obviously meant to express the very nature of

---

the reliefs of the Black Obelisk. To us this interpretation seems wrong. The part of the vestment thrown over the right shoulder of the Assyrian king and his servants is clearly different from the tassels in the Persian scene.

that revolt. This is also obvious from the repetition of the word, resulting in an *inclusio*, in which v. 13 and 14 render the meaning of *'alah*.

2. In these verses 13 and 14 we find, however, once more the reversal of the Exodus termini, which occurs in Num. xiv 3 f.; Ex. xiv 11 ff.; xvi 3. The fact is so conspicuous that LXX, Aquila and Vulgate left out the negation at the beginning of v. 14. Commentators have unsuccessfully tried to find in the double mention of the Exodus in v. 13 and 14 the two sources J and E respectively. To us, this double mention is an increase in emphasis; the *terminus a quo* is described in v. 13; the *terminus ad quem* in v. 14.

3. We therefore would like to explain *'alah* as a refusal to enter the Holy Land and as the aetiological reflection of a resistance against the canvassing for immigration into Palestine among the wealthy Jews of the Dispersion. This conclusion would be confirmed by the fact that the texts favouring the translation of *'alah* as "to appear before a judge" (Gen. xlvi 31; Dt. xxv 7; Judg. iv 5) always specify the word by means of legal terms. Such a specification is lacking here.

4. Following the traditional JE-attribution no satisfactory explanation has been advanced of *minḥah* in v. 15. As our expositions have shown, it is altogether justified to assume the existence of some forms of cult in the Dispersion.

5. Secondary aspects of the material, too, suggest the late date of the pericope and its attribution to a P-hand in the times of the Dispersion. Commentators have already made a concession for v. 26a, attributing it to P and labelling it as a gloss. But v. 26c with its idea of taboo likewise points to P. Cf. also *nᵉsiᵖej 'edah* in v. 2b, and furthermore, the character of ordeal and its predominance in Persian ritual (see our remarks on Num. v and vi).

6. The symbolism of the divine punishment of Datan and Abiram is far more evident if it is understood in relation to the crime as outlined above. The *earth* is going to swallow them, because they prefer their actual country above the Holy Land.

28. *Num. xvii 6-15*

A clear example of the apotropaeic notion of *kipper*, cf. what we said on Leviticus, *sub* (*a*).

29. *Num. xviii*

The author of the PC is hard put to maintain the great lines of development of his salvation history because of the great number of legislations he has to integrate into his work here. This should not make us blind, however, for small details indicating that the great line is not completely lost sight of. Thus in xviii 5: *w*ᵉ*lo' jihjeh 'od qeseph 'al b*ᵉ*nej jisra'el*; the close parallel to Gen. ix 11b is obvious: *w*ᵉ*lo' jihjeh 'od mabbul l*ᵉ*šahet ha'areṣ*.

30. *Num. xix*

Aetiology has not played a very important role in the classic critical exegesis of the PC. For this reason we were struck by Hol-zinger's [1]) aetiological remark. Referring to v. 9, he indicates that the regulation of the purification water being kept outside the camp and the sanctuary is alien to P; he suggests that we have to do with a rule of non-Israelite origin, this non-Israelite origin being reflected in the expression "outside the camp". V. 4 is then a kind of Israelite recuperation. In our view, the reference to the *gerim* in v. 10 is another helpful indication; it may well be that the non-Israelite origin of the custom is tied up with the customs of the leading classes in Samaria under Persian and Babylonian influence. Gray (i.l.) says that Persian influence upon this regulation is not impossible. The use of the cow in the context of purification is confined to the Arians. In the case of a still-born baby, the Zendavesta orders the mother to drink the urine of an ox mixed with ashes, in order to purify her womb.

31. *Num. xx 1-13; 22-29*

We need not dwell upon the discussions about the interrelationship of P and E or JE in this Chapter. To us, its P-character, even of v. 5, is clear enough (Num. xi 5 is not a JE-text, but a Deuterono-mistic, post-priestly text, and xvi 3 is a P-text, as we have seen). It contains the reversal of the Exodus termini. P must have had a good knowledge of the old Israelite traditions, and this knowledge may well have led to a literary influence of Ex. xvii on our text.

How ever this may be, the correct interpretation of the text is to be read from xx 22-29. The death of Aaron is transformed into a liturgical ceremony; the reader is not left in doubt that his death is the basis of Eleazar's power. All this can only be understood if the

---

[1]) Holzinger, l.c. *Numeri*, p. 80.

importance of the *Landnahme* in P is taken into account. The legislation handed on by the great founders of Israel's religion is of the highest importance; but at the same time it is essential to indicate that the initial period is over now and that under the guidance of their successors social and religious order is establishing itself.

An interesting hint on the Dispersion situation is given by the word *beᶜirenu*, "our cattle". According to Holzinger (i.l.), this detail would not matter to P's history of the cultic community. But it *is* interesting to P as a parenetic Dispersion document, furnishing proof of a tendency towards re-emigration into Palestine.

32. *Num. xxiv 23-24*

Although this is not a P-text, we mention it in connection with the problems of chronology because "one of the most interesting interpretations" (Gray i.l.) says that the poem refers to the events towards the end of the Persian (i.e. "Asshur", cf. Ezr. iv 22) Empire, then under pressure of the growing Greek power; cf. W. E. Addis [1]), whose own solution is not convincing at all. All this has no direct bearing on the date of the PC, but is highly interesting with regard to the Samaritan acceptance of the Pentateuch, which could be much further towards the end of the Persian Empire than is generally accepted.

33. *Num. xxv 1-18; xxxi 1-54*

This section, the interest of which is easily underestimated, will repay close study.

1. As a first point it was noticed by Wellhausen [2]), that the passage is not in line with the pacifism of the PC. There must indeed be a special reason to insert it here because P is always eager to purge the old material of Israel's history from any martial episodes. Wellhausen's formula *"damit es nicht gänzlich an einem Krieg unter Moses fehle"* is therefore thoroughly misleading.

2. Neither do we get an adequate explanation by assuming that the story of the warfare against the Midianites was taken over by P in order to introduce some laws about conduct in war. P's legislation does not foresee in any condition of war.

---

[1]) W. E. Addis, "*Asshur*", in: *Enc. Bibl.*, col. 463.
[2]) J. Wellinghausen, *Prolegomena zur Geschichte Israels*, Berlin 1927, p. 354.

3. As WELLHAUSEN (l.c.) remarks, the section is full of the spirit of the late Jewry, no longer accustomed to warfare. The same is suggested by the nature of the sin involved; in xxv 1-5 (JE) it is idolatry after the seduction by Moabite women; in P it is the sin of mixed marriages (xxv 6). Balaam is no longer the heathen yet true prophet of God, as he is in JE, but the *auctor intellectualis* of the sin of the people (xxxi 16).

4. By changing the name of the Moabites into Midianites the redactors must have intended to draw the story far away from the peoples around Palestine. The Midianites never lived in the region supposed in the story; according to Judg. vi-vii they were by no means exterminated but were rather troublesome to the Israelites in the period ahead. Most of all, in this story they are no nomads, but they possess cattle and live in cities (v. 10).

5. It should be admitted that the redactional situation of Ch. xxv-xxxi is very difficult. The place of Ch. xxvi with its connecting link in xxv 19 is not very clear; neither is the separation of Ch. xxv and xxxi. The text xxvii 1-11 seems to be wholly out of context; the succession scene of Moses in xxvii 12-13 is followed by another series of regulations in Ch. xxviii. NOTH [1] may be right in his opinion that Moses's succession was a suitable place for interpolations. But he is wrong in supposing that these interpolations occurred after the conjunction of P with JED and the Deuteronomist. Historically speaking, there seems to be no room for additions to the Pentateuch after its acceptance by the Samaritan community, since the "common-wealth" of Judeans and Samaritans was so short-lived. EISSFELDT [2] may be closer to the truth in supposing that the Persian supervisors went so far as to amputate the corpus by segregating the Book of Joshua with its non-pacifistic *Landnahme*-traditions. The redactional chaos must have originated before P's completion and legal imposition. This is indicated not only through analysis of its material but also by the literary ties with Ex. xxx (cf. Num. xxxi 50, 54 and Ex. xxx 12-15, 16). Its concern about ritual purity fits in with the main line of P (cf. xxxi 19 ff. and Num. xix).

6. HOLZINGER's commentary (i.l.) is proof how the unity of the

---

[1] M. NOTH, l.c. *Ueberlieferungsgeschichte...*, p. 8, cf. p. 19, n. 62. *Idem, Ueberlieferungsgeschichtliche Studien*, p. 236 (= 194).

[2] EISSFELDT, l.c. *Einl.*, p. 342.

Chapter gets lost if it is not read aetiologically. (According to him there are three shifts; v. 1-12; v. 13-20; v. 21-24).

7. All the available data point to the same direction: the Chapter should be read aetiologically. It records the voice of conscience of the Dispersion Jews about wealth acquired by them in the course of some war-operations in the Dispersion. Kurt GALLING [1]) says that to the Jews in Babylon the fall of the city in 539 B.C. had not appeared as an example of divine wrath and punishment of the Babylonians, for the priests of Marduk had greeted Cyrus as the liberator from the tyrannical yoke of Nabonidus. On the other hand, they may have seen a fulfilment of the prophetical promises regarding the punishment of the Babylonians in the bloody suppression of the revolt of Nidintu-Bel in 522 B.C. (according to the sources the whole population of Babylon was involved). The Jews may quite well have chosen the part of the Persians and have taken an active part in subduing the insurgence. GALLING points to Zechar. ii 1-4, dating about that time; he thinks that a favourable Persian attitude towards the Jews because of their co-operation may have led to the first considerable return of exiles, which according to him, took place shortly after 520 B.C. Is it rash to see in Ch. xxxi the aetiological reflection of the origin of the wealth of the Jews in the Babylonian Dispersion [2])?

34. *Num. xxvii 12-23*

We recognize the reference to the Spirit in xxvii 18 as something characteristic of the basic structure of the PC. The Spirit is present at the turning points of sacred history (see our comment on Ex. xxx 1-xl 35). The Spirit of God is actively present in the creation, in the construction of the tent of meeting and in the organization of the *Landnahme*.

NOTH [3]) advances rather an artificial argument about v. 17: on the one hand he says that P has chosen an expression which necessarily means "guiding the people in war", and he adduces 1 Sam. xviii 16; 2 Sam. v 2 (cf. 1 Sam. xxix 6); on the other hand the fact that no militant *Landnahme* is mentioned means, according to him, that the *Landnahme* as such must have been outside the interest of the PC. This argument is deficient for many reasons. That the expression

---

[1]) GALLING, l.c. *Studien*, p. 55.

[2]) *Ibidem* p. 53, n. 2: "In our view the economic and financial position of the Jews only improved during Darius's reign". (author's translation).

[3]) M. NOTH, l.c. *Ueb. Studien*, p. 233 (= 191).

'aśer jeṣe wa'aśer jabo', also followed here by the *hiphil* of the same words, would mean "guidance in warlike operation", is not only contrary to the second half of the verse, where it is explained as "being a shepherd to the flock" but also to another P-text, Josh. xiv 11. There, *lammilḥamah* is clearly different from its juxtaposition *weláṣet welabo'*. The latter expression is of such a general nature (cf. Dt. xxviii 6; 2 Kgs. xix 27) that a pacifistic use by the priestly authors can hardly be excluded. But what is even more important is the logical mistake in NOTH's argument that P, not being interested in a militant *Landnahme*, should not be interested in a *Landnahme* at all. The notion of a pacifistic version of the *Landnahme* seems to be foreign to NOTH, no doubt because a Persian dating of the Code is unknown to him.

35. *Num. xxviii 1-xxix 39*

The following observation on these Chapters is bound to be very hypothetical; it is dependent upon our exegesis of Ch. xv.

L. ROST [1]), speaking about these two Chapters, stated that the holocaust was expanded into a complete meal for the divinity and that this must have happened under Babylonian influence. He can hardly be right in asserting that this change must have come about during the Exile [2]) because, to begin with, such a friendly attitude towards the Babylonian cult is less understandable during the Exile than in the Dispersion. But in the second place, as the exiled Jews did not live in the Babylonian cities, there was not much opportunity for them to get acquainted with the Babylonian temple-cult [3]).

Hence it is more plausible to assume that the adoption of this legislation occurred in the Dispersion. That it was imposed upon the Palestinian community may have been due to a corresponding influence among the Samaritan leading classes, the *gerim*, as we have defended for Num. xv. Since there is no explicit mention of them here, we have only an indirect indication that our exegesis of Ch. xv is also valid here. That indication is the predominance of the Autumn Feast. No less than 191 animals are to be slaughtered as burnt offerings (not reckoning the *tamid*-sacrifices). It is true that the Autumn Feast had a predominant position in ancient Israel, but this position was lost before the PC; and even in the Code itself the feast is nowhere

---

[1]) Cf. p. 118, n. 1 of the present Chapter.
[2]) L. ROST, l.c. „Zu den...", p. 332.
[3]) Cf. p. 103, n. 4 of the present Chapter.

else privileged to such a degree in the sacrificial system. On the other hand, the New Year's Festival had always remained prominent in Babylon. We suggest that once more the *gerim* were the link between Mesopotamian customs and the priestly legislation. As for the tremendous numbers of sacrifices, we wonder (but owing to lack of evidence this must remain an open question) whether the *gerim* may have had some commercial interest in such an affluent cult (for instance by providing the sacrificial animals).

36. *Num. xxx 1-17*

Vows of abstinence, in this Chapter presumably abstention in sexual matters, point to the Dispersion where such forms of religious behaviour came into use [1]).

A late origin is also suggested by the word *'issar* (v. 3; occurring nowhere else); it is a special word for "vow of abstinence". The same matter is expressed in Num. vi by the classical Hebrew word *neder*.

37. *Num. xxxii 1-42*

We do not think that this text is prior to P. Opinions are divided; according to some (e.g. HOLZINGER i.l.) it is a confluence of JE and P; P being present especially in v. 18-19. The picture of men deliberating among themselves and dividing the land east of the Jordan would not fit in with P. Others (e.g. GRAY i.l.) think that the text has been recast. "The presence of linguistic peculiarities (e.g. *heni'* in v. 7, 9; *tarbut* in v. 14) and Deuteronomic characteristics (*Qadeš Barne'a* v. 8; Deuteronomic sentences in v. 7-13) and the fact that some of the most marked peculiarities of P are embedded in sections that in other respects most closely resemble JE, render it more probable that the whole narrative has been recast than that it is the result of simple compilation from JE and P, such as is generally found elsewhere".

We on our part think that the peculiarities summed up are found in quite a number of texts that suppose both the existence of P and the late conditions of the Jews at the end of the Persian times (e.g. Ex. xxxii 7-14; Num. xi 4-30; xii 1-8; Josh. viii 30-35; Josh. v 13-15; Josh. xxiii 1-16). We propose to call this group "post-priestly Deuteronomist".

---

[1]) Cf. p. 114, n. 4 of the present Chapter.

We think the present Chapter has a relationship with Josh. xxii. If aetiologically read, it is both concerned with the Dispersion and its appreciation in Palestine. Since it does not belong to P, the Chapter does not come immediately within the scope of our study.

38. Num. xxxiv

Some things are noteworthy in the list of names in Ch. xxxiv. "Parnak" (v. 25) might be the Persian name of Pharnakès (cf. Herod. viii 126). It could also be from a Semitic root *fnk* with inserted r (cf. GRAY i.l.). GRAY concludes that the list as a whole is hardly more ancient than that of Ch. i, though the evidence in the present case is less conclusive. Interesting is the name of Yogli in v. 22. GRAY remarks about it: "This hardly means 'led into Exile'; if it did, it would be a late name". To us the latter alternative is more probable. A late dating of the text is even made more plausible by the fact that the person mentioned is the *son* of Yogli; such a fact would indicate an even greater distance in time from the Exile.

This Chapter, especially v. 3-12, is generally attributed to P, but NOTH [1]) disagrees with this view. His argument—surely a surpirsing one—is that the Chapter is closely connected with Josh. xiii ff., which Chapters, according to him, have nothing to do with P. Is it not far more obvious that Ch. xxxiv constitutes the most acceptable of links between P in Num. and in Josh.? The most characteristic link found in P is eaxctly the one formed by the divine regulations and the carrying-out of them.

Summary

The detailed analysis of the text of the PC itself, presented in the present Chapter, produced an unusually large number of places pointing to a late date. In the following list undoubtedly the most valuable evidence is headed: ethnical and geographical indications, because they provide non-theological and methodically unbiased material. Next in value ranks the material headed aetiological parenesis, because it reveals a permanently maintained reinterpretation of traditional material. Thirdly, the evidence listed under the heading "community" is interesting because our hypothesis on the *gerim*, as far as we can see, stands up to a check from all the material available.

---

[1]) M. NOTH, l.c. *Ueb. Studien...*, p. 236 (= 194).

Ethnical-geographical indications: Gen. x; Gen. xxv 13, 20; Lev. xi-xvi (closest analogies to the Persian cult); Num. xv 37-39; Num. xix; Num. xxiv 23-24; Num. xxxiv 25.

Aetiology of the Dispersion: Gen. xi 31; Gen. xii 15; xiii 6 (wealth and pacifism); Gen. xvii (covenant); Gen. xxiii (buying of land in Palestine); Gen. xxxi 35 (wealth); Gen. xxxvii-l (unity and wealth); Ex. x 23-26 (dwellings); Ex. xxx 11-16 (collections); Num. i 18b (genealogies); Num. xx 1-13; 22-29 (authority); Num. xxv 1-18; xxxi 1-54 (wealth); Num. xxxii (relations to the homeland).

Aetiological parenesis: Gen. xvii (covenant); Gen. xxxvii-l (fraternal unity); Ex. vi 2-vii 2 (against "shortness of mind"); Ex. xvi (reversal of the Exodus termini); Num. xiii-xiv (the value of the Holy Land); Num. xvi (against the refusal to migrate to the Holy Land);

Aetiology of the cult: Gen. xxviii 3; Gen. xxxv 11-12; Ex. xii 16; Ex. xxv 1-Lev. xxvii (apotropaeic conception of cult); Num. ix 15-23 (interruptions and resumptions of cult); Num. xix 9.

Community: Gen. xvii 14; Gen. xlviii 6; Ex. xii; Num. i 1-iv 49; Num. vii; Num. ix 1-14; Num. xv 14-16, 29.

Literary indications: Gen. i (catechetical; polemical); Ex. xxx i-xl 35 (inner coherence of the section and its belonging to the main body of P); Num. i 5-15 (late names); Num. xiii 4-16 (late names); Num. xviii 5 and xxvii 18 (unity of the PC); Num. xxxiv 21 (late name); Num. xxxiv (link with P in Josh.).

Theological developments: Gen. i (dualism) (no prospect of temple building; pacifism); Gen. ix (pacifism); Gen. ix 6-7 (world-wide propagation of the Jewish race); Num. v and vi (vows of abstinence).

V. THE PRIESTLY CODE IN BIBLICAL THEOLOGY

At the end of this inquiry it may be useful to compare its results with the data of the history of the biblical religion so as to check the reliability of the investigation and, if possible, to illustrate its correspondence with recent trends in this field of study.

1. First of all the idea of *amphictyony*. Recent studies tend to do away with the concept altogether. They date the traditions of all-Israel no further back than to the Davidic period. This amounts to a rejection of Noth's theory of the amphictyony. A first step in this direction was made by Rud. Smend [1]. He himself still stuck to

---

[1] Rud. Smend, *Jahwekrieg und Stämmebund*, Göttingen 1963.

Noth's thesis of 1930 that the amphictyony of the twelve tribes was the religio-juridical structure of Israel between the *Landnahme* and the monarchy. But he robbed the theory of one of its main pillars, viz the Holy War, reputedly waged on behalf of the amphictyony. The only evidence left for this theory in Smend's work is (a) the title of "Judge" applied to the Minor Judges [1]) and explained as indications of amphictyonic office, and (b) the special kind of war in Judg. xix-xxi, said to be a war of sanctions after an infringement of the amphictyonic rules [2]) (although Smend has to admit that a good deal of the story is legendary).

An all-out attack on the amphictyonic hypothesis was launched by H. M. Orlinsky [3]). He maintains that there is no evidence of any amphictyonic function of "Judges" nor of any connection between them and the shrines. No amphictyonic league ever met at a shrine to decide on a course of action or to choose a Judge. It is an error of method to assume the existence of an amphictyonic league as soon as the Bible mentions a shrine. According to Orlinsky [4]), Judg. xix-xxi is not the story of an amphictyonic war at all. Note that the *two* sanctuaries of Mispah and Bethel are mentioned here. In Judg. iv-v, on the other hand, there is no reference to any shrine at all.

We agree with Orlinsky's view, not with Noth's widespread theory. But it is necessary to supplement the former's study by the more positive approach of Siegfried Herrmann [5]). We should not underestimate, Herrmann points out, the deep influence of the two geographical and ethnico-political cross-beams or barriers (*Querriegel*) that split up the Israelite tribes into three groups during the period of the Judges. At the same time those barriers were a challenge to the tribes and finally led up to the monarchy. The mere common belief in Yahwe was not enough to effect close political ties. It is not even certain that, apart from this common worship of Yahwe, they shared an identical body of historical traditions [6]). There are grounds to link up Judah with the Qadesh-traditions, and the house of Joseph with those of Exodus and the Mountain of God. The merit therefore of bringing the tribes together into a single tight system and also of

---

[1]) *Ibidem* p. 33-55.
[2]) *Ibidem* p. 26.
[3]) H. M. Orlinsky, "The tribal system of Israel and related groups in the period of the Judges", *OA* I 1962, pp. 11-20.
[4]) *Ibidem* p. 15.
[5]) S. Herrmann, „Das Werden Israels", *ThLZ* LXXXVII 1962, pp. 561-574.
[6]) *Ibidem* p. 573.

unifying their traditions is due to the towering figure of David. We cannot really speak of the traditional concept of Israel [1]) before David's time. Not until then were the conditions created under which the Pentateuchal Yahwist (J) could make a first effort at unifying the tribal traditions [2]).

2. The principal contribution to this new anti-amphictyonic approach is made by Johann MAIER [3]). Of the textual material about *the Ark* he only retains 1 Sam. iv 3-4, as seen in relation with 1 Sam. iii 3 and iv 11-13. It is his thesis that before David the Ark had no significance and value of its own, but was a depository for documents or a treasury of an anti-Philistine league of a number of tribes. It was carried into battle (1 Sam. iv 1b-4a) as *ultima ratio* in a desperate situation because it was thought to share in the numinous power of the ritual of benediction and malediction and possibly of the inscription of the name of Yahwe. It was lost in that battle and later forgotten by Saul. This could only have happened if the Ark was not an object of cult of its own. To David, however, the recuperated Ark became a symbol by means of which he connected his reign with Shiloh, beyond Saul and his failures [4]). We agree with MAIER about the critical analyses of the references to the Ark in Num. x 33-36 and xiv 44 [5]), Ex. xxxiii 1-6 [6]), Josh. vii 6 and viii 33 [7]), in Josh. iii and iv [8]), Josh. vi [9]), Judg. xx 27-28 (where NOTH is shown to be inconsistent by admitting the literary composition of the Chapter and nevertheless explaining it as amphictyonic) [10]), 1 Sam. vii 2; xiv 8, 1 Kgs ii 26,

---

[1]) An analogous conclusion about the twelve-tribe system on the ground of the different types of lists of tribal names was reached by J. HOFTIJZER, „Enige opmerkingen rond het israelitische 12-stammen-systeem", *NTT* XIV 1959, pp. 241-263.

Cf. also W. H. IRWIN, „Le sanctuaire central israélite avant l'établissement de la monarchie", *RB* LXXII 1965, pp. 161-184.

The theory of the amphictyony is also rejected by G. FOHRER, „Altes Testament — 'Amphiktyonie' und 'Bund'?", *ThLZ* XCI 1966, pp. 301-316, 893-904; and by B. D. RATHJEN, „Philistine and Hebrew Amphictyony", *JNES* XXIV 1965, pp. 100-104.

[2]) HERRMANN, l.c. „Das Werden...", p. 572.

[3]) Johann MAIER, *Das altisraelitische Ladeheiligtum*, Berlin 1965.

[4]) *Ibidem* p. 64.

[5]) *Ibidem* p. 4.

[6]) *Ibidem* p. 13.

[7]) *Ibidem* p. 18.

[8]) *Ibidem* p. 23.

[9]) *Ibidem* p. 33.

[10]) *Ibidem* p. 41.

1 Sam. iii 3 [1]), and, finally, of the stories in 1 Sam iv-vii 1 and 2 Sam. vi containing two strata, distinguishing between the titles of *'aron (berit) jahweh* on the one hand and *'aron ha'elohim* on the other [2]). We agree especially with his remark that only the critical reappraisal of the amphictyony-thesis has cleared the way for a true understanding of the text-material about the Ark. Really epochal seems to us MAIER's excursion into the term *jahweh ṣeba'ot* [3]). This term is explained by him as a dualis; comparing it with 1 Kgs. ii 5 (cf. 2 Sam. xi 11), he says that it refers to the double *Heerbann* or people's army under David. 1 Sam. iv 4a and 2 Sam. vi 2 would be brilliantly explained by this hypothesis and testify to the *Neubenennung* or new politico-cultic function of the Ark. This new function of the Ark would have been part of David's programme of unification of the two Israelite regions and the largely non-Israelite city-state of Jerusalem.

All this is of great importance to the study of the PC. If MAIER is right—and in our view he presents a strong case—a number of theories on the origin of the Code are henceforth ruled out. The twelve tribe system seems to be so tightly interwoven with P's structure that we cannot trace back P to pre-Davidic times, for instance as a shrine-legend of the mobile sanctuary of the Ark [4]). Moreover, KOCH's theory about the *Vorlage* of the Code being the cult-legend of a non-Jerusalemite sanctuary having an Ark of its own [5]) would be no longer valid.

Furthermore, if there is no recourse to pre-Jerusalemite amphictyonic traditions to explain P's emphasis on the twelve-tribe system and its localization of people and cult in the desert, we have far more reason to look for a deliberate theological purpose behind these two data. They may indicate an essential change in the theological evaluation of the Jerusalemite cult. This would strengthen our exegesis of many details of the Code in the light of a new world-wide Jewish cult (see n. 5 of the present Chapter, p. 141 f.).

This does not mean that P was the originator of the retrojection of the cult of the Ark into the desert. The *Heerbann* was revived in the Deuteronomic reform under Josiah. The Ark then became the symbol of the new codification of royal rights and duties. It became an

---

[1]) *Ibidem* p. 42-45.
[2]) *Ibidem* p. 46-50.
[3]) *Ibidem* p. 50-54.
[4]) Cf. Ch. I, p. 10, n. 4.
[5]) Cf. Ch. IV, 18 on Ex. xxv 1 — Lev. ix 21 and p. 100, n. 3 and 4; p. 101, n. 1.

essential part of the desert story as the depository of the Law of God [1]). The PC is an analogous effort of reformation and revival of the twelve-tribe system.

This post-Deuteronomic character rules out another theory on the origin of the PC, viz J. HEMPEL's attribution of P to the priesthood of Hebron [2]).

3. The central cultic position of *Aaron* is specific for the PC. His place in pre-exilic biblical literature has always struck scholars as being curiously ambiguous. In the ancient texts Aaron's function is not a cultic one. He is mentioned in the battle against the Amalekites (Ex. xvii 8 ff.), he is present on the Mountain of God and on Mount Sinai (Ex. xviii 12; xxiv 1-2, 9-11), and accompanies Moses into Egypt (Ex. v ff.; Mich. vi 14; 1 Sam. xii 6, 8). But most famous and difficult of all is his connection with the cult of the Golden Calf (Ex. xxxii) and his part in the rebellion against Moses (Num. xii).

Many have been the efforts to reconstruct Aaron's early history from these materials. An interesting recent hypothesis by H. SEEBASS explains Aaron's dominating cultic position in later times from the fact that he had been the mediator of cultic laws and revelation in the nomadic period, contrasting and clashing with the Mosaic religion [3]). Whereas the Mosaic religion centered around the Word and the Promise, the Aaronite cult is thought by this author to have found its focus in the Image or rather Picture of God. The integration of this religion into Yahwism would have been brought about in two ways; first by creating a strong link (of subordination) between Aaron and Moses (Ex. iv 10-16) and secondly by means of a so-called *Enteignung* or expropriation of Aaronite traditions in favour of Moses. The tradition of the Holy Rod, symbol of divine power, was originally Aaronite (cf. the parallel reference to the signs of Moses in Ex. iii 12 and iv 17) [4]); the Mountain of God was the original site of Aaron's revelation (Ex. iv 27) [5]). SEEBASS's exposition on the expropriation of the central Aaronite pericope Ex. xxxii is noteworthy [6]). Ex. xxxii is not a mere retrojection of 1 Kgs. xii [7]). It has certainly had a *Vorlage*

---

[1]) MAIER, l.c. *Das...*, p. 74 f.

[2]) Cf. Ch. I, p. 10, n. 3.

[3]) H. SEEBASS, *Mose und Aaron. Sinai und Gottesberg*, Bonn 1962.

[4]) *Ibidem* p. 28.

[5]) *Ibidem* p. 30.

[6]) *Ibidem* p. 33-36.

[7]) Cf. A. H. J. GUNNEWEG, *Leviten und Priester*, Göttingen 1965, p. 89, n. 4.

in which the Calf was absent (otherwise such a cult could not have presented itself to Jeroboam as authentically Yahwistic), as is also apparent from v. 20; a Golden Calf would not have been subject to pulverization and combustion. V. 4a suggests that the *Vorlage* mentioned a pictorial representation of God, *wajjaṣar 'oto* (accus. masc.!) *baḥeret*, "and he designed him with a slate-pencil". For the translation "designed" cf. 1 Kgs. vii 15. A recent study [1] still overlooks the importance of the masculin accusative. Originally, no doubt, it referred to *'elohim* in v. 1, not to the gold of v. 3 as in the actual arrangement of the text. If this is correct, the object would have been a panel representing a drawing of God like those with which we are familiar from ancient Egypt. When being expropriated in favour of Moses the table was then converted into a carrier of the Words of God, inscribed by God himself [2].

Although not all Seebass's examples of expropriation are convincing, it seems to us that his new aetiological approach to the biblical figure of Aaron offers a way out of the dilemma of conflicting traditions and merits serious discussion.

Where are we to place Aaron in pre-exilic history? Seebass concludes from an analysis of Ex. xvii (by the same methodical approach of "expropriation") that Aaron was a mediator for some form of religion and revelation, probably in the region of Qadesh [3].

It is useful to point out that the localization of certain traditions in the desert or the oasis does not necessarily refer to a nomadic setting in the pre-*Landnahme* period of Israel.

With regard to the first point, we agree with Seebass that there are far more indications that the origin of the traditions about Aaron go back to the desert than that it should be traced to such local

---

[1] M. Noth, „Zur Anfertigung des 'Golden Kalbes' ", *VT* IX 1959, pp. 419-422. His reference to 2 Kgs. v 23 does not away with that failure. The occurrence of both the root *ṣur* and the root *ḥrt* is no convincing proof that "stringing the gold into a pouch" is the correct translation here. Could it not have been the other way round, viz that the resemblance of Ex. xxxii 4a and 2 Kgs. v 23 gave rise to the interpreting insertion of Ex. xxxii 2-4a?
For a reference to Jewish exegetical literature, anticipating Noth's proposal: J. J. Petuchowsky (short note in:) *VT* X 1960, p. 74.

[2] This explanation of Ex. xxxii seems to us to be more convincing than Kenneth's thesis (cf. Ch. II, p. 59, n. 1), maintained by W. Beyerlin, l.c. *Herkunft...*, p. 146-150, viz that Ex. xxxii is the cult legend of Bethel. This does not do justice to 1 Kgs. XII 31 f. (cf. Beyerlin, p. 149, n. 1).
Kenneth's thesis is also followed by Moses Aberbach and Leivy Smolar, „Aaron, Jeroboam and the Golden Calves", JBL LXXXVI 1967, pp. 129-140.

[3] Seebass, l.c. *Mose...*, p. 64.

Palestinian shrines as (*a*) an anonymous sanctuary in the monarchical period, as suggested in KOCH's frequently cited study, or (*b*) to both Shiloh and Bethel, as MOWINCKEL [1]) says, or (*c*) to Bethel alone, as KENNETH and BEYERLIN contend [2]).

Our own thesis on the origin of the Aaronite traditions concurs with the recent approach to the twelve-tribe system and the Ark. In our view Aaron, too, undubitably belongs to the *Heerbann*-traditions of Davidic times.

The main evidence for this thesis is the remarkable terminological connection between Ex. xxxii 17-18 and Ex. xvii 8-16 (and xxiv 13a-14) [3]) by means of *gabar* and *ḥalaš*, "to be victor" and "to be defeated". The connection between Ex. xxxii and xvii based on these *hapax legomena* has been noticed, but we do think that a much more specific conclusion can be drawn: Ex. xvii is a text about Yahwe's War, which suitably fits in with the Davidic period.

According to NOTH [4]), Aaron and Hur have a firmer place in the text of Ex. xvii 8 ff. than have Moses and Joshua. Of all texts about Aaron this one probably gives the most reliable information about Aaron's origin: he may have been a southern Judean chieftain in a local war against the Amalekites.

In our view, however, the final verses 14-16 clearly refer to a War of Yahwe, not to a local war, and all the biblical evidence of the Holy War against the Amalekites points to the Davidic period. As Rud. SMEND [5]) indicates,—basing himself on an analysis of 1 Sam. xxv 28; cf. 1 Sam. xxx 26 and also 2 Sam. viii 12—the Davidic war against the Amalekites in 1 Sam. xxx may be called a War of Yahwe already in that early period of the king's career.

Now if we put side by side Ex. xvii 8 ff. and Ex. xxxii, there is ground for the hypothesis that Aaron's biblical stature is a retro-jection of some cultic functionary taken into David's service and connected with the warfare against the Amalekites.

Our thesis is more or less dependent upon the new view of the amphictyony, viz that we must not relate any tribal traditions to Israel as a whole until the time of David. This view is also founded

---

[1]) S. MOWINCKEL, l.c. *Erwägungen* ..., p. 127. He points to Judg. xviii 30 (Dan parallel to Bethel) and 1 Sam. iv 4, 19.

[2]) Cf. p. 133, n. 2.

[3]) Cf. W. BEYERLIN, l.c. *Herkunft* ..., p. 26, with a reference to EISSFELDT.

[4]) NOTH, l.c. *Ueberlieferungsgeschichte* ..., p. 195-199.

[5]) Rud. SMEND, l.c. *Jahwekrieg* ... p. 62.

on SEEBASS and NOTH, except that we have assumed a relatively late, i.e. a Davidic chronology. SEEBASS's "expropriation" theory is correct, especially with regard to the Holy Rod and to the visionary revelation. NOTH is right in supposing a connection between Aaron and the war against the Amalekites but owing to his amphictyonic approach he dates it too early.

Our view of Aaron is confirmed by the cultic material of the PC. It explains the curious fact that so many cultic objects are mentioned in the story of David that afterwards disappear from the biblical record to turn up again in the PC; e.g. the table of the bread of the Presence, Ex. xxv 23-30, cf. 1 Sam. xxi 2-7; furthermore Ex. xxviii 6, 7, 12, cf. 1 Sam. ii 18; xxii 18 and the *Urim* and *Tummim*, Ex. xxviii 30, cf. 1 Sam. xxiii 9-12.

It surely is not far-fetched to assume that the traditions of the *Heerbann* continued to lead a sort of underground existence, to surface again in a later period (compare what had happened during Josiah's reign).

As for Aaron's name, there is no consensus about its etymology. Its derivation from *'aron*, the Ark, is still defended by MOWINCKEL [1]), but an Egyptian etymology is not incompatible with our hypothesis.

If we are right in supposing that in P traditions of the *Heerbann*, and therefore of the *'am ha'ares* [2]), come to the fore, ALT's thesis [3]) about prominent Judeans looking forward to their return form Exile and hence keeping alive their traditions, would be happily confirmed.

One might object that Aaron would certainly have left some traces in David's biblical record. In 2 Sam. xviii 24-29, with regard to the Ark only Sadok and Ebjathar are mentioned. But as appears from 2 Sam. xix 12-13 both of them have links with Judah. The biblical record of David is mainly occupied with the rivalry between North and South, and certainly not complete. How many traditions of the *Heerbann*, i.e. the first "appearance of Israel" as a historical entity, may have gone into the story of Israel's *Urzeit*? [4])

---

[1]) MOWINCKEL, l.c. *Erwägungen...*, p. 127.

[2]) Note that Aaron is mentioned in Micah vi 4.

[3]) Cf. Ch. II, A: „Exile and Return in Israel and Judah".

[4]) Cf. about „Abraham" as representative of David: Herbert SCHMID „Melchisedek und Abraham, Zadok und David", *Kairos* VII 1965, pp. 148-151, summary in *IZBG* XIII 1966-1967, n. 249.

Cf. furthermore Num. xxxi 27 related to 1 Sam. xxx 21-25.

Cf. also R. KNIERIM, „Exodus 18 und die Neuordnung der mosaischen Gerichtsbarkeit", *ZAW* LXXIII 1961, pp. 146-171, where a juridical reformation

4. A no less specific function is assigned in P to the *tent of meeting*, but here the old material on which the Code is relying is even more scanty. It is limited to Ex. xxxiii 7-11, because we doubt whether Num. xi 24b-30 and Dt. xxxi 14-15 contain any old material. Scholarly opinions may roughly be classified in two groups; there are those who think that the tent is a sanctuary originated from Israel's nomadic past (*Wanderheiligtum*) and those who regard it as a Palestinian cultic institution of some kind (*Kulturland-Heiligtum*).

To the first group, the nomadic nature of the *tent* is decisive. DE VAUX [1]) adduces a good many parallels from the pre-Islamite Arabs. He thinks this nomadic sanctuary was lost during or after the *Land-nahme* (he agrees with the "classic" rejection of Josh. xviii 1); during the nomadic period it was most probably the depository of the Ark [2]). Johann MAIER [3]) quotes DE VAUX and agrees with him as far as the nomadic character of the tent sanctuary is concerned, but of course he cannot agree with DE VAUX that it should have contained the Ark; presumably we have to do here with traces of an old tradition about an oracle tent, cf. *bqš* [4]).

Scholars of the second group, which apparently is the larger one, think that this is an instance of a southern Judean sanctuary, without the Ark, or even somehow in rivalry with the Ark [5]). In VON RAD's view the Ark embodies the idea of prosperity of the agricultural regions, (mostly in the North) and is due to Canaanite influence, whereas the tent would be the exponent of Yahwism proper. The adherents of this second group, however, have not got any convincing evidence that the tent should belong to southern Judean tribes. Probably this conclusion is based on a kind of parallelism between the Ark and northern Israel on the one hand and the tent and southern Judah on the other [6]).

A particular position is taken up by W. BEYERLIN. He regards the tent of meeting as an amphictyonic sanctuary containing the Ark,

---

in the period of the Kingdom (possibly during Josaphat: 2 Chr. xvii-xix, Dt. xvi 18-20, xvii 8-13) is defended to be aetiologically reflected in the story about Moses.

[1]) DE VAUX, l.c. *Institutions*, p. 126.
[2]) *Ibidem* p. 133.
[3]) MAIER, l.c. *Das* . . ., p. 1 f.
[4]) *Ibidem* p. 17, n. 114.
[5]) G. VON RAD, „Zelt und Lade", in: *Gesammelte Studien zum Alten Testament*, München 1961, p. 109-129, esp. p. 122-125.
[6]) Cf. the bibliography in BEYERLIN, l.c. p. 167, n. 2, and p. 131-133.

and locates Shiloh as its place [1]). According to him, Ex. xxxiii 7-11 had an older form in which the tent of meeting was not outside the camp but in its midst (this would still appear to be so from v. 8 and 10, but cf. the objections made by Joh. MAIER [2]) and S. LEHMING [3]). BEYERLIN maintains that the text represents the cult legend of a covenant feast at Shiloh in a camp of tents, with the tent of meeting in its midst [4]). Apart from the above-mentioned weaknesses, this thesis depends on an early dating of the Ark and of the twelve-tribe system and consequently is saddled with the above-mentioned difficulties.

Others will emphasize the *prophetic* character of the tent. M. HARAN [5]) points to the fact that in Ex. xxxiii 7-11 the tent is rather a hiding-place *from* the godhead than a dwelling-place *for* the godhead. Most studies overlook the fact that revelation occurs *outside* the tent, the tent being therefore a place of mental concentration for the worshipper. Against HARAN it can be advanced that no lexicographical or topical links have been found between the tent of meeting and the traditions of the $n^e bi^{\prime}im$. Moreover, it looks as if the passage is aiming at some sort of legitimation when it describes how Moses entered the tent of meeting in the sight of all.

S. LEHMING, however [6]), points to the times of David. (It is interesting indeed to see the Davidic chronology brought up once more). The starting-point of his argument is the shift in terminology here from *'ohel* to *'ohel mo'ed*. LEHMING draws our attention to the fact that the part of v. 7 from $w^e qara^{\prime}$ up to *mo'ed* has no terminological or topical follow-up in the rest of the text [7]). He then tries to find a set of connected texts about the *'ohel* without *mo'ed*. He brings together Ex. xxxiii 3b, 4; xxvi 7-14; 36-37; xxxvi 14-19, 37-38; xxxiii 7a (without the clause $w^e qara^{\prime}$; as far as *mo'ed*), 8-10; Num. ix 17.

---

[1]) BEYERLIN, l.c. *Herkunft...*, p. 137. Cf. also H. J. KRAUS, *Gottesdienst in Israel*, München 1962, p. 206 f. Cf. in the present work: Ch. III, A, ad 2, pp. 63 ff: the critical approach to Josh. xviii 1.

[2]) MAIER, l.c. *Das...*, p. 17, n. 114.

[3]) S. LEHMING, „Erwägungen zur Zelttradition", in: *Gottes Wort und Gottes Land* (Festschrift H. W. Hertzberg, ed. H. Graf REVENTLOW), Göttingen 1965, pp. 110-132, esp. p. 112.

[4]) BEYERLIN, l.c. Herkunft..., p. 130.

[5]) M. HARAN, „The nature of the *'Ohel Mô'edh*" in Pentateuchal Sources", JSS V 1960, pp. 50-65.

[6]) Cf. n. 3 on this page.

[7]) L.c. „Erwägungen...", p. 112.

This part of his investigation is entirely unconvincing, though. It overrides all considerations of Pentateuchal analysis, its impression being that of an arbitrary link-up. LEHMING seems to be far more right when he assumes the clause *wᵉqara'* as far as *mo'ed*, to be a formula of identification. He mentions the term *mᵉbaqqeš* and thinks it has to do with the *Urim-Tummim* oracle (cf. 2 Sam. xxi 1). This oracle must have been a heritage of priestly groups in southern Judah (cf. Libna and Hebron in Num. xxvi 58ab-alpha, compared with Dt. xxxiii 8). Now the earliest reliable records about *Urim* and *Tummim* point to Davidic times [1]).

In LEHMING's view that the oracle tent was given a more cultic function after it had been taken into the temple of Jerusalem in the Salomonic period, this was the way how it came to receive the name of *'ohel mo'ed*. After this emancipation the identification formula could be added to the old story.

In our view LEHMING's thesis is unnecessarily complicated and overburdened with marginal hypotheses. We agree with his reference to the *Urim* and *Tummim* and to the Davidic period. But has he paid sufficient attention to the aspects of aetiology and legitimation in this passage? Important is in this respect the expression "outside the camp" (v. 7). Does this expression hide some polemical reply to those who objected against the consultation by David of reputedly non-Yahwistic oracles? The fact that the people rose up and looked at Moses (v. 8) would make good sense in this hypothesis; likewise would the cultic recognition in v. 10. In this aetiological retrojection, David would have become Moses. (For the aetiological explanation of the expression "outside the camp" cf. n. 30 of the previous Chapter of the present work, p. 121).

Why should not Ex. xxxiii 7-11 be the only remnant of this old aetiological tradition [2]) and why should LEHMING go to the length of elaborating a complete body of cultic traditions, subsequently spread over several contexts? If the text is Davidic—and any hypothesis here is bound to be tentative because of the scanty material—it might well have belonged to the *Heerbann*-traditions, and have become in the Dispersion the nucleus of the cultic system of the PC by way of the *'am ha'areṣ*.

---

[1]) S. LEHMING, l.c. „Erwägungen...", p. 124.

[2]) It is an open question whether even this early text has not been recast into a piece of Mosaic hagiography.

An investigation into these matters is important for the study of the PC, because in our view the priestly authors did not retroject the temple of Jerusalem into the desert period but made a deliberate selection from the pre-exilic material handed on to the Jews in the Dispersion, preferring the 'am ha'areṣ traditions and those of the *Heerbann* to the monarchical and Zadokite traditions of Jerusalem.

In this respect the question also arises why P should go into such a detailed description of the luxury of the tent of meeting and its cult. This in turn leads us to the other problem what sort of programmatic action of P is compatible with the theory of its late chronology. As we have said in Chapter I, we think P is programmatic. In our interpretation of Ezr. vii 18 [1]), one of the aims of Ezra's mission could be a strengthening of the ties between the Persian court and the Palestinian community by renewing the cult in Palestine in such a way that, in its outwards aspects at least, it might shine in the Empire as a magnificent royal sanctuary, constituting at the same time a centre for the wealthy Jews from the Dispersion.

But why should the tent of meeting be located in Shiloh? Two ways are open to us to arrive at an answer to this question. The most plausible solution would seem to be to consider Josh. xviii 1 as the end of the basic primeval period (*Urzeit*) of the tent of meeting in the desert (see the next section of this Chapter) and as the beginning of its proliferation into local sanctuaries. Note that there is no divine rule as regards the location of the tent in Shiloh, as there is for the permanent and essential structure of the cult. The last part of the verse of Josh. xviii 1: "the land lay subdued before them", seems to support this interpretation. The choice of Shiloh to represent the first realization of the tent of meeting within the land is a suitable one, because it was well known for the temporary character of its cultic function.

Its site, too, was well-chosen. Situated half-way between the post-exilic centres of Shechem and Jerusalem, it was a convenient scene for the sacred ceremony of allotting the land, which we defended to be the aetiological reflection of the new late post-exilic settlement.

Another way to solve the problem might be to read Josh. xviii 1 in a programmatic light. In this hypothesis P would have had the plan to found a new (royal) sanctuary in the heart of the country, superseding the existing (or claimed) centres in the North and South on account of its great splendour and wealth, and thus contributing

---

[1]) Cf. p. 39 of the present study.

to the unity of the community. The fact that nothing has come down to us about such a vast project is not necessarily a decisive proof to the contrary; the period following upon Ezra's career was a very troubled one. If it is true that there is no explicit divine order to be found in P, there is indeed a prophetic text which, at least in the redactor's mind, might point to a new flourishing of Shiloh: Gen. xlix 10. Since Gen. xlix 1a is by P, the priestly redactor may have been responsible for the insertion of the benedictions. MT's ʿad ki jaboʾ šiloh is almost unanimously declared to be linguistically possible, but topically impossible [1]) because the sanctuary was in ruins at the moment when Judah began to play a role in Israel's history. But no attempts at text-emendation should be made before one has tried to find out whether the text may have had an acceptable meaning to the redactors. This redactor, on reading the text in its present-day form, which is either authentic [2]) or a corruption or misreading [3]), may have seen in it a prophecy of a new cultic role of the old *maqom*. It cannot be denied that such a project would reveal a considerable alienation from the Palestinian Jews; in our view, however, the hypothesis must not be ruled out for this reason. The analysis of the PC has convinced us that the Dispersion had a spiritual attitude altogether different from that of the Palestinian Jews.

All in all, the first hypothesis seems to be the more plausible one.

5. As regards the *cult*, a main theme of the present work is the importance to be attached to its apotropaeic-exorcistic character. With KAUFMANN pointing the way, we have found that unity of the cult in the Deuteronomic sense was not prescribed nor assumed in the priestly law, nor part of P's programmatic intentions. The tent of meeting is not an *elected* place as it is in D. D assigns the performance of all kinds of cultic duties to that elected place: the reading of the Torah (Dt. xxxi 10 f.), judicial decisions (Dt. xvii 8 f.), the celebration of Passover and the autumn-feast (Dt. xvi 7, 18), the eating of tithes and sacrifices (Dt. xii 17 f.; xiv 23; xv 19 f.; xvi 2 f.).

---

[1]) HOLZINGER, l.c. *Genesis*... p. 258.

[2]) J. LINDBLOM, "The Political Background of the Shiloh Oracle", *VTS* I 1953, pp. 78-87: the text was pronounced by a *nabiʾ* belonging to David's court in Hebron.

[3]) St. LACH, „Sens wyrazu szîlo(h)", in: Annales Theologico-Canonici IX 1962, pp. 5-16; French summary in *IZBG* X 1963-1964, p. 40, nr. 275. After a survey of the opinions, he opts for the translation „à qui appartient"; cf. Hez. xxi 10.

Nothing of this is found in the PC [1]). Outside the camp the following rites took place: the burning of certain sacrificial animals (Lev. iv 12, 21; viii 17; ix 11), the carrying-away of the ashes (Lev. vi 11), the sacrifices of birds for lepers (Lev. xiv 3 ff.) and the burning of the red cow (Num. xix 2 ff.); also, matters concerned with death and sickness (Lev. x 4 f.; xxiv 14 f.; Num. xv 35 f.; Lev. xiii 46; xiv 3 f.; Num. v 2 f.). Only for the eating of *qodeš q°dašim* a place within the precincts of the sanctuary is prescribed; the ordinary "holy" meals are permitted everywhere. It is obvious therefore that the function of the sanctuary in P is not a Deuteronomic one; it has rather to do with an apotropaeic protection against the "demonic" forces of evil, uncleanness and death. That quality is conferred to a *room* by anointing it and is not immutably bound up with a particular chosen *site*. Hence unity of cult in a single place is not only nowhere mentioned in P's laws; obviously, it is not in line with the priestly regulations. As KAUFMANN [2]) says, the uniqueness of the tent of meeting is a "historical" one, not a principle of law. The tent is unique only as a place of *revelation*. It is an *Urbild*, built according to the divine model as shown to the prophet Moses. Numerous prophets came after Moses, a great many high priests succeeded Aaron, and the camp expanded into many villages and cities (cf. Lev. xiv 1 ff. with xiv 33 ff.). In the same way the tent of meeting was followed by a good many cultic places. They all had to meet the requirements of the Law only by the qualification of their *room*, not by any restriction on their number.

We differ, however, from KAUFMANN in the historico-chronological elaboration of this view. A close study of all details of the Code, especially of the archeological, geographical and onomatographical ones, has taught us that this apotropaeic concept of cult was not pre-Deuteronomic, but a late post-exilic one, largely influenced by Persian and Babylonian syncretistic rituals (cf. Ch. iv, n. 19, p. 109ff).

The apotropaeic character of the cult, about which we spoke in our notes on Leviticus *sub* (*a*), has also proved its value as a criterion in literary-critical analysis. Applying it, we have found out that the main body of priestly traditions is not present in Ex. xxv-xxix but rather from Ex. xxx onwards; on the inner coherence of these Chapters we were able to shed some more light.

---

[1]) KAUFMANN, l.c. "Probleme . . .", p. 33 f. Cf. p. 9, n. 2 and p. 75, n. 1 and the commentary on Ex. xii 16, p. 98 f.

[2]) *Ibidem* p. 40.

New, too, is the implicit negative position as regards the temple, which we found in Gen. i. In our view Gen. i should be read in combination with Ex. xii, with the codification about the tent of meeting, and with Num. ix 15-23. Cultic laws and sacred history cannot be separated. The whole universe is created by almighty God. God does not select one special site; his is a cultic community, *q^ehal 'ammim*, spreading itself through the whole of mankind. Such a spreading, a dispersion, implies a good many dangers of contamination, but remedies against it are provided by the Mosaic revelation. A God-given country is the focus of such a wide-spread community; it is here that it has its central sanctuary, safe from heathen inroads (Yeb!).

6. Is the priestly description of *people* and *community* within the structure of a military camp not at variance with P's pacifism? As a matter of fact, the Israelites are called *ṣeba'ot* (e.g. Ex. vi 26; xii 17, 51), a census is taken, the order of camping and marching is firmly established (Num. ii-iv) and each section has its own standard (Num. ii 2-4). Nevertheless, both P's pacifism in the *Landnahme* and in Israel's relations with her neighbouring peoples on the one hand, and P's shaping the community along military lines on the other, are understandable within the framework of the Persian governmental policy. As we have seen, the aim of the Persians in launching the "ecumenical" project of bringing greater unity between the two parts of the Palestinian community was to strengthen that region of their Empire, after the Egyptian stronghold had fallen away. There even exists a terminological parallel with the Jewish military colony at Yeb, viz *'edah*, community, and *degel*, standard [1]).

Under this heading also come our remarks on the concept of *gerim* and our interpretation of the entire priestly Code as a kind of *ecumenical effort*. In other words, the Code's practical aim in bringing together groups of people dominates its doctrinal, catechetical, and theological purposes. This may be the deepest reason why in the PC cultic customs are only rarely explained. The fact that certain customs were highly traditional among Dispersion Jews, Persian authorities or Samaritan leading classes seems to have been enough for them to be introduced into the priestly legal system even if they were, to modern minds, bordering on the regions of magic and superstition. Our study may perhaps be helpful to modern readers by laying bare

---

[1]) KITTEL, l.c. *Geschichte...*, p. 501-516; 505, 507.

this basic inspiration. Particular emphasis might be given to the fact Israelite cultic initiative was most fertile when ecumenical achievement reached its highest peak, viz under the towering figures of David and Ezra [1].

General Summary

At the end of Ch. i, we formulated three questions. An attempt here to answer them, might at the same time provide us with a general summary of our findings.

Josh. xviii was a key text. It taught us that the traditional "face-value" exegesis of priestly texts has often led to an unsolvable dilemma. When, however, the aetiological method was applied, we arrived at solutions of a remarkable coherence. The PC was found to present the characteristics of its time of origin and of a very precise programmatic purpose. Josh. xviii 1 was proved to refer to a period long after the settlement of two well-defined groups in Palestine, viz to the later Persian Period.

The cult turned out to be far less Deuteronomic in character than it had been supposed since WELLHAUSEN. Josh. xxii suggested some sort of compromise in the dispute around the cult in Yeb. The Code is more concerned about the purity of cult, conceived in an apotropaeic spirit, than with a unity of place. The Dispersion was accepted by the priestly authors as a basic fact in Israel's existence; it made Israel into a cultic community throughout the then existing world, with Palestine for its main point.

After a critical analysis of previous theories the notion of *gerim* in the PC was clarified by means of ALT's exposition on the Samaritan leading classes. Along this way we have gained an understanding why so many customs of late Persian flavour were incorporated into it; at the same time we were able to link up the PC with Ezra's

---

[1] By assuming Ezra's main aim to have been a *practical* one, we may overcome the dilemma of prophetical and legalistic types of religion, as expressed by H. H. SCHAEDER, l.c. *Esra...*, p. 3: „Esra und die nach ihm kamen, waren freilich nicht nur die Testamentvollstrecker, sondern zugleich die Totengräber des prophetischen Geistes. Aber sie waren es nicht, weil sie den Geist durch den Buchstaben verdrängen, die Gesinnung durch Formeln und tote Werke ablösen wollten. Sie waren der Ueberzeugung, dass der Geist nur fruchtbar wirkt, wo er sich ans Wort bindet, und dasz die Gesinnung nur taugt, wenn sie sich in geordnetem Handeln auswirkt. Man mag Esra einen blossen Organisator nennen — das Wort hat heute keinen guten Klang —, wenn man nur im Auge behält, dass sein Ziel Ordnung war. Ist Ordnung nicht Geist?"

mission, held by us to have been in 398 B.C. The opinion of CAZELLES and GRELOT was abundantly confirmed: this mission was part of the Persian governmental policy to make Palestine into a stronghold of the Empire.

Our effort was inspired by the idea that we should never cease to challenge suppositions that threaten to become an axioma.

JAKOB SEGNET JOSEPHS SÖHNE
Darstellungen von Genesis XLVIII in der Überlieferung und bei Rembrandt

VON

J. C. H. LEBRAM

Eines der vollkommensten Gemälde aus Rembrandts letzter Periode ist in der Kasseler Gemäldegalerie aufbewahrt. Schon im frühesten Katalog der Sammlung, der aus dem Jahre 1749 stammt, liest man die Eintragung: „Rembrant. Jakobs Einsegnung der Kinder Josephs. Lebens-Groß auf Leinen. Höhe rheinl. Maas: 5 Schuh 6 Zoll, Breite 6 Schuh 8 Zoll" [1]). Das so bezeichnete Bild hat der Kunsthistoriker Herbert VON EINEM mit folgenden Worten beschrieben [2]): „Wir blicken in ein nicht näher bezeichnetes Gemach, in dem — schräg zur Bildfläche und fast den ganzen Raum einnehmend — das Bett steht, über das eine rote Decke ausgebreitet liegt. Der Hintergrund ist eine einfache bräunliche Wand. Links und rechts sind dunkle Vorhänge, die nach den Seiten zurückgeschlagen sind. Der Patriarch, in hellem Rock, darüber einen Fuchspelz, auf dem Kopf eine gelblichweiße Kappe, hat sich mühsam vom Lager aufgerichtet und segnet mit seiner Rechten den größeren der beiden Enkel, die an seinem Bette niedergekniet sind. Die Linke scheint er um seines Sohnes Schulter gelegt zu haben, der in breitem hellfarbigen Turban hinter dem Bette steht, sich dem Vater zuneigt und mit seiner Linken des Alten segnende Rechte führt. Neben ihm steht, reich geschmückt, die Mutter der Knaben in dunklem grünlichblauen Kleid und blauer goldgestickter Mütze. Ein Schleier deckt einen Teil ihrer Stirn und fällt nach hinten herab. Sie hat ihre Hände gefaltet und sieht dem Segensakte mit leise geneigtem Haupte zu." Rembrandt läßt den Beschauer den Höhepunkt der Geschichte von Gen. xlviii miterleben. Aber er gibt die Szene anders wieder, als sie in der Bibel erzählt wird [3]). Nicht nur Einzelheiten, sondern die ganze Stimmung

---

[1]) Herbert v. EINEM, *Rembrandt der Segen Jakobs*. Bonner Beiträge zur Kunstwissenschaft. Band 1. 1950. S. 34.[3]

[2]) v. EINEM, *Rembrandt*. S. 8 f.

[3]) v. EINEM, *Rembrandt*. S. 14: „Wort und Bild decken sich in keiner Weise." Cf. W. STECHOW, „Jakob blessing the sons of Joseph." *Gazette des Beaux Arts*. 6. Series. Nr. 23. New York 1943. S. 193-208.

ist verändert. Die Verwickelung und Spannung, wie auch die uner-
wartete Wendung, die der Handlung ihre Dramatik verleihen, fehlen
bei Rembrandt [1]. Aus dem kräftigen Widerspiel der Figuren, das
die Erzählung kennzeichnet, ist die bewußte Einheit der Familie
geworden.

Um den Unterschied deutlich zu erfassen, lesen wir zunächst den
biblischen Bericht: „Und nach diesen Geschehnissen meldete man
Joseph: „Siehe, dein Vater ist krank." Da nahm er seine beiden
Söhne, Manasse und Ephraim, mit sich. (2) Da sandte man Jakob
Nachricht mit den Worten: „Siehe, dein Sohn Joseph kommt zu
dir." Und Israel nahm seine Kraft zusammen und setzte sich auf
seinem Lager aufrecht hin. (3) Dann sagte Jakob zu Joseph: „El
Schaddaj erschien mir zu Luz im Lande Kanaan, segnete mich (4)
und sprach zu mir: „Ich will dir viel Kinder geben, dich mehren
und zu einem Bund von Völkern machen. Dieses Land gebe ich
deiner Nachkommenschaft nach dir zu ewigem Besitz. (5) Und nun
sollen deine zwei Söhne, die dir im Land Ägypten geboren sind,
bevor ich zu dir nach Ägypten kam, mir gehören. Ephraim und
Manasse sollen mir wie Ruben und Simeon gelten. (6) Aber deine
Nachkommenschaft, die du nach ihnen gezeugt hast, soll dein sein.
Nach dem Namen ihrer Brüder sollen sie in ihrem Gebiet genannt
werden. (7) Und als ich von Padan zurückkam, starb mir Rahel
unterwegs im Lande Kanaan, als ich noch ein Stück Wegs bis Ephrata
hatte. Da begrub ich sie dort am Wege nach Ephrat, das ist Bethlehem.
(8) Und Israel sah die zwei Söhne Josephs und sprach: „Wer sind
diese?" (9) Da sagte Joseph zu seinem Vater: „Meine Söhne sind es,
die mir Gott hier (בזה) geschenkt hat." Und er sprach: „Bringe sie
doch zu mir, damit ich sie segne." (10) Die Augen Israels waren
altersschwach, sodaß er sie nicht sehen konnte. Und er (d.h. Joseph)
führte sie zu ihm hin, und er küßte sie und umarmte sie. (11) Dann
sprach Israel zu Joseph: „Ich hatte nicht vermutet, dich wiederzu-
sehen, und doch ließ mich Gott sogar deine Nachkommenschaft
sehen." (12) Und Joseph nahm sie von seinen Knien weg und beugte
sein Gesicht tief zur Erde. (13) Nun nahm Joseph die zwei, Ephraim
an seiner Rechten, links von Israel, und Manasse an seiner Linken,
rechts gegenüber Israel, und er brachte sie zu ihm. (14) Israel aber
hob seine Rechte und legte sie auf das Haupt Ephraims — und doch
war er der Jüngere — und seine Linke auf das Haupt Manasses;

---

[1] v. EINEM, *Rembrandt*. S. 11 "Die einzelnen Figuren sind wahrhaft zu einer
Familie zusammengeschlossen."

so verschränkte er [1]) seine Hände, wenn auch Manasse der Erstgeborene war. (15) Und er segnete Joseph und sprach: „Der Gott,
in Verantwortung vor dem meine Väter, Abraham und Isaak,
gewandelt sind, der Gott, der mich mit seinem Hirtenstab geführt hat,
solange ich bin, bis auf diesen Tag, (16) der Engel, der mich erlöst
hat von allem Unheil, möge diese jungen Männer segnen. Sie
sollen mit meinem Namen und mit dem Namen meiner Väter Abraham
und Isaak genannt werden. Sie sollen sich vermehren, daß sie zahl-
reich werden mitten im Lande.'' (17) Und Joseph sah, daß sein Vater
die rechte Hand auf das Haupt Ephraims legte, und das erschien
seiner Ansicht nach schlecht. Da ergriff er die Hand seines Vaters
(תמך), um sie vom Haupte Isaaks auf den Kopf Manasses zu führen.
(18) Und Joseph sprach zu seinem Vater: „Nicht so, mein Vater!
Dieser ist doch der Erstgeborene! Lege deine Rechte auf sein Haupt.''
(19) Sein Vater weigerte sich jedoch und sagte: „Mein Sohn, ich
weiß. Auch dieser wird zu einem Volke werden, und auch groß
werden. Aber sein jüngerer Bruder wird größer als er werden, und
seine Nachkommenschaft soll eine Fülle von Völkern bilden. (20)
Und er segnete sie an jenem Tage mit den Worten: „Mit dir soll
Israel sich segnen und sagen: 'Gott mache dich, wie Ephraim und
Manasse.' So stellte er Ephraim vor Manasse'' [2]).

Wir wollen nicht die Unebenheiten, die literarischen und religions-
geschichtlichen Fragen behandeln, die diese Geschichte im Rahmen
der Bibel aufwirft, sondern unsere Betrachtung gilt den Unterschieden zwischen dem alten Bericht und Rembrandts Bild. Von
der veränderten Stimmung des Bildes sprachen wir schon. Joseph
packt nicht die Hand seines Vaters, oder reißt sie gewaltsam zurück,
sondern stützt sie. Vorsichtig beruhigend liegt seine Linke unter des
Vaters segnender Rechten. Der Beschauer wird unsicher, ob er wirklich die Hand Jakobs auf Manasses Kopf führen will, oder ob er schon
— innerlich überwunden von dem Wort des Vaters — der sicheren
Zielstrebigkeit des anscheinend starren, aber doch wissenden Alters
nachgegeben hat. Haltung und Ausdruck des Sohnes zeigen sich verschmolzen in eine bildnerische Einheit mit Jakob ohne Schrecken
noch Abwehr. Mit wohlwollender Spannung und bedächtiger Sorge
verfolgt Joseph die Bewegungen des Alten. Fast möchte man meinen,
er sei über das Ergebnis, die Segnung Ephraims befriedigt.

---

[1]) Das hebr. Wort שׂכל ist schon früh als „überkreuzen, vertauschen'' erklärt
worden, kann vielleicht auch heißen „etwas bewußt tun.''
[2]) Gen. xlviii.

Die Anordnung der beiden Söhne, im biblischen Bericht umständlich beschrieben, ist im Zuge der natürlicheren anatomischen Gestaltung aufgelockert. Manasse steht zwar näher am Großvater; doch erscheint die biblische Aufstellung nicht streng festgehalten. Dafür tritt der konstitutionelle Gegensatz zwischen beiden Enkeln scharf ins Licht. Ephraim, obschon jünger, ist größer als Manasse. Die Weissagung des segnenden Großvaters ist als schon erfüllt dargestellt. Außerdem ist er blond und hell, wie irgendein kleiner holländischer Bub aus der Umwelt Rembrandts. Manasse dagegen ist schwarzhaarig und dunkeläugig, Vertreter des unter den portugiesischen Juden begegnenden Typus, den der Maler in der Umgebung der Jodenbreestraat sah.

Die dritte wesentliche Änderung gegenüber dem biblischen Bericht ist die Einbeziehung von Josephs Frau, der Asenet, in die Szene. Die Bibel berichtet ihre Anwesenheit nicht. Man könnte annehmen, daß sie nur aus kompositorischer Notwendigkeit dargestellt wurde, um gegen die sehr gefüllten andere Bildhälfte ein Gegengewicht zu schaffen. Man hat aber bemerkt, daß Rembrandt noch während des Malens die Gestalt auf alle mögliche Weise abzuschwächen suchte, um ihr Schwergewicht zu verringern [1]). So werden wir doch eher inhaltliche Motive für die Zufügung Asenats suchen, und die Veränderungen als das Unternehmen ansehen, die kompositorische Schwierigkeit, die aus der Forderung des dargestellten Inhalts erwuchs, zu überwinden. Asenet zeigt auf dem Bilde Zufriedenheit, mütterlichen Stolz und zugewandte Aufmerksamkeit. Fragen wir nach dem Typus ihrer Erscheinung, so entspricht er der Art Manasses, nicht der Ephraims.

Diese Einzelzüge, die zur Veränderung des Bildes führten, hat man ikonographisch zu erklären versucht. Dabei ist auch erkannt worden, daß nicht nur christliche, sondern auch jüdische Überlieferungen Anregungen für Rembrandts Darstellung gegeben haben [2]). Unser Ziel ist jedoch kein ikonographisches oder kunsthistorisches, d.h. wir wollen weder eine Geschichte der künstlerischen Darstellung des Jakobssegens geben, noch Material zur Bilderklärung bereitstellen. Der Gesichtspunkt der folgenden Betrachtung ist vielmehr traditionsgeschichtlich. Wir suchen die Wiedergabe einer alten Überlieferung als Ausdruck eines durch den Augenblick der Geschichte bestimmten

---

[1]) C. NEUMANN, *Rembrandt.* II. S. 432.
[2]) Diesem Ziel dient der in S. 145, Anm. 3 angegebene Aufsatz von W. STECHOW.

Verständnisses des Stoffes zu verstehen und zu deuten. Wir fragen: Was für einen geschichtlichen Augenblick bezeichnet die künstlerische Darstellung von Gen. xlviii durch Rembrandt im Flusse der Überlieferung dieser Perikope? Damit ist von uns gefordert, daß wir die Geschichte der Auslegung von Gen. xlviii an uns vorüberziehen lassen. Dabei wird sich zeigen, daß die traditionsgeschichtliche Untersuchung auch die Archaeologie und Kunstgeschichte einbeziehen muß und sich nicht auf die Untersuchung von Wiedererzählungen beschränken darf.

I

Die alten Spuren einer Verarbeitung von Gen. xlviii in der nachbiblischen Überlieferung sehen nicht so aus, als ob die Perikope eine wichtige Rolle im jüdischen Glauben gespielt habe. Josephus berichtet zurückhaltend [1]: „Das höchste Lob aber spendete er (scil. Jakob) dem Joseph, weil derselbe seinen Brüdern nicht nur die erlittenen Untaten verziehen, sondern auch doppelte Liebe erwiesen hatte; hatte er ihnen doch soviel Gutes gezeigt, als man kaum seinen größten Wohltätern angedeihen läßt. Im Hinblick hierauf befahl Jakob seinen Söhnen, sie sollten die Söhne Josephs, Ephraim und Manasse, in ihre Zahl aufnehmen, und das Land Kanaan mit ihnen teilen, worüber wir noch später sprechen werden." Noch kürzer ist das Jubiläenbuch [2]: „Und Israel segnete seine Kinder, ehe er starb, und sagte ihnen alles, was ihnen im Lande Ägypten begegnen würde; und wie es ihnen in den letzten Tagen ergehen würde, tat er ihnen kund. Er segnete sie und gab Joseph zwei Teile im Lande." Diese schweigsame Art, mit der die Segnung der beiden Josephssöhne übergangen wird, ist doppelt erstaunlich, weil er sich um die Weissagung eines Sterbenden und einen für die Heilsgeschichte wichtigen Vorgang handelt. Nach der Gewohnheit der Zeit erwartet man, daß gerade eine solche Bibelstelle eine bevorzugte Rolle spielt. Diese Annahme wird enttäuscht, wenn man nicht eine leichte Akzentuierung in der Art, wie Josephus berichtet, sehen will. Jakobs Segen und Verheißung ist durch die Aktivität der anderen Jakobssöhne ersetzt. Sie sind es, die die beiden Josephssöhne in ihre Zahl aufnehmen, so daß diese Handlung als Gunst der andern Stämme, nicht als Jakobs Verheißung erscheint.

---

[1] Antt. Jud. ii 8, 195.
[2] Jub. xlv 14.

Die Haltung der alten Überlieferer gegen Gen. xlviii ist gut zu begreifen. Ephraim ist schon für Jesaja und Hosea [1]) der Vertreter des abgöttischen Nordreiches und Ziel ihrer Kritik. Der Bericht der Königsbücher ist darauf abgehoben, Jerobeams Abfall und den Untergang des Nordreiches durch die Verbindung von Schuld und Strafe zu verknüpfen. Im Psalm lxxviii 67 finden wir das Urteil über Ephraim gesprochen:

„Er verwarf das Zelt Josephs,
und den Stamm Ephraim erkor er nicht.
Dagegen erwählte er den Stamm Juda,
den Berg Zion, den er lieb hat."

In nachbiblischer Zeit spricht Ben Sira von Jerobeam, „der sündigte und Israel zur Sünde verführte. Und er bereitete Ephraim ein Ärgernis, sodaß sie vertrieben wurden aus ihrem Lande" [2]). Aber Josephus und das Jubiläenbuch sind nicht nur von alter Überlieferung beeinflußt. Sie fanden, wie auch Sirach, in ihrer Gegenwart Anlaß genug, Ephraim und Manasse abzulehnen. Diese galten nämlich als Vorfahren der Samaritaner, denen gegenüber Feindschaft und Ablehnung seit den Tagen Esras bis hin zur Zeit des Zelotismus immer mehr wuchsen. Sirach sprach von dem „törichten Volk, das zu Sichem wohnt" und „kein Volk" ist [3]). Der ehemalige Zelot Josephus schreibt über sie: „Die Samaritaner sind nämlich von Natur solche Leute . . ., die wenn es den Juden schlecht geht, ableugnen, daß sie mit ihnen verwandt sind — und damit sagen sie die Wahrheit. Sehen sie aber einen Lichtblick in deren Los, sind sie sofort zur Gemeinschaft mit ihnen bereit . . ." [4]). Aus dem Fortgang dieser Stelle erkennen wir auch, warum gerade Gen. xlviii für Josephus eine schwer zu bewältigende Bibelstelle war. Er weiß nämlich über den Anspruch der Samaritaner Bescheid, „ . . . die ihren Stammbaum von den Abkömmlingen Josephs, Ephraim und Manasse ableiten." In der Tat berichtet MACDONALD in seiner „Theology of the Samaritans" über die bisher noch unveröffentlichte sog. Chronik II, daß dort auf diese beiden Stämme die Herkunft der Samaritaner zurückgeführt wird [5]). Während Samuel in Mizpa von den übrigen Stämmen

---

[1]) Jes. vii 2-5.8. Hos. v 3.5.9, vi 4 u.ö.
[2]) Sir. xlvii 23.
[3]) Sir. l 25.26.
[4]) *Antt. Jud.* xi 8. 341.
[5]) J. MACDONALD, *The Theology of the Samaritans.* 1964. S. 18.

gezwungen wurde, Saul zum Könige zu salben, blieben Ephraim und Manasse als die einzigen Stämme ihrem Gott treu. Die älteste faßbare samaritanische Quelle, der Memar Marqah, ruft — gewiß nicht ohne Tendenz gegen irgendwelche Andersdenkende: „Exalted are Joseph and *all his descendants*, for they did not forsake the Truth" [1]. Vielleicht ist auch dies eine Anspielung auf 1 Sam. xi. Der nach Deut. xxvii 11 vom Garizim her gesprochene Segen wird als Ermahnung und Belehrung aus dem Munde Josephs und Ephraims gedeutet [2].

Diese Traditionen sind nicht alle von gleichem Alter. Ihre Tendenz ist jedoch schon durch Josephus bezeugt. Wir finden in ihnen den Grund für die Zurückhaltung der alten jüdischen Ausleger gegenüber Gen. xlviii: Dies Kapitel war eine jener Perikopen, die den Anspruch der Samaritaner auf ihre Erwählung stützten.

II

Der geschichtliche Anspruch trennte die Juden von den Samaritanern, doch der Pentateuch war ihnen als Begründung dieses Anspruchs gemeinsam. Darum mußten sich die rabbinischen Erklärer der Bibel doch eines Tages mit Gen. xlviii, und auch mit den daraus abgeleiteten Ansprüchen der Samaritaner, auseinandersetzen. Der Midrasch Tanchuma berichtet von einer Debatte über Gen. xlviii 8 [3]: „Und Israel sah die Söhne Josephs, und sprach: „Wer sind diese?" R. Juda bar Schalom sagte: „Hat er sie denn nicht erkannt, und haben sie denn nicht alle Tage gesessen und sich mit der Tora vor ihm beschäftigt? Und jetzt sagt er: „Wer sind diese?" Nachdem sie ihn 17 Jahre bedient hatten, hat er sie doch nicht erkannt? (Der Grund ist:) Er sah doch Jerobeam, den Sohn Nebats, und Ahab, den Sohn Omris, welche aus Ephraim herstammen, die Anbeter von Sternen und Planeten, und da entfernte sich der Heilige Geist von ihm. Als das Joseph sah, streckte er sich sofort auf den Boden aus, und er erflehte Gnade vor dem Heiligen — gelobt sei er! — und sprach: 'Herr der Welt! Wenn sie geeignet sind für den Segen, dann

---

[1] Das samaritanische Traditionswerk 'Memar Marqah' wird in der Übersetzung MACDONALDS unter Nachprüfung am Originaltext zitiert. Auch seine Einteilung legen wir zu Grunde, wo wir sie erwähnen. Band I enthält den samaritanisch-aramäischen Text, Band II die englische Übersetzung. Im allgemeinen wird dieser Band mit Seitenzahl zitiert. Die Ausgabe heißt: *Memar Marqah* ed. by John MACDONALD. BZAW 84. 1964. Band I und II. Das obige Zitat s. II. S. 94.

[2] *Memar Marqah* II S. 110.

[3] Ausgabe des *Tanchuma* Jerusalem 1960. S. 57b.

laß mich nicht mit Beschämung des Antlitzes wieder umkehren.
Sofort ließ der Heilige — gelobt sei er! — den Heiligen Geist in
Jakob wieder eingehen, und er segnete ihn doch. Und woher wissen
wir das? Weil geschrieben steht: Ich wollte Ephraim gehen lehren
und nahm es auf meine Arme (Hos. xi 3), d.h. Ich ließ den Heiligen
Geist in Jakob gehen um Ephraims willen.' R. Samuel bar Nachman
sagte: 'Zweimal wich der Heilige Geist von Jakob in jener Stunde.
Einmal, als er versuchte Ephraim und Manasse zu segnen, und danach
als er anfing, das Ende zu offenbaren. — „Und Joseph sah, daß sein
Vater die Rechte auf Ephraims Haupt legte ... und er griff an die
Hand seines Vaters, um sie wegzunehmen." (Gen. xlviii 17) Der
aber sagte zu ihm: 'Meine Hand willst du wegnehmen, die die
Engelheere überwunden hat! ... „Und Joseph sprach zu seinem
Vater: Nicht so! (Gen. xlviii 18) "weil er Gideon aus Manasse
entstehen sah. „Aber sein jüngerer Bruder wird größer (Gen. xlviii
19)", das ist Josua, der aus Ephraim hervorgekommen ist." Der
Midrasch setzt sich mit den Schwierigkeiten auseinander, die die
Segnung der Josephssöhne für den rabbinischen Ausleger bringt.
R. Samuel bar Nachman ist der Meinung, daß der Heilige Geist mit
dieser Segnung und der dazugehörigen Weissagung nichts zu tun
hatte. R. Juda bar Schalom sucht die Stelle zu interpretieren. Seine
Erklärung geht von dem prophetischen Verständnis des Wortes
„Sehen" in Gen. xlviii 8 aus. Diese Deutung von Vers 8 ist schon
älter; denn sowohl Philo als der Barnabasbrief [1] setzen sie voraus.
Die Meinung R. Samuels ben Nachman sieht die berichtete Vision
als nicht durch den Geist gegeben an. Damit setzt er sicher die ältere
konservative Tradition des normativen Judentums fort, die — wie
wir oben sahen — die aus Gen. xlviii zu ziehenden Folgerungen
ignoriert. Anders R. Juda Bar Schalom! Er gibt zu, daß es sich
um prophetisches Sehen handeln muß, da anders die merkwürdige
Frage Jakobs „Wer sind diese?" nicht zu erklären ist. Jakob erkannte
die ihm längst bekannten Enkel nicht, weil er in einer Vision ihre
Nachkommen, die nordisraelitischen Könige Jerobeam und Ahab,
sah. Er erkannte sie als das Volk des Abfalls, und darum verließ ihn
die Kraft des Heiligen Geistes. Der Abfall wird nicht als Errichtung
eines Stierbildes oder der Verehrung der Baalim gesehen, sondern
sie werden „Anbeter von Planeten und Sternen genannt." Dieser
Hinweis zielt offensichtlich auf Samarien ab. Die Juden sahen viel-

---

[1] PHILO, *De confusione ling.* 146. *De mutatione nominum* 215. Barn. xiii 4-6.
Philo und der Barnabasbrief werden weiter unten noch genauer behandelt werden.

leicht, wie die Kirchenväter, Samarien als Quellort der gnostischen Bewegung an[1]), und auch die Verbindung zwischen dem Sternglauben und der Entstehung der Häresie finden wir bei den Kirchenvätern[2]). Abwehr der Gnosis kennt auch der Memar Marqah[3]), Nun ist aber Juda bar Schalom der Ansicht, daß der Heilige Geist in Jakob wieder zurückkehrte, und er schließlich doch die Josephssöhne gesegnet habe. Anlaß dieser Veränderung ist nach Juda bar Schalom das Gebet Josephs, dessen Fürbitte die Rückkehr des heiligen Geistes verursachte. Dadurch wurden die Worte aus Hosea xi 3 erfüllt. Der Midrasch betont also, daß Jakob zwar aufgehalten wurde, als er die Segnung vollzog, sie aber schließlich auf Josephs Gebet doch durchführte, weil das Wort Hoseas erfüllt werden mußte.

Durch die Tradentennamen können wir den Midrasch in die Zeit des 4. Jahrhunderts datieren[4]). Der Termin, zu dem wir das erste Mal eine Auseinandersetzung der jüdischen Auslegung mit den Samaritanern finden, ist somit verhältnismäßig spät. Daß es erst nun so weit kam, liegt wohl daran, daß die Umstände jenes Jahrhunderts diese Antwort der Rabbinen erheischten. Jene Zeit muß die Blütezeit der samaritanischen Literatur gewesen sein. Die umfassende Sammlung samaritanischer Traditionen, der Memar Marqah, muß damals entstanden sein. Das Werk zeigt vielfältige Berührung der damaligen Samaritaner mit der griechischen Philosophie der Zeit. Auch eine griechische Übersetzung des samaritanischen Pentateuchs war bekannt[5]). Auch die oben schon genannte Verbindung der Gnosis mit samaritanischen Ursprüngen — sei sie historisch oder nicht — zeigt, wie hoch Samariens Einfluß eingeschätzt wurde. Seine Literatur war deswegen bestimmt nicht nur auf dem engen Boden der Heimat wirksam. Das zeigt sich auch darin, daß Euseb ein offensichtlich

---

[1]) IRENAEUS, *Adv. Haer. I xvi*: 2 (HARVEY I S. 191): Simon autem Samaritanus, ex quo universae haereses substiterunt, habet huiusmodi sectae materiam; ferner Ib. xxv, 2 (S. 219) xxvii, 1 (S. 221) EUSEBIUS, *H.E.* IV 7, 3 (SCHWARTZ, ed. minor. S. 129).

[2]) Hippolyt beginnt das vierte des Elenchos mit einer ausführlichen Darlegung der Astrologie, weil aus ihr die Häresien ableitbar sind.

[3]) *Memar Marqah II*. S. 26. Joseph sagt zu Pharao: "You say that there are two gods in the universe, one in heaven and another on earth; but we say, that there is only one God, sole Creator of heaven and earth.

[4]) Jehuda ben Schalom ist ein palästinensicher Amoräer der 5. Generation (ca. 350 n. Chr.) Samuel bar Nachman gehört zur 3. Generation und lehrte nach 300 in Tiberias.

[5]) In den Anmerkungen zu Origenes Hexapla wird sie mit etwa 50 Zitaten repräsentiert.

samaritanisches Fragment von dem jüdisch-hellenistischen Autor
Eupolemos ableitet [1]).

Es entsteht die Frage, ob wir einen samaritanischen Midrasch
finden können, der die von unserer Tanchumastelle bekämpfte
Ansicht vertritt. Im Memar Marqah liegt — schon aus Gründen des
behandelten Stoffes — eine derartige Überlieferung nicht vor. Wir
haben aber durch Origenes die Nachricht von einer verloren gegan-
genen apokryphen Schrift der Hebräer, die in der Tat gewisse
Berührungspunkte mit der Exegese des Tanchuma hat. Wir finden
die Zitate im Johanneskommentar des Origenes [2]). Der Kirchenvater
zitiert die „ἐπιγραφομένη Ἰωσὴφ προσευχὴ" aus den bei den Hebräern
überlieferten Apokryphen: „Jakob sagt nämlich: 'Ich, der ich zu
euch spreche, Jakob und Israel, bin der Engel Gottes und der herr-
schende Geist; und Abraham und Isaak wurden vor jedem andern
(Schöpfungs-)werk geschaffen; doch ich bin Jakob, als der von
den Menschen Jakob genannte. Aber mein (eigentlicher) Name ist
Israel als der von Gott Israel geheißene, ein Mann, der Gott
sieht, weil ich der Erstgeborene bin von allen Lebewesen, die unter
Gott leben." Und er setzt hinzu: „Als ich von Mesopotamien in
Syrien kam, zog Uriel der Engel Gottes aus, und er sagte: 'Ich bin
herabgestiegen auf die Erde und habe mein Zelt bei den Menschen
aufgeschlagen, und bin genannt mit dem Namen Jakob.' Er geriet
in Eifer und kämpfte mit mir. Er rang mit mir und sagte, daß sein
Name gegenüber dem meinem und jedem Engel überlegen sei. Ich
aber sagte ihm meinen Namen und der wievielte er unter den Gottes
Söhnen sei: 'Bist du nicht Uriel, der achte nach mir, und ich bin
Israel, der Erzengel des Gottesheeres (wörtl. der Kraft des Herrn) und
der oberste Heerführer unter den Söhnen Gottes. Bin ich nicht
Israel, der erste Diener (λειτουργός) vor Gottes Angesicht? Und ich
rief mit dem unzerstörbaren Namen Gott an." Schon JAMES hat die
Vermutung ausgesprochen, daß die Zitate des Origenes aus einem
Midrasch zu Gen. xlviii stammen [3]). Seine Annahme ist überzeugend,
da sich Anknüpfungspunkte an den biblischen Bericht zeigen lassen.
Wie in Gen. xlviii spricht Jakob rückschauend von seiner Heimkehr
aus der Fremde. Paddan ist schon in der LXX zu Gen. xlviii 7 mit
Μεσωποτάμια ἐν Συρίᾳ wiedergegeben, wohl mit Rücksicht auf
Gen. xxxv 9. JAMES macht auch auf die Anrede im Plural aufmerksam,

---

[1]) *Praep. Evang.* IX. 18. cf. RIESSLER, *Altjüdisches Schrifttum*. S. 1266 f.
[2]) ORIGINES, *In Joannem* II, xxxi. 188 ff. *GCS. Origines* IV. S. 88.
[3]) M. R. JAMES, *The lost Apocrypha of the Old Testament*. 1920. S. 26.

was sich in diesem Zusammenhang auf Jakob und seine beiden Söhne Ephraim und Manasse beziehen muß, da der große Jakobssegen in Gen. xlix keine Erinnerung an Mesopotamien kennt.

Neben diesen Anspielungen auf den Grundtext weist das Fragment auch midraschische Erweiterungen von Gen. xlviii auf, die zum Teil Entsprechungen zum Tanchumamidrasch zeigen. Ausgangspunkt für die merkwürdige Selbstprädikation Jakobs am Anfang des Textes — die DANIELOU veranlaßte, daß Stück für judenchristlich zu erklären [1]) — ist die Doppelbezeichnung des Erzvaters in Gen. xlviii, Jakob und Israel. Israel wird mit „ein Mann der Gott sieht" gedeutet. Das ist alte jüdisch-hellenistische Tradition, auf die die Betonung des Sehens im Tanchumamidrasch ebenfalls zurückgeht [2]). Wahrscheinlich ist auch in der Proseuche Joseph von einer Vision Jakob-Israels berichtet, wie sich aus einem weiteren Fragment der Schrift ergibt [3]): „In der Proseuche Josephs mag dies Wort Jakobs so verstanden werden: Denn ich habe auf den himmlischen Tafeln alles gelesen, was dich und deine Söhne treffen wird."

Sowohl durch den Rückblick auf die Heimkehr als durch die Erklärung seines Namens wird in der Proseuche der Midrasch zu Gen. xlviii mit dem biblischen Text in Gen. xxxii 28.30 verbunden. Ausführlich schildert Jakob seinen Kampf mit dem Engel, bei dem auch wieder der Name eine entscheidende Rolle spielt. Eine ähnliche Verbindung hat der Tanchumamidrasch. Als Joseph die rechte Hand Jakobs von Ephraims Haupt wegnehmen will, antwortet der Patriarch: „Meine Hand willst du wegnehmen, die die Engelheere unterworfen hat?"

Die wesentliche Parallele aber scheint mir in der Überschrift des apokryphen Stückes zu liegen. Im Mittelpunkt des Tanchumamidrasch wird von einem Gebet Josephs berichtet, das die Segnung der Josephskinder überhaupt erst ermöglicht. Dieses ist das Kernmotiv, um das all die andern Züge gruppiert sind. Dieses Motiv ist zugleich das Stück des Midrasch, das keinerlei Begründung im biblischen

---

[1]) J. DANIELOU, *Theologie du Judeo-Christianisme*. 1958. S. 183-184. Ich kann hier nicht die Auseinandersetzung mit DANIELOU führen. Daß er mich nicht überzeugte, ersieht man daraus, daß ich unten eine andere These vorlege.

[2]) Israel wird als איש ראה אל verstanden. Für Philo siehe die Hinweise bei S. 152, Note 1.

[3]) Es ist in der *Philokalia xxiii*, 15 (Ausgabe ROBINSON S. 204) wiedergegeben, und stammt aus dem Genesiskommentar des Origines. Cf. JAMES, *Lost Apocrypha*. S. 25.

Text finden kann. Wenn die apokryphe Schrift den Titel „Gebet des Joseph" hatte [1]), dann muß auch sie im Mittelpunkt ein Gebet haben.

Natürlich hat man sich in der Forschung Gedanken über die Herkunft der Proseuche Joseph gemacht [2]). Die christologisch anmutenden Züge sind auch im jüdischen Milieu denkbar. Die Deutung des Israelnamens finden wir bei Philo, der in de confus. ling. 146 Parallelen zur Selbstprädikation Jakobs als „πνεῦμα ἀρχικόν" und der über allen Engeln Stehende hat. Dort heißt es: „ . . . gemäß seinem erstgeborenen Logos, dem ältesten der Engel, als dem, der wohl der Erzengel und Vielnamige ist. Auch „Herrschaft (ἀρχή)" und „Name Gottes" und der „Menschen nach dem Bild" und „der Sehende" -Israel „wird er nämlich genannt." Philo sieht Jakob als eine der Erscheinungen des Logos an. Stein [3]) hat gezeigt, daß der hebräische Midrasch eine ähnliche Hochschätzung Jakobs kennt. So besteht keine Veranlassung, an christliche oder gnostische Herkunft zu denken. Die Proseuche läßt sich als Midrasch zu Gen. xlviii verstehen, dessen dogmatische Anschauungen in der Welt des normativen Judentums durchaus noch Platz haben.

Dennoch denke ich, daß die Proseuche nicht ein Stück jüdischer, sondern samaritanischer Schriftauslegung ist. Den Ausgangspunkt für diese Vermutung bildet die Beobachtung, daß die Tanchumastelle polemischen Charakter hat. Die Vision, die Jerobeam und Ahab zeigt, und das Weichen des heiligen Geistes sind Anzeichen, daß eine falsche Exegese zurückgewiesen werden soll. Die Parallelen zwischen der Proseuche und dem Tanchumamidrasch können darauf beruhen, daß die rabbinischen Ausleger die Proseuchetradition

---

[1]) Man kann einwenden, daß die Asenetgeschichte im Armenischen „Aseneths Gebet" überschrieben ist, obwohl eine ganze Geschichte erzählt wird. C. BURCHARD, *Untersuchungen zu Joseph und Asenet.* = Wissenschaftliche Untersuchungen zum NT. 8 Tübingen. 1965. S. 32 ff. hat gezeigt, daß dieser Titel eine Korruptel ist.

[2]) Außer DANIELOU hat VACHER BURCH, *Journal of Theological Studies* xx. 1918. S. 20. seine Meinung über die Herkunft der Proseuche Joseph geäußert. Er hält sie für christlich, während J. T. MARSHALL in *Hastings Bibl. Dict.* ii, 779 antichristliche Tendenz vermutet. Wir können das Auftreten einer über den Engeln Stehenden himmlischen Gestalt, ebensowenig wie die Logoslehre als Beweis gegen die jüdische Herkunft eines Buches benutzen. Es zeigt sich deutlich, daß dogmatische Strukturen und Topoi nichts über die Herkunft aus einer bestimmten Religion sagen. Sie sind in einer bestimmten Periode allen Gruppen gemeinsam. Das Denken ist eine Lingua Franca. Es gibt kein jüdisches, oder christliches Denken. Wohl aber ist der Glaube verschieden, der sich an unterschiedlichen historischen Erscheinungen fixiert. Wo solche Fixierungen erkennbar sind, ist die Zuweisung zu bestimmten Gruppen möglich.

[3]) E. STEIN, *Philo und der Midrasch.* BZAW. 57. 1931. S. 37.

bekämpfen wollen. Dieser Gedanke liegt besonders nahe, weil wir in der normativen jüdischen Überlieferung keine Vorläufer der Tanchumatradition finden. Da es in diesem Falle um die Segnung Ephraims geht, liegt besonders nahe, daß eine samaritanische Tradition abgewiesen werden soll, und diese würde uns dann in der Proseuche vorliegen.

Nun lassen sich aber auch positive Gründe für eine Herkunft der Proseuche aus samaritanischem Bereich finden. Die Trennung von Jakob und Israel als irdischer und himmlischer Gestalt entspricht besonders gut den Vorstellungen der samaritanischen Theologie der ersten nachchristlichen Jahrhunderte, wie sie uns aus Memar Marqah bekannt sind. Von einer „צורתה" — einer Form Adams, die ein himmlisches Gegenbild zum irdischen Adam ist, spricht MM IV 2.3. In VI 4 finden wir über Jakob die Bemerkung: „Als er in die Welt hinauszog, da war sein Stand hoch, und als er die 'קומה' (Bestätigung? Eid? = Verheißung?) gewann, da beherrschte er alle Weisheit" [1].

Solche Hinweise auf die Denkstruktur sind aber nicht besonders beweiskräftig, solange wir nicht genaue Entsprechungen finden. Hier kann uns die Tatsache weiterhelfen, daß die Schilderung des Kampfes zwischen Jakob und dem Engel Uriel ein wesentliches Fragment des Stückes bildet. Wir wissen aus der apokalyptischen Tradition, daß derartige Engelkämpfe oft als Symbolik geschichtlicher Vorgänge verwendet werden [2]. Um festzustellen, an welche Vorgänge gedacht ist, fragen wir zunächst nach der Bedeutung des Uriel. Dieser identifiziert sich fälschlich mit Jakob. Er gibt vor, auf die Erde herabgestiegen zu sein und sein Zelt bei den Menschen aufgeschlagen zu haben. Nun liegt derselbe Topos dem Weisheitsmythos bei Jes. Sir. xxiv 8 zu Grunde: „Da befahl mir der Schöpfer des All und der, der mich geschaffen hat, brachte meine Wohnung (τὴν σκηνήν μου) zur Ruhe und sprach: 'In Jakob schlage deine Wohnung auf und in Israel sei dein Erbe.' Vor Anfang der Ewigkeit schuf er mich, und bis in Ewigkeit werde ich nicht aufhören. Im heiligen Zelt machte ich vor ihm Wohnung und so bekam ich in Zion Wohnung." Dieser 'hieros logos' der die Weisheit zum Bewohner des Jerusalemer Tempels macht, stimmt mit dem Anspruche Uriels in der Proseuche Joseph in charakteristischen Wendungen

---

[1] *Memar Marqah* II. 139 ff. 226.
[2] Dan. x 13 ff.

überein. Die Proseuche allerdings brandmarkt ihn als falschen
Anspruch. Denn nach ihr ist Uriel nicht der wirkliche Jakob und
auch nicht der oberste Geist. Nur eine sehr untergeordnete himm-
lische Gestalt, in der achten Rangstufe auf Jakob folgend, hat in
Jerusalem Wohnung gemacht. Die Proseuche erklärt den Gegner
Jakobs, mit dem er kämpfte, als er den Jabbok überschritt, als den
Engel, der im Jerusalemer Tempel Wohnung genommen hat und
nun Jakob den Eingang in sein Land verwehren will.

Nachdem wir die Polemik als antijerusalemisch erkannt haben,
fragen wir nach dem Standpunkt, von dem aus sie geführt wird. Die
feindliche Haltung der Samaritaner gegen Jerusalem ist bekannt. Ein
weiteres Argument ist der noch unveröffentlichten Chronik II zu
entnehmen, deren Traditionen MACDONALD bekannt gemacht hat.
In ihr wird von einer Rückkehr der Samaritaner aus assyrischer
Gefangenschaft berichtet, die eine Ausweitung von 2 Reg. xvii 28 ist.
Die dortige Rückkehr eines samaritanischen Priesters ist zu einer
Rückkehr der wahren (samaritanischen) Verehrer Gottes unter ihrem
Hohepriester Serajah gemacht worden. Der Bericht ist weithin den
Schilderungen über die Rückkehr der judäischen Golah von Babylon
nachgeformt, jedoch unter einem assyrischen König datiert. Man
wollte der feindlichen Jerusalemer Golah etwas Entsprechendes
gegenüber stellen. Vielleicht wendet sich diese Überlieferung auch
gegen die aus 4 Esra xiii 39 ff. bekannte Meinung, daß die zehn
Stämme erst bei den Geschehnissen der Endzeit zurückkehren
werden. Ein Zug aus dieser Heimkehrlegende erweckt unsere
Aufmerksamkeit: Der König von Assyrien — entsprechend 2 Reg.
xvii unterrichtet über Trockenheit, Hungersnot und Tierplagen in
Samarien — wendet sich mit seinem Befehl zur Rückkehr an die
Samaritaner, die damals in *Haran* wohnten [1]). Die Samaritaner
ziehen von Haran nach Kanaan. Diese Tradition ist offensichtlich
in Parallele zu Jakobs Aufenthalt in Haran geformt. Die Rückkehr
des Erzvaters mit der anschließenden Gründung des Tempels in
Bethel ist in der samaritanischen Überlieferung der Chronik II als
Prototyp der Rückkehr aus der assyrischen Gefangenschaft verstanden. Da die Proseuche Joseph antijerusalemisch ist und ihre
Tendenz durch den rückkehrenden Jakob vertreten wird, können
wir den erzählten Kampf als Prototyp der Rückkehr der Samaritaner
aus ihrer assyrischen Gefangenschaft deuten, bei der Uriel, der den

---

[1]) MACDONALD *Theology* S. 20.

illegitimen Gottesdienst von Jerusalem vertritt, überwunden wird.
Das Alter dieser samaritanischen Traditionen ist schwer festzustellen. Sie tragen das Kennzeichen einer bewußten Parallelisierung
zur jüdischen Überlieferung. Für ihre Verbreitung werden wir kaum
eine ältere Periode als das zweite bis dritte Jahrhundert nach Christus
annehmen können. In irgendeiner Form ist sie Ursache und Anstoß
der apologetischen Deutung von Gen. xlviii in der Form des Midrasch
Tanchuma geworden. Ursache der Tanchumadeutung ist die literarische Aktivität der Samaritaner in jener Zeit. Die jüdische Bibel-
auslegung ist zur Auseinandersetzung über unsern Text gezwungen.

III

Einen andern Brennpunkt der exegetischen Diskussion über Gen.
xlviii finden wir in der Formung, die der Midrasch zur Stelle in der
Sammlung Pesiqta Rabbati erhalten hat [1]). Die Sammlung ist wohl
jünger als die Tanchuma-Kompilation. Das sagt jedoch über das
Alter der darin erhaltenen Traditionen nicht viel. Doch entstammt
ein für uns wichtiger Einzelzug wohl einer Weiterentwicklung der
Tanchumaform. Die Überlieferung in Pesiqta entspricht im Großen
und Ganzen der in Tanchuma vorliegenden. Jedoch findet sich an
der Stelle, wo in Tanchuma vom Gebet Josephs berichtet wird, eine
bezeichnende Abänderung. Nachdem Jakob den Segen nicht voll-
ziehen kann, berichtet der Midrasch: „Da begann Josef zu bitten und
sagte zu ihm: 'Vater, meine Söhne sind so gesetzmäßig (geboren)
wie ich; sie sind Söhne, die mir Gott durch *diese* gegeben hat. „Durch
diese" (בזה) steht in der Schrift, weil er Asenet, ihre Mutter, vor
seinen Vater führte und zu ihm sagte: 'Ich komme mit der Bitte zu
dir, wenn auch nur wegen der Gerechtigkeit von *dieser*." An Stelle
des Gebetes steht in Pesiqta Rabbati also eine Bitte Josephs an Jakob,
er solle die Söhne wegen der Frau Josephs, Asenet, segnen. Die
Bedeutung dieser Passage wird deutlicher durch das Targum Jeruschalmi I zu Gen. xlviii 8 f.: „Und Israel sag die Söhne Josephs
und sprach: 'Von wem sind diese dir geboren?' Und Joseph sagte
zu seinem Vater 'Meine Söhne sind sie, die mir das Wort Jahwes gab.
Gemäß dieser Urkunde, die sie betrifft, habe ich Asenet geheiratet
als Tochter des Gesetzes." In Pesiqta Rabbati und im Targum
Jeruschalmi I ist also eine weitere Person in die Handlung eingeführt,

---

[1]) Ed. FRIEDMANN. III. S. 12a.

die zwar in der Bibel vorkommt, aber in Gen. xlviii nicht auftritt. Sie wird beigezogen, um die gesetzmäßige Abkunft der Josephs- söhne und zugleich ihre eigene Gesetzmäßigkeit dartun zu lassen. Das geschieht durch die Deutung des בזה, in Gen. xlviii = hier, als "wegen dieser".

Damit stehen wir in einem anderen Komplex der exegetischen Auseinandersetzung. Der Midrasch setzt sich mit Überlieferungen auseinander, die zur Legende von Joseph und Asenet gehören. Diese geht von der biblischen Überlieferung aus, daß Josephs Frau Asenet die Tochter eines ägyptischen Priesters in Heliopolis war. Sie schildert Josephs Frau als ideale Proselytin, die aus Liebe zu Joseph und durch eine himmlische Erscheinung zum jüdischen Glauben bekehrt wird. Bei ihrem Übertritt gewinnt sie zugleich den siegreichen Helden Joseph zum Manne. Der Gedanke, daß die erwählten Josephs-söhne von einer heidnischen Mutter aus der hamitischen Völkerfamilie stammen sollten, erschien den rabbinischen Überlieferern nicht tragbar. So entwickelt die jüdische Haggada die Theorie, Asenet sei nur ein Adoptivkind gewesen; ihre tatsächliche Mutter sei Dina, die Schwester der Josephsbrüder Simeon und Levi[1]. In späterer Weiterüberlieferung wird Dinas Kind auf wunderbare Weise nach Ägypten gebracht, um dort Josephs Frau zu werden. In der Linie dieser Abwehr liegt auch die Betonung der Legitimität Asenets in unserem Midrasch.

Gegen wen richtet sich aber die polemische Betonung der legitimen Abstammung Asenets? Für die dem Asenetbuch zu Grunde liegende Tradition möchte ich samaritanischen Ursprung nicht für unmöglich halten[2]. Nach manchen Bemerkungen samaritanischer Literatur genoß der Proselyt eine gewisse Wertschätzung[3]. Der samaritanische

---

[1] Trakt. Soferim 21, Weiteres siehe bei APTOWITZER, „Asenat, the wife of Joseph." *HUCA*. I. 1924. S. 239-307.

[2] Über die Herkunft der Asenetlegende ist viel diskutiert worden. C. BUR-CHARD, *Untersuchungen* (cf. S. 156. Anm. 1) will sie aus einem proselytenfreund-lichen Milieu des hellenistischen Judentums ableiten. Das wäre an sich denkbar, und wir haben Veranlassung, die Existenz solcher Kreise zu vermuten. Wenn wir über ihre literarische Tätigkeit nur etwas mehr wüßten. PHILONENKO, „*Ini-tiation en mystère dans Joseph et Asenet.*" *Initiation.* Contributions of the Study Conference of the International Association for the History of Religions. 1964. denkt an essenische Entstehung. Wirklich begegnet sind wir all solchen Ge-schichten bisher nur in der rabbinischen Haggada, dem Samaritanismus und der christlichen Volksüberlieferung. Ich erfinde darum nicht gern eine umfangreiche Literatur für irgendeine neue Gruppe. Was ist in Qumran wirklich qumranische Literatur?

[3] *Memar Marqah* II S. 118.

Bibelausleger Ibrahim kämpft im Mittelalter gegen die rabbinische Tradition, daß Asenet von Dina abstamme, da die Ehe zwischen Onkel und Nichte nach samaritanischer Auffassung illegitim sei [1]). Die Asenettradition ist also in dieser Periode zwischen Juden und Samaritanern diskutiert worden. Außerdem ist es zum mindesten vorstellbar, daß die Samaritaner, die Joseph als ihren König ansahen, die Stammutter seines Hauses in Parallele zu Ruth, der Ahnfrau Davids, als bekehrte Heidin ansahen. Doch kommen wir über Vermutungen nicht hinaus.

Sicher aber fand die Asenetgestalt in der christlichen Welt bald Interesse. Von der Legende haben wir später Versionen bis hin zu niederländischen Übersetzungen im hohen Mittelalter. Sie war zu einem Volksbuch der Christenheit geworden. Auch auf den frühen christlichen Darstellungen des Jakobssegens tritt Asenet auf. So finden wir sie unter den christlichen Malereien des IV. Jahrhunderts in der San-Callisto-Katakombe [2]), und ebenfalls in der herrlichen Buchmalerei des VI. Jahrhunderts in der Wiener Genesis [3]). Ohne Zweifel sollte damit eine christliche Interpretation der Perikope verdeutlicht werden. Die Josephssöhne hatten einen jüdischen Vater und eine heidnische Mutter und wurden so als Symbol des von Juden und Heiden abstammenden Gottesvolkes aufgefaßt. Durch den Jakobssegen wurden sie in die Zahl der zwölf Stämme aufgenommen, und die beiden Eltern aus den beiden Teilen der nichtchristlichen Menschheit wurden Symbolfiguren in dieser bedeutsamen prototypischen Handlung.

Merkwürdigerweise verschwand Asenet mit dem Beginn des Mittelalters aus den christlichen Darstellungen des Jakobssegens, und so kennen wir keinen *literarischen* Beleg von christlicher Hand für ihre Anwesenheit bei der Segnung ihrer Söhne. Jedoch ist die Erweiterung der Segnungsgeschichte in Pesiqta Rabbati offensichtlich gegen diese Deutung der Asenetgestalt gerichtet. Der Midrasch stimmt der in der christlichen Tradition bekannten Meinung zu, Asenet habe der Segnung der Söhne beigewohnt. Jedoch, so betont der Mischna polemisch, ist sie keine Heidin, sondern die gesetzmäßige Frau des Josephs, und auch ihre Söhne sind Söhne des Gesetzes, keiner von ihnen ist ein Prototyp der Christenheit.

---

[1]) APTOWITZER S. 251.
[2]) Cf. STECHOW S. 195.
[3]) Abgebildet bei v. EINEM Abb. 6.

IV

Das Mittelalter hat die Asenetfigur vielleicht aus ästhetischen Gründen wegfallen lassen. Die Handlung wird meist in ornamentalem Zusammenhang dargestellt: Auf Emailkreuzen, Glasfenstern und Buchillustrationen [1]). Das mag zur Reduktion des Materials geführt haben, um eine vollkommenere Form zu erreichen. Auch Joseph fehlt, und später war Asenet vergessen. Aber auch ikonographisch ist der Fortfall der Frauenfigur zu erklären. Man hatte ein Mittel, um die Erwählung viel konzentrierter, auch schärfer polemisch gefaßt, darzustellen, und zugleich dem Verlangen nach einer ästhetisch symmetrischen Formung entgegenzukommen. Es bestand in der Kreuzung der Arme Jakobs [2]).

Der schwer verständliche Ausdruck in Vers 14 'שׂכל' wird als 'flechten, verdrehen' gedeutet und mit dem akkad. Wort šakkilu in Verbindung gebracht. Dieses bedeutet einen „gedrehten Turban” [3]). So kann man das Verb in Gen. xlviii als 'vertauschen, überkreuzen' übersetzen. Die LXX setzen diese Deutung mit 'ἐναλλάξ' = austauschend, über Kreuz' voraus. Auch das Targum Jeruschalmi I folgt dieser Tradition mit seiner Übersetzung 'פרג'. Die so beschriebene Haltung bekommt in der christlichen Zeit einen symbolischen Charakter als Anspielung auf die Kreuzigung Christi. Die Wiener Genesis zeigt das bereits, und auf den Emailkreuzen des Mittelalters erhält die Kreuzung der Hände immer stärkere ornamentale Betonung. Neben den Darstellungen der bildenden Kunst stehen die literarischen Quellen, die die Verschränkung der Arme ebenfalls mit der Kreuzigung in Verbindung bringen [4]).

Mit der Vertauschung der Arme ist eine andere Tradition verbunden, die ebenfalls auf dem Boden des Christentum entwickelt worden ist. Sie führt in die Überlieferung eine gewisse Schärfe ein. Nach dieser ist der jüngere bevorzugte Bruder Ephraim der Typos der Christenheit, während der ältere mit dem geringeren Segen bedachte

---

[1]) v. EINEM, *Rembrandt*, Abbildungen 6-22.

[2]) Die älteste sichtlich betonte Überkreuzung der Arme finden wir in der Abbildung der Wiener Genesis. Das Mittelalter gibt die Haltung der Hände Jakobs fast durchgängig in dieser Form. Merkwürdiger Weise hat der Psalter der Queen Mary (Französ. Buchmalerei aus dem Hochmittelalter. Abgebildet bei E. Abb. 20) ein anderes Moment gewählt. Die Szene hat nicht so sehr symbolischen, als vielmehr genrehaften Charakter. Jakob und Joseph tragen Judenhüte. Hat hier die jüdische Überlieferung eine Rolle gespielt?

[3]) KÖHLER-BAUMGARTNER. 1. Auflage. S. 922.

[4]) TERTULLIAN, de baptismo VIII, 2 u.a.

das Judentum vertritt. Jakob segnete Ephraim mit dem Erst-
geburtssegen, weil er in ihm die kommende Christenheit vor sich
sah. Auch Ambrosius und Augustin [1]) deuten die beiden Gestalten
auf diese Art. So wurde durch die gekreuzten Arme die Kreuzigung
symbolisiert, und zugleich Erwählung der Christenheit und Zurück-
setzung des Judentums in einem Akt dargestellt. Das machte die
Gestalt der Asenet überflüssig. Sie verschwand und wurde vergessen.

Die Exegese, die Ephraim zum Typos der Christenheit macht,
geht bekanntlich bis in die Anfänge der Kirche zurück. Im Barnabasbrief wird Gen. xlviii folgendermaßen gedeutet: „Und in einer
anderen Prophezeiung sagt Jakob zu seinem Sohn Joseph: 'Siehe,
der Herr hat mich nicht deiner Gegenwart beraubt; führe deine
Söhne zu mir, damit ich sie segne. Und er führte Ephraim und
Manasse herbei, und wollte, daß Manasse gesegnet würde, weil er
der ältere war. Joseph führte ihn nämlich an die rechte Hand des
Vater Jakob. Aber Jakob sah im Geiste das Vorbild des λαός (d.h.
des späteren christlichen Gottesvolkes). Und was sagt die Schrift?
„Und Jakob vertauschend seine Hände — ἐναλλὰξ τὰς χεῖρας —
legte die Rechte auf den Kopf des Ephraim... Und Jakob sprach
zu Joseph: 'Ich weiß, Sohn, ich weiß; aber der Ältere wird dem
Jüngeren dienen, und dieser wird gesegnet sein." Schaut, auf welchen
er (die Hände) legte, das Volk ist der erste und Erbe des Bündnisses [2]).

Formal schließt sich die christliche Auslegung an Traditionen an,
die wir im jüdischen Hellenismus finden. Auch Philo stellt diese
Stelle hinter Gen. xxv 23 wie der Barnabasbrief [3]). Der Unterschied zwischen beiden Söhnen ist ebenfalls bei Philo herausgestellt.
Ephraim, der jüngere, bezeichnet die wertvollere μνήμη, = Gedächtnis, während der ältere Manasse die unbedeutendere Seelenkraft
der ἀνάμνησις, = Erinnerung, symbolisiert: „Symbolisch wird
nämlich Ephraim „μνήμη" genannt, mit Fruchttragen übersetzt: das
Gedächtnis der Seele des Weisheitsliebenden, die die eigenste Frucht
trägt, wenn sie durch das Gedächtnis die Objekte des Sehens in sich
festhält. Manasse aber ist die „ἀνάμνησις", man sagt übersetzt heiße
er „ἐκ λήθης" (= aus dem Vergessen); wer der Lethe entflieht,

---

[1]) Ambrosius, *De benedictione Patriarcharum.* MPL xiv, 673 ff. Augustin, *De
civitate Dei.* XVI, XLII. MPL. XLI, 520 f. Alles ist zusammengestellt bei Stechow
S. 194 ff.

[2]) xiii 4-6.

[3]) Cf. Robert A. Kraft, *Barnabas and the Didache.* The Apostolic fathers III.
1965. 123 ff.

erinnert sich an alles. Mit großem Recht grüßt der Überwinder der Leidenschaften und Geübte in der Tugend die „fruchtbringende" μνήμη Ephraim mit der Rechten und wertet an zweiter Stelle die ἀνάμνησις Manasse" [1]. Die Deutung der hebräischen Namen ist offensichtlich eine alte symbolische Exegese, die Philo, der kaum selber Hebräisch konnte, aus einer Tradition übernommen hat. Die Deutung des Namens Ephraim ist klar. Sie ist dem hebräischen Stamm פרה, = Fruchttragen, entnommen. Hingegen die Erklärung des Namens Manasse ist schwierig. Sie deutet die erste Silbe des Namens mit מן, = von, aus, während die anderen Teile mit 'Vergessen' übersetzt werden. Das muß aber auf das Verbum 'נשא' = hochheben, aufnehmen, bezogen sein. Nun gibt es eine Stelle in der LXX, wo נשא mit ποιεῖν λήθην übersetzt wird, nämlich Job vii 21 LXX. Die von Philo übernommene Exegese entstammt der Tradition, die in der griechischen Übersetzung des Hiobbuches am Werk ist. In dieser sind in der Tat Züge einer stoisierenden Interpretation des Hiobtextes zu bemerken. Auch die Deutung von Ephraim und Manasse benutzt die Terminologie der stoischen Psychologie. In stoisierenden griechisch sprechenden Kreisen jüdischer Schriftgelehrten wurde Gen. xlviii 14 also nicht heilsgeschichtlich, sondern ethisch-psychologisch gedeutet.

Das Sonderbare ist nun, daß auch der rabbinische Midrasch für diesen Teil von Gen. xlviii ethische Tendenz aufweist. Im Midrasch Bereschith Rabba haben wir eine Überlieferung des R. Huna [2], die folgendermaßen lautet: „Wissen wir nicht aus den Geburtsurkunden, daß er jünger war? „Jünger" (צעיר) bedeutet doch, daß er seine Bedeutung verkleinerte (מצעיר)." Hier ist Ephraim nichts als ein ethisches Vorbild, und das allein ist der Grund für seine Erwählung. Huna interpretiert Gen. xlviii von Prov. iv 34 aus, das auch sein Echo in Jac. iv 6 gefunden hat: „Gott widersteht dem Hoffärtigen, aber dem Demütigen schenkt er Gnade." Auch die Weisheitsgeschichten von Tobit und Nebukadnezars Fall exemplifizieren diesen Grundsatz. Rabbi Hunas Exegese setzt also die alte Weisheitsmaxime voraus, die an den Bezeichnungen „klein" und „groß" in Gen. xlviii entwickelt ist. Aber auch die bei Philo vorliegende stoische Deutung schließt an diese Begriffe an, so fremd gerade dem stoischen Denken diese Weisheitsmaxime ist. Zwischen der Exegese von Gen. xxv 23

---

[1] *Legum Allegor.* Lib. III. 93. C-W I.S. 127.
[2] Ein babylonischer Amoräer aus der 2. Generation, gest. 297 v. Chr.

und unserer Stelle erklärt Philo: „Tatsächlich nämlich zeigt auch
ein kleiner Hauch die Herrschaft und Führung, nicht allein die
Freiheit der Tugend an, und andererseits knechtet die erst beginnende
Entstehung die Vernunft, auch wenn ihre vollständige Frucht noch
nicht hervorgebrochen ist." Die Ausdrücke 'klein', 'Frucht' und
'hervorbrechen' zeigen, daß jene ältere Exegese wiedergegeben wird,
die auch sonst in diesem Midrasch bei Philo vorliegt. Wir dürfen
vermuten, daß sie eine Umdeutung der alten weisheitlichen Auslegung
ist, die bei Huna noch wirksam ist. Beide — der von Philo zitierte
stoisierende Tradent in griechisch sprechender Exegese und R. Huna
— gehen auf die eine Tradition zurück, die Gen. xlviii 14 ethisch
deutete. Ihr vorchristlicher Ursprung ist wahrscheinlich. Diese
Neutralisierung der heilsgeschichtlichen Deutung war gegenüber
den Samaritanern, wie den Christen, gleich brauchbar.

Obwohl die Juden die christliche Deutung von Gen. xlviii 17
gekannt haben müssen, finden wir keine Polemik gegen diese.
Wahrscheinlich war es schwierig, einen antichristlichen Sinn heraus-
zuarbeiten, ohne einen der beiden suspekten Jakobssöhne herabzu-
setzen oder zu sehr zu erhöhen. Vielleicht besitzen wir aber doch
einige leichte Spuren einer Abwehr der christlichen Deutung der
Stelle. In Tanchuma ist die ethische Deutung der Stelle aufgegeben
und die Bevorzugung Ephraims mit seinen Nachkommen Josua
begründet. Diese auf Num. xiii 8 basierende Erwähnung könnte
man vielleicht mit der Abwehr des Jesusnamens in Verbindung
bringen. Nicht Prototyp der Jesusgemeinde, sondern des Jesus —
wie die LXX seinen Namen wiedergibt —, des Sohnes Nuns, ist
Ephraim. Deutlicher als diese sehr unsichere Beziehung scheint die
Abänderung der in den alten Übersetzungen gebräuchlichen ‚vertauschen, überkreuzen' im Targum Onkelos zu sein. Dieses Targum
gibt das biblische שׂכל mit אתכם 'weise gebrauchen' wieder. Nach
Pesiqta R. hat schon Rabbi diese Deutung. Gegenüber der bis dahin
einheitlichen Tradition fällt diese Verbindung von שׂכל mit dem
Verbalstamm סכל auf. Hier könnte der Gedanke im Hintergrund
stehen, daß Jakob seine Hände nicht gekreuzt hat. Man wollte die
Stützung der christlichen Deutung vermeiden.

Die Auslegung von Gen. xlviii ist die verschiedensten Wege
gegangen. Ihre Geschichte ist keine isolierte Entwickelung im
Rahmen des Judentums, sondern eine Wechselwirkung verschieden-
ster Gruppen. Die Gedanken über die Rolle Josephs wurden im

Anschluß an die altjüdische Überlieferung von der Vision Jakobs
im Gespräch zwischen Judentum und Samaritanismus entwickelt.
Die Beteiligung der Asenet kam durch christliche Übernahme und
Verwendung vielleicht samaritanischer Traditionen in den Vorder-
grund. Das Judentum veränderte dieses Motiv apologetisch. Die
Debatte über die Haltung der Hände Jakobs und der Bevorzugung
Ephraims, die in der älteren Weisheitsüberlieferung ethisch gedeutet
wurde, empfing ihre Scharfe durch die christliche Exegese von
Gen. xlviii 17 im Barnabasbrief. Es war ein Kampf um die Bibel,
die jede Gruppe als ihren Besitz ansah, als den Adelsbrief ihrer
Familie.

Wenn wir nun mit unserm auf langem Wege erworbenen Wissen
zu Rembrandts Bild zurückkehren, dann ist unsere erste Frage, aus
welchen Überlieferungen diese Darstellung ihre ikonographischen
Anstöße empfängt. Das Auffälligste ist, daß Rembrandt von verschiedensten Traditionen beeinflußt ist, die nicht aus einer einheitlichen Information stammen können. Der kräftig akzentuierte
Unterschied zwischen den beiden Knaben ist ein Erbe christlicher
Überlieferung. Er kann nicht aus jüdischer Überlieferung kommen.
Man hat angemerkt, daß 1646 bei Isaak Voß in Amsterdam eine
Ausgabe der Barnabasbriefes erschien [1]). Solche Gedanken waren
also in Amsterdam bekannt. Daneben stehen Züge, die Rembrandt
durch jüdische Überlieferung — durch christliche Polemik oder
durch die Bekanntschaft mit Manasse ben Israel — zugeflossen sein
mögen. Die Anwesenheit der Asenet, der älteren christlichen Ikono-
graphie noch bekannt, konnte ihm auf archäologischem Wege nicht
zugekommen sein. Auch ist Asenet nicht als der Typus gezeichnet,
den Rembrandt bei Ephraim als christlichen darstellt. Sie ähnelt
dem als jüdischen Knaben dargestellten Manasse. Nicht die heidnische
Asenet der samaritanisch-christlichen Legende steht vor uns, sondern
die gesetzestreue Frau Josephs, als die sie im jüdischen Bereich
geschildert wird. Bei der Darstellung der Hände sind wir nicht
sicher. Auf älteren zeichnerischen Entwürfen ringt Rembrandt stark
mit dem Problem der Hände [2]). Die Haltung der Hände Jakobs
könnte also die bildnerische Auflösung eines lang überlegten Problems sein, in Wahrheit eine meisterhafte Lösung! Aber auch diese
kann durch ikonographische Anweisungen gefunden sein. Einige

---

[1]) STECHOW, S. 207.
[2]) Die Zeichnungen sind abgebildet bei v. EINEM Abb. 25-28.]

Graphiker der Renaissance übergehen die Kreuzung [1]) der Hände.
Vielleicht können wir sogar noch einen Schritt näher an Rembrandts
Quelle kommen. Auf dem Bild sind nicht nur Jakobs Hände auffällig,
sondern auch die Art, wie Joseph die Hand Jakobs berührt. Er greift
nicht gewaltsam nach ihr, packt sie nicht, sondern stützt sie von
unten und sucht sie dabei auf das Haupt Manasses zu leiten. Die
Bewegung ist so vorsichtig, daß man gemeint hat, Rembrandt wolle
gar keine Gegenbewegung Josephs schildern [2]). Das scheint mir
nicht beweisbar, aber die Handhaltung des Sohnes entspricht der
Übersetzung der Targumim. Gen. xlviii 17 steht das hebräische
'תמך', das 'ergreifen, halten, festhalten' bedeutet. Die LXX übersetzen den Ausdruck mit ἀντιλαμβάνειν. Auch im palästinischen
Aramäisch kommt der Ausdruck in derselben Bedeutung vor. Die
Targumim aber übersetzen mit dem Stamm סעד, „stützen". Damit
bekommt die Quelle, aus der Rembrandt die jüdischen Traditionen
empfing, sichtbare Kontur. Alle Züge, die dem Maler nur aus dem
Judentum zugeflossen sein können, sind in einer sogenannten
Rabbinerbibel zu finden, die den hebräischen Text mit den verschiedenen Targumim nebeneinander abdruckte. Dort konnte Rembrandt
von der Anwesenheit Asenets, von ihrer Gesetzmäßigkeit und von
der Haltung der Hände Jakobs und Josephs unterrichtet werden.
Natürlich hat Rembrandt nicht hebräische oder gar aramäische
Studien betrieben, um eine solche Bibel zu lesen. Aber es gab in der
Umgebung von Rembrandts Wohnung gewiß Rabbinen, die ihm
über die Schilderung der Szene in den Targumim Aufschluß geben
konnten [3]). Eine solche Quelle besaß für Rembrandt genug Autorität,

---

[1]) Holbeins Holzschnitt in „Historia veteris testamenti icones ad vium ex-
pressae", und ein Glasgemälde von Jörg Breus d. J. in Berlin, das von Holbein
abhängig ist, übergehen die Kreuzung der Hände. v. EINEM S. 23 f., STECHOW
S. 200.

[2]) v. EINEM S. 31 f.: (Josef) ist aus dem Gegenspieler zum Mitspieler geworden.
Mit seinem rechten Arm scheint er den Oberkörper des Greises zu stützen, mit
der Linken führt er Jakobs Hand."

[3]) Die große Amsterdammer Rabbinerbibel konnte noch nicht in den Händen
der zeitgenössischen Rabbinen sein, sie erschien erst 1724-27. Die Venediger
Ausgabe 1618-1619, bei Pietro & Lorenzo Bragadin unter Leitung von Leon von
Modena und Abraham Chaber-Tob ben Solomon Chajim Sopher herausgegeben,
kommt eher in Frage. Aber 1640 erschien in Amsterdam im Hause Manasse ben
Israels selbst ein Auszug der Rabbinerbibel, der den Pentateuch und die Megillot
mit einigen liturgischen Beigaben umfaßte.* Diese handliche und erschwingbare
Ausgabe war gewiß bei manchen der Gewährsmänner Rembrandts zu finden.
Wie wesentlich der damaligen, auch christlichen, Theologengeneration die
Kenntnis der Rabbinerbibel erschien, sieht man an ihrer 1618-1619 erfolgten

um als Vorbild für seine Darstellung zu dienen, war sie doch nichts anderes als eine alte Übersetzung der Bibel.

Es geht uns aber hier letztlich nicht ums Ikonographische. Uns bewegt die Frage, ob Rembrandt eine bestimmte Haltung gegenüber der Tradition ausdrückte, als er seine Darstellung auf die Leinwand brachte. Wer Tradition verarbeitet, steht selber in der Traditionsgeschichte. Darum interessiert es uns, warum und mit welchem Ziel Rembrandt diese verschiedenen Traditionen nebeneinandersetzte. Vergleichen wir seine Darstellung mit der ihm vielleicht bekannten Darstellung der biblischen Szene durch Guernico, dann fällt der gewaltige Gegensatz der Stimmung auf. Bei Guernico ist das Ganze ein titanenhafter Ausbruch entfesselter Gefühle. Enttäuschung, Entsetzen, Triumph werden in gewaltigen Bewegungen geschildert [1]). Rembrandts Bild zeigt eine Einheit. Es ist die Einheit einer Familie, die in all ihren Gegensätzen doch letztlich Harmonie und Geborgenheit darstellt. H. v. EINEM hat betont, daß auf diese Weise Rembrandt den biblische Vorgang säkularisiert d.h. vermenschlicht, ihn zum Ausdruck menschlicher Beziehung macht. Man muß ihm, schon aus kunst- und kulturgeschichtlichen Gründen, zustimmen. Dennoch möchte man sich fragen, ob diese Darstellung einer Familie nicht auch eine Idee ausdrücken soll. Der Gedanke kommt dem Betrachter, wenn er den absichtsvollen Gegensatz zwischen den beiden Söhnen erkennt. Dieser ist der christlichen Tradition entnommen und widerspricht dem Gedanken der einheitlichen Familie. Wenn diese beiden, so verschiedenen Typen, deren geschichtssymbolischer Gehalt gegenüber der Tradition noch gesteigert ist, hier im Mittelpunkt dieses Familienbildes stehen, dann wollte Rembrandt damit vielleicht doch das Programm einer Einheit, oder besser eines Zusammenlebens von Christentum und Judenheit ausdrücken. Die aus Spanien vertriebenen Juden hatten in den Niederlanden Aufnahme gefunden. Rembrandts Wohnung stand in dem Viertel, wo überall neue Häuser für die zugewanderten Juden gebaut wurden. Die gewaltige Synagoge der portugiesischen Juden war noch nicht erstellt, aber die Bedeutung dieser Zuwanderung war deutlich. Was den Manasse auf Rembrandts Bild am stärksten gegen den auf Guernicos Gemälde dargestellten abhebt, ist die

---

Ausgabe durch den reformierten Theologen J. BUXTORF d.Ä. [*Mitteilung von J. SMIT SIBINGA, Leiden].

[1]) v. EINEM Abb. 30 S. 29 f. Nach v. EINEM hat Rembrandt Guernicos Bild gekannt und vielleicht sogar in seiner späteren Periode noch einmal studiert.

kindliche Fröhlichkeit, mit der er zum Beschauer hinausblickt. Jakob segnet den jüngeren Bruder, aber Manasse ist fröhlich, denn durch den gesegneten Ephraim findet er auch eine Heimat.

Rembrandt hat gelegentlich symbolische Darstellungen gemalt [1]). Vielleicht finden wir auch hier eine Symbolik seiner Gedanken. Es ist ein sehr hoffnungsvolles Programm. Das neue Europa, das nicht mehr das Abendland ist, soll Raum und Heimat für beide, für Juden und Christen sein. Beide sollen an der neuen kulturellen, wirtschaftlichen, künstlerischen und wissenschaftlichen Entwicklung mitarbeiten, die das 'Goldene Jahrhundert' in den Niederlanden einzuleiten schien. Darum konnte Rembrandt das Material für sein Gemälde auch aus der Überlieferung beider Bekenntnisse schöpfen. Er steht in einer neuen traditionsgeschichtlichen Situation, in der nicht mehr die Polemik, Abgrenzung und Verurteilung die Überlieferung bestimmt, sondern das Wissen, daß beide in einem Hause, in einer Familie wohnen. Der Europäer des zwanzigsten Jahrhunderts, für den manches von Rembrandts Hoffnungen erfüllt, vieles jedoch zerstört ist, kann nur mit Beschämung vor diesem Bild in der Kasseler Galerie stehen.

---

[1]) Ich denke an das, allerdings früh entstandene Gemälde 'De eenheid van het land' im Museum Boymans-van Beuningen, Rotterdam, oder auch an die helle weibliche Kindergestalt auf der ‚Nachtwache'.

SOME TRANSLATION PROBLEMS

BY

CHR. H. W. BREKELMANS

1. *Judges v 29*

In the last part of the song of Debora, the mother of Sisera is introduced, while she together with other prominent ladies is looking forward to the return of her son and his army. The ladies who surround her attempt to encourage her. But as soon as these ladies enter the scene, the translators get into trouble.

1. The translation of *ḥakmôt śārôtêhā* is disputed. Everyone seems to accept that actually the text has a plural. Consequently, some of them maintain this plural in their translation. So for instance E. DHORME: "les plus sages de ses dames" [1]) or the Revised Luther-Version: "die Weisesten unter ihren Fürstinnen" [2]). Most commentators and translators, however, take the line that, with the following verb in they singular, the subject should be translated as singular. They then think to be obliged to introduce a small textual change, reading *ḥakmat* for massoretic *ḥakmôt* [3]).

2. In v. 29b almost all translations hold, that with *'af hî* the subject changes: *hî* is being understood of Sisera's mother and not of the wise lady in 29a. This interpretation is already to be found in the Septuagint translation: καὶ αὐτὴ ἀπεκρίνατο. Nevertheless, some scholars have maintained, that *hî* refers to the wise lady of the first stichos. "*Hî* bezieht sich auf die klügste der Fürstinnen, nicht auf die Königinmutter", wrote ZAPLETAL [4]). The same view finds expression in the translation of H. GRESSMANN: "Die klugste der Fürstinnen erwidert ihm, die gibt ihr zu Antwort" [5]). Last mentioned

---

[1]) *La Bible. L'ancien Testament* Tome I (Bibliothèque de la Pleiade), Paris, 1956, 737.
[2]) *Die Bibel nach der Übersetzung M. Luthers.* Redivierter Text, Stuttgart, 1964, 478.
[3]) See f.i. KÖHLER-BAUMGARTNER, *Lexicon*, s.v. The new third edition retains this alteration.
[4]) V. ZAPLETAL, *Das Buch der Richter* (EHAT), Münster, 1923, 92.
[5]) H. GRESSMANN, *Die Anfänge Israels* (SAT), Göttingen, 1922, 185.

writers, however, represent merely a very small minority and have not been able to influence the opinion of the majority.

3. With those who take that in v. 29b Sisera's mother is the subject there is difference of opinion about the explanation of the stichos. Two trends are to be distinguished.

a) Sisera's mother allows herself to be comforted by the words of the wise lady and repeats her words to encourage herself. In this conception the words of v. 30 are, so to say, put in the mouth of the wise lady as well as in Sisera's mother's. So the revised Luther version has: "und sieselbst wiederholt ihre Worte"[1]). Some commentators object to the translation of *hēšîb* as "repeat" and prefer: "Elle-même se répond à elle-même"[2]). K. Budde formulated this objection explicitly as follows: "Nicht "sie wiederholt sich", sondern "sie gibt sich selber ihre Antwort", d.h. sie beschwichtigt sich sofort mit demselben Gedanken"[3]). This objection has not prevented, that the translation "repeat" has remained the most common.

b) The same translation is also used by a second trend of opinion, but in an almost opposite explanation. Sisera's mother, it is said, refuses to be encouraged by the wise lady; she proceeds to repeat her own anxious words of v. 28[4]). In this case v. 29b cannot be considered as an introduction to v. 30. The translator is almost obliged to put the stichos in brackets or dashes[5]).

From the preceding it is obvious that the traditional translations of v 29 of Debora's Song still contain several difficulties. The following may be a contribution to their solution.

1. The Hebrew plural *hakmôt* plus following verb in the singular occurs also in Prov. xiv 11. Almost to the same effect *hokmôt* plus singular verb is used in Prov. i 20 and ix 1. In both last instances we have an intensifying plural or a kind of pluralis majestatis[6]). *Hakmôt* in Prov. xiv 1 and Judg. v 29 is followed by a further adjunct: *hakmôt šārôtêhā* and *hakmôt nāšîm*. In both cases from the group of princesses or women one is preferably indicated as being wise. Here

---

[1]) L.c.

[2]) M. J. Lagrange, *Le livre des Juges* (EB), Paris, 1903, 102.

[3]) K. Budde, *Das Buch der Richter* (KHC), Freiburg, 1897, 48.

[4]) See f.i. C. J. Goslinga, *Het Boek der Richteren* (KV), Kampen, 1933, 114.

[5]) Cf. G. Moore, *Judges* (ICC), Edinburgh, 1895, 167-8.

[6]) P. Joüon, *Grammaire de l'hébreu biblique*, Roma, 1923, 211. According to M. Dahood *hokmôt* is a Phoenician singular form (*Psalms* I, Anchor Bible, New York, 1966, 275.279).

too, therefore, the plural seems to have an intensifying or elative meaning. The plural translation of v. 29a, found occasionally, therefore seems to be inexact. On the other hand there is no reason to modify the text. It is possible to maintain the traditional Hebrew text and translate: "her wisest lady (or: the wisest of her ladies) speaks to her".

2. Whether Sisera's mother or the wise lady is the subject of v. 29b depends on the interpretation of '*af hî*' at the beginning of the stichos. Now '*af* actually introduces a change of subject. From the poetical texts of the OT can be quoted:

> Ps. lxxxix 27-28
> He (*hû*) will say to me: You are my father,
> my God, the Rock who saves me.
> And I ('*af ānî*) will make him my firstborn,
> the highest of the kings of the earth.
> Hiob xv 4
> You even ('*af* '*attā*) subvert religion
> and deprecate devotion toward God.

But there is also another use of '*af*, notably in poetry, where it serves as introductory particle of the second stichos of a verse. Then it does not point to a change of subject but resumes the subject of the first stichos.

> Jes. xxvi 9
> my soul (*nafšî*) longs for thee in the night
> yea my spirit ('*af rûḥî*) in me aches for thee.
> Jes. xxxiii 2
> be thou our help [1] in the morning
> thou ('*af*) our salvation in the time of distress.

The same use of '*af* occurs, when it is followed by a personal pronoun; see f. i.

> Prov. xxiii 27-28
> A harlot is a deep pit,
> a strange woman a narrow well;
> Yea, she ('*af hî*') will rob you like a bandit
> and be worse than the most treacherous of mankind [2].

---

[1] The *mem* of $z^e ro^c$-*m* is an enclitic *mem* which balances the suffix -*nû* of the second stichos.

[2] So with R. B. Y. Scott, *Proverbs* (Anchor Bible), New York, 1965, 141-142.

The translation of the last line may be uncertain to some extent, it is no matter of doubt, that the same harlot is the subject of both v. 27 and v. 28. *'Af hî'* then resumes the subject of v. 27. We saw that this use is very common in Hebrew poetry. Thus it appears that *'af hî'* in Judg. v 29b can very well resume the subject of 29a. This dispenses us with the so complicated translations of Lagrange and others.

3. A next item where translations differ is the rendering of *tāšîb 'amārêhā*. The same connection of *hēšîb* and *'amārîm* we find only in Prov. xxii 21. More commonly *hēšîb dābār* is used (28 times). Then there are *hēšîb debārîm* (Prov. xxiv 26) and *hēšîb millîn* (Hiob xxxiii 32; xxxv 4). All these expressions are used with the same meanings:

a) of an envoy or spy, who returning from his mission gives an account of the experiences on the spot (Gen. xxxvii 14; Deut. i 22.25; Jos. xiv 7; xxii 32).

b) of an envoy or messenger, who after carrying a message and receiving an answer, transfers this answer to the person who sent him. (Ex. xix 8; 1 Kings ii 30; xx 9; 2 Kings xxii 20).

c) of someone who gives an answer to a question (1 Sam. xvii 30; 2 Sam. xxiv 13; Jes. xli 28).

d) finally of someone who in a conversation, in which the word goes from one person to the other, begins to speak, answers, retorts, either in a normal conversation, in court or in dispute (1 Kings xii 6.9; Prov. xviii 13; xxvii 11; Hiob xxxv 4).

In none of these texts is there any reason for translating "to repeat". *Hēšîb 'amārîm* parallels the verb *'ānāh* in the first stichos. One should compare Amarna *awata turru* and Ugaritic *rgm ṯṯb*, which occur with the same meaning: to reply, to answer, to speak [1]).

We may conclude: There is everything to be said for returning to the translation of V. ZAPLETAL and H. GRESSMANN:

> "The wisest of her ladies speaks up,
> and replies to her."

2. *Psalm cxx 7*

The massoretic text of this verse has caused many difficulties as may be apparent from some of the most recent commentaries. The

[1]) J. A. KNUDTZON, *Die El-Amarna-Tafeln*, Leipzig 1915, Letter 81, 23; 83,78-and 48; 145,24-26; 170,33-34; 251,11-13, etc. C. H. GORDON, *Ugaritic Textbook*, Glossary, Roma, 1966, nr. 2661.

expression *'anî šālôm* at the beginning of the verse is, according to
WEISER [1]) "eine merkwürdige Formulierung". DEISSLER [2]) finds the
whole verse "sprachlich und sachlich wenig plausibel". No wonder
that textual alterations have been proposed. KRAUS [3]) f.i. reads
wᵉkēn for *wᵉkî* and translates: "Ich sprach von Frieden und Wahrheit,
sie aber wollten den Krieg" [4]). Nevertheless, most translations have
maintained the traditional Hebrew text. Now one must admit, with
WEISER, that the first part of the verse *'anî šālôm* is indeed a very
curious formulation. Moreover, the contrast between *'anî* and *hēmā*
does not receive the emphasis which it seems to have in the Hebrew
text. No wonder, that KRAUS a.o. changed the text to this effect. One
may ask, however, if these difficulties can be avoided, without
changing the traditional Hebrew text. The starting point in the study
of this verse is the twofold contrast in both parts of the verse:
'anî-hēmā on the one side, *šālôm* and *milḥāmā* on the other. Then
remain the words *wᵉkî 'adabbēr*. It is possible, that *'anî* is the subject
of the verb *'adabbēr*, both being the first person singular. This possibility has been accepted by SCHMIDT, HERKENNE, KRAUS, DEISSLER
and others. The expression *dibbēr šālôm* is, indeed, a common one
in biblical Hebrew (Ps. xxviii 3; xxxv 20; lxxxv 9; Jer. ix 7; Sach.
ix 10; Esth. x 3).

But when one links *šālôm* with *'adabbēr*, then the result is, that
wᵉkî separates the verb and its object. This needs not to be an insur-
mountable problem. First of all, emphatic *kî* before a verb thrown to
the end of the clause occurs in Ugaritic [5]) and several examples of
this usage have been found in Biblical Hebrew [6]). Secondly, the
existence of a waw asseverativum in classical Hebrew is widely
accepted. WERNBERG-MØLLER [7]) who cites several instances of its
usage before prepositions, wrote: "Although we may not yet be
able to account satisfactorily for this use of waw, yet one thing is
quite clear: the letter does not indicate separation from what precedes;
on the contary, it indicates the closest possible connection" [8]). It

---

[1]) A. WEISER, *Die Psalmen* II (ATD), Göttingen¹, 1959, 512.
[2]) A. DEISSLER, *Die Psalmen* III (Kleinkommentar), Düsseldorf, 1965, 144.
[3]) H. J. KRAUS, *Psalmen* (BK XV 2), Neukirchen, 1961, 830.
[4]) KRAUS, l.c.
[5]) C. H. GORDON, *Ugaritic Textbook*, Grammar, Roma, 1966, 9.17 and 13.51.
[6]) Cf. M. DAHOOD, „Hebrew-Ugaritic Lexicography", *Biblica* 46 (1965) 327.
[7]) P. WERNBERG-MØLLER, „'Pleonastic' *Waw* in Classical Hebrew", *JSS* 3
(1958) 321-326.
[8]) A.c., 322.

seems therefore not impossible, that the waw before the particle *kî*
has the same connective and asseverative meaning as it has before
prepositions.

If this should be accepted, one might translate, the first part of the
verse in this way:

As for me, I talked peace.

In the second stichos *hēmā* is the subject of the same verb *dibbēr*,
which has to be supplied from the first part of the verse. *Milḥāmā*,
then, becomes the object of this verb in parallelism with *šālôm* in
the first part. The *lamed* before *milḥāmā* may be a lamed objecti or
an emphatic lamed.

The translation of the whole verse thus should be:

As for me, I talked peace,
but they, they spoke only of war.

3. *Jona iv* 4.9

Jona, the prophet, had left Nineve and it displeased him exceedingly
that the Lord was sparing the city. Then the Lord asks Him: *hahêṭēb
ḥārā lāk*. This has been rendered almost without exception:

Do you well to be angry? [1]
As-tu raison de te fâcher? [2]
Meinst du dass du mit Recht zürnst? [3]
Zijt gij terecht vertoornd? [4]

This same translation is to be found in the commentaries. One
may ask, nevertheless, if it does justice to the Hebrew text. It is, as
far as I can see, the only place in which *hêṭēb* is translated: to do well,
to be justified. Moreover, from the traditional translations one might
expect ro tead in Hebrew: *hahêṭabtā (le)ḥārôt lāk*. There is, therefore,
every reason to study again the question of the Lord to Jona.

Now, the classical grammars of biblical Hebrew have two remarks
on Jona iv 4 and 9. The infinitif absolute of several verbs, they say [5],
especially the hifᶜil-form, is used as a pure adverb (cf. *harbē*, *harḥēq*,
haškēm). This also the case with the infinitif absolute *hêṭēb*, which
is adverbially used "von dem sorgfältigen und gründlichen Vollzug

---

[1] RSV.
[2] Bible de Jérusalem.
[3] Revidierte Lutherübersetzung.
[4] Nieuwe Vertaling van het NBG.
[5] GESENIUS-KAUTZSCH, 113k; JOÜON 123 r.

einer Handlung" [1]). This use is clear in expressions like: *dāraš hêṭēb*,
šā'al hêṭēb, = to ask, search diligently (Deut. xiii 1e; xvii 4; xi 18),
šibbēr hêṭēb = to break utterly in pieces (2 Kings xi 18). This same
adverbial meaning is, according to GESENIUS-KAUTZSCH, to be
accepted in Jona iv 4 as well.

Secondly, JOÜON remarks [2]) that the interrogative particle *ha* in
many cases may have an exclamatory nuance. He cites Jona iv 4 and
translates the Lord's question to Jona: "Tu es bien en colère!"
According to the foregoing remarks, this seems more according
to the usage of *hêṭēb* in biblical Hebrew. It seems therefore, better
to translate the question of the Lord in Jona iv 4 and 9:

> It seems, you are really angry.

Jona's answer should then be rendered:

> Yes, indeed, I am angry to death.

Or if one would avoid the hebraism "to death" and translate it
as a superlative:

> Yes, indeed, I am most angry.

---

[1]) GES.-K., l.c.
[2]) JOÜON 161b.

DER ZORNESBECHER

VON

H. A. BRONGERS

Unter den vielen bildhaften Ausdrücken, deren das Alte Testament und besonders das Corpus Propheticum sich für Begriffe wie Urteil und Gericht zu bedienen pflegt, (gemeint sind Wendungen wie Seuche, Hunger, Schwert, Exil, usw.) hat die Wendung „der Becher voll schäumenden Weines" oder kürzer „der Becher", der von den zum Untergang Verurteilten bis zur Hefe geleert werden soll, eine besondere Stelle inne. Sehen wir uns das vorliegende Material, das leider ziemlich dürftig ist, an, so fällt sofort auf, daß vor allem dem Propheten Jeremia eine gewisse Vorliebe für die Wendung schwerlich abgesprochen werden kann, mögen der gleiche Ausdruck oder verwandte Formulierungen gegebenenfalls auch bei anderen Propheten nachzuweisen sein [1]. Die Stelle, die sich zwangslos als Ausgangspunkt der Untersuchung nach dem Sinn und Ursprung der Wendung anbietet, ist Jer. xxv 15.16, weil die meisten Exegeten darüber einig sind, daß diese Verse, nebst Hab. ii 16, den ältesten Beleg der Wendung abgeben. Die übliche Übersetzung der Perikope ist folgende: „Denn also spricht zu mir der Herr, der Gott Israels: Nimm diesen Becher Wein voll Zorns von meiner Hand und schenke daraus allen Völkern, zu denen ich dich sende, daß sie trinken, taumeln und toll werden vor dem Schwert, das ich unter sie schicken will." Diese Übersetzung stützt sich auf die Lesung der Syriaca und der Vulgata, die an Stelle des grammatikalisch harten *kōs hayyayin haḥēmāh* für die Lesung *kōs yēn haḥēmāh* optieren. Vielleicht war die ursprüngliche Lesart *kōs* (hayyen) *hazzō't* und ist (*hayyayin*) *haḥēmāh* als erklärende Glosse zu betrachten. In diesem Zusammenhang sei hingewiesen auf die Tatsache, daß LXX hier τὸ ποτήριον τοῦ οἴνου τοῦ ἀκράτου τούτου: *diesen Becher ungemischten Weines* liest. Mit vielen anderen möchte RUDOLPH das Versende *mipnē haḥereb 'ašer 'anōkī šōlēaḥ bēnōtām* als eine Insertion aus V. 27b betrachten. Dem Hitpolel von *gā'aš* begegnen wir noch einmal in xlvi 8, wo dieses Verb verwendet wird für das Wogen des Nilwassers. Das Bild eignet sich besonders gut

---

[1] Jer. xxv 15 ff.; li 7; Ob. xvi; Ez. xxiii 31 ff.; Jes. li 17, 22; Hab. ii 16; Sach. xii 2; Klgl. iv 21; Ps. lxxv 9.

zur Charakterisierung des Beneh- mens eines Trunkenboldes, der von
der einen Strassenseite zur anderen herumtaumelt. Das Hitpolel von
III *hālal* bedeutet irrsinnig sein oder werden, sich wie ein Geistes-
kranker benehmen (1 Sam. xxi 14; Jer. l 38, li 7).

Wiewohl nicht *expressis verbis* erwähnt, wird allgemein angenom-
men, daß es sich hier um eine Vision handelt, ist es doch schwer
vorstellbar, wie sich ein derartiger Auftrag in der alltäglichen Wirklichkeit hätte ausführen lassen. Wir brauchen jedoch hierbei nicht
lange zu verweilen, wie es sich auch erübrigt, besonderen Wert auf
die Liste der Völker zu legen, die diesen Zornesbecher leeren sollen.

Das Bild des Bechers in der Hand Jahwes erscheint auch in Jer. li 7
als symbolische Andeutung der Stadt Babel und weiter in Jes. li 17;
Hab. ii 16; Ps. lxxv 9. Statt *kōs* hat Sach. xii 2 *saf* (Schale).

Der Inhalt des Bechers wird nicht eindeutig angegeben. Akzeptieren
wir die von Rudolph empfohlenen Übersetzung von Jer. xxv 15,
so wäre an einem mit Wein gefüllten Becher zu denken [1]. Die Glosse
hēmāh will jedoch dartun, daß es sich um etwas mehr als Wein handle.
In diesem Zusammenhang muß Ps. lxxv 9 erwähnt werden:

Ja, ein Kelch ist in Jahwes Hand —
schaumender Wein, voller Würze. . .

Hāmar heißt gären, schäumen (Js. xxvii 2; Deut. xxxii 14). Daß
hier jedoch nicht von jungem Wein die Rede ist, erhellt aus Vs 9b,
wo es heißt, daß die *riš'ē 'āreṣ* den Becher bis zur Hefe (*šèmèr*) leeren
sollen. Das kann sich nur auf abgelagerten Wein beziehen. Tatsächlich
sind *šemārīm* alte, abgelagerte Weine (Jes. xxv 6). *Mālē' mèsèk* heißt
reichlich gewürzt. Man war gewöhnt dem Weine Gewürze oder
Honig beizumischen zur Erhöhung des Aromas (Jes. v 22, xix 14;
Spr. ix 2.5). In Ps. Sal. viii 15.16.19 ist jedoch der Zornesbecher mit
ungemischtem Wein (οἶνος ἀκράτος) gefüllt, wie auch in Apok. xiv
10. Das Bild unterlag vielen Wandlungen, wie z.B. erhellt aus Apok.
xviii 6, wo der Stadt Babel zur Bestrafung ihrer Sünden gerade ein
Becher doppelt gemischten Weines dargereicht werden soll. Nur ist
darauf zu achten, daß an allen Stellen, wo von Urteil und Gericht die
Rede ist und der Becher Jahwes ins Gesichtsfeld rückt, der Begriff
Wein immer metaphorisch verwendet wird. So wird in Jes. li 21
nachdrücklich betont, daß diejenigen, die vom Becher Jahwes getrunken haben, nicht vom Wein betrunken geworden sind [2]. Der

---

[1] W. RUDOLPH, *Jeremia*, Tübingen, 1947, S. 140.
[2] Siehe auch Jes. xxix 9; Sach. ix 15.

Becher ist gefüllt mit *ḥēmāh* (Jes. li 17.21), dargestellt als eine flüssige Substanz, die von den Verurteilten wie Wein aus einem Becher getrunken werden soll. Einleuchtend ist hier Hiob xxi 20:

Mit eigenen Augen sollte er sein Unglück sehen
und den Zorn des Allmächtigen trinken.

In Jer. vi 11 begegnen wir dem seltsamen Vorgang, daß der Prophet sich selbst wie ein Faß voll Zornes Jahwes fühlt, das über alle Einwohner Jerusalems ausgegossen werden soll [1]). Wiederum heißt es in vii 20: „Darum so hat Adonay Jahwe gesprochen: siehe mein Zorn und mein Grimm (*'appī waḥ*ᵃ*mātī*) ergießt sich (*nittèkèt*) über diesen Ort, auf die Menschen und auf die Tiere ..." In x 25 fordert der Prophet Jahwe auf, sein *ḥēmāh* auszugiessen über die Völker, die sich für Ihn nicht interessieren (*lō' y*ᵉ*dā'ūkā*) [2]). In den letztgenannten Stellen erstreckt sich jedoch die Übereinstimmung nicht weiter als bis zu der Tatsache, daß die *ḥēmāh* oder *'af* Jahwes als eine Flüssigkeit dargestellt wird. Vom Trinken aus einem Becher ist hier nicht die Rede. An den Stellen, wo dies der Fall ist, hat das Trinken Folgen, die am besten mit Trunkenheit zu vergleichen sind [3]). Das von dem Propheten Jeremia auf Jahwes Geheiß betrunken gemachte Moab soll in sein eigenes Gespei hineinstürzen und sich selbst zum Gespött werden (xlviii 26). Nicht nur fremde Völker werden von Jahwe in dieser Weise lächerlich gemacht, u.U. fällt auch Israel selbst dem gleichen Geschick anheim (Ez. xxiii 32). An dieser Stelle wird der Becher ein Becher des Entsetzens und der Verheerung genannt.

Das Trinken kann aber gelegentlich auch eine Art von Wahnsinn hervorrufen. In diesem Zusammenhang wurde schon auf Jer. li 7 hingewiesen, wo von der Stadt Babel ausgesagt wird, daß sie die ganze Welt tollgemacht hat (*yithōl*ᵉ*lu*). Das Trinken aus dem Becher versetzt die Verurteilten u.U. auch in einen Zustand völliger Betäubung. Der *kōs ḥ*ᵃ*mātō* steht Jes. li 17 in Parallele zu dem Taumelkelch (*qubba'at hattar'ēlāh*). Vs. 22 ist ein Beweis dafür, daß *kōs* und *qubba'at* Wechselworte sind [4]). Sach. xii 2 macht Jahwe Jerusalem zur Taumel-

---

[1]) Vgl. Hos. v 10; Ps. lxix 25.
[2]) Siehe auch Jer. xlii 18, xliv 16 (*nātak*); Ez. xiv 19, xx 8, xxii 22, xxx 15, xxxvi 18 (*šāfak*).
[3]) Stellen wie Jes. lxiii 6 und Nah. iii 11 sind hinsichtlich des unsicheren Textbestandes besser außer Acht zu lassen.
[4]) Auch in Ugarit (1 Aqht. 216) werden *qubba'at* und *kōs* promiscue verwendet.

schale für alle Nachbarvölker [1]). Hat an diesen Stellen das Trinken
aus dem Becher Jahwes noch den Charakter einer zeitbedingten
und vorübergehenden Strafe — von einer Berauschung kann man
sich ja noch erholen —, in den nunmehr zu besprechenden Stellen ist
das bestimmt nicht mehr der Fall. Ob. xvi heißt es in einer an Israel
gerichteten Heilsprophetie, daß die Völker als Strafe für alles, was
sie Israel im Laufe der Zeiten angetan, unaufhörlich (*tāmīd*) trinken
werden und schwelgen (*welāʿu*) und werden sollen, als seien sie nie
gewesen (*wehāyu kelōʾ hāyu*). Das Trinken führt hier demnach den
Tod herbei. Inhaltlich handelt es sich hier um den völligen Untergang
der Bedränger Israels, und zwar im Rahmen des Tages Jahwes (v 15),
der diesmal für Israel das Heil kündet.

Mit dieser Stelle ist Jer. xxv 27 zu vergleichen, wo Jahwe an die
Feindesvölker die Einladung ergehen läßt: „trinket, daß ihr trunken
werdet und speiet und hinfallet und nicht wieder aufsteht von wegen
des Schwertes, das ich zwischen euch sende". Auch hier ist das
Trinken metaphorisch als die völlige Vernichtung dieser Völker
zu betrachten. Jer. li 39 begegnen wir einer ähnlichen Situation. Hier
verspricht Jahwe, daß er den Babyloniern ein Mahl bereiten und sie
trunken machen werde, daß sie „umsinken" (leg. *yeʿullāfu* pro
yaʿalōzu), in ewigen Schlaf sinken und nicht mehr erwachen (vgl.
auch das sekundäre v 57). Daß auch hier das absolute Ende beab-
sichtigt wird, beweist die angehängte Metapher: „ich schleppe sie
wie Lämmer zur Schlachtbank". Zu beachten ist auch Jer. xlix 13, wo
Jahwe in einer Prophetie über Edom das Trinken aus dem Becher
erläutert im Drohwort: „ich habe bei mir geschworen: zum Entsetzen,
zur Schmach, zur Öde und zum Fluch [2]) soll Bozra werden, und alle
seine Städte sollen zu ewigen Ruinen werden" [3]). Schließlich ist
die Perikope von den gefüllten Weinkrügen (Jer. xiii 12-14) zu
erwähnen, wo der Gottesspruch lautet: „siehe ich fülle mit Trunkenheit alle Bewohner dieses Landes..., die Könige, die auf dem
Throne Davids sitzen, und die Priester und die Propheten und alle
Bewohner Jerusalems. Sie werden sich dann gegenseitig zerschmet-

---

[1]) In Ps. lx 5 wird die Klage erhoben, daß Jahwe dem Volk Taumelwein zu
trinken gegeben hat. In Jes. xix 14 heißt es, daß Jahwe den Beamten von Zoan
einen Schwindelgeist (*ruʿah ʿiwʿīm*) eingegeben hat, infolgedessen sie Ägypten
irreführen. Das Versende „wie ein Trunkener torkelt" zeigt, daß man auch hier
den Taumel mit dem Rausch der Betrunkenheit gleichgestellt hat. Vgl. auch
Jes. xxviii 7.

[2]) *Leḥōreb* wohl als Dittographie zu vermerken (deest in lxx).

[3]) Das *Wāw* vor *liqlālāh* möchten wir als ein *Wāw explicativum* betrachten.

tern, und zwar die Väter zugleich mit den Söhnen". Gemeint ist, daß wie es unter Betrunkenen leicht zu Balgereien kommt, auch die Bewohner Jerusalems, nachdem Jahwe sie berauscht gemacht hat, einander in gegenseitigen Kämpfen vernichten werden [1]).

Dieser Musterung des leider nicht sehr ergiebigen Materials möchten wir nunmehr eine Übersicht der Versuche folgen lassen, die in der Vergangenheit unternommen worden sind mit dem Zweck, die Herkunft dieser Metapher aufzudecken. Welcher ist der „Sitz im Leben" dieses Zornesbechers? Ist die bildliche Rede als genuin israelitisch zu betrachten oder haben wir es mit einer Entlehnung aus dem Ausland zu tun? Mit dieser Frage hat Hugo GRESSMANN sich zweimal in seinem Leben befaßt. Das erste Mal im Jahre 1905 und zwar im Rahmen seines Aufsatzes *Der Ursprung der israelitisch-jüdischen Heilserwartung* und dann noch einmal, 1927, in einem Beitrag zu der Sellin-Festschrift, unter dem Titel *Der Festbecher*. In der erstgenannten Veröffentlichung ist die Folgerung, daß aufgrund der Tatsache, daß in Jer. xxv 15 ff. die Vorstellung des Trinkens vom Becher Jahwes und das Bild vom fressenden Schwert schon miteinander verschmolzen sind, davon auszugehen ist, daß die bildliche Rede schon in den Tagen Jeremias abgeschliffen war und folglich nicht als von diesem Prophet geprägt betrachtet werden kann. Die Metapher stütze sich auf ein viel höheres Alter. Mit dieser Auffassung erklärten sich bald viele Ausleger einverstanden. Dennoch mutet es ein wenig naiv an, wenn GRESSMANN behauptet, das Bild des vom Wein gefüllten Bechers ertrage sich kaum mit der vom Propheten gemalten Lage: „Vom Wein kann man zwar trunken werden, speien und hinfallen, aber man steht wieder auf, man stirbt nicht davon, noch gerät man durch ihn in Raserei. Der Wein ist überhaupt völlig ungeeignet, das Unheil zu symbolisieren, welches er hier symbolisieren soll. Denn er ist in erster Linie ein köstlicher Trank, ein Freudenspender und Sorgenlöser, und er behält diesen Charakter trotz der unangenehmen Wirkungen, die sich an den übermäßigen Genuss knüpfen" (S. 131). GRESSMANN übersieht hierbei jedoch, daß es sich in den einschlägigen Stellen niemals um Wein ohne weiteres handelt. Selbst da, wo die bildliche Rede noch möglichst lange beibehalten wird, legt man Wert darauf, zu erwähnen, daß der Wein durch Beimischung von bestimmten Gewürzen eine derartige Wirkung bekommen hat, daß die Folgen des Trinkens nicht mehr als normal

---

[1]) W. RUDOLPH, a.a.O. S. 81.

zu betrachten sind. In weitaus den meisten Fällen zeigt sich, daß der Becher mit *ḥēmāh* oder *'af* Jahwes gefüllt worden ist.

An allen diesen Stellen haben wir es nach GRESSMANN mit einem *terminus technicus* zu tun. Der Becher ist nur, wie das neutestamentliche ποτήριόν, eine andere Benennung für Unheil (Mt. xx 22, xxvi 39). Hier erhebt sich die Frage nach der Herkunft des Bildes. Zur Beantwortung der Frage möchte GRESSMANN von der Stelle Jes. xxv 16 ausgehen. Die hier erwähnte Mahlzeit, zu der alle Völker der Welt eingeladen werden, gehe auf eine sehr alte Vorstellung zurück, nämlich auf die Feste, die im Tempel begangen wurden in der Gestalt einer Mahlzeit, wobei Jahwe selbst Gastgeber war: „Beim Hauptfest, das nach der Weinlese stattfand, zogen die Scharen . . . in die Festhallen der Heiligtümer (1 S. ix 22; Jes. xxx 29). Wenn dann der Festbecher, der Becher Jahves, von Hand zu Hand gereicht ward, herrschte ausgelassene Freude . . ." (S. 134).

Dieser unter den Gästen herumgehende Festbecher ist nach G. von den Propheten ins Groteske verdreht worden. Für sie ist der Tag Jahwes ein Unheilstag und folglich wandelt sich bei ihnen das Bild der Ausgelassenheit in ein Bild des Entsetzens: „Auch sie stellen . . . jenen Tag als ein Opferfest dar, an dem der Becher Jahves kreist, aber sie übertreiben die Wirkungen des Weines, als würde ein Rauschtrank oder gar Giftwasser von Jahve kredenzt" (S. 135).

In diesem Aufsatz wird also versucht, den Hintergrund des Bildes aus einer genuin israelitischen Lage heraus aufzuhellen. In der Abhandlung von 1927 ist dies nicht mehr der Fall. Hier schaut G. eifrig nach babylonischen Parallelen um. Nachdem er darauf hingewiesen hat, daß der Becher, der den Tod herbeiführt, als notwendiges Pendant den Leben spendenden Becher neben sich haben muß, weist er auf Beispiele aus dem mesopotamischen Kulturkreis hin. Tatsächlich begegnen wir hier in der bildenden Kunst gelegentlich Göttern, die in der rechten Hand einen Becher oder eine Schale festhalten. In diesem Zusammenhang weist G. auf das Weihbecken Gudeas hin, das eine Göttin mit zwei Lebensbechern in ihren Händen zeigt [1]. Seiner Meinung nach sind die Vorstellungen von Lebens- und Todeswassern seit uralten Zeiten in Babylonien bekannt gewesen. Daher wurde der Becher das „Rangzeichen" des höchsten Gottes, des Schicksalgottes, des Herrn über Leben und Tod, zuerst des Individuums, später auch der Völker. „Daher ist es schwerlich ein Zufall,

---

[1] E. UNGER, *Sumerische und akkadische Kunst*, Breslau, 1926, Abb. 47.

wenn Jeremia (xxv 15 ff.), genau so wie Gudea den Schicksalsbecher aus der Hand des Weltengottes empfängt, von dem alle Nationen abhängen" (S. 61). Soweit GRESSMANN. Wir werden später auf seine Auseinandersetzungen Bezug nehmen.

Auch bei P. VOLZ (*Der Prophet Jeremia*, 1928, S. 392 ff.) spielt das Schicksalsmotiv eine große Rolle, mag er es in auch einer anderen Richtung herausarbeiten. V. möchte die Herkunft des Bildes von dem Gebrauch, der in der Mantik vom Becher gemacht wird, herleiten und erinnert an Gen. xliv 5, wo vom Becher Josephs die Rede ist. „Der Becher als Weissagungsmittel ist die Schicksalsmacht, und so entsteht der Gedanke, daß der Becher das Geschick darstellt und das Trinken des Bechers die Wirkung des Schicksals bedeutet und bringt...". Wir können uns kaum dem Eindruck entziehen, daß hier versucht wird, den Sinn der einen Metapher mittels einer anderen aufzuhellen. Hat doch der mit Wasser und Öl gefüllte Becher, woraus die Zukunft gedeutet werden soll, einen ganz anderen Sitz im Leben als der mit Wein gefüllte Becher in Jer. xxv 15 und in den anderen von uns aufgeführten Stellen [1]). Der Inhalt dieses Bechers ist todbringendes Gift und wer daraus trinkt, muß auf sein baldiges Ende gefaßt sein. Dieser Becher steht völlig für sich da, weshalb die von V. vorgenommene Verbindung mit dem Weissagungsbecher etwas forciert anmutet.

Mit dieser mantischen Interpretation läßt sich die Auffassung Hans SCHMIDTS (*Die Psalmen*, Tübingen, 1935) und anderer, die den in Ps. lxxv 9 erwähnten Becher von dem in Num. v 11 beschriebenen Ordal aus erklären wollen, vergleichen. S. geht dabei soweit, daß er aus diesem Ordal ein Giftordal herausbekommt. Gegen diese Interpretation erheben sich dieselben Einwände, die schon gegen Volz hervorgebracht worden sind. Ist es doch ziemlich klar, daß das Trinken des mit heiligem Wasser und Staub des Stifthüttenbodens gefüllten Bechers der des Ehebruches verdächtigten Frau nicht unbedingt den Tod herbeizuführen braucht. Sie ist nicht zum Trinken des Giftbechers verurteilt worden. Es handelt sich um ein Ordal, das die Schuld oder Unschuld der Frau zutage bringen soll. Damit gibt es auch eine Chance, daß die Frau heil davonkommt. Dagegen ist in den von uns besprochenen Stellen die Folge des Trinkens vom Bechers im voraus zu bestimmen. Wer zum Trinken dieses Bechers verurteilt worden ist, weiß daß er hoffnungslos dem Tode ausgeliefert ist. Hier gibt es keine einzige Chance mehr.

---

[1]) Der in Ps. xvi 5 erwähnte Becher hat eine ganz andere Bedeutung. Er diente zum Werfen der Lossteine.

In die juristische Sphäre versetzt uns die Auffassung anderer Gelehrten, die den Zornesbecher als den Giftbecher, der auf richterlichen Befehl von dem Verurteilten geleert werden soll, betrachten möchten. Jahwe reicht dem Beteiligten den Zornesbecher als Richter dar. Der Kronzeuge ist hier wieder Ps. lxxv 9.

L. GOPPELT bemerkt zu dieser Stelle: „In der Hand des heiligen und gerechten Bundesgottes wird der Becher des Schicksals zum Gerichtsbecher. Der Becher Jahwes ist Bild der richtenden Geschichtsmächtigkeit Gottes oder seiner Gerichtsmacht" [1].

Hierbei soll aber beachtet werden, daß, soweit wir wissen, das Trinken des Giftbechers zur Vollstreckung der Todesstrafe im israelitischen Recht nicht vorgesehen war, wodurch GOPPELTs These den Boden entzogen wird.

In diesem Zusammenhang sei auch auf den von DE LIAGRE BÖHL zu dieser Stelle vorgetragenen Kommentar hingewiesen. Schon in 1939 hatte mein verehrter Lehrmeister in einer Besprechung des Rituals VAT 10126 (= KAR 214) in *JEOL* 6, 110 ff. unsere Aufmerksamkeit auf die Übereinstimmung zwischen der in diesem Ritual geschilderten Göttermahlzeit und dem Inhalt der israelitischen Stellen, womit wir uns jetzt befassen, gelenkt. In seinem Psalmenkommentar bemerkt er: „Der Dichter spielt in V. 8 ff. auf einen eigentümlichen Brauch im assyrischen Kult an, dem anscheinend unter Manasse in dem Tempel Jerusalems ein Platz eingeräumt worden war. Zu den Feierlichkeiten anläßlich des Neujahrfestes (Thronbesteigungsfest) gesellte sich dort das Göttermahl: ein Trinkgelage, zu dem alle Götter, von ihren Statuen und Symbolen repräsentiert, vom Hauptgott Assur eingeladen waren." Nach DE LIAGRE BÖHL ließe sich Ps. lxxv 9 im Lichte dieser Beobachtung derart verstehen, daß nicht der Gott der assyrischen Herrscher, sondern Jahwe selbst alle Völker samt ihren Göttern einladen wird, um ihnen den mit Wein gefüllten Becher darzureichen. Dabei wird es sich aber herausstellen, daß ihnen kein Freudenbecher kredenzt wird, sondern ein Zornesbecher, eine Taumelschale, die sie bis zur Hefe leeren sollen, bis sie am Ende dahinsinken [2]. Davon abgesehen aber, daß in diesem Psalm zwar von einem Becher die Rede ist, *expressis verbis* jedoch nicht ausgesagt wird, daß dieser mit einer Mahlzeit verbunden war, sei noch darauf hingewiesen, daß die angebliche Parallele inzwischen schon erheblich an Überzeugungs-

---

[1] L. GOPPELT, in: *Th. Wb.* VI, 150, s.v.
[2] F. M. Th. BÖHL, *De Psalmen*, II, Groningen, 1947, S. 134 ff.

kraft eingebüßt hat. In seiner These über das assyrische Königsritual hat R. FRANKENA nämlich nachgewiesen, daß bei der in diesem Ritual erwähnten Göttermahlzeit nicht der Hauptgott Aššur Gastgeber ist, sondern der König selbst, der dieses Mahl anläßlich seiner Thronbesteigung den Göttern Assyriens anbietet, in der Hoffnung, daß diese ihm, von dieser Geste gerührt, „alles, was lang, viel und weit ist" gewähren werden [1]. Aus der Tatsache, daß Aššur nicht genannt ist unter den Göttern, die zum Initialtrunk eingeladen werden, meinte DE LIAGRE BÖHL damals schließen zu können, daß Aššur hier selber Gastgeber war. LANDSBERGER möchte aber die Omission von der Tatsache her erklären, daß Aššur schon unter Šamši-Addu I Enlil gleichgestellt worden war. Das col. I, r 30 aufgeführte *e-am-kur-kur-ra* wäre also als den Tempel Aššurs zu betrachten [2].

H. RINGGREN möchte den Sitz im Leben des Zornesbechers ganz bestimmt im Kult suchen (*Vredens Kalk*, Svensk exegetisk Årsbok XVIII, 1953, 19 ff.). Er weist darauf hin, daß einerseits das Bild des Bechers die Strafe Gottes oder das Unglück als einen Taumel, der den Beteiligten erfaßt und hilflos macht, darstellt, andererseits aber auf das zugeteilte Geschick abzielt und so ein Bild des Schicksals wird. Für die Deutung des Rausches schließt R. sich der Meinung WIDENGRENS an, der hierin ein Tammuz-Motiv aufdecken möchte [3]. Daß es bis heute noch nicht gelungen wäre, das Rausch-Motiv in den Tammuz-Texten nachzuweisen, daran hätte vor allem die Tatsache schuld, daß man dieser Möglichkeit während der Übersetzung keine Rechnung getragen hatte. Die Deutung WIDENGRENS wurde angeregt von der Stelle Ps. lxxviii 65, wo es heißt:

Da erwachte Adonay aus einem Schlaf,
wie ein vom Wein übermannter Held [4].

Schlaf und Betäubung weisen beide auf die Ohnmacht des Gottes im Zustand der Erniedrigung hin [5]. Schon an sich darf, nach W.,

---

[1]) R. FRANKENA, *Tākultu, De sacrale maaltijd in het assyrische ritueel*, Leiden, 1954, S. 45.

[2]) B. LANDSBERGER, *Balkan*, Belleten XIV, 54, 250 ff.

[3]) G. WIDENGREN, *Sakrales Königtum im Alten Testament und im Judentum*, 1955, S. 67 ff.

[4]) Vielleicht besser statt *mitronēn*, *mitromēm* zu lesen: wie ein Held, der aus dem (Rausch des) Wein(es) erwacht.

[5]) Auch H. J. KRAUS (*Die Psalmen*, z.St.) möchte den Sitz des Lebens dieses Verses im Kult suchen: „Die Vorstellung vom Erwachen Jahwes könnte auf Anschauungen des kanaanäischen Kultes vom Schlaf der Gottheit Bezug nehmen (vgl. 1 Kö xviii 27)."

diese Stelle als ein Beweis für das Vorkommen des Motivs in Israel
gelten und für die Assoziation mit dem Kreis der Tammuz-Motive.
Hieraus schließt RINGGREN: „Der Rausch ist also ein Chaosmotiv,
das eingebettet ist in den Neujahrsriten, die ihrerseits durch die
Ideologie der Tammuz-Religion gekennzeichnet sind. Er erscheint
in unseren Texten aber in zwei Zusammenhängen, teils mit der
Erniedrigung des König-Gottes verbunden, teils mit dem Gericht
über die Feinde''.

Für die Interpretation des Bechers als Schicksalssymbol ruft auch
RINGGREN, wie viele andere, Babylonische Texte zu Hilfe. Die dritte
Tafel des babylonischen Schöpfungsepos enthält, so betont er, einen
Passus, worin die Götter zum Schmaus zusammentreffen und nachher
das Geschick Marduks bestimmen:

> Die großen Götter allesamt, die das Schicksal bestimmen,
> traten vor Anšar, machten voll den Saal;
> sie herzten sich, traten zusammen, redeten mit einander,
> setzten sich am Tisch, aßen das Brot und kosteten den Wein,
> schanken sich den süßen Most in ihre Becher ein.
> Beim Biertrinken erfreute sich ihr Leib.
> Eine schreckliche Zügellosigkeit stieg in ihre Herzen empor;
> für Marduk, ihren Retter, das Geschick bestimmten sie.

Nach R. haben wir es hier mit einem genuinen Ritus des babylonischen Neujahrsfestes zu tun. Ein sakrales Festmal mit reichlichem
Weingenuß sollte der Schicksalsbestimmung vorangegangen sein
oder deren Hintergrund gebildet haben. Anzunehmen wäre also, daß
ein spezieller Becher mit der eigentlichen Schicksalsbestimmung
verbunden war. Die Frage ist nun ob wir berechtigt sind auch für
Israel einen solchen Brauch zu vindizieren. In diesem Zusammenhang
möchte R. darauf hinweisen, daß NYBERG die Aufmerksamkeit auf
eine Hosea-Stelle (Hos. vii 5) gelenkt hat, die einen derartigen Ritus
zu enthalten scheint: „Den Tag unseres Königs beginnen die Fürsten
damit, daß sie sich erhitzen vom Wein, dessen Gewalt die Schwätzer
hinreißt'' [1]). R. bemerkt hierzu: „Der Tag des Königs weist sicherlich
auf das Neujahrsfest hin und aus der Stelle ist zu entnehmen, daß
das Weintrinken mit der Begehung des Festes verbunden war''.
So weit RINGGREN, der uns leider von der Richtigkeit seiner Ausführungen nicht hat überzeugen können. Auch hier begegnen wir

---

[1]) Statt „sie schwächen'' mit den Versionen *bēḫellu* zu lesen.

noch einmal der bekannten Beweisführung der skandinavischen ritualistischen Schule, die jede beliebige Hypothese von einer anderen unterbauen läßt. Nachdem zuerst das Berauschungsmotiv für die Tammuz-Religion postuliert worden war, erfolgt jetzt die Verbindung dieser Liturgie mit den alttestamentlichen Becher-Stellen. Unbeachtet bleibt dabei, daß in Israel der Becher nicht von Jahwe geleert wird und folglich seine von den Skandinaviern behauptete Erniedrigung völlig dahinfällt, und weiter, daß in den einschlägigen Texten nur von einer Darreichung des Bechers an die israelfeindlichen Völker die Rede ist. Die Exegese der Bibelstellen, die für die Aufrechterhaltung der These herangeführt werden, mutet daher nicht gerade überzeugend an. Die Lage in Ps. lxxviii 65 ist vielmehr dahin zu deuten, daß Adonay hier als ein Soldat erscheint, der sich nach der Schlacht am erbeuteten Wein gütlich getan hat und nur mühsam vom Rausche erweckt werden kann. Mag diese bildliche Rede uns Modernen zuwider sein, es ist genügend bekannt, daß die alttestamentlichen Autoren vor oft sehr kühnen Gleichnissen nicht zurückschrecken, auch dann nicht, wenn Jahwe selbst Subjekt ist. Es erübrigt sich daher anzunehmen, der Psalmist habe einen Ritus der Tammuz-Liturgie im Sinne gehabt. Unter dasselbe Verdikt fällt die Exegese von Hos. vii 5, wo die Wendung *yōm malkēnū* auf das Neujahrsfest bezogen wird und das Weintrinken als ein essentielles Detail der Feier erscheint. Man kann aber nicht umhin anzuerkennen, daß die Wendung *yōm malkēnū* befriedigender als den Geburtstag des Königs gedeutet werden kann.

Angesichts des rein hypothetischen Charakters der RINGGRENschen Auseinandersetzungen ist sein Versuch, die Herkunft des Bechermotivs vom Kult her zu erklären, als mißlungen zu betrachten.

So weit das Literaturverzeichnis, dem wir jedoch noch einige Bemerkungen beigeben möchten. Es ist auffallend, daß so viele Autoren das Bechermotiv sozusagen vom Mahlzeitsmotiv absorbieren lassen und das Kosten des Bechers höchstens als ein Detail der Mahlzeit anzuerkennen bereit sind. Unserer Meinung nach haben wir es hier jedoch mit zwei selbständigen Motiven zu tun, mögen sie auch, wie wir noch sehen werden, inhaltlich miteinander verwandt sein. Genau so bemerkenswert ist die häufige Heranziehung von babylonischen Parallelen, wobei mehr Wert auf angebliche Übereinstimmung als auf die Unterschiede gelegt wird, ein Verfahren, das sich, wie wir gesehen haben, gerächt hat und schon im voraus den Verdacht der Willkür hervorrufen mußte.

In unseren vorangehenden Auseinandersetzungen blieb die bildende Kunst noch unbeachtet. Es gilt jetzt diese Lücke auszufüllen. Leider muß auch hier wieder die Klage über die Dürftigkeit des Materials laut werden. Die Rollsiegel sollen hier zuerst herangezogen werden. Es handelt sich um die Vorstellung eines stehenden oder sitzenden Gottes oder Königs (die Figur ist nicht immer genau zu bestimmen), der in der rechten Hand einen Becher oder eine Trinkschale festhält. Da auf diesen Siegeln ein *legendum* immer fehlt, kann der Sinn der Vorstellung nur erraten werden. Weiter gibt es einige Reliefs in den assyrischen Königspalästen, worauf der König, am Tisch liegend, mit einem Becher in der rechten Hand dargestellt ist. Hier bietet die Interpretation selbstverständlich keine Schwierigkeiten. Andererseits tragen sie zur Deutung des einschlägigen Problems nicht das Geringste bei. Merkwürdig sind jedoch zwei Vorstellungen, denen wir uns nun zuwenden möchten. Die erste ist ein Detail des wohlbekannten schwarzen Obeliskes Salmanassars III (859-824). Auf diesem Relief ist der König aufrecht stehend dargestellt, mit dem knieenden Jehu von Israel zu seinen Füßen. In seiner rechten Hand hält er eine Trinkschale, während seine Linke den Griff seines Schwertes umklammert [1]. Der zweiten Vorstellung, die sich in vielen Punkten mit der ersteren berührt, begegnen wir auf einer Stele Asarhaddons (681-669), aus Sendschirli. Der König erscheint hier überlebensgroß. In seiner rechten Hand hält er einen Becher und mit der linken Hand umklammert er eine Keule. Vor ihm liegen kniend einige Gefangene, die mit gehobenen Händen zu ihm aufblicken. Damit die königliche Würde und Majestät möglichst eindrucksvoll hervortreten möge, hat der Künstler die beiden Gefangenen, die, es sei nebenbei bemerkt, auch unter sich stark in Größe differieren, ganz klein dargestellt [2].

Die beiden Vorstellungen bieten also die auffallende Kombination Trinkschale/Becher — Gefangene. Nun erhebt sich die Frage nach der Interpretation dieses Faktums. Sie erinnern stark an Ps. lxxv 9:

Ja, ein Kelch ist in Jahwes Hand —
schäumender Wein, voller Würze;
und er reicht 'von einem zum andern',
auch seine Hefen müßen sie schlürfen.

Bei näherem Zusehen scheint sich jedoch kaum eine Parallele zu ergeben, weist doch nichts daraufhin, daß die Schale oder der Becher

---

[1] B. Meissner, *Babylonien und Assyrien*, I, Heidelberg, 1920, Taf. Abb. 29.
[2] *Ebenda*, Taf. Abb. 38.

gleich den Gefangenen darzureichen ist. Im Gegenteil, auf der Stele
Sendschirlis scheint Asarhaddon selbst im Begriff, den Becher zu
leeren. Das Totalbild der Darstellung erlaubt jedoch kaum eine
Deutung der Geste, es sei denn, daß wir uns damit begnügen anzunehmen, der König bringe einen Toast auf seinen Sieg aus. Sind wir
aber der Meinung, diese Deutung sei als all zu banal abzulehnen,
verbleibt noch die Möglichkeit, den Becher als Abzeichen der
Königswürde aufzufassen. Es ist z.B. seltsam, daß, wo in diesen
Abbildungen die Waffe des Königs immer wechselt (Schwert, Keule,
Bogen), der Becher oder die Trinkschale immer da ist. Über mehr als
eine Vermutung kommen wir hier aber nicht hinaus.

Angesichts der Tatsache, daß auch die bildende Kunst Babyloniens
und Assyriens zum Beschaffen brauchbarer Parallelen außerstande zu
sein scheint, ist es an der Zeit, zum alttestamentlichen Material
zurückzukehren und nachzugehen, ob das Bechermotiv sich doch
nicht mit mehr Aussicht auf Erfolg von Israel selbst her verstehen
ließe. Leider ist hier im voraus zu befürchten, daß die Aussicht auf
Erfolg sich als überaus klein erweisen wird. Schon bei der Besprechung von Ob. xvi erhob WEISER die Klage: „Die Herkunft dieser
vielleicht auf mythologische Wurzeln zurückgehenden Vorstellung
vom göttlichen Zornesbecher, der den Tod bringt, ist nicht mehr
zu ermitteln" [1]. Ebenso pessimistisch urteilte Th. KLAUSER in
seinem Aufsatz „Becher", in RAC II, S 48: „Wie dies wohl wesentlich
eschatologische Motiv entstand, ist noch ungeklärt".

Erscheinen also die Aussichten auf ein erfolgreicheres Resultat als
nicht gerade vielversprechend, so möchten wir doch die Aufmerksamkeit auf einige Aspekte lenken, die in den besprochenen Veröffent-
lichungen vernachlässigt worden sind. Zwei Umstände sind unserer
Meinung nach daran schuld, daß die Forschung auf die falsche
Fährte geraten ist. Einmal dadurch, daß einige Gelehrten sich von
der Tatsache, daß in den Texten von einem mit Wein gefüllten
Becher die Rede ist, haben verführen lassen, den Sitz des Lebens
dieses Bechers in einer etwaigen Mahlzeit oder einem Gelage zu
suchen und zweitens dadurch, daß es ihnen, nachdem sie diese
falsche Richtung eingeschlagen hatten, nicht mehr vergönnt war, die
Einsicht zu gewinnen, daß es sich in allen Becherstellen nur um eine
Symbolsprache handelt.

Es ist von der *ḥēmāh* Jahwes die Rede. Es hat sich schon heraus-

---

[1] A. WEISER, *Das Buch der zwölf kleinen Propheten*, Göttingen, 1949, S. 186.

gestellt, daß man sich diese *ḥēmāh* als eine flüssige Substanz vorstellte, die entweder auf die Verurteilten ausgeschüttet (*šāfak*, *nātak*), oder ihnen zum Trinken dargereicht wurde (Hi. xxi 20). Im letzten Falle wäre dabei am ersten an eine Darreichung mittels eines Bechers zu denken. Hier konnte man aber nicht umhin den abstrakten Begriff *ḥēmāh* zu konkretisieren, wozu die Vorstellung des vom gewürzten Wein gefüllten Bechers, dessen Genuß dem Beteiligten unangenehm war, verhalf. Faktisch hatte der Becher damit schon den Charakter des Giftbechers bekommen (Hab. ii 15) [1]).

Man kann auch nicht umhin, ein offenes Auge zu haben für das Gewicht, das dem symbolischen Sprachgebrauch in den einschlägigen Texten beizumessen ist. Daß das biblische Hebräisch in einer erstaunlichen Abundanz Metaphern und Symbole zu verwenden gewohnt ist, darf als allgemein anerkannt gelten. Nicht alles Ausgesagte soll auf die Goldwaage gelegt werden. Demzufolge ist u.E. der von Jahwe mit *ḥēmāh* gefüllte Unheilsbecher genau so symbolisch zu interpretieren wie z.B. der mit Wein gefüllte Heilsbecher in Ps. xxiii 5. Auch dieser Becher ist faktisch niemals dargereicht worden. Er bringt, gleich wie der mit herrlichen Speisen beladene Tisch, von dem in demselben Vers die Rede ist, das Glück und die Wonne zum Ausdruck, womit der Dichter beschenkt worden ist.

Besonders hoch zu werten ist auch die Konstatierung, daß das Unheilsbechermotiv im A.T. nicht vereinzelt dasteht, sondern seine Stelle im ganzen Komplex der Vorstellungen hat, die das Erleiden des Zornes Jahwes mit dem Bild des gezwungenen Kostens von giftigen Speisen und Getränken symbolisieren. Neben der Gegenüberstellung Heils-/Unheilsbecher begegnen wir auch der Antithese Heils-/Unheilsmahl. Ein gutes Beispiel der ersteren bietet Jes. xxv 6 ff., wo angekündigt wird, daß Jahwe Zebaot auf dem Zionsberg für alle Völker der Erde ein Mahl von fetten Speisen und süßen Weinen bereiten wird. Wäre hier noch die Möglichkeit eines wirklichen Mahles zu erwägen, schwieriger wird es schon, das Gleiche für sein Gegenstück, das Unheilsmahl, anzunehmen. Es handelt sich um Stellen, wo Menschen, die den Zorn Jahwes zu erleiden bekommen haben, darüber klagen, daß er sie mit *mēy rōš* getränkt und mit *laʿanāh* gespeist hat [2]). Das häufige Vorkommen dieser Redensart

---

[1]) Vgl. W. Lotz, „Das Sinnbild des Bechers", *Neue Kirchliche Zeitschrift* XXVIII 1917, S. 396-407.

[2]) *La ʿanāh* = artemisia (I. Low, *Die Flora der Juden*, I-IV, 1924-1934, S. 386 ff. Nach *Köhler-Baumgartner Lexikon* ist *rōš* eine unbekannte giftige Pflanze.

(Deut. xxix 17; Am. vi 12; Jer. ix 14, xxiii 15; Hoh. iii 19) läßt
vermuten, daß wir es auch hier wieder mit einem fest geprägten
Ausdruck zu tun haben, der nur bildlich zu interpretieren ist. Einige
dieser Stellen verhelfen dieser Vermutung fast zur Sicherheit:

Jer. ix 14
Darum, so hat Jahwe Zebaot, der Gott Israels, gesprochen:
siehe, ich gebe ihnen Wermut zu essen und Giftwasser zu trinken.
Ich zerstreue sie unter die Völker, die weder sie noch ihre Väter
kannten und sende das Schwert hinter ihnen drein, bis ich sie
aufgerieben habe.

Daß es sich auch hier nur um eine bildliche Rede handeln kann,
die mit der Realität nichts zu tun hat, erhellt aus der Tatsache, daß
das Essen der Wermut und das Trinken des Giftwassers bildlich
verwendet wird für die Erprobungen des Exils und der Kriegs-
gewalt. Hiermit ist zu vergleichen Jer. xxiii 15, wo derselbe Ausdruck
für die Hinrichtung der falschen Propheten erscheint.
Hierzu gehört auch Thr. iii 19:

Zu gedenken meiner Not (ʿanwīy) und Unrast (mᵉrūdī)
ist Wermut und Gift.

Daß es sich auch hier um eine poetische Stilfigur handelt, braucht
nicht weiter hervorgehoben zu werden. Es erübrigt sich nach einem
etwaigen Sitz im Leben auszuschauen.
Wir hoffen gezeigt zu haben, daß die Lage angesichts des Bechermotivs genau dieselbe ist. Aus der Tatsache, daß das Substantiv in
einigen markanten Stellen determiniert erscheint, wird ersichtlich,
daß der Zornesbecher schon bei seiner Ersterscheinung im A.T.
einen klaren metaphorischen Charakter zeigt und offenbar ein
allbekannter Begriff ist. So heißt es Jer. xlix 12 in einem Drohwort
an Edom:

Denn so hat Jahwe gesprochen: siehe, die, denen es nicht
gebührt, den Becher (hakkōs) zu trinken, die müssen ihn trinken,
und da solltest du frei ausgehen?

Und weiter: Jes. li 17:

Mach dich auf, mach dich auf, stehe auf, Jerusalem, die du von
der Hand Jahwes den Becher seines Zorns (ʾet kōs ḥᵃmātō)
getrunken hast . . .

Schließlich Hab. ii 16, wo den Chaldäern angesagt wird:
Auch zu dir kommt rund der Becher in der Rechten Jahwes
(*kōs y^emīn jhwh*), d.h. übler Schmutz auf deine Ehre.

Man muß sich darüber wundern, daß diese Metapher, die sich so
ganz vorzüglich zum Sichtbar- und Fühlbarmachen des Zorns
Jahwes eignete, so spät im prophetischen Sprachidiom vorkommt.
Wie schon hervorgehoben, sind Jer. xxv 25 und Hab. ii 15, 16 als
die ältesten Stellen zu betrachten. Von da an aber ist die Popularität
des Bildes ständig im Wachsen begriffen. Über das N.T. hinaus
(Mark. x 38 par.; Matth. xxvi 42; Joh. xviii 11) hat es sich dann,
sei es als stark abgeschliffene Andeutung für Schmerz und Mühsal
im allgemeinen, bis in die Gegenwart behauptet.

EZEKIEL XIV 1—8

J. SCHONEVELD

In Ez. xiv 1-8 there are a number of expressions that have a concrete meaning, but have not been recognized as such. Even if their literal meaning was sometimes understood they were too rashly given a figurative explanation.

The first expression occurs with minor variations in vss. 3, 4, and 7 [1]). In vs. 3 JHWH says: *hā ʾᵃnāšîm hāʾēllę hęʿᵉlû gillûlêhęm ʿal libbām*. The various translations that have been given are: "these men have raised their idols in their heart" [2]); or: "these men carry their idols in their heart" ("deze mensen dragen hun afgoden in het hart") [3]); or: "these men carry their gods of infamy high in their heart" ("deze mensen dragen hun schandgoden hoog in het hart") [4]); or: "diese Männer hängen ihren Götzen nach, wörtlich: liessen in ihr Herz hinaufkommen" [5]). Of other translations the sense is virtually the same.

With MESNIL DU BUISSON we should here like to plead for taking this expression as a statement of a concrete fact. In an article of "Une tablette magique de la Région du moyen Euphrate" [6]) MESNIL DU BUISSON treats a tablet, 8.2 cm long, 6.7 cm wide, and maximally 2.2 cm thick, having a rounded top and a hole with traces of a suspension chord. This tablet was apparently intended to be worn as an amulet. In a note he comments: „Ezechiel xiv 3 et 7: l'expression *ʿal libbām* "sur son coeur" nous paraît à comprendre ici à la lettre. Les gilloulim étaient sans doute portés sous le vetement" [7]). He does, however, not adduce arguments for this literal interpretation. He is opposed by ZIMMERLI: "so spricht die Parallele 38, 10, auch

---

[1]) The most important variation is that vs. 3 has *ʿal libbām*, whereas vs. 4 and vs. 7 have *ʾęl libbô*. It is not correct to alter *ʾęl* into *ʿal*, as the use of these two prepositions in alternation belongs to the style of Ezekiel. Cf. A. SPERBER, *A Historical Grammar of Biblical Hebrew*, Leiden, 1966, pp. 58-63.

[2]) G. A. COOKE, *The Book of Ezekiel* (I.C.C.C.), Edinburgh, 1936, p. 150.

[3]) Translation of the Netherlands Bible Society (*Nederlands Bijbelgenootschap*).

[4]) *Canisius Translation.*

[5]) W. ZIMMERLI, *Ezechiel* (Biblischer Kommentar — Altes Testament), p. 300.

[6]) An article which appeared in *Mélanges Syriens*, offerts à M. R. DUSSAUD, 1939.

[7]) *Art. cit.* p. 419.

11,5 20, 32, wo *rûᵃḥ* statt *lēb* steht, deutlich dagegen". ZIMMERLI also points to Jes. lxv 17 and to Jer. iii 16, vii 31, and xliv 21 [1]). In all these parallels the operative term is *'ālâ 'al*, which means "to rise in the heart". In the hiph. this would become "to raise in the heart", and the translation in Ez. xiv 3 would be: "they raise their *gillûlîm* in their heart". Although this is not quite impossible, VAN DEN BORN rightly calls this causative a forced construction [2]). But more evidence would be needed to disprove MESNIL DU BUISSON's literal reading.

We shall start from other parallels having the hiph. of *'ālâ* together with an object and an adjunct with *'al*. Several instances of this occur: in 2 Sam. i 24, it says that Saul attached (hiph. of *'ālâ*) ornaments of gold (object) upon (*'al*) their apparel (i.e. on that of the daughters of Israel); in Jos. vii 6; Ez. xxvii 30; Lament. ii 10 people cast up (hiph. of *'ālâ*) dust upon (*'al*) their heads; in Ez. xxxvii 6 JHWH will bring up (hiph. of *'ālâ*) flesh upon the bones; in Amos viii 10 JHWH will bring up sackcloth upon the loins; in 1 Kings x 16 and 17 Salomon put up gold on the shields, in 2 Chron. iii 5, he put up fine gold on fir trees, and in iii 14 he put up cherubim upon the veil of the house of the Lord. So the hiph. of *'ālâ* with object and *'al* means in a most general sense: "to put something upon something else", and this can be carried out in various ways. Thus, here in Ez. xiv the translation should be, that "the elders of Israel have put their *gillûlîm* upon . . .".

But upon what? The answer is: upon (*'al*) *libbām*! The term *lēb* is usually translated as: heart. However, this should not be taken in an anatomical sense, as the pump that causes the blood to circulate through the body. In O.T. no relation can be discovered between the heart and the blood [3]). It is moreover hard to say where exactly in the body they located the heart, and how they pictured it to

---

[1]) ZIMMERLI, *op. cit.*, p. 300.

[2]) A. VAN DEN BORN, *Ezechiël* (De Boeken van het O.T.), Roermond and Maaseik, 1954, p. 88.

[3]) See F. H. VON MEYENFELDT, *Het hart (leb, lebab) in het Oude Testament*, Leiden, 1950, p. 137. In the Gilgamesh epic a connection is made between blood (*damu*) and heart (*libbu*). In xi 294 Gilgamesh says: „*ana mannija ibali damu libbija*": „for whom did blood run out of my heart?" Yet, not here either is meant by *libbu* the heart in its anatomical sense, but in a wider meaning: the blood went out of Gilgamesh' inside. On the basis of this text E. DHORME incorrectly asserts that: „Les anciens n'ignoraient pas qu'il etait le moteur essentiel de la circulation du sang". (E. DHORME, *L'emploi metaphorique des noms de parties du corps en hébreu et en akkadien*, Paris, 1963, p. 113).

themselves. In the Babylonian medical texts published by LABAT [1]), the prognosis of the sick man is made in the order of literally from top to toe, on the basis of the symptoms. Thus the diseases of the *rêš libbi* (i.e. the top of the *libbu*) are dealt with between those of the breast and those of the belly; so the *rêš libbi* is located in between these two. The morbid symptoms also indicate that by *rêš libbi* cannot possibly be meant what we call the region of the heart: "if he has a thickening [?] at his *rêš libbi* and vomits black blood and the temples [of his head] are pressed [?] then he will die. When he has a swelling and a thickening [?] and has black blood [in his motions] then he will die" [2]). By *libbu* in these texts is meant the belly. The diseases of the *libbu* itself among others also show the symptoms named [3]). And what are we to think of the location of the *lēb* when the poet of Ps. xxii 15 says that his *lēb* is melted in the midst of his bowels?

Generally, however, in O.T. the *lēb* is considered to be higher up in the body, namely in the space behind the breast. The heart is noticeable from the energy of life which it gives to man as a whole. When Nabal's heart "died within him" he became as a stone. No less than ten days later he actually deceased [4]). Joab thrust three darts into the *lēb* of Absalom [5]). If it actually was his heart that was meant, one dart would have sufficed; as it is, after the three darts were thrust into his "heart", he still showed signs of life, whereupon ten of Joab's soldiers "smote Absalom, and slew him". A better translation therefore would be: Joab thrust three darts into the *breast* of Absalom. There would then no longer be any need for explanatory comment on this passage like: "according to the present context Absalom is killed twice over", nor for considering, as a consequence, 2 Sam. xviii 11-14 as secondary [6]).

In several other cases, too, the translation "breast" for *lēb* is to be preferred [7]). In Ex. xxviii 29 Aaron bears the breastplate of

---

[1]) René LABAT, *Traité accadien de Diagnostics et Pronostics médicaux*, Paris-Leiden, 1951.

[2]) *Op. cit.* p. 114 f.

[3]) *Op. cit.* p. 120 f.

[4]) 1 Sam. xxv 37f.

[5]) 2 Sam. xviii 14f.

[6]) A. VAN DEN BORN, *Samuël* (De Boeken van het O.T.), Roermond and Maaseik, 1956, p. 195 f.

[7]) See P. JOUÖN, „Locutions Hebraïques avec la preposition ʿal devant leb, lebab", *Biblica*, V, (1924), pp. 49-53.

judgement upon his *lēb*, i.e. his breast. In Nah. ii 8 the women are tabering upon their *lēb*, so on their breast. In the Song of Solomon viii 6 the bride says: "Set me as a seal *'al libbękâ*: i.e. on your breast. Prov. vi 21 should be translated: Bind them (sc. the *miṣwâ* of the father and the *tôrā* of the mother) continually upon your breast (*lēb*), hang them about your neck. "Hang them about your neck" is a figurative expression derived from the habit of hanging trinkets or amulets round the neck; in the same way the "bind them continually upon your breast" "*lēb*" refers with equal concreteness to the custom of wearing amulets on the breast.

When Prov. vii 3 exhorts: "Bind them upon your fingers, write them upon the table of your *lēb*, in the latter clause should be seen, as much as apparently in the former, an allusion to a concrete custom, even if the sens would be figurative here [1]). But what is the table of the breast? Is it the surface of the breast itself? It is thus that the LXX took it, translating ἐπὶ τὸ πλάτος τῆς καρδίας. In that case we have to think of tattooing. But it is equally possible that "breasttable" means a tablet hanging on the breast, in the same way as the Amarna Letters speak of *lêḫu* (= *lêʾu*) *ša tikki*: neck tablets [2]).

The elders of Israel, then, have put their *gillûlîm* on their breasts. But the next question is: in what way? If Mesnil du Buisson thinks of amulets worn under the clothes [3]), it is perhaps on account of 2 Macc. xii 40, which relates how sacred objects devoted to the idols of Jamnia were found under the shirts of killed Jews. However, the elders of Israel, especially when they were at their idolatrous practices, may just as well have worn their *gillûlîm* on their breasts above their clothes, in a manner, comparable to the Babylonian method of hanging amulets with the image of Lamastu round the necks of children [4]). Little Ishtar images were also worn this way.

---

[1]) In Jer. xvii 1 it says that the sin of Judah is engraved with a pen of iron, with a diamond point on the table of their heart and into the horns of their altars. Just as the last part (engraved into the horns of their altars) represents something concrete, so the first part (engraved on the *lûaḥ* of their hearts) must refer to a custom. Judah's sin has been "recorded" on the cultic symbols and through signs or representations applied to the breast. As far as the iron pen and the diamond point are concerned, the custom was to apply the tattooings with needles, sharp burins, which were dipped into the ink (See H. Lilliebörn, *Ueber religiöse Signierung in der Antike*, 1933, p. 15). The LXX has: „engraved on the breast of the heart". The Vulgate: "super latitudinem cordis eorum".

[2]) J. A. Knudtzon, *Die El-Amarna-Tafeln*, I, p. 110 (Tablet no. 14, col. 2, 2).

[3]) *Art. cit.* p. 429.

[4]) B. Meissner, *Babylonien und Assyrien*, Heidelberg, Vol. I, 1920, p. 391, Vol. II, 1925, p. 223.

Of old, trinkets, such as necklaces, could also serve as amulets which were hung round the neck. Excavations have shown that in Palestine amulets were abundantly used, for instance, those of the Horus eye, scarabees and little representations of bulls. In Ez. vii 20 is told that the inhabitants of the country of Israel have made ornaments and images (*šiqqûṣîm*) out of their silver and gold. With the former, amulets may have been meant.

Yet, this is not the only explanation possible. The *gillûlîm* may also have been applied to the breast directly. When Saul put ornaments on the dresses of the Israelitish women, this would mean that these ornaments were hung loose upon the dress or attached to it. But when Solomon put palmtrees and serpentines upon the walls of the big house, what is meant, is reliefwork applied to the cypress wood, in the same way as in Ez. viii 10 all *gillûlîm* of the house of Israel were drawn on, or engraved in (*mᵉchuqqê*) the wall all round. In 2 Chron. iii 14 the same verb, *hiph.* of ʿalâ, with ʿal is used for the application of cherubs on the veil. There it means, as in Ex. xxvi 31, that they were woven into it. Considered in this light the *gillûlîm* put upon the breast could also mean, that they were applied by tattooing.

In the Semitic world itself tattooing has indeed been very customary, and today it still is, for instance, in the Arab world. The symbols tattooed were the sign that one was the property of the god. JHWH set a mark on Cain who was thereby protected by Him [1]). Ezekiel must set a mark on the foreheads of those faithful to JHWH (Ez. ix 4). Jacob's offspring will write upon their hand: (property) of JHWH (Is. xliv 5). JHWH Himself is said to have engraved Zion on the palms of His hand while her walls were continually before Him. (Is. xliv 16). The prophet of Zechariah xiii 6 has scars on his breast, remainders of the incisions that he made for his God. In 1 Kings xx 41 Ahab recognizes a certain man as a prophet, when the latter removes the bandage from above his eyes: apparently a sign then became visible. The expressions in Ex. xiii 9: an ʾôt on the hands and a ẕikkārôn between the eyes (the forehead) probably are reminiscences of the ancient habit of tattooing. In Lev. xix 28 it is expressly forbidden to make incisions into one's flesh and tattoo oneself as a sign of mourning (cf. Lev. xxi 5; Deut. xiv 1).

The wording of the text admits of both interpretations, the wearing

---

[1]) Gen. iv 15.

of amulets as well as the tattooing of the breast. A definite choice cannot be made. But the place of the *gillûlîm* is at any rate the breast in its literal sense.

The second expression that requires a literal, concrete interpretation is that of the elders who have placed their *mikšôl* right opposite themselves (xiv 3, 4, 7). Both the verbs *nātan* in vs. 3 and *śîm* in vs. 4 and 7 first of all command literal meanings. The word *nôkah*, too, points in that direction. But then the term *mikšôl* must also have indicated something concrete. Its actual meaning does not contradict this: in Lev. xix 14 it is forbidden to put a *mikšôl* before a blind person. Here in Ez. xiv it is meant literally as well as figuratively. In vii 19 the manufacture of these gods out of silver and gold is mentioned, a very real thing, but the people will — figuratively — stumble over these idols and their silver and gold will not be able to save them on the day of JHWH's wrath. It will be robbed by strangers to pollute it [1]). This, of course, again refers to the silver and gold of the idols and ornaments. AALDERS quite rightly says: "The stumbling-block which caused them to fall to unrighteousness is here the concrete idol" [2]). But he weakens this interpretation again by writing: "When it says about this: *nāt^enû nôkah p^enêhem* it is questionable whether this should be taken literally, which would imply that they had placed idols in their houses; one might also very well think of a figurative expression, meaning that the images of the gods . . . were . . . always vividly before their eyes" [3]). That he weakens the literal meaning, is owing to the *gillûlîm* that occur in a parallel construction, and in AALDERS' opinion must not be taken literally either ("clung inwardly to the idols") [4]). The literal interpretation is, however, supported by Ez. viii 7-13. There, too, Ezekiel sees the elders engaged in idolatry quite concretely. On Assyrian, Babylonian and Hethitian cylindrical seals the worshipper is represented as standing opposite his god. [5]) Besides these there are many more examples of representations of a worshipper and his god facing each other. We need not even go outside the Book of Ezekiel to find this situation: In the temple Ezekiel sees seventy of the elders of

---

[1]) Ez. vii 21 f.

[2]) G. Ch. AALDERS, *Ezechiël* I, (Commentaar op het O.T.), Kampen, 1955, p. 240.

[3]) *Op. cit.* p. 240.

[4]) *Op. cit.* p. 240.

[5]) Otto WEBER, *Altorientalische Siegelbilder* (Der alte Orient), Leipzig, 1920, *passim*.

Israel standing in the temple while facing the *gillûlîm* portrayed upon the wall, and having each of them a censer in his hand [1]).

The third expression to be examined is *t^epōś ʾet bêt jiśrāʾēl b^elibbām* in vs. 5. In judging the various existing translations, as given below, it should be premised that *tāpaś b^e* never means "to catch in (something)" but "to catch with (something)" or "to catch (someone) by his . . ." or "to catch (something or somebody)" [2]).

The translations of "*t^epōś ʾet bêt jiśrāʾēl b^elibbām*" show many variations: The *Leiden translation* and the *Canisius translation* render this very freely; the former: "to wound the heart of the house of Israel" ("om het hart te wonden van Israëls huis"); the latter: "to wound the house of Israel in the heart" ("om het huis Israëls in het hart te wonden"). AALDERS translates "to catch in the heart" ("in het hart grijpen") [3]). He interprets it as: "to cause a benificial shock which urges [Israel] to conversion". There are also some translations that give a good, literal reading, as, for instance, ZIMMERLI's: "an seinem Herzen zu packen" [4]); VAN DEN BORN's: "in order to catch the house of Israel by the heart" ("om het huis van Israël bij het hart te grijpen") [5]); and BERTHOLET's: "um das Haus Israel am Herzen zu fassen" [6]). COOKE, TROELSTRA and KRAETZSCHMAR give translations very similar to the ones just quoted [7]). In his comment ZIMMERLI starts from the verb *tāpaś*, meaning "das kräftige, gar hart Zupacken bei der Gefangennahme eines Menschen oder eines Tieres". In this way JHWH "behaftet" Israël [8]). ZIMMERLI, however, leaves

---

[1]) Ez. viii 11.

[2]) *Tāpaś* with preposition *b^e* (in qal; niph; pi.) occurs 13 times in O.T. *b^e* indicates an object 7 times (Deut. ix 17; xxi 19; 1 Kings xi 30; Jes. iii, 6; Jer. xxxvii 14; Ez. xxix 7; xxx 21), 5 times it means "with" (Ez. xxi 16; xxi 29; xxix 7; Jer. xxxviii 23; Prov. xxx 28), and twice it means "at, by" (Gen. xxxix 12, Ez. xiv 5). So the successive meanings are: 1. to catch somebody; 2. to catch with e.g. the hand, 3. to catch (somebody) by e.g. his garment or his heart. Outside this enumeration were kept: Ez. xix 4 and 8: "in (*b^e*) their pit he was caught"; and Ps. x 2 "let them be caught in the devices that they had plotted". These prepositions do not belong to *tāpaś*, but indicate the time or the place, at which the catching occurred.

[3]) AALDERS, *op. cit.* p. 241.

[4]) ZIMMERLI, *op. cit.* p. 310.

[5]) VAN DEN BORN, *op. cit.*, p. 88.

[6]) A. BERTHOLET, *Hesekiel* (Handbuch zum A.T.), Tübingen, 1936, p. 50.

[7]) COOKE, *op. cit.* p. 151; A. TROELSTRA, *Ezechiël* I (Tekst en Uitleg), Groningen, 1931, p. 44; R. KRAETZSCHMAR, *Das Buch Ezechiel* (Handbuch zum A.T.), Göttingen, 1900, p. 138.

[8]) ZIMMERLI, *op. cit.* p. 310.

the word *b^elibbām* quite out of account. VAN DEN BORN for an interpretation of the expression points to Gen. xxxix 12, where Potifar's wife catches (from the verb *tāpaś*) Joseph by (*b^e*) his garment. This is quite correct. But he explains: "the purpose is to compel Israel to stay with JHWH, like Joseph with the woman" [1]). In my opinion this is very far-fetched. For VAN DEN BORN generalizes the particular case of Joseph in order to push the expression here in the same direction: Israel has to stay with JHWH. This method is not correct: one can, of course, catch somebody by the hand to conduct him somewhere, but in an other context the same act may be intended to keep someone who slips or stumbles on his legs. Therefore the meaning and purpose of "catching Joseph by his garment" cannot simply be transferred to "catching Israel by the heart", as JHWH does. It is moreover to be doubted whether the idea that Israel is *compelled* (cf. above, AALDERS: "urged") to stay with JHWH is correct. This is not in keeping with Ezekiel's appeal to Israel to be converted. COOKE rightly reads a threat in this expression [2]). HITZIG, on the other hand, views it quite differently again: "Ihr Herz zu rühren und zu bessern" [3]).

The comparison with Gen. xxxix 12 is, in itself, correct. The expressions are perfectly parallel. Just as Potifar's wife catches Joseph by his garment, so does JHWH catch the house of Israel by their *lēb*. Of course, this has a figurative meaning. But before it can be established, the literal meaning of the term should be known. And consequently one wonders how someone can be literally caught by the heart, if by *lēb* an internal organ, or more generally, the inside is meant. If the *lēb* can be caught like a garment, it must again stand for something external: the region of the heart or the breast. JHWH will, in a figurative sense, catch the house of Israel by the breast as one catches somebody by the neck (Job xvi 12: *'āḥaz b^e*) or by the head (2 Sam. ii 16: *ḥzq* hiph. with *b^e*) or by the beard (1 Sam. xvii 35: *ḥzq* hiph. with *b^e*). Now imagine the reaction of somebody who is caught by the breast. It can hardly be experienced otherwise than as a threat, an expression of vehement anger, which will cause in the victim fright and alarm. And that JHWH will catch the house of

---

[1]) VAN DEN BORN, *op. cit*. p. 88.
[2]) COOKE, *op. cit*., p. 151.
[3]) F. HITZIG, *Der Prophet Ezechiel* (Kurzgefasstes exegetisches Handbuch zum A.T.), Leipzig, 1847, p. 94. The same opinion is held by VON MEYENFELDT, *op. cit*., p. 60.

Israel thus, should be related to the fact that they had just applied their *gillûlîm* to their breast. To speak of the *breast* of the *house* of Israel is a strong personification indeed, and to our minds almost a false metaphor, but there is a precedent in a similar image, which we find in Ez. iii 7, where the house of Israel is referred to as having a forehead.

The expression, then, should be interpreted as an agressive act. JHWH will jump at his people because of their idolatry. The imagery is powerful and expressive, and can be compared to Job xvi 12, where Job says that God has taken him by his neck, or to Ps. iii 8, where JHWH is said to have smitten the enemies upon the cheeckbone and broken the teeth of the ungodly, or to Hos. xiii 8, where JHWH is compared to a bear that rends his victim's chest (*segôr libbām*).

The text, however, does not state that it is the house of Israel who have applied the *gillûlîm* of their breast, but only the elders. Why then should JHWH yet catch the house of Israel by the breast? Apparently because the sins of the elders were not restricted to that group. As early as in vs. 4 there is no longer question of the elders only, but of everyone who performs the injustices denounced, while vs. 5b even says that the house of Israel are all estranged from JHWH through their *gillûlîm*. Thus is it quite justified that finally the threat is uttered against the house of Israel as a whole.

The expression *na'ᵃnê lô bî* occurs twice in the pericope, in vs. 4 with the verb in the perfect tense, and in vs. 7 as a participle. ZIM-MERLI says: "Das niph. von *'ānâ* macht Mühe" [1]). As it corresponds with *dāraš*, we should certainly start from the meaning "to answer". But how should the niph.-form be explained and what does it mean? In O.T. a few cases of *'ānâ* niph. have the passive meaning of "to be answered" [2]). But this does not fit in our pericope. Usually the niph. is the reflexive or passive form of the qal. But another possibility is that the niph. is the reflexive or passive of the pi. or hiph. [3]). As

---

[1]) ZIMMERLI, *op. cit.*, p. 301.

[2]) See Job xi 2; xix 7; Proverbs xxi 13.

[3]) P. Paul JOUÖN S. J., *Grammaire de l'Hébreu Biblique*, Rome, 1947, p. 115: "Bien que le nifal soit proprement le réfléchi (et souvent le passif) du *qal*, on le trouve aussi comme le réfléchi (ou passif) du hifil." It does not matter whether the hiph. actually occurs, it might just happen to be absent. Of the verb *ḥarar* (to be glowing), for instance, neither pi. nor hiph. are to be found in O.T. but the niph. has a causative meaning with respect to the qal: to be made to glow, to burn oneself. The restriction is sometimes made, that this phenomenon only

the niph. of ʿānâ must apparently have two meanings, we could here try to start from the hiph. The hiph. would mean: to let (somebody) answer; in the niph. this becomes: to let (somebody) be answered. The translation of these words in vs. 4 and 7 then should be: "I, JHWH, shall let him (*lô*) be answered by Me (*bî*)", or in a somewhat easier construction: "I shall let him have an answer from Me".

It would be much easier still, if we could start from the form *naʿanē* of the Babylonian Talmud Qid. 40b. There the question is posed, which is more important, study or action: "Rabbi Tryphon answered (*naʿanâ*) and said: study; rabbi Akiba answered and said: study; they all answered (*naʿanû*) and said: study". But this text may be a little less than a thousand years younger than that of Ezekiel. However this may be: in the text of Ezekiel, too, *naʿanê* can mean nothing else but that those who come to consult JHWH will receive an answer. But what kind of answer! JHWH will fall upon them.

One more difficulty is the connection of vs. 4 to vs. 5 through *lemaʿan*. With an infinitive this means: "in order to", denoting a purpose. This is the reason why *tepōś ʾet bêt jisrā ʾēl belibbām* has been translated by: "in order that I may catch the house of Israel in the heart". But this translation we had to reject on grammatical grounds, and because the expression should be understood as a threat. JHWH will let the idolators have an answer from Him by catching them by the breast, i.e. by storming violently against them. JHWH's answering does not bring the oracle so much coveted, but, in its stead, a fear-inspiring deed, just as in Ps. lxv 6 God will answer by terrible things. *lemaʿan* does not only serve to indicate the aim, but in certain cases also the result [1]).

Attention has yet to be paid to the first *hāšîbû* of vs. 6. The text runs: *šûbû uehāšîbû mēʿal gillûlêkẹm ûmēʿal tôʿabôtêkẹm hāšîbû penêkẹm.* The word by word translation is: "return and turn away from your idols, and from all your abominations turn away your faces". The first *hāšîbû* requires an object: turn away... (object) from your idols. This "object" could be the same as the one used in the second part: "your faces". COOKE considers this also possible: "and turn

---

occurs in intransitive verbs (H. BAUER-P. LEANDER, *Historische Grammatik der hebräische Sprache*, 1922, p. 289) but the only example of it given by JOUÖN, is precisively the transitive verb *šmʿ* (*op. cit.* p. 115, n. 3).

[1]) P. JOUÖN, *op. cit.* p. 521.

(your faces), supplying in thought the object expressed in cl. b" [1]).
The author may well have left it out on stylitics grounds. The two
parts of the sentence, without *peněkęm*, form a pure chiasm. The
object of both parts is placed at the end, outside the chiasm. Grammatically speaking it is indeed not impossible, though seldom
occurring, that the joint object of two clauses is only named in the
second [2]).

ZIMMERLI sees in *šûbû û hăšîbû* a rhetorical duplication in which,
otherwise than in the second part of the verse, the hiph. only serves
as a variation of the qal [3]). For this he points to Ez. xviii 30, but
apart from the fact that that *locus* is grammatically doubtful, in the
present case we meet the preposition *mē'al*, which recurs in the
second part in a completely parallel way.

The clause in vs. 8: "I will set my face against that man (*bā'îš*)
otherwise only occurs in Lev. xvii 10, xx 3, 5, 6 and xxvi 17; in Jer.
xxi 10 and xliv 11 and in Ez. xv 7. It is always used in a depreciatory
sense.

The translation, then, of the pericope discussed, would have to
run as follows: "When certain of the elders of Israel came to me and
sat before me, the word of JHWH came to me, saying: Son of man,
these men have applied their idols to their breast and set up the
stumbling-block of their iniquity right opposite themselves: should
I then let myself be consulted by them? Therefore speak to them
and say to them: Thus the Lord JHWH has spoken: Every man of
the house of Israel that applies his idols to his breast and sets up the
stumbling-block of his iniquity right opposite himself and then
comes to the prophet: I, JHWH, shall let him have an answer from
me in accordance with the multitude of his idols, so that I shall catch
the house of Israel by the breast, because they have all turned away
from me through their idols. Therefore say to the house of Israel:
Thus the Lord JHWH has spoken: Return and turn away (your
faces) from your idols, and from all your abominations turn away
your faces. For every man of the house of Israel and of the sojourners
sojourning in Israel, who withdraws himself from Me and applies
his idols to his breast and sets up the stumbling-block of his iniquity

---

[1]) COOKE, *op. cit.* p. 151.
[2]) Cf. Carl BROCKELMANN, *Hebräische Syntax*, Neukirchen, 1956, p. 136.
[3]) ZIMMERLI, *op. cit.* p. 301.

right opposite himself and then comes to the prophet in order that he should consult Me for him: I, JHWH, shall let him have an answer from Me, and I shall set my face against that man, so that I shall make him a sign and proverbs and shall cut him off from the midst of my people. And thus you will know that I am JHWH".

אנשי דמים IN THE PSALMS

BY

N. A. VAN UCHELEN

The expression which will be the subject-matter of this article, occurs in the Old Testament in three different forms, a: איש דמים; b: איש הדמים; c: אנשי דמים [1]). All together there are eight instances. In each case the context is markedly poetical; this is certainly true as far as the Psalms and Proverbs are concerned, and the scene in which the Benjaminite Shimei opposes David the Judaean (2 Sam.) derives its dramatic force from the imaginative vocabulary used by the author.

All translations make clear that the translators have interpreted the phrase literally. Thus the rendering is virtually always: "man of blood", or something similar [2]). These literal translations (including LXX: ἀνὴρ αἱμάτων) although not offensive, do not give any clue to the real meaning of the expression. A literal translation seems to contrast with the strongly poetical context. In order to trace the nature and the meaning of the expression one has to check whether this contrast is real. Such an investigation is twofold: lexicological in so far as the use and the combination of words is concerned, and stylistic in so far as one has to estimate the context.

I. *The use of the expression and its construction*

In singular the word דם means blood running out of man or animal [3]): in the case of man it is usually connected with circumcision and menstruation, in the case of animals with slaughter. In plural

---

[1]) For (a) cfr. Ps. v 7; 2 Sam. xvi 18; for (b) cfr. 2 Sam. xvi 7; for (c) cfr. Ps. xxvi 9; lv 24; lix 3; cxxxix 19; Prov. xxix 10.

[2]) E.g. N. H. Ridderbos, *De Psalmen* I, Korte Verklaring, Kampen 1962, p. 94, 98: "man vol bloedschuld"; H. J. Kraus, *Psalmen* I¹, Neukirchen 1961, p. 36: "Mörder".

[3]) Koehler-Baumgartner, *Lexicon*, p. 212, s.v.; Gesenius-Kautsch, *Grammatik* 28 Aufl., p. 418 (124n); *R.G.G.*, s.v. Blut; — M. Dahood's suggestion (in: *Psalms* I, The Anchor Bible, New York 1966, p. 31) to derive דמים from the root דמה to be like, and to translate the whole phrase by "man of idols" (coll. Latin similis and simulacrum) is unacceptable for two reasons. Firstly, OT Hebrew does not know of any substantive which, being derived from this root, shows

the word gets a wider meaning, various shades of which can be prominent. It then means generally "bloodshed" (Num. xxxv 33), with the derived meaning of "bloodstain" (Isa. i 15) or "pool of blood" (Isa ix 51) [1]). In legal texts the word, both in singular (Lev. xvii 4) and plural (Deut. xix 10), tends to be used rather metaphorically: "bloodguiltiness" [2]). It is characteristic Hebrew idiom to express by means of one word two stages of one and the same process [3]); for the word דם this is exemplified in Lev. xvii 4 and Deut. xix 10. Because of this correlation between the performance of a deed and the undergoing of its effects, between the deed envisaged as actually being done and the result of the deed, the expression אנשי דמים can be translated in two ways: men of bloodshed or men of bloodguilt.

The phrase is formally one of the genetive constructs typical for the compounds with איש, בעל and בן [4]). In such cases the "nomen regens" denotes the *person* who is in a particular situation or possesses a particular quality [5]): e.g. איש דברים (Ex. iv 40), איש חמה (Prov. xv 18), איש לבב (Job. xxxiv 34). The genetival forms constructed with איש can obviously be classified under the heading of gen. qualitatis because they (the nomina recta) point to characteristic qualities of the person concerned.

Although the Hebrew Grammar of GES. K. (128 s.t.) ranges איש דמים (ein mit Blutschuld befleckter) under the grammatical category of gen. qual., one cannot maintain that דמים has to be considered as a distinctive quality of a person, certainly not if the whole expression is literally translated by "ein mit Blutschuld befleckter". A survey of the current translations and of the grammatical interpretations make it clear that אנשי דמים always has been understood

---

the form דמים in plural. Secondly, there is no instance of the phrase where the context allows for this interpretation. This will be substantiated in the present paper.

[1]) GES.-K. 124n "Plural des Produkts", "der räumlichen Ausdehnung".

[2]) H. G. REVENTLOW, "Sein Blut (komme) über sein Haupt", *V.T.* 10 (1960), p. 311-327, illustrates the semantic development of דם in the OT.

[3]) The same wide range of meaning is seen e.g. in the case of חטאת (Num. xxxii 23) and עון (Gen. iv 13); cfr. generally K. KOCH „Gibt es ein Vergeltungsdogma im A.T.?", *Z. Th. K.* 52 (1955) p. 1-42; G. VON RAD, *Theologie* I, p. 264 who uses the terms "synthetische Grundvorstellung" and "synthetische Lebensanschauung".

[4]) GES.-K. 128s, t.

[5]) For similar genetival constructions cfr. C. BRÖCKELMANN, *Hebräische Syntax*, Neukirchen 1956, p. 70 (76b), 71 (77 f.).

as a description of men who actually did shed blood and who consequently, are bloodguilty. In this sense they are (just) *murderers* [1]).

It appears, however, that in the legal passages of the Old Testament another term is used to denote a murderer. In particular the passages dealing with cities of refuge frequently use רֹצֵחַ as a terminus technicus for murderer [2]). The verb רצח, as opposed to more general verbs like הרג and המית, means "to kill violently, crudely" [3]). In 1 Kings xxi 19 Elijah uses it to express exactly how Ahba "killed" Naboth. The use of רעח in the passages dealing with cities of refuge indicates that the man concerned is quilty, according to the law. The רֹצֵחַ has shed blood, דם, violently; he now bears bloodguilt (דם); therefore he must fear the avenger of blood (גאל דם). The act of avenging the blood, too, is described with the root רצח (Num. xxxv 27).

The expression אנשי דמים (mainly Psalms) does *not* occur in legal passages of the Old Testament [4]). The only instance outside the Book of Psalms (and Proverbs) is 2 Sam. xvi 7, 8 (the encounter of David and Shimei). When seen in the context (vv. 5-14), the expressions איש הדמים (v. 7), and איש דמים (v. 8) do *not* hint at an actual criminal offence committed by David. The Benjaminite puts forward only one argument against the Judaean, and this is found in a causal sentence, viz. אשר מלכת תחתו. In this utterance can be heard the wrath of a fellow-tribesman and partisan of Saul. It is the predicament of David which encourages Shimei to utter this unflattering remark. The preceding passage about Ziba, the servant of Saul's son Mephibosheth, suggests that Shimei is not the only one in nursing this wrath and desire for revenge [5]).

Shimei's argument in v. 8 indicates, that the resentment gravitates around the fact that David did put Saul's dynasty to an end, a dynasty which according to the tradition had been elected by YHWH and established by Samuel, and thus had acquired full legitimacy. This

---

[1]) The Accadian language possesses the phrase "bēl dami" "etwa Mörder", cfr. W. von Soden, *Akkadisches Handwörterbuch*, s.v. dāmu; the *Assyrian Dictionary*, Chicago (*C.A.D.*) does not contain the phrase.

[2]) Num. xxxv has 14 instances of רֹצֵחַ; Deut. iv and ix have respectively one and three instances; Joshuah xx, 3 instances.

[3]) B. Maarsingh, *Onderzoek naar de ethiek van de wetten in Deuteronomium*, Winterswijk 1961, p. 12-13.

[4]) Forms of the root רצח occur three times in the Psalms: in xlii 11 the sense is figurative; in lxii 4 the text is dubious; in xciv 6 the literal meaning is evident, paralleled by הרג.

[5]) J. Bright, *History of Israel*, London 1962, p. 188.

explains why some people had always regarded David's political
and dynastic machinations as illegal. This point of view is expressed
more particularly by the invective איש חבליעל immediately after
איש הדמים. "Son of Balial" occurs 27 times in the Old Testament;
in 1 and 2 Sam. it denotes especially men who revolt against the
social order [1]) which is authorized by YHWH and vindicated by
the King; therefore men who undermine the authority represented
by the king. E.g. when Saul has been proclaimed king at Mizpah,
some אנשי הבליעל are said to have their doubts about Saul, to despise
him and not to bring any presents (1 Sam. x 27). Sheba is called
איש בליעל because he blew the trumpet and said: "We have no
portion in David"; together with "all the men of Israel" he revolted
against the king (2 Sam. xx 1) [2]).

When it comes to competing tribes and rival dynasties, there are
many sore points. According to many people David had not been
considerate in avoiding them being cocksure and relentless in his
politics. He had been scheming all the time to get a position to which
many people thought he had no claim. Long-repressed resentment
transpires in the phrase אשר מלכת תחתו; therefore David is a איש
הבליעל. This trend of thought is likely to determine at least partially
the meaning of the neighbouring expression איש הדמים.

This interpretation gains force where it is taken into account that
in the context there is no hint at any criminal offence; nor does the
tradition accuse David of having aimed at the extermination of
Saul's house [3]). Admittedly 1 Chron. contains an explicit tradition
that David had shed much blood, but the only contact between
2 Sam. xvi and 1 Chron. xxii 8, xxviii 3 is to be found in the word דם
and the passages have been written with such a different aim that it
is simply not right to bring them together exegetically. In 1 Chron.
the elaborate characterisation of David as a warrior as opposed to
Solomon the man of peace serves the underlying purpose of the
author, viz. to stress the actual importances of the restoration of the
temple and cult. In this purposefully contrived context David's
description as איש מלחמות has its own special function and meaning.

---

[1]) V. MAAG, "Belijaʿal im A.T.", *Theologische Zeitschrift* 21, 4 (1965), p. 287-299.
[2]) In 2 Sam. xxiii 6; 2 Chron. xiii 7 the expression is used to decry similar
revolutionary activities.
[3]) E.g. 2 Sam. i 17-27, David's lamentation over Saul and Jonathan; and
2 Sam. iv 11, David's reaction after the murder of Ishbosheth; and 2 Sam. ix 1-13,
David's mild attitude towards Mephibosheth, the son of Saul.

II. *The expression and its context*

To trace the nature and meaning of אנשי דמים it is necessary to determine exactly the nature and meaning of its context in each particular case. In a Psalm the context is not only the few verses which precede and follow but also the song as a whole. The structure of the song (i.e. the literary form, the stylistic means and the factual date as forming one closed system) forms the material which expresses by all its different aspects the intention of the poet [1]). Inside this structure as it is created by the poet a single phrase has its own function. According to *this* point of view the following contexts will be analysed.

a) Psalm v 7. The general designations הוללים (the blinded) and פעלי און (evildoers) of vs. 6 are followed up in vs. 7 by a more precise description: they are דברי כזב, and this expression is put as parallel to אנשי דמים ומרמה. The parallel is accentuated in vs. 10 in terms about which there can be no misunderstanding:

כי אין בפיהו נכונה קרבם הוות
קבר־פתוח גרונם לשונם יחליקון

b) Psalm xxvi 9. The אנשי דמים are referred to in this verse in one breath with the חטאים, while vs. 10 characterizes them by זמה; this term sheds some considerable light on the inquiry insofar as it proves that no (bloody) offence is referred to, but a shameful sexual offence (Lev. xix 29 etc.).

c) Psalm lv 24. About the אנשי דמים ומרמה, a preceding verse (22) had said חלקו מחמאת פיו־רכו דבריו משמן, an attitude which is already described in vs. 10 by a reference to לשונם.

d) Psalm lix 3. As in Ps. v here the phrase פעלי און is used as parallel; the activities of this category of people are described most clearly in vv. 8 (יביעון בפיהם חרבות בשפתותיהם) and 13 (חטאת פימו דבר שפתימו). The verb נבע in vs. 8 can have אולת as subject (Prov. xv 2), רעות (Prov. xv 28), און (Prov. xix 28) but also תהילה (Ps. lxxviii 2) and דבר (Ps. cxlv 7).

e) Psalm cxxxix 19. The אנשי דמים, here paralleled by רשע are typified in v. 20 with ימרוך למזמה: "who maliciously defy Thee"; according to Ps. x 2, 4 the malicious thought and utterance is: אין

---

[1]) R. WELLEK and A. WARREN, *Theory of Literature*, London 1962, Ch. 12, The Mode of Existence of a Literary Work of Art, p. 140, 141.

אלהים! In the second half of this verse שׁוא is found, a word which occurs several times constructed with words like שׂפה and חלק (Ps. xii 3) and פה (Ps. cxliv 8, 11).

f) Proverbs xxix 10. A text which can not give any clue to a critic who wants the man to shed blood actually. This bird's eye view of the contexts in which אנשׁי דמים usually occurs, does yield a result which is not unimportant from a lexicological point of view. Often the same words appear to denote their activities:

    a. the root   דבר   three times (Ps. v 7; lv 22; cxxxix 19).
    b. the root   חלק   twice   (Ps. v 10; lv 24).
    c. the word   פה   four times (Ps. v 10; lv 24; lix 8, 13)
    d. the word לשׁון   twice   (Ps. v 10; lv 10).
    e. the word שׂפה   twice   (Ps. lix 8, 13).
    f. the word גרון   once   (Ps. v 10).

Briefly, the phrase appears to be situated in a fairly complete physiological inventory of the organs of speech. This lexicological clue is confirmed by another point, this time a stylistic one. Twice the group of words אנשׁי דמים ומרמה occurs (Ps. v 7; lv 24). The word מרמה in the Old Testament always has the following words in the immediate context: פה (four times, Ps. x 7; xxxvi 4; xic 2; Jes. liii 9), דבר (four times, Ps. xxxiv 14; xxxv 20; xxxvi 4; Jer. ix 2), לשׁון (twice, Ps. l 2; lii 6), שׂפה (Ps. xvii 1) and כזב (Prov. xiv 25).

The nature and meaning of the contexts in which אכשׁי דמיא is used, indicate that the phrase has to be interpreted in a figurative sense. By figurative it is meant that the expression in these contexts obviously does not describe man who actually did shed blood. It is not possible to interpret the expression as a poetical circumlocution to denote what in other instances is called רצֵח [1]), because the phrase is too much interwoven with a stereotyped context which points to a different reality of its own. By the nature and meaning of its context the expression is given a figurative meaning, which is different from the literal meaning.

In order to come to an adequate translation one has to ascertain the background which is common to all contexts. This background

---

[1]) From a legal point of view it is clear that these men would be continuously exposed to the attacks of the גאל-דם, and only the cities of refuge could offer some protection. From a practical and social point of view it is unthinkable that a murderer is still enjoying liberty and forming the menace to public safety about which the Psalmist speaks.

can be described as follows: the Psalmist feels constantly threatened by the slander and calumny of his enemies. Their tongue is like a sharp razor (Ps. lii 4), their bitter words are like arrows shot from ambush (Ps. lxiv 4) and under their lips is the poison of vipers (Ps. cxl 4). The Psalmist's honour is robbed, his reputation is lost, his God is denied. "The terrors of death have fallen upon me" (Ps. lv 4), "for the waters have come up to my neck" (Ps. lxix 2) [1].

It need not be surprising that the rabbis, so much given to an actualizing and historicizing exegesis were able to give the names of those people who made themselves guilty of treacherous slander and calumnious dishonouring: the tongues of Ahithophel, Balaam, Doëg and Gehazi were full of lethal venom [2].

The impious man ambushes the pious Psalmist by his slander: as a matter of fact, the latter uses repeatedly the verb ארב to denote their activity [3]. Psalm lix illustrates how this ambush is arranged: after vs. 4 כי הנה ארבו לנפשי, vv. 7 and 8 continue "howling like dogs they prowl about the city, bellowing with their mouths, and swords in their lips"; and in vs. 11: "full of cursing and lies". The illustration of Psalm lix is put into a brief formula in Prov. xii 6: דברי רשעים ארב־דם. The verb ארב thus appears to be used alternatingly with נפש and דם [4]); this is shown, too, in Prov. i 18.

Lev. xix 16 presents a picture of slander, how it threatens the life of the righteous: the activities of a רכיל are given in the preceding verses: one shall do no injustice in judgment; not be partial to the poor or defer to the great; these are exactly the ways in which the impious is forbidden to stand forth against the life of the righteous. This is the reason why vs. 16b says: לא תעמד על־דם רעך.

In Ezekiel xxii the word רכיל points to the same phenomenon:

---

[1] About the function of the words spoken by one's enemies, cfr. N. H. Ridderbos, *De werkers der ongerechtigheid in de individuele Psalmen*, Kampen 1939, p. 80-93, who rightly objects to Mowinckel's arguments of "Seelenmacht" and "seelische Voraussetzungen", which allegedly enforce the spoken word; id. *Psalmen* i o.c. p. 29-31 where he omits to refer to newer anthropological views concerning the so-called "primitive mentality" and "magic" which conflict with Mowinckel's position. These newer views are discussed in Th. van Baaren's *Wij Mensen*, Religie en wereldbeschouwing bij schriftloze volkeren, Utrecht 1960, p. 196-220.

[2] For the rabbinical interpretation cfr. A. Wünsche, *Midrash Tehillim*, Trier 1892, esp. ad Ps. v 7; for the actual words spoken by these men cfr. 2 Sam. xvi 23; Num. xxxi 8; 1 Sam. xxi 7; 2 Kings iv 12, viii 4.

[3] For the Psalms, cfr. Ps. x 9²; lix 4.

[4] For the construction with דם, cfr. Prov. i 11, 18; Micah vii 2.

here, too, the actual behaviour of the slanderer is put in relation to his neighbour's blood: vs. 9 אנשי רכיל היו בך למען שפך־דם. The offences, none of which is equivalent to actual bloodshed, are enumerated in vv. 7, 8, 10, 11, 12b and c; they are all of the same kind as the offence hinted at in Lev. xix, but classified, all the same, under the stereotyped heading למען שפך־דם [1]). Both Lev. xix and Ezek. xxii list long series of offences which threaten the life of the neighbour. In both passages the slanderer רכיל is mentioned explicitly, in immediate relation with דם, blood. This figurative context of the word דם (and of the expression אנשי דמים) is found, too in the book of Ecclesiasticus. Besides the Greek text ἄρτος ἐπιδεομένων ζωὴ πτωχῶν ὁ ἀποστερῶν αὐτὴν ἄνθρωπος αἱμάτων there is the Hebrew text which says לחם חסר חיי עני העושקו איש דמים [2]).

All texts which have been discussed individually, must not be considered as arguments but as illustrations; each in its turn shows how the meaning of a word (c.q. combination of words) is determined at least partly by the impact of the whole context and the mental images evoked by it. In the case of אנשי דמים the context bears abundant witness that no literal meaning is aimed at. The complex of meaning in which the phrase fulfils its part, gives it a figurative sense; which amounts to saying that the phrase is not so much a "figure linguistique" as rather a "figure de pensée". Because of the metaphorical nature of the expression it is evident, "dass es nicht nur auf die Bedeutung ankommt, sondern dass gefühlmässige Wirkungen und Nebenvorstellungen aller Art beteiligt sind" [3]).

The current translations (man of blood; man of bloodguilt) are correct from a merely linguistic point of view. But a theoretical linguistic criterion is insufficient to guarantee an adequate translation of a whole sentence, because one and the same word, used in a different context, is not the same word. Therefore, given due consideration to the (usual) context, the expression אנשי דמים must be rendered by: "bloodthirsty men" [4]).

---

[1]) H. G. REVENTLOW, o.c. p. 319, 320.
[2]) For the Greek text, cfr. RAHLFS, Septuaginta³, Ecclus. 34; 21; for the Hebrew text, cfr. M. H. SEGAL, Sefer Ben-Sira Haššalem, Jerusalem 1953; ad xxxiv 25.
[3]) W. KAYSER, Das sprachliche Kunstwerk, Bern 1965, p. 125.
[4]) This translation is found in H. LAMPARTER's Das Buch der Psalmen I, 1959 Ps. v 7 ("mit Blutgier befleckt"); and also in the Revised Standard Version London Oxford U.P. 1963 Prov. xxix 10 ("Bloodthirsty men").

DIE THEOPHANIE IN PS. L 1—6

VON

NIC. H. RIDDERBOS*

Bei der Behandlung dieses Themas stoßen wir auf sehr viele
Fragen, die gegenwärtig bei der Untersuchung der Psalmen und
anderer Bücher des AT Anlaß zu mancherlei Diskussionen sind und
nicht mit Gewißheit beantwortet werden können. Ich lege das
Resultat meiner Untersuchungen zur Theophanie in Ps. l 1-6 denn
auch nicht ohne die nötigen Vorbehalte vor, da ich mir bewußt bin,
daß viele meiner Behauptungen hypothetischen Charakters sind.
Selbstverständlich können hier nur bestimmte Aspekte dieses Themas
behandelt werden.

I A

Weniger Vorbehalte macht der Verfasser des l. Psalms, als er sich
an seine Zuhörerschaft richtet.

In der Entstehungszeit dieses Psalms gab es Israeliten — und zwar
durchaus nicht wenige —, die auf den Bund, den Jahwe mit Israel
geschlossen hatte, stolz waren (V. 16, 5) und den Opferdienst gewissen-
haft versahen (V. 8), die es jedoch beim Umgang mit dem Nächsten
nichts weniger als genau nahmen mit den Geboten Jahwes (V. 17-20).
Der Verfasser des l. Psalms fühlt sich berufen, gegen diese Lebens-
haltung zu protestieren. Er kleidet seinen Protest in ein überaus
auffälliges Gewand und scheut sich nicht, im Volke Israel den Eindruck hervorzurufen, *seine Botschaft sei von so großer Wichtigkeit, daß
ihre Übermittlung soviel bedeutet wie eine Wiederholung des Offenbarungs-
geschehens am Sinai.*

V. 1-6 beschreiben eine Theophanie. In diesen Versen läßt sich
ein Fortschreiten der Handlung beobachten. Theophanieschilderungen nennen wiederholt Erscheinungen, die zum Ausbruch eines
Gewitters gehören. Auch in diesen Versen ist das in sehr starkem
Maße der Fall.

---

*) Aus dem Holländischen von K. E. Mittring, Amsterdam.

Zunächst wird Gottes Stimme vernommen; wir dürfen wohl
sagen: sein Donnerruf erschallt:

> Gott, die Gottheit, Jahwe spricht
> und er ruft die Erde
> vom Aufgang der Sonne bis zu ihrem Niedergang.

V. 2 nennt das Erscheinen Gottes:

> Vom Zion her, vollkommen in Schönheit,
> erscheint Gott in seinem Glanz.

הוֹפִיעַ [1]): vielleicht ist bei diesem Wort speziell an Lichterschei-
nungen zu denken, indessen scheint mir das nicht unbedingt notwendig zu sein (vgl. Ez. xxviii 7, 17); jedenfalls würde ich hier
lieber nicht, wie es des öfteren begegnet, von den Strahlen der
aufgehenden Sonne sprechen.

V. 3 enthält eine genauere Ausarbeitung von V. 2:

> Unser Gott kommt und er wird keineswegs schweigen.
> Feuer vor ihm her verzehrt
> und rings um ihn stürmt es gewaltig.

Feuer und Sturm sprechen von Gottes Anwesenheit. Bei „Feuer"
ziehe ich es vor, an das Feuer des Blitzes zu denken. Aber diese
Auffassung kann bestritten werden (vgl. Ps. xcvii 3).

Sodann läßt Jahwe seine Stimme, seinen Donnerruf erneut er-
schallen:

> Er ruft zum Himmel dort droben
> und zur Erde, nun, da er sein Volk richten wird.

Er befiehlt, V. 5, Israel vor ihm zu versammeln:

> Sammelt mir meine Frommen,
> sie, die meinem Bund beim Schlachtopfer beitreten [2]).

In V. 6 lesen viele Exegeten unter Berufung auf die alten Übersetzungen: וְיַגִּידוּ, Und der Himmel wird (oder: möge) seine Gerechtigkeit verkünden. Mir scheint es richtiger, der Massoretischen

---

[1]) Vgl. F. SCHNUTENHAUS, „Das Kommen und Erscheinen Gottes im Alten
Testament" (*ZAW* LXXVI, 1964, 1-22), 8 f.

[2]) Mit Recht äußert L. KÖHLER, *Theologie des Alten Testaments*³, 1953, 45 Bedenken gegen die Übersetzung „den Bund mit mir schließen".

Vokalisation zu folgen — wie etwa auch D. Michel [1]) —, und demgemäß zu übersetzen:

> Und der Himmel verkündet seine Gerechtigkeit:
> siehe, es ist Gott, der Richter ist.

Vielleicht läßt sich die Bedeutung dieses Verses folgendermaßen umreißen: in den vorhergehenden Versen ist die Rede vom Rufen Gottes, wobei die Vorstellung eines Donnerschlags hervorgerufen wird. Dem Donnerschlag folgt der am Himmel entlangrollende Donner, in dem der Dichter gleichsam die Akklamation des Himmels zu Gottes Einschreiten hört. Der Himmel verkündet im voraus, daß das bevorstehende Urteil gerecht sein wird, denn — so bezeugt er voll Ehrfurcht — „es ist Gott, der Richter ist".

B

Die in Ps. l gebotene Theophanieschilderung erinnert, so meine ich, in stärkerem Maße als andere an Gottes Erscheinen auf dem Sinai; es ließe sich selbst behaupten, daß diese Theophanie soviel bedeutet wie eine Wiederholung des Sinaigeschehens. Indessen bedürfen diese Behauptungen näherer Betrachtung.

In diesem Zusammenhang erscheint es mir nicht erforderlich, auf die von der Sinai-offenbarung handelnden Erzählungen der Thora einzugehen. Über diese Erzählungen werden sehr unterschiedliche Betrachtungen angestellt. Aber man kann jedenfalls dies kaum bestreiten: in der Entstehungszeit dieses Psalms war in Israel ganz allgemein der Glaube verbreitet, daß Jahwe sich am Sinai in sehr besonderer Weise geoffenbart habe und mit Israel in die Beziehung eines Bundes getreten sei. Niemand wird M. Noth allzu großer Leichtgläubigkeit gegenüber Israels Traditionen mit Bezug auf die mosaische Zeit zeihen wollen. Jedoch hält Noth es für wahrscheinlich, daß das „Fest der Bundschließung bzw. Bundeserneuerung mit seiner Vergegenwärtigung des Themas 'Offenbarung am Sinai'" „ein Stück ältester uns noch erhaltener Überlieferung im Alten Testament" genannt werden müsse [2]).

An dieser Stelle möchte ich einige Bemerkungen über die Monographie von Jörg Jeremias [3]) einflechten. Jeremias behandelt „das

---

[1]) D. Michel, *Tempora und Satzstellung in den Psalmen*, 1960, 29.
[2]) M. Noth, *Überlieferungsgeschichte des Pentateuch*², 1960, 65 f.
[3]) J. Jeremias, *Theophanie*. Die Geschichte einer alttestamentlichen Gattung, 1965.

Verhältnis der Berichte von der Sinaitheophanie zu den Texten der Gattung der Theophanieschilderungen" (vgl. vor allem S. 100-111). Nach seiner Meinung machen es die „Unterschiede und Abweichungen und die nur recht geringen Übereinstimmungen zwischen beiden Gruppen von Theophanietexten . . . unmöglich, in der Sinaitheophanie den Prototyp aller anderen Theophanieschilderungen zu sehen; sie machen daneben auch jeglichen literarischen Einfluß der Berichte von der Sinaitheophanie auf die Theophanietexte der Gattung äußerst unwahrscheinlich" (S. 110).

Dem wäre gleich etwas hinzuzufügen. JEREMIAS ist der Ansicht, daß die ursprüngliche Form der „Gattung der Theophanieschilderung" aus zwei Elementen bestanden habe, deren erstes vom Kommen Jahwes handle, während das zweite den „Aufruhr der Natur" zum Thema habe. Das zweite Element habe Israel von der Umwelt übernommen, dagegen sei es sehr wahrscheinlich, daß „der Kern des ersten Gliedes, . . . der von einem Kommen Jahwes von seiner Wohnung — präziser: vom Sinai — sprach, den Einflüssen der Sinaitradition seine Entstehung verdankt" (vgl. S. 151-155).

Es würde im Rahmen dieses Aufsatzes zu weit führen, JEREMIAS' Standpunkt als Ganzes zu behandeln. Dies würde erfordern, zunächst die terminologische Frage zur Diskussion zu stellen — was zumindest im Blick auf das Anliegen dieses Artikels nicht eben ein vielversprechendes Unterfangen scheint[1]). Hier sei nur bemerkt, daß Jeremias dem 1. Psalm in seinen Darlegungen meiner Meinung nach nicht gerecht wird. Soweit ich sehe, läßt sich von der Theophanieschilderung in Ps. 1 sicherlich sagen, daß sie ihren Prototyp in der Theophanie am Sinai hat.

---

[1]) Jedes Erscheinen Gottes kann als „Theophanie" bezeichnet werden; verbindet sich ein Erscheinen Gottes mit einem Aufruhr der Natur, so kann man von einer „Theophanie im engeren Sinne" sprechen. Diese Unterscheidung wird hier lediglich bequemlichkeitshalber eingeführt, ohne irgendeinen weiteren Anspruch zu erheben.

Heute wird von einigen Autoren unterschieden zwischen Theophanie und Epiphanie, siehe etwa C. WESTERMANN, *Das Loben Gottes in den Psalmen*[3], 1963, 74; F. SCHNUTENHAUS, a.a.O., 2; Th. C. VRIEZEN, *Hoofdlijnen der Theologie van het Oude Testament*[3], 1966, 206. Wenn Gott erscheint, um seinem Volk (durch einen Mittler) etwas zu sagen, spricht man von einer Theophanie; erscheint Gott zur Rettung seines Volkes im Kampf mit den Feinden, so handelt es sich um eine Epiphanie (die Definitionen des Unterschieds weisen bei den einzelnen Verfassern gewisse Abweichungen auf). Eine solche Unterscheidung kann gewiß klärend wirken, siehe jedoch auch S. 217, Anm. 1.

Man vergleiche für JEREMIAS' Definition der Theophanie die zitierte Monographie, 1 f.

Die Theophanieschilderung in Ps. l erinnert stärker als andere an Gottes Erscheinen am Sinai. Von den Theophanien im A.T. gilt gewöhnlich — sofern wir den Begriff „Theophanie" nicht zu weit fassen —: Gott erscheint, um handelnd einzugreifen, um seine Feinde zu vernichten, um sein Volk zu befreien. In Ps. l erscheint Gott nicht, um handelnd einzugreifen, sondern um zum Volke zu sprechen; so verhielt es sich auch bei der Sinaitheophanie [1].

Ferner: in Ps. l wird der Bund zwischen Gott und Israel nachdrücklich betont. Gott wird "unser Gott" genannt (V. 3), Israel heißt „sein Volk" (V. 4), „mein Volk" (V. 7); בְּרִית steht sowohl in V. 5 wie in V. 16.

Dreierlei ist in diesem Zusammenhang besonders hervorzuheben.

1. In V. 5 findet sich der auffallende Ausdruck כֹּרְתֵי בְרִיתִי עֲלֵי־זָבַח, der zu verschiedenen Fragen Anlaß gibt. Hier genüge die Bemerkung, daß er wohl stark an die Bundesschließung am Fuße des Sinai erinnert, wie sie in Ex. xxiv 3-8 beschrieben wird.

2. V. 16-17 lauten:

Und zum Gottlosen spricht Gott:
Wie kommst du dazu, meine Satzungen aufzuzählen
und meinen Bund in deinen Mund zu nehmen,
wo doch gerade du die Zucht hassest
und meine Worte hinter dich wirfst?

Anschließend (V. 18-20) ist die Rede von Diebstahl, Ehebruch und Lästerung. Es liegt zweifellos sehr nahe, bei „meine Worte" vor allem an „die zehn Worte" (Dtn. iv 13) in Ex. xx und Dtn. v zu denken.

3. Dies wird um so akzeptabler, wenn wir V. 7c hinzuziehen: אֱלֹהִים אֱלֹהֶיךָ אָנֹכִי. Auch dieser Ausdruck ist in verschiedener Hinsicht bemerkenswert. Wie man im übrigen auch über den Gebrauch des Gottesnamens אלהים in der Elohistischen Psalmensammlung denken mag, an dieser Stelle jedenfalls ist es sehr wahrscheinlich, daß statt אלהים ursprünglich יהוה gebraucht worden ist. יהוה אליך אנכי: nach den obigen Ausführungen kann behauptet werden, daß es sich

---

[1] Dasselbe läßt sich auch sagen, wenn man das Unterscheidungspaar Theophanie-Epiphanie verwendet. VRIEZEN schreibt (a.a.O.): „bijv. de Sinaï-verhalen zijn naar hun tekening veel meer verwant aan epifanieschilderingen, maar wel bedoeld als theofaniebeschrijving"; eine Bemerkung dieser Art ließe sich auch zu Ps. l machen.

hierbei um eine Erinnerung an die Einleitung des besagten Dekalogs handelt. Am Rande sei erwähnt, daß, wie W. ZIMMERLI [1]) mit Recht feststellte, Ps. 1 7c ein starkes Argument für die Auffassung liefert, daß die Übersetzung von Ex. xx 2 nicht „Ich, Jahwe, bin dein Gott" lauten müsse, sondern „Ich bin Jahwe, dein Gott".

C

Die Theophanieschilderung in Ps. 1 greift, so glaube ich folgern zu können, sehr offensichtlich auf das Geschehen am Sinai zurück. Der Zion wird ein zweiter Sinai, wie dies nach Jes. ii 2-4, Mi. iv 1-3 auch in der großen Zukunft der Fall sein wird. Ps. 1 schildert einen Vorgang, der demjenigen am Sinai gleicht. Diese Behauptung liegt meinen weiteren Ausführungen zugrunde. Dann aber müssen wir auch sagen: indem der Verfasser des 1. Psalms der Botschaft, die er verkündigen will, eine solche Form gibt, *bekundet er, daß die Übermittlung dieser Botschaft soviel bedeutet wie eine Wiederholung der Offenbarung am Sinai.* Es ist eine große Sache, wenn ein Mensch es wagt, das כה אמר יהוה in den Mund zu nehmen, wie Israels Propheten dies immer wieder tun. Was sich hier ereignet, ist noch größer. Dem Bewußtsein des Verfassers des 1. Psalms und dem seiner Zuhörer galt das Ereignis am Sinai sicherlich als eine der fundamentalen Heilstaten, die Jahwe für Israel verrichtet hatte. Und nun sagt der Psalmist: jenes große fundamentale Ereignis wird jetzt wiederholt. Wodurch? Durch die Übermittlung der Botschaft des Psalmisten an das Volk. Es ist dies zweifellos eine Vorstellung von unfaßbarer Kühnheit. „Unfaßbar" im vollen Sinne des Wortes. Sie enthält etwas, was von uns niemals völlig durchschaut werden kann, was wir niemals zur Gänze werden verstehen können. Indessen können wir wohl trachten, etwas näher an die Dinge heranzukommen.

Zu diesem Zweck empfiehlt es sich, zwei Aspekte besonders zu beachten (im zweiten Teil dieses Aufsatzes wird noch von einem weiteren dritten Aspekt die Rede sein). In beiden Fällen geht es um Fragen von weitreichender Bedeutung, die ich nur kurz behandeln kann.

1. Hier führt, so meine ich, nicht eine Privatperson auf eigene Verantwortung das Wort, sondern ein Sänger des Heiligtums, der diesen Psalm bei irgendeiner kultischen Begehung von Amts wegen

---

[1]) W. ZIMMERLI, „Ich bin Jahwe" (in: *Geschichte und Altes Testament*; Festschrift-Alt, 1953, 179-209), 204 f.; vgl. auch J. L. KOOLE, *De tien geboden*, 1964, 22.

zu Gehör brachte. Ob man dies zu akzeptieren bereit ist, hängt selbstverständlich von der Auffassung ab, die man von den Psalmen im allgemeinen hat. Mir scheint zwischen den Psalmen und dem Kultus ein enger Zusammenhang zu bestehen[1]). Man kann hierüber geteilter Meinung sein, es läßt sich jedoch schwerlich leugnen, daß zwischen Ps. l und dem Kultus ein ursprünglicher Zusammenhang bestanden hat. Dafür spricht schon die Überschrift מִזְמוֹר לְאָסָף. Bei GUNKEL-BEGRICH lesen wir[2]): „Die Frage nach dem Zwecke der einzelnen Sammlungen ist beim Korahiten- und beim Asaph-Psalter leicht zu beantworten. Es ist von vornherein wahrscheinlich, daß die Liederbücher der Tempelsängergilden für den Tempeldienst zusammengestellt und bestimmt waren." Und etwas weiter: „Die Hauptmasse der in den Tempelliederbüchern vereinigten Lieder sind für den Kultus gedichtet." Auch der Inhalt dieses Psalms macht wahrscheinlich, daß er für den Kultus gedichtet wurde. Im zweiten Teil werde ich hierauf noch näher eingehen. An dieser Stelle sei bereits darauf hingewiesen, daß der Psalmist sich an ganz Israel richtet; er nennt die Israeliten „sie, die meinem Bund beim Schlachtopfer beitreten" und stellt Betrachtungen über den Opferdienst an; bei all dem spricht er mit großer Autorität. Gerade ein Psalm wie dieser berechtigt uns, mit MOWINCKEL, JOHNSON und vielen anderen Exegeten von „Tempelpropheten, kultischen Propheten" zu sprechen.

Der Verfasser des l. Psalms macht zwar keine Andeutungen darüber, daß er inspiriert sei — wie es etwa der Dichter des xlix Psalms tut, und zwar vor allem in V. 5. Er ist jedoch offensichtlich davon überzeugt, daß die Worte, die er spricht, nicht seinem eigenen Herzen entstammen. Seinen Worten haftet sogar ein visionärer Zug an. Bei Hab. iii, wo ebenfalls eine ausführliche Theophanieschilderung gegeben wird, kann mit Recht von einer Vision gesprochen werden. Bei Ps. l jedoch möchte ich nicht weiter gehen, als bis zu der Konstatierung eines „visionären Zuges". Es gibt zu wenig Gründe zu der Annahme, daß der Psalmist eine ausgesprochene Vision gehabt habe. Wenn man, wie etwa J. VAN DER PLOEG[3]), die Verben der Verse 1-6 sich auf die Vergangenheit beziehen läßt ("sprach", „rief" usw.), erscheint der Gedanke an eine Vision viel berechtigter. Ich ziehe es

---

[1]) Vgl. vom Verf.: *Psalmen en Cultus*, 1950.
[2]) GUNKEL-BEGRICH, *Einleitung in die Psalmen*, 1933, 444.
[3]) J. VAN DER PLOEG, *De Psalmen*, 1963, z.St.

jedoch vor, die betreffenden Verben mit den meisten Exegeten durch
Präsentia zu übersetzen.

2. Sodann möchte ich, um das Phänomen, daß Ps. 1 von einer
Wiederholung des Geschehens am Sinai spricht, wenigstens einiger-
maßen verständlich zu machen, darauf hinweisen, daß dies im A.T.
keineswegs eine Ausnahme darstellt. Wir berühren hier wiederum
ein vielumfassendes Thema, nämlich die israelitische Geschichts-
auffassung. Soviel scheint mir ohne weiteres ersichtlich: das A.T.
lehrt nicht, daß alles in einem ewigen Kreislauf begriffen sei. Die
Geschichte, wie das A.T. sie sieht, bewegt sich eher in einer geraden
Linie als in einem Kreis. Indessen ist auch das Bild der Geraden
sicherlich unzulänglich, u.a. deswegen, weil das A.T. eben betont,
daß die Geschichte sich in gewissem Sinne stets wiederholt [1]. Das
Wort „Typus" möchte ich in diesem Zusammenhang vermeiden,
und wäre es nur, weil dieses Wort gegenwärtig in recht verschiedenen
Bedeutungen verwendet wird. Kaum zu bezweifeln scheint mir
jedoch, daß atl. Autoren Ereignisse der Gegenwart wie der Zukunft
des öfteren in einer Weise beschreiben, die deutliche Assoziationen
an wichtige Ereignisse der Vergangenheit hervorruft. So läßt sich
sicherlich sagen, daß das A.T. von einem neuen Auszug, einem
neuen Einzug und von einem zweiten David spricht. Warum bedient
es sich dieser Darstellungsweise? Ich gebe ein ziemlich willkürlich
gewähltes Zitat. W. ZIMMERLI (*BK*) schreibt zu Ez. xxxiv 23 f.,
einem Text, in dem von dem kommenden David die Rede ist: „Von
einem 'David redivivus' mag BEGRICH insofern mit Recht sprechen,
als zweifellos der Gedanke der Gleichartigkeit des verheißenen
gerechten Herrschers mit dem David der Vorzeit unterstrichen sein
will. Darüber hinaus aber wird man auch den Hinweis auf die Treue
Jahwes, der seine anfängliche Verheißung über Davids Haus nicht
fahrenläßt, darin finden." Überlegungen derselben Art lassen sich
auch zu Ps. 1 anstellen. Indem der Autor den Eindruck hervorruft,
daß sich das Geschehen am Sinai gleichsam wiederholt, bringt er
sehr nachdrücklich zum Ausdruck: noch lebt der Gott des Sinai, noch
kümmert er sich um Israel. Der Verfasser des 1. Psalms will seinen
Hörern einprägen: der Tag, an dem Jahwe am Sinai seinen Bund
mit dem Volke schloß, war ein großer Tag, ein Tag von entschei-
dender Bedeutung; aber von dem heutigen Tag gilt dasselbe.

---

[1] O. JAGER, *Het eeuwige leven*, 1962, 498 spricht unter Berufung auf W. BAR-
NARD von dem Wendeltreppencharakter, der Spirale in der biblischen Geschichte.

II

Im zweiten Teil meiner Ausführungen befasse ich mich mit der Frage nach dem *ursprünglichen Sitz im Leben* und mit der damit zusammenhängenden Frage nach der *Entstehungszeit* des Psalms. Verschiedene Punkte, die im ersten Teil bereits berührt wurden, werden in diesem Zusammenhang noch eingehender betrachtet werden müssen.

A

Was den Sitz im Leben [1]) anbelangt, so sei zunächst daran erinnert, daß verschiedene Exegeten eine kleinere oder größere Anzahl Psalmen mit einem Fest in Verbindung bringen, das hauptsächlich anhand von den Psalmen selbst entnommenen Angaben rekonstruiert wurde. So wird von einem Thronbesteigungsfest, einem Fest der Bundeserneuerung, einem Bundesfest gesprochen. Bei all dem beruht besonders viel auf Hypothesen. Der konkreteste Anknüpfungspunkt für die Annahme eines Festes der Bundeserneuerung ist im A.T. Dtn. xxxi 9-13: „Und Moses schrieb dieses Gesetz auf und gab es den Priestern, den Söhnen Levis, die die Lade von Jahwes Bund trugen, und allen Ältesten Israels. Und Moses gebot ihnen: nach Ablauf von sieben Jahren, zu der bestimmten Zeit des Erlaßjahres, am Laubhüttenfest, wenn ganz Israel kommt um das Angesicht Jahwes, deines Gottes, zu sehen an dem Ort, den er wählen wird, sollst du dieses Gesetz vor den Ohren von ganz Israel verlesen. Etcet." Es ist kaum denkbar, daß diese Bestimmung völlig in der Luft schwebte und keinerlei Verbindung mit der Realität hätte. Zumindest in einer bestimmten Periode der Geschichte Israels hat diese Gesetzeslesung alle sieben Jahre stattgefunden. Nun versuchen verschiedene Forscher, eine mehr oder weniger enge Verbindung zwischen dieser Gesetzeslesung, dieser Bundeserneuerung und Ps. l herzustellen. Zweifellos ist dieser Gedanke nicht ohne Anziehungskraft. Auf diese Weise ließe sich die Frage, warum der Verfasser des l. Psalms den Eindruck hervorruft, daß das Geschehen am Sinai sich gleichsam wiederhole, viel einleuchtender beantworten. Die Verlesung des Gesetzes nämlich bedeutete soviel wie eine Wiederholung des Geschehens am Sinai. Und es läßt sich denken, daß nach der Thoralesung — was diese Thora im einzelnen auch enthalten haben mag — ein Tempelsänger das Wort ergriff um eine Auslegung, eine Vertiefung und Anwendung des Gesetzes vorzutragen.

---

[1]) Für eine gute Übersicht der zu dieser Frage bestehenden Meinungen vgl. etwa H. J. KRAUS, *Psalmen*, I (*BK*), 370 ff.

Hier scheint mir ein Wort über den Inhalt, die Tendenz am Platz, die Ps. 1 auf das Ganze gesehen hat. G. von Rad, einer der Forscher, die eine Verbindung zwischen Ps. 1 und dem Fest der Bundeserneuerung hergestellt haben, schreibt: „Man kann freilich nicht sagen, daß Ps. 1 unmittelbar und direkt eine kultische Begehung widerspiegele; dagegen sprechen schon die folgenden Verse (nämlich die auf V. 5-7 folgenden Verse), die in bekannter Weise den materiellen Opferdienst zugunsten des geistigen Dankopfers und einer geistigen Gehorsamsleistung ablehnen. Der Psalm hat sich also innerlich schon vom Kultus gelöst." [1]) Diese Ansicht ist m.E. nicht haltbar. Mit Recht behauptet S. Mowinckel [2]): „Ps. 1 actually emphasizes that one thing must be done, and the other not left undone", „das eine", d.h. das Darbringen von Opfern, „das andere", d.h. die Erfüllung der ethischen Gebote. Der Verfasser des 1. Psalms verwirft nicht den materiellen Opferdienst, geschweige denn den Kultus überhaupt. Andernfalls hätte er nicht gesagt (V. 2): „Vom Zion her, vollkommen in Schönheit, erscheint Gott in seinem Glanz", und ebensowenig (V. 5): „Sammelt mir meine Frommen, sie, die meinem Bund beim Schlachtopfer beitreten", oder (V. 8): „Nicht um eurer Schlachtopfer willen will ich euch bestrafen; und eure Brandopfer, sie sind ständig vor mir" [3]), dann hätte er sich auch bei den positiven Forderungen, die er erhebt, nicht einer so ausgesprochen kultischen Terminologie bedient (V. 14 f., 23).

Soviel scheint mir deutlich: *wenn* man zwischen einem Psalm und dem Kultus eine Verbindung herstellt, so kann von einer *Nachahmung* der kultischen Begehung nur gesprochen werden, wenn dem Inhalt des betreffenden Psalms Argumente entnommen werden können, die dafür sprechen; wenn man etwa beweisen kann: „Der

---

[1]) G. von Rad, *Das formgeschichtliche Problem des Hexateuch*, 1938, 21 (*Gesammelte Studien zum A.T.*, 1958, 30).

[2]) S. Mowinckel, *The Psalms in Israel's Worship*, II 1962, 22.

[3]) V. 8 hat m.E. zu bedeuten: Israel ist nicht schuldig, weil es zu wenig Opfer darbrächte. H. J. Kraus, a.a.O., 377, schreibt: „In 8 wird zunächst ausdrücklich hervorgehoben, daß Schlachtopfer und Brandopfer, wie sie in der kultischen Praxis Israels dargebracht werden, nicht einfach pauschal verworfen und verdammt werden (wie viele Exegeten aus Ps. 1 entnehmen wollen)". Mir erscheint diese Formulierung nicht zutreffend. Der Gedanke an eine "pauschale Verwerfung und Verdammung" der Opfer lag völlig außerhalb des Gesichtskreises derer, an die Ps. 1 gerichtet ist. Und Ps. 1 befaßt sich gewiß nicht mit der Widerlegung moderner Exegeten. Zudem läßt Kraus' Paraphrase dieses Verses sich mit V. 8b nicht in Einklang bringen.

Psalm hat sich innerlich vom Kultus gelöst." Derartige Argumente lassen sich m.E. in Ps. 1 jedoch nicht finden.

B

Wie gesagt, es ist an sich reizvoll, Ps. 1 mit der Gesetzeslesung in Verbindung zu bringen, wie diese nach Dtn. xxxi 9-13 alle sieben Jahre stattzufinden hatte. Nun wissen wir jedoch so gut wie nichts darüber, inwieweit Israel der Vorschrift von Dtn. xxxi 9-13 Folge geleistet hat. Es ist indessen höchst unwahrscheinlich, daß Israel diese Vorschrift unter dem König Josia nicht befolgt hätte. Man kann über das Alter des Buches Deuteronomium im allgemeinen, über das von Dtn. xxxi 9-13 im besonderen, und über das zur Zeit Josias gefundene Gesetzbuch geteilter Meinung sein, indessen dürfte kaum zu bestreiten sein, was H. J. Kraus zu Ps. 1 schreibt (S. 374): „Unter dem judäischen König Josia wurden die altisraelitischen Bundestraditionen neu in das kultische Leben des Zentralheiligtums Jerusalem eingeführt (2 Kö. xxiii 1 ff.)".

So gelangen wir zu der als Experiment gemeinten Frage: ist es möglich, daß Ps. 1 zur Zeit Josias entstanden ist?

Um zunächst dies zu sagen: verschiedene Forscher lassen Ps. 1 auf Grund seines Inhalts — ohne die Gesetzeslesung von Dtn. xxxi zu erwähnen — aus der Zeit der großen Propheten, aus dem 8. oder 7. Jahrhundert datieren. A. Cohen (Soncino BB) macht selbst die — übrigens zu weit gehende — Bemerkung: „It is now generally agreed that the conditions denounced in the Psalm relate to the eight century which called forth a similar censure from Isaiah, Hosea and Micah." Kraus, der das Fest der Bundeserneuerung wohl erwähnt, gelangt hinsichtlich der Datierung des Psalms zu der Feststellung (S. 374): „Vieles spricht dafür, daß man an die Zeit Josias denken könnte." Er läßt jedoch die Möglichkeit offen, daß in Ps. 1 „kultische Vorstellungen und Formen sekundär nachgebildet worden sind". Die Frage der Nachbildung wurde oben bereits berührt. Abgesehen davon möchte ich gegen Kraus' Standpunkt folgenden Einwand erheben. Kraus denkt offenbar an die Zeit von Josias Reform, was mir verfehlt erscheint. Wenn man Ps. 1 in die Zeit Josias ansetzen will, so muß sicherlich an die Zeit nach der Reform gedacht werden. Das Volk nämlich, gegen das sich Ps. 1 richtet, macht sich weder der Abgötterei noch anderer illegitimer kultischer Bräuche schuldig. Äußerlich gesehen entspricht der Kultus den Vorschriften bis ins Detail. Daneben aber nimmt man es beim Umgang mit dem Nächsten mit den Vorschriften Jahwes nichts weniger als genau. Wie wir Jeremia wohl entnehmen können, wird in Israel eine solche Situation nicht lange nach der Reform des Josia geherrscht haben.

Spricht etwas dagegen, dasz Ps. 1 aus der Zeit Josias datiert? Die Argumente, die H. GUNKEL (*HK*), S. MOWINCKEL (a.a.O., S. 69-71) und andere für eine nachexilische Datierung ins Feld führen, scheinen mir nicht überzeugend. Das stärkste Argument, das sich für eine nachexilische Datierung anführen ließe, wäre vielleicht, daß V. 9-13 gewissermaßen rationalisierend über das Opfer sprechen. Es ist gewiß verständlich, daß HANS SCHMIDT (*HAT*) schreibt: „Ein eigentümlich aufklärerischer Ton, wie er etwa auch in Jes. xl 16 ff. begegnet, verständlich genug bei Menschen, die weit umher gekommen sind, liegt in dem Spott über die Vorstellung von einem Gott, der Tierfleisch ißt, wo er doch die ganze Welt vom Aufgang zum Niedergang zu eigen hat." Indessen dürfte bei der Berufung auf den „aufklärerischen" Ton eine gewisse Behutsamkeit am Platze sein. Von einer Aufklärung wird auch schon im Hinblick auf die Zeit Salomos gesprochen [1]). Hier wäre auch darauf hinzuweisen, daß der Ton, der in Jes. xl 16 ff. anklingt, auch in Jer. x 1-16 hörbar wird; dabei ist jedoch zu bedenken, daß viele Forscher die Stelle Jer. x 1-16 für unecht halten [2]).

Lassen sich nun *positive Argumente* für eine Datierung des 1. Psalms aus der Zeit Josias finden? Es ist von vornherein nicht zu erwarten, daß sich hierfür sehr konkrete Argumente finden lassen. Sie müßten in erster Linie im Deuteronomium, das zur Zeit Josias besonderen Einfluß besessen haben muß, gesucht werden, sowie in den Prophetien Jeremias, der unter Josia wirkte. Was das Deuteronomium angeht, so wurde Dtn. xxxi 9-13 bereits einige Male genannt. Dem wäre noch folgendes hinzuzufügen: in Ps. 1 5 lesen wir: „sammelt mir meine Frommen (אִסְפוּ)"; in Dtn. xxxi 12: „versammel(t) das Volk usw. (הַקְהֵל)", und in Dtn. xxxi 28: „versammelt zu mir alle Ältesten eurer Stämme usw. (הַקְהִילוּ)", vgl. auch Dtn. iv 10. Einen solchen Aufruf zur Versammlung des Volks, um ihm das Gesetz oder etwas diesem Vergleichbares vorzutragen, habe ich an keiner

---

[1]) Siehe etwa G. VON RAD, *Theologie des Alten Testaments*, I 1957, 61.

[2]) Siehe jedoch auch etwa C. J. LABUSCHAGNE, *The Incomparability of Yahweh in the Old Testament*, 1966, der über Jer. x 2-16 (ausgenommen V. 11) schreibt (68): "In its present form the pericope is a unit, so much so that we may assume the possibility that Jeremiah himself uttered the prayer and the confession at some cultic occasion — perhaps at the renewal of the covenant during the time of Josiah."

anderen Stelle des A.T. finden können. Und weiter: Ps. 1 4 lautet:
„Er ruft zum Himmel dort droben und zur Erde, nun, da er sein
Volk richten wird". Himmel und Erde werden als Zuhörer, vielleicht
können wir auch sagen: zu Zeugen des Bevorstehenden aufgerufen.
An vier Stellen des Deuteronomium finden sich die engsten Paral-
lelen dieser Ausdrucksweise. In Dtn. iv 26, xxx 19 und xxxi 28 ruft
Jahwe Himmel und Erde ausdrücklich zu Zeugen gegen Israel auf,
siehe auch Dtn. xxxii 1 und außerdem Jes. i 2 ¹).

Beachten wir die Übereinstimmungen zwischen Ps. 1 und Dtn.
xxxi, so spricht in der Tat einiges dafür, Ps. 1 mit einer Gesetzeslesung
wie sie in Dtn. xxxi vorgeschrieben wird in Verbindung zu bringen,
siehe vor allem Dtn. xxxi 9-13 (eine Wiederholung des Geschehens
am Sinai), V. 12 und 28 (Aufruf zur Versammlung des Volks, um
ihm das Gesetz oder etwas diesem Vergleichbares vorzutragen) und
V. 28 (das Zum-Zeugen-Rufen von Himmel und Erde).

Was schließlich das Verhältnis des 1. Psalms zu Jeremia angeht,
so kann sicherlich von Übereinstimmungen und Verwandtschaft
gesprochen werden, obschon bei Jeremia schärfere Akzente gesetzt
werden. Vielleicht ist es der Erwähnung wert, daß מוּסָר dreißigmal
in den Sprüchen vorkommt, viermal im Buche Hiob, einmal in den
Psalmen, Ps. 1 17, einmal in der Thora, Dtn. xi 2, nirgends bei den
„früheren Propheten" und vierzehnmal bei den „späteren Propheten"
(und zwar achtmal bei Jeremia, zweimal bei dessen Zeitgenossen
Zephanja). In Ps. 1 18-20 finden wir einen Anklang an die „zehn
Worte" aus Ex. xx und Dtn. v, desgleichen in Jer. vii 9. Ps. 1 nimmt
dem Kultus gegenüber eine kritische Haltung ein; ebenso, und
zwar noch radikaler, Jeremia, siehe vor allem Jer. vii 21 ff. Ps. 1 16
lautet: „Wie kommst du dazu, meine Satzungen aufzuzählen und
meinen Bund in deinen Mund zu nehmen?", Jer. viii 8: „Wie wagst
du zu sagen: wir sind weise, und die Thora Jahwes ist mit uns?".
Von Dtn. xxxi 9-13, der Vorschrift, dem Volk die Thora des Sinai
zu bestimmten Zeiten vorzulesen, ließe sich über Ps. 1, der eine
Anwendung und Vertiefung der Sinaithora gibt, eine Linie zu Jer.
xxxi 31-34 ziehen: „Ich werde einen neuen Bund mit ihnen schließen,
nicht wie der Bund vom Sinai war; ich werde meine Thora in ihr
Innerstes legen und sie in ihr Herz schreiben." Der Autor des 1.
Psalms kann ein kultischer Prophet genannt werden. In der Zeit

---

¹) Eine gute Behandlung dieser Ausdrucksweise findet sich bei H. WILDBERGER
(*BK*) zu Jes. i 2.

Josias und Jeremias scheint es viele kultische Propheten gegeben zu haben. Ich erinnere nur an 2 Reg. xxiii 2, wo berichtet wird, daß Josia mit „den Priestern, den *Propheten* und dem ganzen Volk, mit klein und groß" zum Tempel ging, und an die Parallelstelle 2 Chr. xxxiv 30, wo die Aufzählung lautet „mit den Priestern, den *Leviten* und dem ganzen Volk, mit groß und klein".

Im vorstehenden habe ich natürlich keineswegs *bewiesen*, daß der ursprüngliche Sitz im Leben des l. Psalms die Verlesung der Thora war, wie diese gemäß der Vorschrift in Dtn. xxxi unter Josia stattgefunden haben muß. Aber ich habe darzulegen versucht, daß dies eine *Möglichkeit* ist, der ernsthaft Rechnung getragen werden muß.

Insonderheit der zweite Teil meiner Ausführungen hat weitgehend den Charakter einer Hypothese, eines Experiments— oft konnte ich mich dabei Experimenten anschließen, die andere Exegeten bereits früher unternommen haben. Die Dinge liegen nun einmal so: für das wirkliche Verständnis eines Psalms ist die Kenntnis seines ursprünglichen Sitzes im Leben oft von unschätzbarem Wert. Und da das A.T. hierüber in der Regel keine direkten Angaben macht, ist es zulässig, ja notwendig, auf diesem Gebiet Hypothesen aufzustellen und Experimente zu wagen.

HUIBERT DUIFHUIS (1531-1581) ET L'EXÉGÈSE DU PSAUME LXXXIV 4

PAR

M. J. MULDER

Récemment a paru dans le *Bulletin Museum Boymans-van Beuningen* un article de N. van der Blom, intitulé „De plaque met de titel „De preek van Duyfhuis" " [1]). Dans cet article l'auteur discute une „plaque", acquise par le musée Boymans-van Beuningen à Rotterdam en 1955. Cette „plaque" répresente des fidèles écoutant attentivement a un prédicateur dans une église. Van der Blom démontre dans son article que ce pasteur doit être l'ancien curé réformiste Huibert Duifhuis (1531-1581). D'abord curé de Saint-Laurens à Rotterdam, ensuite, à partir de 1575 de Saint-Jacob à Utrecht, il se convertit dans cette dernière ville au protestantisme [2]).

La chaire, figurée sur la „plaque", porte le nombre 84 [3]). C'est la désignation du Ps. lxxxiv et c'est ce psaume que Van der Blom rattache au nom de Duifhuis en se référant à une petite strophe de quatre vers sous une copie d'un portrait du ministre précité. Dans ces vers il y a une allusion évidente au nom de Duifhuis (littéralement „maison du pigeon") [4]). C'est le pigeon du Ps. lxxxiv selon l'auteur, puisque dans la Vulgate Ps. lxxxiv (lxxxiii) 4 est conçue en ces termes: „Etenim passer invenit sibi domum; et turtur nidum sibi, ubi ponat pullos suos. Altaria tua Domine virtutum: rex meus, et Deus meus". Dans la „Vorstermanbijbel" (1532) „turtur" est traduit par „tortelduyve" (littéralement „tourterelle") [5]), bien que vers cette époque apparaissent des traductions qui rendent *d*e*rôr* par „hiron-

---

[1]) N. van der Blom, „De plaque met de titel „De preek van Duijfhuis". Kerkelijke tegenstellingen in de kunst van de zeventiende eeuw", *Bulletin Museum Boymans-van Beuningen* 15 (1964), pp. 39-52.

[2]) Cf. J. Wiarda, *Huibert Duifhuis, de prediker van St. Jacob.*, Amsterdam 1858 et W. F. Dankbaar, „Duifhuis", *RGG³* II, col. 282.

[3]) N. van der Blom, *l.c.*, repr. 1 (p. 21).

[4]) N. van der Blom, *l.c.*, pp. 42 s. et représentation 16 (p. 43). Ces vers sonnent:
„In 't wezen straalt de minzaamheid,
Gekent in 't woord en 't wijs beleid
En 't doen des mans. Dees kracht betoonde
De Hemel-DUIF, die 't HUIS bewoonde".

[5]) N. van der Blom, *l.c.*, p. 44.

delle" [1]). Beaucoup de traductions du 16me siècle s'appuient sur la
Vulgate, qui s'appuie à son tour sur la version de la Septante: καὶ
γὰρ στρουθίον εὗρεν ἑαυτῷ οἰκίαν καὶ τρυγὼν νοσσιὰν ἑαυτῇ, οὗ θήσει
τὰ νοσσία αὐτῆς, τὰ θυσιαστήριά σου, κύριε τῶν δυνάμεων, ὁ βασιλεύς
μου καὶ ὁ θεός μου.

Cette traduction de *dᵉrôr* par „tourterelle" (ou „pigeon") dans la
Septante, la Vulgate et d'autres versions invite à examiner de plus
près la signification du nom hébraïque de cet oiseau. Etant donné
que *dᵉrôr* est incorporé dans un contexte il est nécessaire de mettre en
cause tout le verset 4 (dans d'autres traductions le verset 3). Notre
article, résultat de cette investigation est arrangé comme suit: la
première partie donne un bref aperçu des quelques dizaines de
traductions et d'explications de ce verset dans le cours de l'histoire,
surtout à partir du 16me siècle avec par ci par là un exposé un plus
détaillé de certains commentateurs. Cette partie se termine par une
tentative d'explication et de traduction du verset 4. La seconde
partie de cette étude s'occupe plus spécialement de la signification
du mot *dᵉrôr* et de la traduction de ce mot par τρυγών dans la Septante.

I

La consultation des quelques dizaines de traductions et de commentaires du passé et du présent montre facilement que le Ps. lxxxiv 4
est une vraie *crux interpretum* [2]). A côté de quelques questions d'importance secondaire telles que la signification de גם au commencement
du verset, la signification de אשר, la traduction correcte des parfaits
מצאה et שתה, des problèmes se posent surtout pour les points suivants: 1. la signification et la fonction de את—מזבחותיך, avec (a) la
signification de *'èt* et (b) la valeur du pluriel de *mizbeaḥ*. Dans le
cadre de ce problème il est nécessaire de relever l'opinion de ceux
des savants qui croient nécessaire d'introduire dans notre verset des
changements *metri causa* par exemple; 2. faut-il prendre notre verset
littéralement, symboliquement, allégoriquement ou bien faut-il y
voir une comparaison?; 3. le problème de la traduction des mots

---

[1]) Pour les Pays-Bas nous ne mentionnons que la „Statenvertaling". Cf. la
suite de cette étude.

[2]) Cf. H. VENEMA, *Commentarius ad Psalmos LXV-LXXXV*, Leeuwarden
1766, p. 772: „Multi in *sensu* et *scopo* versus constituendo multum laborarunt,
cum nec qua ratione *passeres* et *oves* in tabernaculo, quin altari, nidificare dicantur,
nec quid hoc ad rem faceret, explicare potuerunt . . .".

ṣippôr et *dᵉrôr*. A la fin de cette partie nous essayerons de proposer une interprétation personnelle du psaume et plus spécialement du verset 4 [1]).

1a. Le problème que posent le caractère un peu isolé de את–מזבחותיך et l'interprétation correcte de *'èt* (comme préposition ou comme *nota objecti*) a attiré l'attention de presque tous les traducteurs et interprétateurs. *'èt* conçu comme une préposition se trouve surtout à l'époque moderne: „Statenvertaling"; Venema; De Wette; Wutz; Gunkel; De Liagre Böhl; Eerdmans; Baumann [2]); Podechard; Weiser; Ridderbos; Kraus; Maillot-Lelièvre; Dhorme (Bible de la Pléiade) et la „Revised Version". On traduit le plus souvent: „auprès" ou „tout près". C'est Ridderbos qui souligne que *'èt* dans notre verset ne peut pas figurer comme *nota objecti* (*accusativi*) et dans des études modernes sur le *'èt*-syntagmème notre verset n'est pas mentionné [3]). A l'opposé des traducteurs cités plus haut il y a toute une série de traducteurs et d'interprétateurs et cela dès une époque réculée, qui n'y voient pas la préposition *'èt*, mais la *nota objecti* ou peut-être autre chose encore. Nous mentionnons:

---

[1]) Nous avons consulté les commentaires suivants sur les Psaumes. Nous ne les mentionnons brièvement qu'avec le nom d'auteur et avec l'année de l'édition. Les noms, mentionnés sans référence dans le texte, se rapportent au commentaire du Ps. lxxxiv (4). Inutile de dire qu'il nous a été impossible d'entrer dans les détails. Le choix des commentaires suivants est de toute évidence plus ou moins arbitraire. Voici les noms des commentateurs du Ps. lxxxiv (4): Luther (voir note 3, p. 230); Calvin (éd. J. J. Schipper 1667); H. Venema (1766); W. M. L. de Wette (1836); E. W. Hengstenberg (²1851); J. Olshausen (1853); H. Graetz (1882); S. R. Hirsch (1882); F. Delitzsch (⁵1894); H. Keszler (²1899); J. J. P. Valeton (1903); F. Baethgen (³1904); C. A. et E. G. Briggs (1907; ³1925); B. Duhm (²1922); R. Kittel (³ ⁴1922); A. Bertholet (⁴1923); F. Wutz (1925); H. Gunkel (⁴1926); E. König (1927); W. E. Barnes (1931); H. Schmidt (1934); H. Herkenne (1936); W. O. E. Oesterley (1939); F. M. Th. De Liagre Böhl (1947); B. D. Eerdmans (1947); A. Cohen (1950); A. Clamer (1950); E. G. Kissane (1954); E. Podechard (1954); R. J. Tournay et R. Schwab (1955); A. Weiser (⁴1955); W. S. Mc Cullough et autres (1955 *The Interpreter's Bible*); J. Ridderbos (1958); H. J. Kraus (1960); A. Maillot et A. Lelièvre (1966). En outre, les traductions suivantes sont consultées: *Statenvertaling*; *Leidse vertaling*; *Nieuwe Vertaling van het Ned. Bijbelgenootschap*; *Naslaan-Bybel*; *King James Version*; *Revised Version*; *Die Echter-Bible* (F. Nötscher); *Die Schrift-werke verdeutscht von* M. Buber; *La Sainte Bible* (L. Segond); *Bible de la Pléiade* (E. Dhorme). Commentaires et traductions, qui ne sont pas énumérés ici, sont référés sur la manière usuelle dans notre exposé.

[2]) E. Baumann, „Struktur-Untersuchungen im Psalter II", *ZAW* 62 (1950), p. 135; cf. p. 134.

[3]) Cf. l'étude de J. Hoftijzer, „Remarks concerning the use of the particle 'T in classical Hebrew", *OTS* 14 (1965), pp. 1-99.

La Septante; Aquila[1]); la Vulgate, la „Coverdale translation"[2]); la „King James version"; Luther[3]); la „Leidsche vertaling"; la „Naslaan-Bybel"; la Sainte Bible (Segond); la „Nieuwe Vertaling van het Ned. Bijbelgenootschap"; Buber; la Sainte Bible (de Jérusalem) (Tournay-Schwab) et les commentateurs suivants: Hengstenberg; Graetz; Hirsch; Delitzsch; Keszler; Valeton; Kittel; Bertholet; König; Barnes; Schmidt; Oesterley; Clamer[4]) et aussi Nötscher (Echter-Bibel). Quelques exégètes hésitent: Briggs par exemple traduit: „At Thy altars, they praise Thee ever...", mais il voit ʾèt comme une glose explicative. Selon lui, il est incorrect de rattacher la dernière partie du verset à ce qui précède, il voudrait placer ici deux mots du verset suivant. Il fait partie d'une catégorie de traducteurs qui croient devoir, en transposant ou en complétant, donner plus de relief à את–מזבחותיך isolé. Nous mentionnons de ceux qui complètent la phrase: Münster et Clarius[5]) (qui signalent cette correction comme une possibilité); Graetz („setzt eine Lücke voraus": את–מזבחותיך à compléter avec המציאני ou הראני); Segond („Fais-moi trouver..."); Cohen („(thus do I find my resting-place) by Thine altars"). Duhm met le verset 4b immédiatement après le verset 3 („Mein Herz und mein Fleisch jubeln zu dem lebendigen Gott, deinem Altare...") suivi du verset 4a. Il n'y a pas d'unanimité parmi ceux qui ne considèrent pas ʾèt comme préposition, mais comme nota objecti. Delitzsch appelle ces mots את–מזבחותיך un objet supplémentaire des verbes précédents. On a l'impression que beaucoup de traducteurs sont de cette opinion

---

[1]) F. Field, *Origenis Hexaplorum quae supersunt etc.* II, Oxford 1875, p. 235. C'est bien connu qu' Aquila rend la particule את par σύν, par exemple Gen. i 1.

[2]) E. R. Smothers, "The Coverdale translation of Psalm LXXXIV", *HTR* 38 (1945), pp. 245-269. Cette traduction, descendante de la réformation protestante en Angleterre, date de 1535. C'est elle qui a influencé entre autres la „King James Version". Smothers compare dans cette étude le texte du Ps. lxxxiv dans la „Coverdale translation" avec celui de la Vulgate, celui du Psautier de Luther (1524), celui de la version latine de Sante Pagnini (1528) et celui du Psautier de Zurich (1531).

[3]) E. Mülhaupt, *D. Martin Luthers Psalmen-Auslegung* II, Göttingen 1962, pp. 490 s. et p. 493. Cf. aussi *Stuttgarter Jubiläumsbibel: Die Bibel ... nach der deutschen Übersetzung D Martin Luthers*, Stuttgart 1931.

[4]) A. Clamer pense que la particule את est un signe de l'accusatif malgré sa traduction par „auprès (de tes autels)".

[5]) Cf. pour l'opinion de Münster et Clarius: *Criticorum sacrorum sive annotatorum ad librum psalmorum etc.* III, Londres 1660, cols. 473s. Cf. aussi M. Polus, *Synopsis criticorum aliorumque S. Scripturae interpretum* II, pars I, Londres 1671, col. 1106, responsio V: „Alii locum aliter accipiunt, et supplementum addunt". On donne plusieurs exemples.

quand ils ajoutent „c'est-à-dire" ou bien mettent deux points avant
la traduction de מזבחותיך-(את). Il est important de citer l'opinion de
CALVIN qui voit ces mots comme une exclamation: „ô altaria tua".

La traduction de ces deux mots dépend aussi de l'opinion que se
fait le traducteur du problème de savoir s'il est possible que les
oiseaux nichent près de l'autel. HENGSTENBERG, DUHM, HERKENNE
et BAUMANN le considèrent comme impossible. Chez un nombre
beaucoup plus élevé de commentateurs se trouve l'opinion contraire:
DE WETTE; VALETON; BRIGGS; BERTHOLET; GUNKEL; WUTZ;
OESTERLEY; DE LIAGRE BÖHL; EERDMANS; RIDDERBOS; KRAUS;
MAILLOT-LELIÈVRE. Un argument souvent cité est la croyance que
la région du temple formait un asile pour l'homme et l'animal. Pour
justifier cette opinion on allègue entre autres des parallèles du monde
arabe [1]). Sous ce rapport il n'est pas inutile, cependant, de rappeler
que selon la Mišna il y avait des pointes sur le toit du temple [2]). Mais
DE WETTE n'est pas sûr que cette information d'une époque tardive
s'applique au temple salomonique.

A côté de cette question concernant la nidification des oiseaux près
de l'autel les exégètes se posent aussi la question suivante abordée
par nous sous le numéro „2" et liée à notre problème: est-ce qu'on
doit prendre ce verset au sens littéral ou au sens figuré (symbolique
ou allégorique)? En effet, la question de savoir si les oiseaux nichent
près des autels du temple ne joue pas un rôle très important quand on
sait que sous les mots ṣippôr et dᵉrôr se cache le poète lui-même ou
une autre personne ou même un groupe entier. HENGSTENBERG, un
de ceux qui suivent cette opinion, a des réactions assez émotionnées
devant les exégètes plus récents qui, selon lui, partent de la „un-
glückliche Vorurtheil" selon laquelle notre psaume serait l'expression
de la nostalgie de quelqu'un, qui, loin du temple, se rappelle les
oiseaux nichant près des autels et qui se dit alors: ces oiseaux sont
plus heureux que moi qui suis séparé de votre sanctuaire ... [3]).

---

[1]) Cf. HERODOTUS, *Historiae* I, 159; W. ROBERTSON SMITH, *The Religion of the
Semites*[2], Edinburgh 1894 (= Meridian Library edition 1956), p. 160 et note 1.
La question de savoir comment il était possible que les oiseaux aient fait leur nids
près des autels est aussi posée par M. POLUS, *ibidem*.
[2]) Middoth iv 6: כלה עורב, cf. Ch. ALBECK, ששה סדרי משנה, סדר קדשים,
Jérusalem Tel Aviv 5719, p. 332: שפודי זהב נעוצים בגג, להבריח את העורבים.
On parle ici surtout de l'expulsion des oiseaux de proie (des corbeaux).
[3]) Cf. H. VENEMA, *o.c.*, p. 772: „Interpretes in errorem abduxit, quod *passerem*
et *palumbum* proprie et litteraliter acceperint, cum emblematice et inproprie hic
occurrant: quid enim *passeribus* cum *altari*? quid *aves* memorasse adtinet? aves

Il y a des exégètes qui veulent entendre les autels *synecdochice* pour
tabernacle ou temple: un des lieux les plus saints est nommé comme
une *pars pro toto* (DE WETTE; OLSHAUSEN; DELITZSCH; BARNES).
Cette opinion ne nécessite pas une prise de position sur la question de
l'interprétation de '*èt* comme préposition ou comme *nota objecti*.

Nous terminons cette partie de notre sommaire en rappelant
l'opinion de KISSANE. Celui-ci traduit את–מזבחותיך par „dans vos
autels". Il suppose qu'au moment de la composition du psaume le
temple était détruit de sorte que les oiseaux pouvaient librement faire
leurs nids dans les autels éteints [1]).

1b. Beaucoup de personnes ont cherché une solution pour le
problème du pluriel מזבחות dans notre verset. VENEMA et HENGSTEN-
BERG pensent à l'autel des holocaustes et à l'autel des parfums. Etant
donné qu'ils croient que le poète se voit sous l'image des oiseaux, cette
opinion est possible, sinon l'autel des parfums donnerait bien des
difficultés. La „Interpreter's Bible" interprète le pluriel comme „dans
les environs de vos autels" et dit: „il y a deux autels, à savoir l'autel
des parfums à l'intérieur et le grand autel à l'extérieur du temple".
Un troisième autel fut construit par le roi Achaz de Judée, selon la
„Interpreter's Bible" (cf. 2 R. xvi 10-16). JOH. DE GROOT a consacré
une étude aux autels du temple salomonique [2]). Dans cette étude il
montre qu'il a dû y avoir deux autels dans le parvis du temple jusqu'au
règne d'Achaz. Il accueille notre verset comme un appui, pas très
sûr pourtant, pour sa thèse. Par là le psaume pourrait être du même
coup daté approximativement comme pré-exilique [3]). Sur l'opinion
de DE GROOT s'appuie par exemple RIDDERBOS. D'autres exégètes
rejettent catégoriquement les deux autels dans le parvis du temple
comme interprétation possible en se référant au pluriel משכנותיך
dans le verset 2 („Leidse vertaling"). D'autres encore pour interpréter le pluriel ont pensé à une „indication de catégorie" („soort-
aanwijzing") (VALETON) ou croient que le pluriel est employé pour
des raisons rhétoriques ou euphoniques (BARNES).

---

nidificantes in altari nos ad desolationem domus Dei potius, quam frequentiam
et prosperitatem ducerent".

[1]) Cf. M. POLUS, *o.c.*, col. 1106, responsio IV et déjà RAŠI: I. MAARSEN, *Parshan-
datha The Commentary of Rashi on the Prophets and Hagiographs* III, Jérusalem 1936,
p. 84.

[2]) Joh. DE GROOT, *Die Altäre des salomonischen Tempelhofes* (*BZWAT*, NF 6),
Stuttgart 1924.

[3]) Joh. DE GROOT, *o.c.*, p. 9.

Il est clair que dans l'énumération sous „1a" et „1b" on n'a pas su expliquer de façon satisfaisante את-מזבחותיך. Ceux qui dans leurs commentaires s'intéressent au mètre de ce verset du psaume trébuchent sur l'irrégularité que présente notre verset dans l'ensemble du psaume (avec le verset 7). C'est ainsi qu'on en vient à transposer ou à omettre un ou plusieurs mots dans notre verset. Par exemple BAUMANN qui lit, en omettant אשר: „Auch der Vogel hat ein Haus gefunden und die Schwalbe ihr Nest, hat ihre Brut bei deinen Altären gelegt . . ." [1]). KRAUS ainsi que plusieurs autres auteurs proposent d'omettre *metri causa*: יהוה צבאות מלכי ואלהי. Enfin, HERKENNE est d'opinion que „tes autels, Yahvé Sabaot" est une variante moins réussie de „tes demeures, Yahvé Sabaot" (le verset 2) et pour cela doit être omis. Il suppose que nos mots sont une note marginale d'un copiste et que cette note a dû s'introduire plus tard dans notre texte.

2. L'opinion qu'on s'est faite sur le „Sitz im Leben" de ce psaume est assez importante pour la question de savoir si on doit comprendre notre verset littéralement ou bien symboliquement ou allégoriquement. On peut envisager ce psaume, selon RIDDERBOS, d'un point de vue liturgique ou historique. Beaucoup d'exégètes de jadis (par exemple CALVIN; HENGSTENBERG; DELITZSCH; KÖNIG) ont identifié le poète de notre psaume avec David fuyant devant Saül ou Absalom. Beaucoup d'exégètes modernes, qui professent l'opinion liturgique, considèrent notre psaume comme un chant de pèlerinage chanté pendant le pèlerinage de Jérusalem ou dans le temple. Dans une des plus récentes études qui s'occupent de notre psaume, on dit que le chant „am Ende einer Wallfahrt gesungen worden ist. Der Ausdruck des Staunens über die Wohnungen Jahwes, gepaart mit einem Rückblick auf die in der Vergangenheit liegende Sehnsucht nach dem Heiligtum, sowie die Schilderung der Wallfahrt zu diesem, verbunden mit einer Betrachtung über die Vorzüge des Weilens am Ort des Tempels, lassen keine andere Deutung zu" [2]). Tout de même selon WANKE, à qui nous empruntons le passage précédent, il n'est pas facile de résoudre le problème de savoir qui a chanté ce psaume, étant donné qu'à côté d'expressions individuelles il y a aussi des tournures didactiques. Lui-même pense que le psaume „ausschliesslich f ü r Wallfahrer gedichtet wurde; und zwar von einem an einer

[1]) E. BAUMANN. *l.c.*, pp. 134 s.
[2]) G. WANKE, *Die Zionstheologie der Korachiten in ihrem traditionsgeschichtlichen Zusammenhang* (*BZAW*, 97), Berlin 1966, p. 18.

Zionstheologie orientierten Verfasser, der wechselweise die Pilger und sich selbst zu Wort kommen lässt" [1]).

Il serait trop long de traiter en détail les opinions qu'ont émises les savants et les commentateurs sur le psaume lxxxiv (4) et les motifs qui les ont conduits à cette opinion. Qu'il nous soit permis de nous contenter d'un exposé plus détaillé de quelques opinions curieuses. En outre nous donnerons un résumé de plusieurs autres commentaires que nous avons consultés.

LUTHER [2]), dans la paraphrase de sa première „Psalmenvorlesung" (1513-1515) a vu dans „le passereau" l'image de lui-même et de tout fidèle [3]), dans „la maison" l'église ou lui-même, dans „la tourterelle" le pénitent et dans „les autels" la croix et la passion de Jésus-Christ. Dans les scolies de la première „Psalmenvorlesung" il approfondit encore selon la même méthode [4]). CALVIN pense que David a composé le psaume et il commence la discussion de notre verset par la remarque: „Versum hunc quidam uno contextu legunt: acsi diceret Propheta, aves prope altaria nidulari". La particule 'èt semble renforcer cette opinion. Lui-même pense autre chose. Sa traduction du verset 4b est: „ô altaria tua Jehovah exercituum Rex meus et Deus meus". Selon lui il y a ici une exclamation, qui interrompt le cours des pensées du poète. „Primum ergo David passeribus se et hirundinibus comparans, miseriam suam amplificat: quia indignum est ab haereditate sibi promissa expelli Abrahae filios, quum aviculae nidos alicubi reperiant". Il est compréhensible que David ait poussé des exclamations: „Nam quia objicere promptum erat, multos esse angulos in mundo ubi tuto quiesceret... respondet, se malle toti mundo renunciare, quam privari sacro Tabernaculo: nullum locum sibi iucundum esse procul a Dei altaribus, imo nullum usquam domicilium extra terram Sanctam sibi placere".

L'exégèse de CALVIN comparée à la paraphrase de LUTHER excelle par sa sobriété. Mais que l'interprétation symbolique ait prospéré plus tard c'est ce que nous montre une étude du 18me siècle, assez importante pour que nous nous y arrêtions un instant: l'étude de NIC. NONNEN, *Dissertatio theologico-exegetica de Tzippor et Deror symbolis proselytorum sub Josaphati regno conversorum ad psalmi lxxxiv.*

---

[1]) G. WANKE, *ibidem.*
[2]) E. MÜLHAUPT, *o.c.,* p. 491.
[3]) Israel par exemple: RAŠI: I. MAARSEN, *o.c.,* p. 84.
[4]) E. MÜLHAUPT, *o.c.,* p. 493.

vs. 4 [1]). Selon lui le psaume lxxxiv a été écrit au temps du roi Josaphat. C'est aux actes de celui-ci que le psaume fait allusion tout le temps. Le psaume aurait été chanté par un Israélite du royaume des dix tribus qui se serait converti à la vraie religion. Il voit les oiseaux du verset 4 comme symboles des Édomites et des Qénites, qui habitaient parmi les Moabites. Quelques-uns de ceux-ci se sont convertis sous Josaphat au peuple d'Israël, parmi eux Yonadab, fils de Rékab et père des Rékabites. Notre verset aurait chanté la conversion de ces derniers [2]). Car: „aves proprie dictas ad altaria Iehovae nidulasse florente republica Iudaica, et cultu in templo, est ἀδύνατον" [3]). Par conséquent il voudrait entendre notre verset dans un sens strictement allégorique, car dans la Bible les animaux sont plus souvent „emblemata gentium". Pour le prouver il cite les exemples nécessaires. Les oiseaux dans le verset 4 désignent des „aves montanae", qui nichent dans les crevasses des rochers quoique „species harum volucrum nondum satis sint notae" [4]). Que ces oiseaux doivent être pris réellement comme symboles des Édomites et Moabites c'est qu'il essaie de montrer en alléguant d'autres versets de la Bible [5]). Ensuite il montre que Yonadab, qui vivait au temps de Josaphat, descendait des Qénites (cf. 1 Chr. ii 55) et qu'il embrassa la religion juive avec sa famille. On emploie pour caractériser le prosélyte le terme „positus in altaribus" [6]). Les petits des oiseaux sont les descendants de ces peuples cités sous le symbole des oiseaux qui peuvent servir Dieu „près de ses autels" [7]). Comme conclusion de son argumentation Nonnen pose que dans notre verset un Israélite du royaume des dix tribus prie de ne plus jamais être arraché à la proximité de Dieu. C'est le poète qui emploie l'image des prosélytes et de leurs descen-

---

[1]) Nic. Nonnen, *Dissertatio theologico-exegetica etc.*, Brême 1741. La consultation de cette étude a été rendue possible par la bienveillance de la „Bayerische Staatsbibliothek" à Munich.

[2]) Nic. Nonnen, *o.c.*, pp. 4 s.

[3]) Nic. Nonnen, *o.c.*, p. 17.

[4]) Nic. Nonnen, *o.c.*, p. 20. Pour צפור comme oiseau de montagne par exemple Ps. xi 1; civ 17 etc.; pour דרור Pr. xxvi 2 „ubi cum tzippor itidem conjuncta est huic נוד divagatio, illi עוף volatus adscribitur, pernix adeoque fuit. Si Deror palumbus aut turtur fuit, seu columbarum ferarum species ut volunt Bochartus ... et Malvenda .... montana fuit avis, cum illis in rupium fissuris habitaculum et nidus sit Cant. II. 14".

[5]) Nic. Nonnen, *o.c.*, pp. 20-23.

[6]) Nic. Nonnen, *o.c.*, pp. 34 ss.

[7]) Nic. Nonnen, *o.c.*, p. 36. Il prétend aussi que les psaumes xxiii-xxix „ad usum proselytarum fuisse destinatos": *o.c.*, p. 35.

dants: si ces derniers sont déjà admis près de Dieu dans son sanctuaire, à plus forte raison le serait un descendant de Jacob [1]).

Pour autant que nous avons pu le constater l'opinion de NONNEN n'a pas reçu l'approbation des générations suivantes. Mais celui qui lit son argumentation très détaillée que nous n'avons fait que résumer brièvement, ne pourra pas lui dénier des dons remarquables d'invention et d'originalité, même s'il ne persuade certainement pas les exégètes modernes de la justesse de ses opinions exégétiques souvent très curieuses.

Plusieurs commentateurs supposent que l'auteur du psaume s'identifie avec *ṣippôr* et *dᵉrôr* (HENGSTENBERG; DELITZSCH; KESZLER). On rencontre aussi plusieurs fois l'idée d'une comparaison, „abrégée" ou non (VENEMA; DUHM; KITTEL; PODECHARD) [2]): le poète est *comme* un oiseau . . . D'ailleurs parmi les savants, énumerés sous „1", qui estiment possible que les oiseaux nichent dans les autels du temple, il y en a beaucoup qui voient un parallèle entre les oiseaux qui ont trouvé un nid et le poète lui-même. MAILLOT et LELIÈVRE disent par exemple: nous avons ici une image double: 1. le Seigneur protégeant les oiseaux est pour le psalmiste le symbole de la protection qu'il trouvera lui-même dans le temple. 2. En outre: „l'auteur n'ignore pas quelle voyageuse est l'hirondelle; elle aussi fait son pèlerinage annuel à Sion. Le psalmiste y voit un accueil de toute la nature animée, bienheureuse, elle aussi, d'être accueillie à Sion".

Actuellement la conception allégorique ou symbolique n'a presque plus d'adhérents. KÖNIG a deux objections contre cette opinion:

1. si l'oiseau était le poète, on n'aurait pas employé le fémenin et

2. avoir des petits serait contre nature sous ce rapport. Mais NONNEN a, selon nous, prouvé d'avance, que l'explication allégorique de notre verset ne doit pas se laisser arrêter par de telles objections.

3. Voici un bref résumé de la traduction des mots désignant les oiseaux cités dans le verset 4. Pour une recherche plus détaillée sur la

---

[1]) Nic. NONNEN, *o.c.*, pp. 36 s.

[2]) Cf. A. CLAMER, *a.l.*: „C'est ainsi que les anciens et les Pères de l'Église coupaient et expliquaient ce verset, regardant ces noms comme de simples métaphores, les passereaux pour désigner ceux qui mènent la vie religieuse, et les tourterelles ceux qui se sanctifient dans la vie du monde, les uns comme les autres trouvant leur repos auprès des autels de Dieu". Cf. aussi H. VENEMA, *o.c.*, p. 773: „*Prius* si obtineat, apodosios et protasios particulae deerunt, et pertinebit ad classem *similium implicitorum*, ut Gejerus recte observavit; *posteriore* sensu, vox *passeris* et *palumbi*, non proprie, sed figurate erit intelligenda . . .".

signification des mots hébraïques nous renvoyons à la deuxième partie de cet article. Dans les traductions du passé et du présent que nous avons consultées on voit que proportionnellement trois traduisent *ṣippôr* par „oiseau” ou „oiselet” contre quatre qui le traduisent par „passereau”. On trouve la traduction „oiseau” déjà chez Aquila (ὄρνεον) et saint Jérôme („avis”) [1], mais aussi chez Luther et chez beaucoup de commentateurs du 19me et 20me siècle, comme Hengstenberg; Graetz; Hirsch; Keszler; Baethgen (comme „Kosewort”); Duhm; Briggs; Gunkel; Nötscher (Echter-Bibel); Buber; Kraus et Wanke [2]. On trouve la traduction „passereau” aussi chez des traducteurs et des commentateurs anciens: la Septante; la Vulgate; Psalterium romanum [3]); Münster, Sante Pagnini et autres chez Polus [4]); Calvin; „King James version”; „Statenvertaling”; „Coverdale translation” [5]); Venema; De Wette; Olshausen; König; Barnes; Oesterley; Kissane; Podechard etc. Parfois on hésite, par exemple Kraus, qui bien qu'il traduise „oiseau” pense que la traduction „passereau” est aussi possible.

En ce qui concerne *derôr* il y a une plus grande unanimité pour les traductions plus modernes. Nous notons une cinquantaine de traductions de *derôr* par „hirondelle” contre une dizaine d'autres traductions, notamment par „colombe” („pigeon”) ou „tourterelle”. On rencontre cette dernière traduction surtout dans les traductions plus anciennes, comme dans la Septante (τρυγών); la Vulgate („turtur”); Psalterium romanum; mais aussi chez Luther; Venema et Baethgen („Wildtaube”), tandis qu'il y a d'autres commentateurs qui hésitent entre „colombe” et „hirondelle” (Valeton; Kraus) ou montrent leur hésitation par un „?” (Herkenne; Maillot-Lelièvre). A côté de la traduction „colombe” à la place de „hirondelle” on voit aussi στρουθός (Aquila) et „passer” (St. Jérôme).

Si on veut arriver à donner une exégèse exacte de notre verset on doit, selon nous, partir de l'ensemble du psaume. Les *cruces* de notre psaume sont si nombreuses que cela nous prendrait trop de

---

[1] Cf. pour la traduction d'Aquila: note 1, p. 230; pour celle de saint Jérôme: Dom Henri de Sainte-Marie, *Sancti Hieronymi Psalterium iuxta Hebraeos* (*Coll. Bibl. Lat.*, XI), Rome 1954, p. 121.

[2] G. Wanke, *o.c.*, p. 16.

[3] Dom R. Weber, *Le psautier romain et les autres psautiers latins*, Rome 1953, *a.l.*

[4] Cf. M. Polus, *o.c.*, col. 1106. En outre il énumère Muis, Ainsworthus et Piscator.

[5] E. R. Smothers, *l.c.*, pp. 257 s.

temps de les examiner toutes. Si on laisse de côté le premier verset
qui attribue le psaume comme מזמור aux fils de Coré[1]), on pourrait
voir le verset 2, le début du psaume, comme un titre qui présente
habilement le thème du psaume. Le מה par lequel commence le verset
provoque la réaction naturelle d'un „למה", qui sera développé plus
loin pour trouver son point culminant dans le verset 8: voir Dieu
dans Sion (ou: sur le Sion)[2]). Ce psaume n'est pas qualifié à tort d'un
„chant de Sion"[3]: Sion est au sens propre comme au sens figuré le
centre du psaume Sion cependant doit toute son importance à Dieu,
dont plusieurs noms ou combinaisons de noms sont groupés pour
ainsi dire concentriquement autour du mot Sion: יהוה צבאות (les
versets 2, 4, 9[4]) et 13); יהוה (3, 12); חי)אל((3, 8[5])); אלהים (4, 8[6]),
9 avec יעקב), 10, 11, 12 (avec יהוה)). Il est frappant que dans les
versets 5 et 6 Dieu soit seulement désigné par des suffixes pronomi-
naux et que dans les versets 7 et 8a, où l'on fait probablement allusion
au pèlerinage, toute désignation de Dieu manque, jusqu'à ce que,
dans les versets 8b et 9a (le centre du psaume), tous les noms de Dieu
s'accumulent autour de Sion. Vu le contenu des versets 7 et 8a il
est stylistiquement et objectivement explicable que Dieu n'est pas
nommé dans ces versets (cf. les mots בעמק הבכא et יעטה), quoique
ces stiches posent beaucoup de problèmes exégétiques. Le verset
6b forme après les versets 5 et 6b la transition au pèlerinage. Dans ces
derniers versets le poète a célébré ceux qui ont le privilège d'habiter
sur le Sion. Dans une image hardie, où, selon notre avis, il n'est
pas nécessaire de corriger מסלות[7]), le chanteur passe des יושבים aux
עוברים, pour arriver à une apogée dans le verset 8b pour les יושבים
ainsi que pour les עוברים.

Cependant il y a encore une autre raison qui explique l'importance
de Sion et qui joue un rôle important dans notre psaume. Sur le
Sion se trouve la demeure de Dieu. Tout le monde doit se diriger
vers cette montagne qui est le point sûr, où tout peut trouver la

---

[1]) Cf. pour les psaumes des fils de Coré: M. J. Buss, „The Psalms of Asaph and
Korah", *JBL* 82 (1963), pp. 382-392 et G. Wanke, *o.c.*

[2]) A lire avec la Septante, Aquila et Pešitta יראו, cf. H. J. Kraus, *a.l.* et
G. Wanke, *o.c.*, p. 17.

[3]) Par H. J. Kraus, M. J. Buss et G. Wanke.

[4]) Littéralement: יהוה אלהים צבאות

[5]) A lire אֶל au lieu de la préposition (cf. aussi la note suivante).

[6]) אֶל אלהים. Il n'est pas nécessaire de rayer אלהים *metri causa* (contre H. J.
Kraus et G. Wanke).

[7]) Par exemple dans כסלות (H. J. Kraus) ou מעלות (G. Wanke).

paix et la certitude. Aussi voyons-nous que la notion de „demeure"
joue un rôle important dans notre psaume: משכנותיך (le verset 2);
חצרות (3, 11); בית ((4), 5, 11). Le pluriel de משכן et חצר est notable
et on peut probablement l'interpréter comme un „pluriel de généralisation" [1]. On constate un rapport étroit entre le lieu où demeure
Dieu et Dieu même (cf. les versets 3, 5, 11). L'immobilité et la
certitude de ce lieu dépendent de la certitude de Dieu. Serait-ce un
hasard si le mot משכנות, qui est en rapport avec כון, est employé dans
le verset 2? Et est-il vraiment nécessaire d'émender le verset 11 en
remplaçant le mot בחרתי par le mot בחדרי [2]) et le mot רשע par le mot
עשר [3])? Parfois אהל peut contraster avec בית, parce qu'une tente est
mobile [4]) et en outre רשע fait un beau contraste avec le mot טוב
précédent et suivant. Dans le cadre de cette étude nous ne pouvons
pas discuter en détail les questions qui restent à résoudre relativement
à la signification des versets 9 et 10 [5]). Il vaut la peine pourtant de
nous arrêter un instant à la fin du psaume: dans le verset 13b sont
appelés „bienheureux" ceux qui se confient en Dieu (בטח). La douceur
de la demeure de Dieu et surtout de Dieu Lui-même aboutit à la
bénédiction de celui qui a mis pour toujours sa confiance en ce Dieu
du Sion.

Si dans ce qui précède nous avons bien saisi le sens de cette œuvre
d'art qu'est notre psaume, on se pose la question: quelle est alors
la fonction du verset 4 dans cet ensemble? On parle d'oiseaux. Ṣippôr
est une indication générale pour „l'oiseau" [6]) et vu le parallélisme

---

[1]) Cf. le pluriel de généralisation: P. Joüon, *Grammaire de l'hébreu biblique*[2],
Rome 1947, § 136 j.

[2]) Ainsi entre autres H. J. Kraus et G. Wanke.

[3]) Ainsi entre autres G. Wanke.

[4]) Cf. entre autres 2 Sam. vii 2; Is. xxxviii 12 etc.

[5]) Pour la signification de משיח et de מגן: G. Wanke, *o.c.*, pp. 19s. Cf. mainte-
nant aussi pour מגן: W. von Soden, „Vedisch *Magham*, „Geschenk"-neuarabisch
Maǧǧānīja, „Gebührenfreiheit" ", *JEOL* 18 (1964), pp. 339-344 et M. Dahood,
„Hebrew-Ugaritic Lexicography IV", *Bibl.* 47 (1966), p. 414.

[6]) C'est צפור qui a souvent la signification d'un collectif: Gen. vii 14; Dt. iv 17
etc., mais aussi de l'oiseau simple: Lev. xiv 4 et *passim*; Dt. xiv 11; Ps. xi 1 etc.;
cf. L. Koehler-W. Baumgartner, *Lexicon in Veteris Testamenti libros*, Leyde
[1]1953, *s.v.* Dans d'autres langues sémitiques se trouve ce mot aussi, par exemple
dans l'ugaritique: C. H. Gordon, *Ugaritic Textbook* (*An. Or.*, 38), Rome 1965,
p. 460 nr. 1905: *ʿṣr*. A côté de ce mot on trouve *ṣpr*: C. H. Gordon, *o.c.*, p. 475
nr. 2186. Il est possible que ce mot soit analogue au mot accadien *ṣibâru*. Un
autre mot encore plus analogue dans l'accadien c'est *iṣṣūru*: W. von Soden,
Akkadisches Handwörterbuch I (= *AHw*), Wiesbaden 1965, *s.v.* Dans l'arabe il y a
le mot عصفور (cf. C. H. Gordon, *o.c.*, p. 460 nr. 1905). Nous terminerons
cette énumération par l'araméen: cf. L. Koehler-W. Baumgartner, *o.c.*, s.v.

dans notre verset il est possible dans notre cas de voir *derôr* comme
un synonyme de *ṣippôr* et de le traduire par „oiselet" par exemple.
Nous entrerons plus loin dans les détails pour l'explication du mot
derôr. Il est important de noter déjà ici que dans Pr. xxvi 2 *ṣippôr* et
derôr sont cités l'un à côté de l'autre dans un aphorisme dont la
deuxième partie pose des problèmes exégétiques, il est vrai, mais où
les deux mots doivent être considérés nettement comme synonymes [1]).
On ne doit pas exclure la possibilité que, par exemple dans la langue
du peuple, *ṣippôr* et *derôr* aient été étroitement unis et se soient
rencontrés dans certaines expressions. On pourrait se souvenir ici
du צפור דרור de l'hébreu d'une époque ultérieure. Le parallélisme
synonymique invite à considérer *bayit* et *qen* [2]) comme ayant un sens
voisin. Donc dans le verset 4a on dit: un oiseau même trouve une
demeure (= un nid) et un oiselet un nid où il dépose ses petits [3]).
Cela ne veut pas dire seulement que l'oiseau trouve un nid pour ses
petits, mais encore qu'il trouve un endroit fixe où il peut couver en
paix ses œufs et soigner ses petits. Le petit animal, souvent faible,
surtout vagabond, qu'est un oiseau, doit de temps en temps trouver
où se fixer de façon permanente et il trouve cet endroit effectivement.
Le poète veut suggérer: combien plus sûre n'est pas la demeure de
Dieu pour ceux qui sont en route. Ainsi le verset 4a a une fonction
stylistique: le poète *soupire* après la sécurité („les parvis") de son
Dieu (v. 3), un oiseau *trouve* (parfait) son nid (v. 4a), bienheureux
ceux qui *habitent* la maison de Dieu (v. 5).

Enfin quelle est la fonction de את־מזבחותיך dans notre verset?
La place de ces mots étonne. On a voulu émender le verset 4 par
exemple *metri causa*, comme nous l'avons fait remarquer plus haut.

צפר pour l'araméen biblique; CH. F. JEAN-J. HOFTIJZER, *Dictionnaire des Inscriptions sémitiques de l'Ouest*, Leyde 1965, p. 246 s.v. (surprenante est la forme צנפר
dans l'araméen d'Empire: Aḥiqar 91, 98, 199); C. BROCKELMANN, *Lexicon Syria-
cum*², Halle (la Saxe) 1928 s.v. {ܨܦܪ} pour le syrien. Qu'on compare aussi G. R.
DRIVER, „Birds in the Old Testament", *PEQ* 87 (1955), p. 130.

[1]) Avec raison a démontré O. BAUERNFEIND, „στρουθίον", *ThWzNT* VII,
p. 730 note 5, que dans la langue de tous les jours ou dans la langue des poètes
il n'y a souvent pas de distinction exacte entre les différents genres d'oiseaux.
Dans le patois d'Amsterdam un pinson („vink") est une désignation de chaque
(petit) oiseau.

[2]) La lettre ק de קן est grande dans plusieurs MSS; selon HIRSCH „vielleicht
um den Gedanken hervorzuheben: Den Vogel zieht es nicht nur zu dem Hause
hin, *wo* er *ein* Nest gebaut, sondern zu dem Neste hin, *das* er sich gebaut". En
outre קן est précédé et suivi par un *paseq*.

[3]) Pour le parfait cf. P. JOÜON, *o.c.*, § 112d.

Mais vu l'incertitude qui règne toujours en ce qui concerne le mètre dans la poésie des Hébreux, l'émendation *metri causa* reste souvent incertaine et peu satisfaisante. Selon nous il y a deux moyens pour arriver à une bonne solution: 1. originairement מזבחותיך את fait partie du texte, mais alors on ne doit pas lier directement ces mots à ce qui précède; on peut les considérer par exemple comme une exclamation (CALVIN) [1]: le poète interrompt la suite de ses idées pour se rappeler les autels, c'est-à-dire la demeure de Dieu sur le Sion: ce n'est que là qu'il peut trouver la paix et la sécurité; 2. nous avons à faire ici à une glose, qui fut d'abord placée dans la marge du texte par un copiste et qui entra plus tard dans le texte même [2]). Ceci a dû se passer très tôt déjà, parce que les traductions anciennes, parmi lesquelles la Septante, ont trouvé sans aucun doute ces mots dans leur „Vorlage" [3]). Nous préférons la deuxième possibilité. Premièrement les mots מזבחותיך את interrompent le développement régulier de notre verset logiquement aussi bien que syntaxiquement: gênants et ambigus, ils obscurcissent plutôt qu'ils n'éclaircissent. Deuxièmement il n'est pas si certain qu'on puisse traduire 'èt (préposition) si facile-ment par „auprès de", comme on le fait ici. 'èt comme une préposition est plutôt „avec", „en relation avec" et est alors souvent employé pour des personnes [4]). Si on voit dans 'èt la *nota objecti* il est possible qu'on y voie une glose „explicative" d'un copiste (. . . c'est-à-dire Tes autels . . .), parce qu'on ne s'attend guère à trouver un commen-taire du poète lui-même dans ses vers. Cependant on ne peut que deviner l'intention réelle du copiste avec cette glose. D'ailleurs nous ne voudrions pas nous prononcer sur la possibilité du nichement

---

[1]) F. NÖTSCHER (*Echter-Bibel*) et autres pensent à une comparaison abrégée; cf. aussi note 1, p. 236.

[2]) Cf. H. HERKENNE, *a.l.*

[3]) Plusieurs MSS écrivent מזבחתיך (*scriptio defectiva*), cf. C. D. GINSBURG, *The Old Testament . . . with various readings from MSS etc.*², Londres 1926, *a.l.*

[4]) La préposition 'et demande une recherche plus détaillée. Nous avons rapide-ment vérifié les données concernant cette préposition chez S. E. LOEWENSTAMM et J. BLAU, *Thesaurus of the Language of the Bible* I, Jérusalem 1957, pp. 400 ss. Selon notre avis il n'y a qu'un verset, qui est comparable à notre verset: Ez. xliii 8: ספם את־ספי וגו'; mais ici את = אצל. Sauf pour déterminer des personnes la signification „près de", „auprès" ne se trouve que dans l'expression אשר את־ avec un nom d'un lieu: Jug. iii 19; iv 11; 1 R. ix 26; 2 R. ix 27. 'et avec des noms de choses doit être traduit par „avec" ou un mot pareil, par exemple: Gen. vi 13; Dt. xxix 19; Is. xxviii 15 etc. Cf. encore l'expression את־פני, c'est „devant", „près de" (Lev. iv 6, 17; Ps. xvi 11; xxi 7 etc.). En outre, la confusion avec la *nota objecti* est assez grande.

des oiseaux dans le temple. Selon nous le poète lui-même n'attache aucune importance à ce fait.

La signification de cette glose את מזבחותיך est liée à la deuxième partie de notre étude: quelle est la signification de d*e*rôr et pourquoi la Septante traduit-elle ce mot par τρυγών?

II

Dans beaucoup de dictionnaires d*e*rôr est mis en rapport avec le radical drr [1]). Ce radical drr est lié au darāru accadien: „donner libre cours à" [2]) et au darra arabe: „couler en abondance (du lait)" [3]). Dans le (nouveau) dictionnaire de l'Ancien Testament de (KOEHLER et) BAUMGARTNER ([3]1967) le mot d*e*rôr est cité trois fois: 1. l'oiseau que nous discutons ici („.e. Vogelart, trad. Schwalbe od. Taube . . ."); 2. la myrrhe vierge („Klumpenmyrrhe, Stakte, d. körnerartigen erstarrten Tropfen d. Myrrhe, dickflüssiges Salböl") (Ex. xxx 23); 3. la manumission (des esclaves) (Lev. xxv 10; Jer. xxxiv 8, 15, 17; Ez. xlvi 17; Is. lxi 1). Ces trois mots sont, selon le même dictionnaire, derivata de drr [4]).

Toutefois l'étymologie, si importante qu'elle est, ne nous renseigne pas nécessairement sur la signification précise qu'a eue tel ou tel mot dans un certain contexte et dans un certain temps. Qu'est-ce-que c'est qu'„un oiseau libre" par exemple? Dans la littérature post-biblique on trouve la combinaison צפור דרור. Dans Nega'im xiv 1 deux exemplaires de cette espèce d'oiseau sont cités relativement au rituel de purification d'un lépreux décrit dans Lev. xiv [5]). La cinqui-

---

[1]) Cf. W. GESENIUS-F. BUHL, Hebr. und Aram. Handwörterbuch über das A.T.[17], Leipzig 1921, s.v. et p. 169 s.v. דרר; L. KOEHLER-W. BAUMGARTNER, o.c.[3], Leyde 1967, s.v.

[2]) The Assyrian Dictionary of the University of Chicago, D, Chicago 1959, p. 109 s.v.; W. VON SODEN, AHw, s.v.

[3]) E. W. LANE, An arabic-english lexicon I, part 3, Londres 1867, s.v. ﺟﺲ; A. DE BIBERSTEIN KAZIMIRSKI, Dictionnaire Arabe-Français I, Paris 1960, s.v. ﺟﺲ.

[4]) Cf. déjà W. GESENIUS-F. BUHL, o.c., s.v. דרר. On pense que le mot d*e*rôr III („manumission") fut emprunté de l'assyrien andurārum „délivrance de charges". Ici „an" est une préformante qui se trouve seulement devant les racines mediae geminatae (dans l'accadien); cf. W. VON SODEN, Grundriss der akkadischen Grammatik, Rome 1952, § 56a. Ce mot andurārum on le fait dériver de drr; W. VON SODEN, AHw, s.v.; L. KOEHLER-W. BAUMGARTNER, o.c.[3], s.v. III. Cf. en outre A. G. BARROIS, Manuel d'Archéologie biblique II, Paris 1953, p. 223; G. R. DRIVER-J. C. MILES, The Babylonian Laws II, Oxford 1955, p. 207 note 2; J. LEWY, "The biblical institution of D*e*RÔR in the light of akkadian documents", Eretz-Israel 5 (1958), pp. 21+-31+.

[5]) Cf. aussi Tosephta, Naz. vi 1 (éd. M. S. ZUCKERMANDEL, Pasewalk 1880, p. 291) et en outre bTal, Beṣa 25a.

ème mišna du chapitre précité du Nega'im prouve que les rabbins ont interprété *derôr* comme indiquant la „liberté" dans laquelle vivait l'oiseau [1]). Dans le Talmud babylonien (Šabb. 106b; Beṣa (= Yom ṭob) 24a) on propose deux explications de *ṣippôr derôr*, la première due à Rabba b. R. Hona: „parce qu'il n'accepte pas qu'on règne sur lui" [2]); l'autre explication vient de l'école de R. Ismael: „parce qu'il habite dans une maison aussi bien que dans les champs" [3]). Ici on pratique, selon notre avis, un jeu de mots à propos de *derôr* et de *drh*. Dans 'Aboda Zara 38b on donne comme mesure d'une petite chaudière (יורה קטנה) une chaudière si petite qu'un *ṣippôr derôr* n'y pourrait pas entrer [4]). D'autres pensent que même la tête de l'oiseau n'y pourrait pas entrer. Le prix de cet oiseau est modéré: un as romain seulement (environ 0.03 N.F.) [5]). Ces indications rabbiniques donnent l'impression que les mots *ṣippôr derôr* ne désignent probablement pas la colombe, mais un autre oiseau [6]). Tout comme dans l'Ancien Testament, on disposait d'autres mots pour ''colombe'', comme *yônā* (*bèn-yônā*) [7]); *tôr* [8]) et aussi *gôzāl* [9]). Dans la première partie de notre étude nous avons envisagé la possibilité que le fait que *ṣippôr* et *derôr*

---

[1]) Ch. Albeck, סדר טהרות, Jérusalem 1959, p. 247; cf. aussi Tosephta, Neg. viii 7 (éd. Zuckermandel, p. 628).

[2]) לפי שאינה מקבלת מרות.

[3]) מפני שדרה בבית כבשדה :Cf. Tosephta, Neg. viii 3: היה מביא שתי צפרין דרור ואלו הן הדרות בעיר (éd. Zuckermandel, *ibidem*). Chez autres auteurs aussi „liberté", par exemple Sixt. Amama, *apud: Criticorum sacrorum ... ad librum psalmorum etc.* III, Londres 1660, col. 475 et M. Polus, *o.c.*, col. 1106.

[4]) ודלמא אדמויי. א'ר ינאי כל שאין צפור דרור יכול ליכנס בתוכה :La suite est אדמוה ועיילוה אלא כל שאין ראש צפור דרור יכול ליכנס בתוכה Cf. aussi Soṭa 16b.

[5]) Men. 99b: אתה שאם (משל ל) אדם שמסר צפור דרור לעבדו אמר כמדומה אתה מאבדה שאני נוטל ממך איסר בדמיה וגו'

[6]) Cf. G. Dalman, *Arbeit und Sitte in Palästina* VI, Gütersloh 1939, pp. 97 s. et *idem*, VII, Gütersloh 1942, p. 267. Cf. aussi W. G. Braude, *The Midraš on Psalms* II, New Haven 1959, p. 65.

[7]) Cf. M. Jastrow, *A dictionary of the Targumim etc.* I, New York 1903 (réimpression 1950), s.v. יונה II: יונה = „dove"; בן־יונה = „pigeon". Cf. L. Koehler-W. Baumgartner, *o.c.*[1], s.v. I יונה = „dove"; „for offerings בן־יונה etc ..... single(male?) dove(s) ...".

[8]) M. Jastrow, *o.c.* II, New York 1903 (réimpr. 1950), s.v. תור II = „turtle-dove"; L. Koehler-W. Baumgartner, *o.c.*[1], s.v. II תור „turtle-dove".

[9]) M. Jastrow, *o.c.* I, s.v. גוזל = „brood, chick, esp. pidgeon". Dans l'Ancien Testament on trouve ce mot deux fois; cf. L. Koehler-W. Baumgartner, *o.c.*[3], s.v. „Turteltaube Gn 15₉, junger Adler Dt 32₁₁''. La Septante traduit גוזל dans Gen. xv 9 par περιστερά, dans Dt xxxiii 11 par νεοσσός. Cf. encore par exemple Šek. vi 5: קנין וגוזלי עולה et M. Jastrow, *o.c.* II, s.v. קן = 1) „nest; birds in a nest"; et 2) "the couple of sacrificial birds".

244 M. J. MULDER

voisinent dans notre psaume et Pr. xxvi 2 soit lié à la fonction de ces deux mots dans des expressions populaires. Peut-être ce rapport est devenu de plus en plus étroit pour donner naissance à l'unité *ṣippôr dᵉrôr*, qu'on rencontre dans la littérature talmudique. Alors *dᵉrôr* III „manumission" pourrait avoir influencé aussi la signification de *ṣippôr dᵉrôr*.

Le désir de déterminer le sens de *dᵉrôr* a fait couler beaucoup d'encre depuis des siècles. SAM. BOCHART par exemple dit dans son *Hierozoicon* [1]), consulté par beaucoup de générations: „Avem *dᵉrôr* non esse Hirundinem, ut volunt, sed columbae ferae speciem, puta Turturem, aut palumbum". Il fonde cette opinion principalement sur la traduction de la Septante du Ps. lxxxiv 4. Il avance aussi des arguments empruntés à d'autres langues sémitiques, avant tout des arguments étymologiques. Mais l'autorité de BOCHART, si grande soit-elle, n'a pas réussi à imposer son point de vue. Déjà l'éditeur de l'œuvre de BOCHART, E. F. C. ROSENMÜLLER [2]) se montre d'un autre avis: „In tota hac disputatione feliciorem ego Bochartum versatum esse putem in aliorum commentis refellendis, quam in sua sententia stabilienda". Selon lui „דרור *turturis* nomen ὀνοματοποιητικόν crediderim, quum in eo consentiant interpretes veteres omnes". Un de ses contemporains I. H. MICHAELIS [3]) était moins catégorique: il hésite dans son choix entre „hirundo" et „palumbum s. columba silv.".

Une des excursions qui suivent le *Biblischer Kommentar über die Psalmen* de F. DELITZSCH, écrite par J. G. WETZSTEIN, a pour titre „Ueber den Vogelnamen דרור" [4]). Ici WETZSTEIN démontre qu'à bon droit SAADIA dérive *dᵉrôr* du mot arabe دورِيّة et que le moineau ordinaire est appelé *dûrî* en Syrie et en Palestine. Cependant on se demande si le mot *dᵉrôr* correspond réellement au *dûrî* de l'arabe moderne. Cela serait impossible si on traduisait *ṣippôr* par moineau. Toutefois *ṣippôr* est l'oiseau en général, l'espèce „passereau" dans

---

[1]) SAM. BOCHARTUS, *Hierozoicon sive de animalibus S. Scripturae* (rec. etc. E. F. C. ROSENMÜLER) Tom. II, Leipzig 1794, pars II liber I cap. viii, pp. 590 ss.

[2]) Note dans SAM. BOCHARTUS, *o.c.*, p. 595; cf. aussi E. F. C. ROSENMÜLLER, *Scholia in Vetus Testamentum* IV 3, Leipzig 1804, pp. 2245 s.

[3]) Io. H. MICHAELIS, *Uberiorum Adnotationum philol.-exegetic. in Hagiographos (in Psalmos)*, Halle 1720, p. 633. Cf. aussi H. VENEMA, *o.c.*, p. 773: „. . . posterior vero (sc. vox, M.J.M.) *palumbum*, vel *turturem*, columbae sylvestris genus, uti Vir in hoc studiorum genere summus, Bochartus, docuit".

[4]) J. G. WETZSTEIN, „Ueber den Vogelnamen דרור", in: F. DELITZSCH, *Biblischer Kommentar über die Psalmen* I³, Leipzig 1873, pp. 385-388.

la langue de tous les jours. Là où on n'avait pas besoin de préciser l'espèce, ṣippôr était employé pour désigner „passereau" („moineau") dans la langue arabe moderne comme dans l'Ancien Testament, toujours selon WETZSTEIN. Ensuite il montre que le Talmud, en donnant le participe darā, cité ci-dessus (Beṣa 24a), ne donne pas une étymologie du mot dᵉrôr, mais que ce passage du Talmud et l'exégèse de Saadia sont liés historiquement et „dass ihn die Worte שדרה בבית כבשדה direkt auf den dûrî geführt haben". Selon la définition talmudique il est possible de songer aussi à côté de „moineau" à „colombe" ou „hirondelle", mais SAADIA a rejeté sciemment cette possibilité: quant à „hirondelle" parce que Lev. xiv ne peut citer pour la purification des lépreux que des oiseaux purs, et que d'autre part l'hirondelle (סנונית) tout comme quelques autres oiseaux cités nommément, était impure selon Sifra (sur Lev. xiv). Quoique le dûrî de SAADIA repose, selon WETZSTEIN, sur l'autorité plus ancienne de la Mišna, il est quand même douteux que cette explication soit juste. „Nach einigen Stellen, die mir vorliegen, dachte man sich unter dem dᵉrôr nicht eine bestimmte, sondern mehrere Gattungen kleiner und ... menschenscheuer Vögel ...". WETZSTEIN lui-même est d'accord avec l'opinion de GESENIUS [1]), qui interprète dᵉrôr comme „hirondelle" en se basant sur la racine drr entre autres. Si on trouve aussi dans l'Ancien Testament un autre mot pour „hirondelle" [2]) cela vient peut-être de ce que ces deux mots „ursprünglich zwei verschiedenen palästin. Völkerschichten angehören". Enfin il rejette la traduction „tourterelle".

G. R. DRIVER a abordé le problème d'un autre côté [3]). Selon lui le mot dᵉrôr est composé de la dentale d, allongée par des r sonants „from the dental „hwit-hwit" or „tit-tit-tit-tit" which that bird gives forth". Lui aussi traduit le mot par „hirondelle". Il pense que cette identification est conforme aux deux versets où l'oiseau est appelé un symbole de paix et de certitude (notre verset); à côté de cela il mentionne le vol inquiet (Pr. xxvi 2).

Des biologistes se sont aussi occupés de l'oiseau. Nous avons déjà cité BOCHART, nous voulons citer pour l'époque moderne entre

---

[1]) GUIL. GESENIUS, *Thesaurus philol.-critic. linguae hebraeae et chaldaeae V.T.* I, Leipzig 1829, p. 355.

[2]) En question סוס ou סיס: Is. xxxviii 14 et Jer. viii 7, cf. L. KOEHLER-W. BAUMGARTNER, *o.c.*[1], s.v. סיס = martinet noir (Apus Apus L.).

[3]) G. R. DRIVER, l.c., p. 131, cf. aussi W. S. McCULLOUGH, „Swallow", *IDB* IV, p. 468.

autres Mlle ALICE PARMELEE [1]), qui pour le mot *dᵉrôr* pense à l'hirondelle qui pouvait nicher dans le temple sans être dérangée et J.
FELIKS [2]), qui pour *ṣippôr dᵉrôr* pense au „passer domesticus biblicus"
et qui est d'avis que la traduction de *dᵉrôr* par „hirondelle" ne fait
pas droit à la description qu'en donnent la Bible et le Talmud.

Ce qui précède montre qu'on n'arrive pas facilement à identifier
dᵉrôr avec une espèce déterminée parce que ni l'étymologie du mot,
ni une interprétation onomatopéique ne peuvent compter comme
des preuves convaincantes pour une identification définitive. Selon
nous le plus vraisemblable est de voir la signification de *dᵉrôr* parallèlement à *ṣippôr*, donc comme désignation du genre „oiseau",
probablement des plus petits oiseaux. Le caractère onomatopéique
du mot est douteux. Les dictionnaires et les commentaires qui
s'abstiennent de se prononcer ou mettent un point d'interrogation
font preuve d'une réserve prudente.

Reste la question de savoir comment la Septante et les autres
traductions anciennes à l'instar de celle-là ont pu penser à „tourterelle". Bien sûr on peut nommer quelques possibilités qui ont inspiré
à la Septante sa traduction. Une de ces possibilités est qu'elle ait eu
une „Vorlage" où on ne rencontre pas *dᵉrôr*, mais un autre mot, par
exemple *tôr* [3]). Dans tous les autres cas où on trouve τρυγών le texte
hébraïque emploie le mot *tôr*. Une deuxième possibilité est que les
traducteurs de la Septante aient connu parfaitement l'oiseau précis
avec lequel on pouvait identifier *dᵉrôr*, quoique la traduction de
Pr. xxvi 2 (στρουθός) semble un peu étonnante [4]). Qui prouvera que
le traducteur de ce dernier verset a tort, puis qu'AQUILA l'approuve
dans le Ps. lxxxiv 4? Si on veut partir — et selon nous ce serait
juste — du fait que la Septante avait la même „Vorlage" en ce qui

---

[1]) A. PARMELEE, *All the Birds of the Bible*, New York 1959, pp. 160 ss.
[2]) J. FELIKS, *The animal world of the Bible*, Tel-Aviv 5722/1962, p. 61; *idem*,
„Sperling", *BHH* III, cols. 1830 s. Mais aussi „hirondelle", par exemple
R. PINNEY, *The Animals in the Bible*, Philadelphia/New York 1964, p. 170 (répr.
nr. 62). Nous mentionnons aussi un des plus anciens biologistes H. B. TRISTRAM,
The Fauna and Flora of Palestine (The Survey of Western Palestine), Londres 1884,
p. 61: „hirundo rustica".
[3]) Cf. E. HATCH-H. A. REDPATH, *A Concordance to the Septuagint etc.* II, Oxford
1897 (réimpr. Graz 1954), p. 1377 s.v. τρυγών. Pour Ps. lxxxiii (lxxxiv) 3 on
donne un"†". Cf. aussi J. Fr. SCHLEUSNER, *Novus Thesaurus Philol.-Crit. etc.* V,
Leipzig 1821, p. 547 s.v. τρυγών.
[4]) Le plus souvent στρουθός est la traduction de היענה (בת), cf. E. HATCH-
H. A. REDPATH, *o.c.*, p. 1297 s.v. On compare pour la traduction d'AQUILA
dans Ps. lxxxiv 4 F. FIELD, *o.c.*, p. 235.

concerne notre verset que nous avons avec notre texte massorétique, et si on veut supposer ensuite qu'elle ne sait pas plus que nous de quel oiseau il s'agissait, alors il faudra chercher la solution, si tant est qu'elle soit trouvable, dans une autre direction.

On sait que la colombe a joué un rôle important dans les mythes et les rites du Proche Orient. Elle était aussi dans l'antiquité grecque un attribut des dieux (par exemple les colombes de l'oracle de Zeus de Dodone) et surtout des déesses (par exemple l'Aphrodite cyprienne) [1]. Mais alors elle a déjà fait le voyage de l'est à l'ouest. Les auteurs classiques le savent, comme DIODORE, qui dit: ἔνιοι δὲ μυθολογοῦντές φασιν αὐτὴν γενέσθαι περιστεράν, καὶ πολλῶν ὀρνέων εἰς τὴν οἰκίαν καταπετασθέντων μετ' ἐκείνων ἐκπετασθῆναι· διὸ καὶ τοὺς Ἀσσυρίους τὴν περιστερὰν τιμᾶν ὡς θεόν, ἀπαθανατίζοντας τὴν Σεμίραμιν.[2]) ou TIBULLE, qui chante: „quid referam, ut volitet crebras intacta per urbes alba Palaestino sancta columba Syro" [3]).

Cette colombe d'Aphrodite est en rapport avec la colombe d'Astarté, Atargatis (Derketo) comme on l'appelle surtout dans l'ancien Hiérapolis [4]). LUCIANE sait que pour elle les colombes sont sacrées et qu'elles ne sont pas mangées [5]). Des philologues ont même prétendu que le mot grecque pour colombe περιστερά doit être en rapport avec Ištar, c'est-à-dire *peraḥ-Ištar* [6]), mais aujourd'hui on doute de cette étymologie [7]).

Bien qu'on ne puisse pas dire que la colombe est un animal sacré en Israél, elle était considérée comme pure, c'est-à-dire qu'elle était propre à la purification et au sacrifice [8]). Le plus souvent le sacrifice

---

[1]) Cf. entre beaucoup d'autres études J. G. FRAZER, *Adonis Attis Osiris*³ I, Londres 1914, pp. 33 s. et p. 147; STEIER, „Taube", *PW* (Zweite Reihe) IV, cols. 2479-2500, surtout cols. 2490-2500; H. GREEVEN, „περιστερά", *ThWzNT* VI, pp. 63-72, surtout pp. 64 s. Dans cettes études on peut trouver une bibliographie vaste sur notre sujet. Cf. aussi J. PEDERSEN, *Israel its Life and Culture* III-IV, Copenhague 1940, index.

[2]) DIODORUS, *Bibliotheca Historica*, II 20.

[3]) TIBULLUS, I 7, 17 s.

[4]) STRABO, *Geographica*, XVI c. 785: Ἀταργάτιν δὲ τὴν Ἀθάραν, Δερκετὼ δ'αὐτὴν Κτησίας καλεῖ. Cf. G. DALMAN, *o.c.* VII, pp. 267 s.

[5]) LUCIANUS, *De dea Syra*, c. 14 et c. 54; Cf. XENOPHON, *Anabasis*, I 4, 9. Que cela n'était pas une habitude persique: HERODOTUS, *Historiae*, I 138.

[6]) E. ASSMANN, „περιστερά", *Philologus* 66 (1907), pp. 313 s.; cf. E. BOISACQ, *Dictionnaire étymologique de la langue grecque*², Heidelberg/Paris 1923, p. 773 s.v.

[7]) H. FRISK, *Griechisches Etymologisches Wörterbuch*, Lief. 16, Heidelberg 1965, p. 514 s.v.

[8]) Cf. entre autres G. DALMAN, *o.c.* VI, p. 95 et VII, p. 226; H. GREEVEN, *l.c.*, p. 66.

d'oiseau se composait d'une ou de deux jeunes colombes [1]) ou de
quelques tourterelles [2]). Elles ne sont pas citées parmi les sacrifices
qu'on pouvait manger [3]). D'autre part elles ne sont pas rangées dans
Lev. et Dt. sous les soi-disant „oiseaux impurs", si bien qu'on a
l'impression que, du moins à une époque ultérieure, on les mangeait [4]).
La colombe est citée aussi dans le récit du déluge, parallèlement au
récit dans le onzième chant de l'épopée de Gilgameš [5]) et dans
plusieurs tours et comparaisons poétiques [6]). Cela nous mènerait
trop loin d'entrer dans les détails pour déterminer la signification
et la fonction de la colombe dans le judaïsme postérieur, mais pour
le but de notre étude il n'est pas tout à fait inutile de relever qu'on
établit dans la littérature talmudique un rapport entre l'Esprit de
Dieu et la colombe, par exemple là où on entend dans le temple la
bat qôl comme le roucoulement d'une colombe [7]). Lorsque GREEVEN
attire l'attention, dans son article, intitulé „περιστερά", sur ce fait,
il ajoute dans une note: „Bezeichnend ist auch, dass das Gurren der
Taube als κύριε κύριε gedeutet wurde bChull 139b... Ähnliche
Gedanken mögen bewirkt haben, dass Ps. 84, 4 דרור (Schwalbe?)
in LXX mit τρυγών wiedergegeben wird..." [8]). Il est dommage,
qu'il n'ait pas développé ces „ähnliche Gedanken".

A côté de la colombe et de la tourterelle, comme nous l'avons
déjà vu, „l'oiseau vivant" était prescrit dans Lev. xiv en rapport
avec le rituel de la purification d'un lépreux. Partant du fait que
ṣippôr est le nom générique pour „oiseau", on peut se livrer à toutes
sortes de spéculations concernant l'espèce d'oiseau désigné ici, à

---

[1]) בני־יונה: Lev. i 14; v 7, 11; xii 6, 8; xiv 22, 30; xv 14, 29; Nu. vi 10.

[2]) תור: les mêmes versets comme dans la note précédente, en outre Gen. xv 9.
Cf. aussi Luc. ii 24: ζεῦγος τρυγόνων ἢ δύο νοσσοὺς περιστερῶν. Il y a aussi des
merchands de colombes dans le temple: Matth. xxi 12; Marc. xi 15; Jean ii 14, 16.
Cf. en outre H. L. STRACK-P. BILLERBECK, *Kommentar z. N.T. etc.* I, Munich
1922, pp. 850 ss.

[3]) W. ROBERTSON SMITH, *o.c.*, p. 219 note 2; G. DALMAN, *o.c.*, VII, p. 266.

[4]) Cf. pour les oiseaux impurs Lev. xi 13-19 et Dt. xiv 12-18.

[5]) Épopée de Gilgameš XI 146 s.: *summatu*; ensuite on mentionne l'hirondelle:
sinūntu (149 s.) et le troisième oiseau c'est le corbeau: *āribu* (152 s.). Pour des
autres exemples on compare H. GREEVEN, *l.c.*, p. 65.

[6]) Cf. R. ZEHNPFUND, „Tauben in den biblischen Büchern", *PRE³* XIX,
p. 396 et H. GREEVEN, *l.c.*, pp. 66 s.

[7]) Berakot 3a: שמעתי בת קול שמנהמת כיונה וגו'; cf. Ḥull. 139b: ici le roucoulement des colombes est expliqué comme קירי קירי, c'est à dire κύριε κύριε:
G. DALMAN, *o.c.* VII, p. 268 et H. GREEVEN, *l.c.*, p. 66 note 37. Ici il s'agit d'une
sorte spéciale des colombes à savoir les הרדסיאות ou הדרסיאות.

[8]) H. GREEVEN, *ibidem*.

condition pourtant qu'on se restreigne aux oiseaux „purs". La Septante a choisi ὀρνίθιον, employé exclusivement dans Lev. xiv (d'ailleurs 13 fois). Il est clair qu'elle a pensé à un petit oiseau. Le Targum d'Onqelos et la Pešiṭṭa suivent de près le texte hébraïque, tandis que la Vulgate traduit par „passer". Dans le judaïsme postérieur on n'est pas sûr de quel oiseau il peut s'agir, quoi qu'on pense aux oiseaux „gazouillants" [1]). Et pourquoi ne penserait-on pas ici à une espèce de colombe [2])?

Compte tenu de ce qui précède on peut dire que les colombes, les tourterelles et les ṣippôrîm ḥayyîm sont propres au sacrifice et à la purification. Autrement dit: elles pouvaient se trouver sur l'autel ou près de l'autel. D'autres oiseaux sont exclus. N'est-il pas évident que le traducteur de la Septante en rencontrant notre verset avec la glose את מזבחותיך, qui faisait déjà partie du texte, a pu penser tout de suite aux oiseaux purs? S'il a choisi pour ṣippôr στρουθίον au lieu de ὀρνίθιον, on pourrait en déduire que pour le traducteur du psaume le mot général στρουθίον pour ṣippôr lui était présent à l'esprit [3]), tandis qu'il voyait dans le mot de'rôr une autre espèce d'oiseau pur [4]). Cette supposition est considérablement renforcée, selon nous, par la traduction du Targum [5]): לחוד יונתא אשכחת ביתא ושפנינא שרכפא ליה די כשרין גוזליה לאתקרבא על מדבחתך יי צבאות מלכי ואלהי („la colombe aussi trouve une maison et la tourterelle un nid pour elle parce que ses petits sont légitimes pour être sacrifiés sur Tes autels . . .").

Il est vrai que dans cette traduction paraphrasante on cite d'abord la colombe et après la tourterelle, mais on retrouve ici deux éléments importants pour bien comprendre la traduction de la Septante:

---

[1]) Cf. Ḥull. 139 b, 140 a et Raši sur Lev. xiv 4: טהרות: לפי שהנגעים באים על לשון הרע שהוא מעשה פטפוטי דברים לפיכך הוזקקו לטהרתו צפרים שמפטפטים תמיד בצפצוף קול

[2]) Selon S. Kraus, *Talmudische Archäologie* II, Leipzig 1911, p. 138 on trouve dans la littérature talmudique 10 espèces de colombes. F. Frank, „Tierleben in Palästina", *ZDPV* 75 (1959), p. 86 dit qu'il n'existe que trois espèces de colombes dans la Palestine moderne.

[3]) C'est souvent la traduction de צפור: Ps. x(xi) 2(1); ci(cii) 7(8); ciii(civ) 17; cxxiii(cxxiv) 7; Eccl. xii 4; Thr. iii 52; cf. O. Bauernfeind, *l.c.* VII, pp. 730 s.

[4]) Il est peut-être possible, mais selon nous invraisemblable, que la traduction de la Septante soit fondée sur une erreur d'audition par laquelle le scribe aurait compris deʿrôr comme tôr. Cf. entre autres pour les questions relatives à la traduction de la Septante J. L. Seeligmann, „Problemen en perspectieven in het moderne Septuaginta-onderzoek", *JEOL* 7 (1940), spéc. p. 367, p. 373 et pp. 376-384.

[5]) P. de Lagarde, *Hagiographa Chaldaice*, Leipzig 1873, *a.l.*

אתקרבא על מדבחתך et כשרין [1]). La |traduction de *dᵉrôr* par τρυγών que donne la Septante, ne pourrait pas compter, selon nous, comme une identification légitime de cet oiseau, mais on peut expliquer cette traduction. Ensuite on peut expliquer aussi que dans les siècles postérieurs plusieurs traducteurs prenaient la traduction de la Septante pour tellement sûr, qu'ils traduisent *dᵉrôr* par „turtur", „tourterelle", „colombe" ou „(tortel)duif". Ce fut l'occasion pour DUIFHUIS de retrouver son nom dans le Ps. lxxxiv et d'autre part, ce psaume lxxxiv (4 s.) a pu mettre VAN DER BLOM à son tour sur la piste de DUIFHUIS.

---

[1]) Cf. pour l'influence juive sur les traductions de la Septante entre autres L. PRIJS, *Beiträge zur Frage der jüdischen Tradition in der Septuaginta*, Leyde 1948 et *idem, Jüdische Tradition in der Septuaginta*, Leyde 1948. Aussi: J. HEINEMANN, דרכי האגדה, Jérusalem 5714, pp. 170 ss. et p. 252 note 35 (bibliographie).